Mothers, Criminal Insanity and the Asylum in Victorian England

History of Crime, Deviance and Punishment

Series Editor:
Anne-Marie Kilday, Vice Chancellor and Professor of Criminal History, University of Northampton, UK

Editorial Board:
Neil Davie, University of Lyon II, France
Johannes Dillinger, University of Maine, Germany
Wilbur Miller, State University of New York, USA
Marianna Muravyeva, University of Helsinki, Finland
David Nash, Oxford Brookes University, UK
Judith Rowbotham, Nottingham Trent University, UK

Academic interest in the history of crime and punishment has never been greater and the *History of Crime, Deviance and Punishment* series provides a home for the wealth of new research being produced. Individual volumes within the series cover topics related to the history of crime and punishment, from the later medieval to modern period and in both Europe and North America, and seek to demonstrate the importance of this subject in furthering understanding of the way in which various societies and cultures operate. When taken together, the works in the series will show the evolution of the nature of illegality and attitudes towards its perpetration over time and will offer their readers a rounded and coherent history of crime and punishment through the centuries. The series' broad chronological and geographical coverage encourages comparative historical analysis of crime history between countries and cultures.

Published:
Policing the Factory, Barry Godfrey
Crime and Poverty in 19th-Century England, Adrian Ager
Print Culture, Crime and Justice in Eighteenth-Century London, Richard Ward
Rehabilitation and Probation in England and Wales, 1900–1950, Raymond Gard

The Policing of Belfast 1870–1914, Mark Radford
Crime, Regulation and Control during the Blitz, Peter Adey, David J. Cox and Barry Godfrey
The Italian Prison in the Age of Positivism, 1861–1914, Mary Gibson
Life Courses of Young Convicts Transported to Van Diemen's Land, Emma D. Watkins
Fair and Unfair Trials in the British Isles, 1800–1940, eds. David Nash and Anne-Marie Kilday
Photographing Crime Scenes in Twentieth-Century London, Alexa Neale
Combating London's Criminal Class, Matthew Bach
Prison and Workhouse Reform in 19th-Century England: Shaping Incarceration, Lewis Darwen and David Orr

Forthcoming:
The Forefathers of Terrorism: Violent Crime in Politics, 1300–1800, Johannes Dillinger
Feminist Campaigns against Child Sexual Abuse: Britain and India, 1860–1947, Daniel Grey
Deviance, Disorder and Music in Modern Britain and America, Cliff Williamson
Crime and Criminal Justice in Early Modern Ireland: Developing a Colonial Institution, Coleman A. Dennehy
Motor Bandits in Interwar England: Criminal Mobility in the Modern Age, Alyson Brown
Prosecuting London's Fraudsters 1760–1820: Swindlers, Tricksters and the Law, Cerian Griffiths
Sex and Violence in 1920s Scotland, Louise Heren

Mothers, Criminal Insanity and the Asylum in Victorian England

Cure, Redemption and Rehabilitation

Alison C. Pedley

BLOOMSBURY ACADEMIC
LONDON • NEW YORK • OXFORD • NEW DELHI • SYDNEY

BLOOMSBURY ACADEMIC
Bloomsbury Publishing Plc
50 Bedford Square, London, WC1B 3DP, UK
1385 Broadway, New York, NY 10018, USA
29 Earlsfort Terrace, Dublin 2, Ireland

BLOOMSBURY, BLOOMSBURY ACADEMIC and the Diana logo
are trademarks of Bloomsbury Publishing Plc

First published in Great Britain 2023
This paperback edition published in 2025

Copyright © Alison C. Pedley, 2023

Alison C. Pedley has asserted her right under the Copyright,
Designs and Patents Act, 1988, to be identified as Author of this work.

For legal purposes the Acknowledgements on pp. xiv–xv constitute an
extension of this copyright page.

Cover image © The Broadmoor Criminal Lunatic Asylum,
female dormitory, 1867. Artokoloro/Alamy Stock Photo.

All rights reserved. No part of this publication may be reproduced or transmitted
in any form or by any means, electronic or mechanical, including photocopying,
recording, or any information storage or retrieval system, without prior
permission in writing from the publishers.

Bloomsbury Publishing Plc does not have any control over, or responsibility for,
any third-party websites referred to or in this book. All internet addresses given
in this book were correct at the time of going to press. The author and publisher
regret any inconvenience caused if addresses have changed or sites have
ceased to exist, but can accept no responsibility for any such changes.

A catalogue record for this book is available from the British Library.

A catalog record for this book is available from the Library of Congress.

Library of Congress Cataloging-in-Publication Data
Names: Pedley, Alison C., author.
Title: Mothers, criminal insanity and the asylum in Victorian England :
cure, redemption and rehabilitation / Alison C. Pedley.
Description: London ; New York : Bloomsbury Academic, 2023. | Series:
History of crime, deviance and punishment | Includes bibliographical
references and index. | Summary: "A history of 'insane' women committed
to criminal lunatic institutions in Victorian England which argues that
they were places of recuperation, recovery and rehabilitation"–
Provided by publisher.
Identifiers: LCCN 2023014135 (print) | LCCN 2023014136 (ebook) |
ISBN 9781350275324 (hardback) | ISBN 9781350275348 (epub) |
ISBN 9781350275331 (ebook)
Subjects: LCSH: Mothers–Mental health–History–19th century. |
Mentally ill women–England–History–19th century. | Psychiatric hospitals–England–
History–19th century. | Insanity (Law)–England–History–19th century. |
Great Britain–History–Victoria, 1837-1901.
Classification: LCC HQ759 .P423 2023 (print) | LCC HQ759 (ebook) |
DDC 362.2/1094109034–dc23/eng/20230501

LC record available at https://lccn.loc.gov/2023014135 .
LC ebook record available at https://lccn.loc.gov/2023014136

ISBN: HB: 978-1-3502-7532-4
PB: 978-1-3502-7535-5
ePDF: 978-1-3502-7533-1
eBook: 978-1-3502-7534-8

Series: History of Crime, Deviance and Punishment

Typeset by Integra Software Services Pvt. Ltd.

To find out more about our authors and books visit www.bloomsbury.com
and sign up for our newsletters.

In loving memory of Charles and Brenda Shakeshaft

Contents

List of charts	x
List of tables	xi
List of illustrations	xii
Abbreviations	xiii
Acknowledgements	xiv
1 'One of the very gravest of crimes': Introduction	1
2 'How criminal lunatics are made': Pathways to the asylum – Court cases, criminal responsibility, insanity defence and the power of medical evidence	27
3 'To be held until her Majesty's pleasure be known': Confinement – opinions, discussions and decisions	57
4 'God bless all hear [sic] for the good nursing I get now.' Dynamics of treatment and care in the asylums	77
5 'They should be … happy and comfortable.' Patient life in the asylums and the impact of behaviour and relationships	99
6 'The paramount importance of gentleness and kindness to all patients.' Therapeutic agency – medical men, chaplains and attendant staff in the asylums	121
7 'She might, without unwarrantable risk, be discharged': Release or retention and the protocols of discharge	139
8 'A depth of sympathy and a breadth of charity': Conclusion	177
Notes	185
Bibliography	234
Index	258

Charts

3.1	Initial place of incarceration for homicidal mothers deemed insane, 1835–63	61
4.1	Recorded causes of insanity from asylum records, 1835 to 1900	84
7.1	Discharges of 302 women admitted between 1835–1900	144
7.2	Discharges by marital status (admissions between 1835 and 1900)	145
7.3	Discharges of pre-1863 Admissions (not Broadmoor) with destination	146

Tables

3.1	Women admitted for the killing of their own children. Broadmoor Criminal Lunatic Asylum, 1863 to 1900	69
4.1	Assigned causes of insanity, 1835 to 1900	84
5.1	Employment extract from Annual Report 1875	109
7.1	'Discharges, Removals & Deaths': admissions between 1863 and 1900	148
7.2	Deaths in the asylums; admissions between 1835 and 1895	169
7.3	Cause of death in incarceration, 1835 to 1895	169

Illustrations

1.1	Bethlem Royal Hospital, 1848	13
1.2	Fisherton House Asylum (Old Manor Hospital)	14
1.3	Broadmoor Criminal Lunatic Asylum, 1867	16
5.1	Plan of Women's Division, 1885	100
5.2	The Airing Court, 1867	112
5.3	Female Dormitory, 1867	120
7.1	Dayroom for infirm female patients, *c.*1910	168
7.2	Broadmoor old burial ground, March 2020	173
8.1	Female Airing Court, *c.*1910	184

Abbreviations

BCLA	Broadmoor Criminal Lunatic Asylum.
BFHS	Berkshire Family History Society.
BMM	Bethlem, Museum of the Mind.
BRO	Berkshire Record Office.
FHA	Fisherton House Asylum.
HO	Home Office.
LCLAR	Lancashire County Lunatic Asylum at Rainhill.
LMA	London Metropolitan Archive.
LRO	Liverpool Record Office.
OBP	Old Bailey Proceedings – online.
TNA	The National Archive.
WC	Wellcome Collection – online.
WHC	Wiltshire & Swindon History Centre, Chippenham.

Acknowledgements

In 1978, I graduated from the University of Liverpool with a BA (Hons) in Modern History. After a break of over thirty years a career in finance followed by motherhood, I decided to return to university. In 2012 I received my MA in Historical Research and in 2020, my PhD, both from the University of Roehampton. When looking for a subject for my MA dissertation, it was suggested that the archive of Broadmoor Hospital (formerly Broadmoor Criminal Lunatic Asylum) to be a source of interesting material. My initial review showed that the majority of women patients between 1863 and 1900 had been committed to the asylum for the killing of their own children. Since then, I have not been able to draw myself away. My research into the lives of nineteenth-century married mothers, who murdered their children and were found to be insane, has been the basis of all my subsequent work. Through engaging in deeper research in and around the subject, I progressed on to my PhD and now this book. I spent eleven years at Roehampton as a part-time postgraduate student attached to the History Department. At the time it was a lively and inclusive department, and I will always value and appreciate studying in such an academically excellent environment. I will be ever grateful to my PhD supervisors, Dr Michael Brown and Dr Meg Arnot. They were unstinting with their help and friendship and were infinitely patient with my idiosyncratic writing style. In particular, Mike's confidence in my ability to get this book written has been magnificent.

While undertaking my studies, I have made lasting contacts with other PhD candidates, now fully blown doctors themselves. In particular, I value the friendship of Dr Tahaney Algrahni, Dr Angela Clark and Dr Helen Rutherford. We propped one another up in tough times, but we all made it in the end! I have been fortunate to have received helpful and interested responses from other scholars. I am very grateful for the encouragement from Professor Anne-Marie Kilday, Professor Joanne Begiato, Professor Hilary Marland, Dr Daniel Grey and Dr Jade Shepherd. I would like to express my gratitude to the two people who reviewed the first manuscript of this book. Your advice and suggestions were wise, valuable and excellent. I hope I have done justice to them all. Additionally, I would like to thank Kim Thomas and Ute Oswald for their kindness in sharing their research; it was appreciated.

Acknowledgements

I would not have been able to complete my PhD and this book without the help of archive staff. Everyone I met gave generously of their time and all were friendly and obliging. I thank Mark Stevens, County Archivist at the Berkshire Record Office, for his generosity in sharing his wide knowledge of Victorian Broadmoor and its records. I also thank Colin Gale at Bethlem, Museum of the Mind, for letting me have a corner of his old office in the Nissan hut at Bethlem in 2013, when I first started my research. It was a privilege to handle and access the original Bethlem case books and files. Thanks, too, to the staff at the Wiltshire History Centre in Chippenham, who provided much help when needed. Amongst my thanks to the archives, I must recognize the staff at the record office of my home city, Liverpool. I will always remember my visits to the Liverpool Record Office, not just for the unprecedented access to records, but also for the special Liverpudlian humour and banter which accompanied my days there.

Finally, I would like to acknowledge the part my family has played. My husband, David, has uncomplainingly borne all the highs and lows of research, been my in-house computer boffin and my rock. My son, Tom and his partner, Jasmine put up with me dropping in on them on research trips to Liverpool, without complaint. All my life, I had support from my parents in whatever I chose to do. Right up to their deaths, they always wanted to know how my writing was going and would listen with close attention to the stories I was telling. Their lifelong support and guidance in my careers and studies was unstinting and invaluable. For that reason, I have dedicated my book to them, with all my love. Charles Shakeshaft 1925–2019 and Brenda Shakeshaft, née M'Cartney, 1926–2021. Without my family and their support, patience and love, that none of this would have happened. Thanks are hardly enough.

1

'One of the very gravest of crimes': Introduction

On her release from Broadmoor in 1870, after seventeen years in confinement, Amelia Burt wrote that she was 'truly sensible of the care and the kindness I have received for so many years'.[1] She had been originally committed to Bethlem Royal Hospital in 1852; then she was transferred to Broadmoor Criminal Lunatic Asylum in May 1863 as one of the first patients. Amelia Burt had been tried at the Old Bailey on 13 December 1852 for the wilful murder, by drowning, of her nine-month-old baby, Annie Philadelphia.[2] The witnesses' descriptions of her behaviour at the time of the crime led the judge, Mr Justice Wightman, to conclude that she must have been insane, and he advised the jury to acquit her on those grounds.[3] Initially, Amelia was sent into Surrey County Gaol, Horsemongers Lane, then, on 27 December, she was admitted into Bethlem as a criminal patient.[4] The casebook notes explain that once in the Hospital, she was a model patient, being 'very good-tempered and obedient ... and her intellect is clear'. This was despite the fact that she 'continued in a low state of mind' and 'only in this way [shows] any symptom of insanity'.[5]

In her first seven months in Bethlem, Amelia had never been seen to smile, and the medical officers were concerned that she could be suicidal. By April 1854, she had become 'almost cheerful ... and frequently smiles', still working with her needle and in 'excellent bodily health'.[6] Despite her apparent tranquillity and unlike other 'less dangerous' patients, Amelia was not removed to the criminal lunatic ward at Fisherton House Asylum in Salisbury. However, she was transferred to Broadmoor on 30 May 1863.[7] In 1870, she was allowed to write to the Home Secretary to petition for her release. In her letter, she described her husband as 'being of unsteady habits' and claimed that she had 'not seen or heard of [him] for the last 16 years'.[8] On their medical certificate, Dr John Meyer and Dr William Orange confirmed that they found 'her to be Sane and in good bodily health'.[9] In turn, in their covering letter to the certificate, the Governors of Broadmoor confirmed that Amelia's mother and sister were willing to receive her after discharge.¹⁰ She was duly discharged on 2 April 1870.¹¹ By April 1871, she was living with her mother in Bermondsey, under her maiden name of Gibson.¹²

At the heart of this book is a discrete set of women, mothers who had killed their children in nineteenth-century England and Wales and who were determined to be criminally insane. Amelia Burt's life story for the years between 1852 and 1870 is a history of one such mother and her experiences of the law, courts and lunatic asylums in Victorian England. As a vignette, it acts as an introduction and lends some colour to the themes and arguments in this book. It was hard to select just one such history to cover a substantial part of the Victorian period; however, Amelia Burt's crime and her incarceration in two separate specialist criminal lunatic facilities make her story a relevant case study. Additionally, Amelia's trial is documented in the Proceedings of the Old Bailey, and it was also widely covered in the press. She was transferred from remand in prison to Bethlem where detailed casebook notes were kept, and then she was one of the first tranche of patients admitted to Broadmoor in 1863.¹³ Amelia Burt spent her final seven years in an institution in Broadmoor and was one of the few early cases to be unconditionally discharged from there. The final part of her incarceral story is contained in the relevant Home Office files which contain her petition for release and other official correspondence detailing her discharge.¹⁴ Her seventeen years in detention covered a period of both consolidation and change in the protocols and procedures surrounding confinement of criminal lunatics. It was also the time when the new, dedicated criminal lunatic asylum became a firmly established part of the medico-legal and asylum landscape.

Notwithstanding the fact that criminally insane mothers had carried out a socially unacceptable deed, they were not inevitably censured by the public, nor by the legal and medical worlds of nineteenth-century England. Prevailing Victorian expectations of motherhood coupled with sociocultural ideas of respectability influenced decisions made about all maternal child homicides. Despite fixed ideas of morally acceptable behaviour, women who had violently attacked their children were not automatically seen as morally reprehensible, nor deviant nor degenerate. If a woman's weakened mental state was believed to be so damaged that her moral senses of maternal responsibility and duty were overridden, then a feasible assumption was that violent, out-of-character behaviour could follow. All collective social principles had the potential to influence interpersonal dealings between the mothers and the male legal, medical and governmental authorities. The concept that considerate humanity frequently drove societal attitudes is examined by chronicling and analysing individual experiences of a dataset of infanticidal and homicidal women deemed to be criminally insane. There was a willingness in society to treat vulnerable women such as infanticidal mothers and suicidal women as mad, but redeemably so. In this book, the lives of mothers who killed their children are explored and analysed with the aim of finding answers to the questions: 'Why were the mothers who had violently assaulted their children, considered to be curable and redeemable? Were they seen as very different from other criminal lunatic women? And what were the cultural and social factors which lay behind the responses and treatment they received on their passage through the legal and asylum systems in Victorian England and Wales?'

Respectability and class

A key strand in the book is the influence of contemporary views of respectability on social perceptions of criminally insane maternal child murderers in Victorian England. Contemporary ideas of 'proper and respectable' class behaviour underlie many of the themes in this book. The social background of all parties, including the women, their families and kin and the men from medical and legal authorities, had an impact on the interpersonal and professional relationships. Respectability in the nineteenth century was a societal gauge by which people were observed and judged, an unwritten set of social rules defined by morality and discipline. The layers of society had differing codes of behaviour and such 'rules' encompassed expectations of personal behaviour, of family life and social interaction. It was generally expected that a respectable person would conduct themselves and their relationships in a decent and proper manner, whatever their background. As a concept of behaviour, respectability was seen as important to an ordered society, although what it meant differed from class to class.[15]

David Cannadine believes that individual views of respectability and acceptable behaviour depended, to an extent, on where people believed they stood in society.[16] As he wrote, 'middle-class observers believed only a minority of workers was respectable: the workers themselves often thought otherwise.'[17] To use class as an impartial appraisal of social position is a complex historiographical issue. The term itself can be emotive and idiosyncratic. In his book, *The Public Culture of the Victorian Middle Class*, Simon Gunn observes that membership of a certain social class is amorphous and changed over historical time periods. If membership of a certain grouping depended on solely income and economic circumstances, then the boundaries became unclear. There is a school of thought that the Victorian class structure, in particular the development of the middle class, was a performative sociocultural construction.[18] Gunn argues that class identity grew from social conduct and attitudes, which behaviours became markers on how each social grouping viewed the other. Urban nineteenth-century society can be defined by a series of opposites, between the educated and the uneducated, or mental and manual labour all underpinning expectations of social status.

As Daniel Grey writes, behavioural propriety and being of good character were an important factor to both lay and professional commentators in cases of maternal infanticide.[19] The research undertaken for this book supports Grey's opinion and shows that the prevailing expectations of female respectability and of maternal behaviour did have an influence on Victorian inter-class interactions and opinions. The hypothesis that Victorian views of female decency and motherhood played a part in nineteenth-century society's views of female criminality is not original. Lucia Zedner suggests that such views were a 'highly artificial notion of the ideal woman – an exemplary moral being', and as such could be detrimental to the way they were viewed in court.[20] She also wrote that condemnation of infanticidal mothers lay less with the crime but more with a woman's social status, for example, whether she was married or not. So, although Zedner states that the moral views of ideal womanhood were 'highly artificial', she does acknowledge that they could influence the middle-class arbiters of legal, medical and governmental opinion.[21] This is borne out throughout this book, in particular in Chapters 2 and 3. All the decisions made about the futures of the women had their roots in, potentially class-driven, subjective characterization opinions voiced during their journeys through the medico-legal and asylum systems. The effect of various class interpretations of moral decorum and respectability impacted on public and official opinions of women's lives both before and after their crime.

Leading on from this, it should be remembered that the male figures of authority with whom the women came into contact were invariably from the middle and, occasionally, upper classes. It is conceivable that their opinions would be coloured by their own backgrounds and that they would have had certain perceptions of domestic life. Nonetheless, as James Hammerton writes, it is a supposition that all middle-class families adhered to the domestic ideology of 'separate spheres'.[22] An ideology which advocated that the 'man of the house' would work outside of the home, providing for the family and that his wife and mother of his children would, in return, create a domestic safe haven for his comfort. Her life would be immersed in caring for the moral and physical welfare of all of her family.[23] As both Anne Digby and John Tosh have suggested, this domestic 'idyll' was not uniformly practised or accepted by all middle-class families.[24] To many middle-class observers, a working-class family was only respectable if the husband was employed, prudent, affectionate and non-violent and the wife was a good housekeeper and a fond mother.[25] Victorian philanthropic commentators and charitable observers adhered to the opinion that the model of a working family should be one of hardworking, caring and thriftful mutual support. Joanne Begiato points out that middle-class observers viewed working-class men and their domestic lives, against their own somewhat judgemental criteria.[26] While Cannadine suggests that 'middle-class Christian virtues' of kindness, decency and prudence, spread to the lower classes over the Victorian period, Begiato (writing as Joanne Bailey) counters the argument. She states that similar cultural expectations of family and of family responsibilities had long existed in the working class too.[27] Jonathan Andrews in his study of Broadmoor's female patients suggests that despite being from differing places in society and showing the occasional lack of appreciation for the socioeconomics of poorer families, the middle-class legal, medical and governmental officials acknowledged that many of the domestic values of lower classes were 'acceptable'. These middle- and upper-class men found that the domestic standards of the lower classes could be as respectable as their own values.[28]

Respectability in working-class society has been discussed in an influential body of scholarship.[29] Ellen Ross's book *Love and Toil: Motherhood in Outcast London* highlights the struggles of poor households in Victorian England and is an invaluable guide to the circumstances of the majority of the women studied. Ross described what respectability might mean to poorer families. It would depend on the father's employment situation, on whether the wife kept a clean house and on whether the children seemed well cared for and adequately fed.[30] At the centre of a respectable, working-class Victorian home was the mother-figure. She could be the wife, mother, stepmother, grandmother, sister of the 'head of the house' with domestic responsibilities falling to the females within a family group. Working-class mothers were seen as the fulcrum of the home, taking pride in capably managing children and the domestic economy – keeping a respectable home was considered an essential quality in a married woman.[31] Working-class principles included loyal extended family relationships and neighbourly support to their contemporaries.[32] Although behavioural emphases differed from class to class, all had their own recognized conventions and knew how their particular society expected them to behave in order to be considered as respectable. [33]

The living conditions of working-class families and the impact these conditions might have on family life, have also been the subject of scholarly discussion.[34] Emma

Cuming writes that a poor home could often be just one or two rooms with shared facilities and families frequently moved accommodation. In order to boost the household economy, it was not unusual to sublet what rooms the family had and take in boarders.[35] From quite an early age, children might be expected to contribute to the running of the household.[36] Middle-class ideals of an innocent childhood, carefree and safe, would be beyond the economic means of many working families.[37] Steven Taylor notes that frequent changes of accommodation and changes in the make-up of a household would have an impact on the children. By the nature of the home situation, they would be exposed to all types of behaviours, many of which which be seen as immoral to some middle-class observers.[38] Many lower-class families were judged by such moralistic observers as being fractured, uncaring and neglectful. Their behaviour was seen as carelessly immoral towards the younger family members. Contemporary commentaries have led to a lasting idea that poorer Victorian parents lacked emotional connection with their children.[39] Julie Marie Strange counters this assumption and suggests that the emotional bonds within Victorian working-class families were not always obvious. Emotional connections and familial affection were more likely to be shown through the work involved in caring for and feeding children.[40] Significantly for married women, careful mothering and good housekeeping skills, which were not dissimilar to middle-class domestic ideals, were the basic expectations to being a fond parent.[41]

What constituted 'good' and 'true' motherliness became increasingly more idealized in Victorian Britain, and these expectations of mothers from all levels of society had elemental differences due to class and cultural viewpoints.[42] Emma Griffin writes that it was expected that a mother should be nurturing, with her maternal love exhibited through good housekeeping abilities and through being closely attentive to the whole family's needs and well-being.[43] The linking thread between all was that mothers were expected to have an emotional bond with their children. As Griffin also states, 'the love between a mother and her child [was and] is one of the most elemental of human emotional experiences,' which is frequently demonstrated in many of the cases studied throughout this book.[44] The lives and background of the accused infanticidal and homicidal mothers and other women discussed in this book were scrutinized and commented on by all quarters, throughout their passages into the criminal lunatic facilities. They had their home lives and characters publicly and medically dissected. The women could face various public appearances where the circumstances of their crimes and the state of their physical and mental health would be pored over. Medical experts, lawyers, coroners, judges, magistrates and juries could all at some point express critical opinions. These views could be countered or supported by witness testimonials from their families, social contemporaries and neighbours, their own kith and kin, each giving contextual and personal explanations for the women's crimes. Despite all that had happened, such scrutinization would frequently show that they were frequently still be considered to be respectable women in all aspects and loving, fond mothers.

Infanticide and moral outcry

In the nineteenth century, there were frequent public outcries and moral anxiety about the rates of child death and infanticide. Victorian society was alarmed by the seemingly steep rise in the reported number of cases of infanticide. With medical campaigners and social reformers presenting infanticide as a widespread social problem, public sentiment was stirred up.[45] The 'moral panic' of the mid-nineteenth century was a public response to what was believed to be social problems of the poor.[46] The term 'infanticide' was used in Victorian medical writings, in the press and eventually in general public consciousness, to describe the killing of children of all ages, from newborn to adolescent.[47] Before the 1922 Infanticide Act, the charges brought in court were 'wilful murder', 'manslaughter' or 'concealment', although in legal papers, the word 'infanticide' could be 'applied to the murder of infants within a year of their birth'.[48] The Victorian press used the word widely, reporting on inquests into suspicious child deaths in detail, thereby drawing the public attention to 'every single case of child murder brought before our coroners'.[49] The reports could be quite shocking and salacious and probably played a part in fuelling the recurrent moral panics about the number of child deaths in the country.

It is not possible to definitively explain the reasons for the high incidence of infanticide and child homicide in Victorian England. There is not one easy applicable answer as the motives and rationales were as diverse and widespread as the incidents themselves.[50] In popular thought, the main reasons for infanticide, in particular, were popularly believed to be desperation, poverty and the shame of illegitimacy.[51] A typical perpetrator was perceived as a young, desperate woman from the servant class, who had probably been seduced and abandoned.[52] Another was the evil baby-farmer who would take the infant and, with or without the knowledge of a desperate mother, destroy it.[53] In 1846, the *Times* carried an editorial on the subject of infanticide which commented on legal trials of newborn child murder. It declared that 'Not a day passes but the disclosures of ... a trial, establish the melancholy truth that human life is losing its value.' The article continued, 'The laxity of the verdicts and leniency of the sentences ... prove ... we are becoming familiarized with the crime [infanticide] and we consider it palliated by extreme provocation of circumstances. Crime ... is crime and its guilt rests somewhere.'[54] Despite opinion such as this, somewhat conversely a society which regarded poverty as self-inflicted or escapable, could accept that mitigating situations of violation, negligence and deprivation could potentially drive a mother to murder her child.[55] The more socially and culturally acceptable verdicts, such as concealment or insanity being given in court, meant that the conscience of all 'decent' society could be considered as salved.

While economic, moral, cultural and social factors of Victorian society might have contributed to the perceived extent of infanticide, they alone do not explain any one particular case. One theory expressed by Leonard Rose in the mid-1980s was that the increase in infant mortality and infanticide was motivated by economic and social pressures. As the birth rate rose, 'surplus' or unwanted children were allowed to die, as a solution to over-population of the poor. Whether such deaths were the result of deliberate neglect or ultimately by parental infanticide, child mortality was a matter of controlling family size and economics. [56] In contra-point to this hypothesis, Anne Marie Kilday points out that, while the idea of newborn child murder was a possible but somewhat extreme, way to limit the size of a family, such cases were difficult to prove and rarely prosecuted. The high rates of infant mortality, whatever the domestic situation of the parents and the household, meant that contemporary opinion tended to accept that a child's unexplained death would be more likely to have been from natural causes, rather than from suspicious parental activity.[57]

The cases where homicidal mothers were charged with killing or assaulting their legitimate children presented a problem to Victorian England and Wales. There were legal dilemmas surrounding the prosecution of married mothers for committing child murder. Kilday highlights the fact that the marital status of a female defendant impacted upon cultural, legal and medical views of all mothers who murdered their legitimate children.[58] The existing legislation was focused upon illegitimacy and as the larger proportion of the women within the studied cases were married, their fate would not be impacted by such legislation. A prevailing, perhaps essentially middle-class, 'moral' view was that mothers with legitimate offspring had no obvious explanation for committing this crime, except, perhaps, insanity. That being said, even cases tried under the existing infanticide legislation frequently received what were deemed lenient verdicts, including verdicts of insanity. Daniel Grey points out that any woman accused of killing her children was repeatedly treated with sympathy by the press and the criminal justice system. [59] He also suggests that this sympathetic leniency towards what was a distressing and tragic crime was based on a stereotyping of the women defendants as normally being 'respectable' and of good character.[60] This theory is borne out by the discourse surrounding the cases researched for this book.

Women and criminal insanity

There was a judicial reluctance to pass a capital sentence for infanticide, both for the killing of infants under twelve months old as well as in its broader meaning of all child murder. The charge would more frequently be concealment of birth or manslaughter. The lenience or benevolent concern would stem from a sympathy for a young, single mother's desperation and possible violation by the father of the child. The accused would be viewed as more sinned against, than a sinner herself. Katherine Watson notes that in her research, she has found that cases of possible madness, if verified by medical opinion, were not heard at assizes and 'diverted from the criminal justice system' or faced a lesser charge.[61] This hypothesis, while maybe applicable to new born murder, is not strictly true in cases involving older children. On many occasions, the records show that patients would admit, whether in truth or in delusion, that they had killed their child to spare it the hardships of life.

There is a large body of scholarship which acknowledges infanticidal mothers would be viewed with sympathy Victorian society and the legal system and thereby receive more compassionate hearings in court than other female offenders.[62] One reason for this might lie in the fact that these mothers tended to not be seen as habitual criminals, but were victims of their weak minds and physiology. Zedner puts forward the idea that the medical profession had 'persuaded' or rather convinced the legal world that the use of the insanity plea for women committing a capital crime, thereby overring true 'legal discourse with that of psychiatry' was the best defence strategy.[63] Leading on from this, Roger Smith and Nigel Walker, to single out two other influential scholars, wrote that the use of insanity as a defence in cases of infanticidal mothers was a convenient legal justification to avoid capital punishment.[64] To interpret the defence of insanity as merely a medico-legal ploy robs it of its nuance. Despite the labelling of the crime of maternal child murder as cruel and atrocious, poverty, domestic violence or indeed the implication of madness were widely accepted as mitigating circumstances for vicious, violent behaviour.[65] To most in Victorian society, then as now, the idea of hanging a mother, even if she had murdered her own child or children, was culturally and morally repugnant.

In cases where the accused women were the biological mothers of the child victims, cultural sensitivities led to a tendency to accept that mothers would only carry out such crimes if it was proved that they were mentally deranged at the time. The source of this perhaps lies in cultural ideals and conventions of female 'natural' behaviour, the received wisdom that women were not naturally prone to violence and would protect their young and not harm them. Insanity gave people a 'bearable' explanation for the abhorrent act of infanticide or child murder and thereby avoid the spectre of capital punishment. Its success has been attributed to the way women were regarded by certain elements of Victorian society. Roger Smith agrees that the perceived fragility of women and their natural closeness to nature allowed 'medico-legal discourse to describe legally exculpatory conditions'.[66] Contemporary understandings of female physical and mental vulnerability impacted on decisions about their futures.[67] An accepted truism was that only a woman suffering from some sort of mental aberration would step away from the role of nurturing motherhood, far enough to attack her own children and commit a deed so outside society's norms of behaviour. Women were regarded as fragile beings whose physical and mental health was at the mercy of their physiology. While it was 'accepted' that the female physiology could place strains on a woman's sanity, so could other mitigating circumstances, such as sexual violation and even drink and insobriety.[68] These mitigations were often considered to be indications of the weakness and vulnerability of the female mind.[69]

In 1852, Dr Charles Hood of Bethlem Royal Hospital published a paper entitled *Suggestions for the Future Provision of Criminal Lunatics*, in which he gave his opinions on and proposals for, the care of the criminally insane.[70] In particular, he referred to mothers who had killed their own children, suggesting that they should be in a facility where they would be helped and cured. He described them as having 'a peculiar claim upon our sympathies' and that it was his experience and belief that, 'the most amiable and gentle of her sex may in the agonies of childbirth or some days afterwards, be attacked with puerperal mania and commit infanticide'.[71] In their extensive work, Martin Weiner and Joel Eigen state that sympathetic views of an infanticidal mother and her circumstances became most noticeable after the 1860s. This is evidenced, they suggest, by the drop in the number of prosecutions for concealment and the shortening of consequent prison sentences were shortened.[72] On this point, I also suggest that having the opening of Broadmoor in 1863, together with evolving theories of psychology and psychiatry, led to a greater willingness to incarcerate 'criminally insane' women in an asylum. As Arlie Loughnan says, the way forward, both legally and medically, was seen to be confinement in the new facility where they would get treatment and hopefully be relieved and cured.[73]

Nearly fifty years after the publication of Hood's paper, Dr John Baker, Medical Superintendent of Broadmoor Criminal Lunatic Asylum, wrote a paper specifically describing and detailing statistics about the female criminal lunatics under his care.[74] He noted:

> It is a sad fact to record but the registers of Broadmoor show that 253 women slaughtered their children. [...] In addition, maternal violence was responsible for attempts on the lives of 33 infants [...] it was only an accident that a fatal result did not ensue. [...] I consider [there to be] 286 cases of infanticide [in Broadmoor][75]

Public perceptions and official opinions of criminality and in particular female criminality were challenged by women whose crime was driven by their mental state and events beyond their control. In turn this impacted on medical and legal attitudes and consequently those opinions often differed on the desirability of incarceral care. There were members of the judiciary who were reluctant to accept that dedicated criminal lunatic asylums were anything but places of imprisonment. To their eyes, incarceration 'until her Majesty's pleasure be known' was an endless sentence, and not a restorative treatment. They did not view the asylum as a place of protection which existed to try to cure and help insane offenders. Such views ran contrary to government and to most medical opinion. As a Home Office official wrote to Lord Alverstone in 1902,

> the kind judicious treatment they receive in the Asylum – which is in no sense a place of punishment – tends to promote rather than retard their permanent recovery and make them better fitted to resume their place in the world. [76]

Once it was established by legal process that the accused women were indeed insane, the next years of their lives would be spent at her Majesty's pleasure, as criminal lunatics, before discharge or death. There was a subtle but clear differentiation between two classes of insane criminals. The delineation between non-convict and convict criminal lunatics was significant in shaping the attitudes of asylum staff, medical and non-medical officers and had an impact on treatment in the asylums. Writing in 1877, Dr David Nicolson, the then Deputy Medical Superintendent at Broadmoor, described 'two distinct classes of criminal lunatics', the 'unconvicted' and the 'convicted' lunatic. He wrote that, in his and the opinion of his superior at Broadmoor, Dr William Orange, the two classes required 'different methods of management and treatment'.[77] In 1902, Dr John Baker, defined the two groups thus: 'Criminal lunatics' were those patients who had been deemed insane by a court on a plea that they were insane at the time the criminal act was committed. Distinct from these patients were 'convicts and felons', who were found to be insane after conviction, during a custodial sentence. He wrote, 'In contradistinction they are termed lunatic criminals.'[78]

In Broadmoor parlance, the classes of criminally insane patient who had been admitted 'until her Majesty's pleasure be known', were known as 'Queen's pleasure patients'. As Jade Shepherd finds in her studies of Broadmoor's male patients, there was definite difference in attitudes towards the insane convict patients, they were generally considered to be immoral and intellectually defective, and their mental states probably incurable. The research for this book reiterates Shepherd's findings that all the medical superintendents at Broadmoor, during their respective tenures, viewed the inclusion of both female and male insane convicts as a hindrance to maintaining the curative functions of the asylum.[79] The length of time the women reviewed for this book remained in the various asylums, depended on different factors which evolved and changed over the Victorian period. Some patients improved quickly and would be released within a short time period, whereas others would be incarcerated for longer, if not for the rest of their lives. For the women's part, consideration for release and discharge could depend on how they conformed to the authorities' expectations of behaviour.

While the attitudes of the medical staff may have impacted on the way patients were treated, in reality, all criminal patients were admitted by warrant from the Secretary of State for the Home Office. Whatever their designation in the asylum might have been, their release, or retention, was also at the behest of the Home Office, even for those admitted from penal custody. Those found to be insane after conviction and while serving a penal sentence, would remain in the asylum until they were certified as being 'of sound mind'. If they had reached the end of their term of imprisonment, they would be released, if not they would be returned to prison to finish their sentences. On the other hand, if they were still considered to be insane at the end of their original penal sentence, they would be admitted to another, non-criminal, asylum as pauper lunatics. It was suggested contemporaneously that the relative comforts of an asylum compared to a county gaol led to a certain amount of shamming or pretence of insanity. Jade Shepherd points out that it was not always as easy to gain a transfer to the specialized institutions as was supposed by the shammers.[80] While her article concentrates on male offenders, the subject of potential playacting and shamming is also relevant to women offenders and appears within various chapters of this book.

As for the genuine patients, Chapter 7 highlights the protocols and procedures involved in being released from the institutions. The process included careful investigation into the suitability and ability of the patients' family backgrounds to look after the, potentially, mentally vulnerable women. Once released, the women would be carefully watched by their kith and kin for incipient signs of instability, effectively considering them as 'invalids' for the rest of their lives. However, whether the potential dischargees had been 'cured' or 'relieved' of their mental illness and so were fit to be at large in the community, was ultimately a decision taken by the Home Office, with medical advice.

Asylums for the criminally insane

In his 1877 treatise, Dr David Nicolson explained what he saw as the defining history of the treatment of criminal insanity. In a contemporary succinct summary of the state provision for the criminally insane, he divided the history into four periods. The first, he believed, was the period up to 1800, when lunatic criminals were in prison. The second period was between 1800 and 1840, when they were recognized as insane and held in asylums. The third, between 1840 and 1860, which he called the 'Reactionary Period', when it was recognized that this state of affairs was unsatisfactory, and something needed to be done. Finally, he came to what he dubbed the 'Broadmoor Period – or Period of Centralization – the present method of disposal'.[81] Certainly, before 1863 and the opening of Broadmoor, the small, specialist provisions at Bethlem Royal Lunatic Asylum and at Fisherton House Asylum in Salisbury, were woefully inadequate.

Image 1.1 Bethlem Royal Hospital, 1848.[82]

Although specialist wards or wings for the criminally insane had been established at Bethlem in 1816, only a small number of patients could be accommodated. The two independent blocks (one male and one female) which constituted the state criminal lunatic asylum stood on either side of the main building. Although administered by the Hospital authorities, admissions to the wings were controlled by the Home Office and they were maintained at government expense.[83] Bethlem remained the sole dedicated facility in England and Wales until 1848. In that year, protected accommodation for less dangerous criminal patients was created at Fisherton House Asylum, near Salisbury.

The background to Fisherton House has been less well documented than that of either Bethlem or Broadmoor; therefore, it is necessary to describe the place and significance of Fisherton House. Fisherton House was acquired

Image 1.2 Fisherton House Asylum (Old Manor Hospital, c.1985).[84]

in the early nineteenth century by William Corbin Finch, senior, and started taking private and pauper patients from 1813.[85] Corbin Finch was a surgeon from London and the proprietor of three other licensed madhouses, namely Kensington House and The Retreat, Kings Road in London and Laverstock House also near Salisbury. In the early years, Fisherton House was managed by Finch's uncle, Charles Finch, who was not medically qualified. William Corbin Finch provided the medical gravitas needed to prove the asylum's worth as a curative institution.[86] Members of the Finch family remained as the proprietors, management and senior medical staff until the middle years of the twentieth century. William Corbin Finch (senior) succeeded Charles Finch as proprietor and, in turn, was succeeded by his son, William Corbin Finch (junior) and son-in-law, John Lush.[87] Dr John A. Lush was a nephew of Finch's wife and he joined the Finches as a co-proprietor and medical superintendent in 1862.[88]

In 1848, Corbin Finch won a contract with the Home Office to construct two wards to house an overflow of criminal patients from Bethlem. As proprietors and medical superintendents, Drs Finch and Lush appear to have responded to the Whitehall authorities in a less deferential manner than their contemporaries and appeared to expect more autonomy in their establishment. The agreement was that they would take in less dangerous criminal patients who would not necessarily need specialist treatment. In reality, when it came to women patients, the transferees from Bethlem were often those who seemed to be recovering and could be soon discharged. In the years when Fisherton House was functioning, they also took cases straight from court and additionally took cases which, it was felt, prisons would not able to cope with, such as pregnant women. By the latter half of the nineteenth century, Fisherton House had become the largest private asylum ever in the UK.[89]

Prior to 1863, there was no coherent pattern of incarceration for the criminally insane as the dedicated facilities could only provide a small number of places for them. Many were housed in county and borough asylums or remained in prison. By 1851, the number of criminal patients in ordinary private or public asylums had increased to such a point that it was said that the borough and county asylums held more criminal lunatics than Bethlem Royal Hospital or Fisherton House Asylum together.[90] The problem of accommodation had been exacerbated by the 1840 *Insane Prisoners Act*. By its terms, two Justices of the Peace could certify that a prisoner was insane, either before or after trial, thereby authorizing a transfer to an asylum. [91] The provision applied to anyone confined by consequence of a capital or a criminal offence, or any summary conviction other than civil process. Many of the county and borough asylums medical superintendents believed that their institutions were unsuitable for the purpose of housing the criminally insane. Their frequent cry, backed by the Commissioners in Lunacy, was for a separate specialized asylum.[92]

Lord Shaftesbury was a keen supporter of having a dedicated institution to house and treat the criminally insane. In a parliamentary debate he gave a speech quoting a list of reasons for not detaining criminal patients in asylums with the other patients. He concluded, 'It is unjust to ordinary patients to associate them with persons branded with crime. The lunatic is generally very sensitive and … [can] feel aggrieved and degraded by association.'[93] This opinion was backed by the reports from the Commissioners in Lunacy. Their reports were based on the canvassed views of various asylum medical superintendents. The so-called convict lunatic or lunatic criminals received much antipathy from the asylum authorities.[94] In their experience and opinion, the presence of criminal patients took attention away from ordinary patients, impinging on and damaging the curative atmosphere of the asylum.[95] Eventually in 1856, the Government announced plans for a state lunatic asylum and, in the same year, a site on the edge of Windsor Forest, near Wokingham in Berkshire, was acquired.[96] Subsequently, the 1860 *Criminal Lunatics Asylum Act* ('The Broadmoor Act') was passed and finally Broadmoor Criminal Lunatic Asylum was opened in 1863.[97]

Image 1.3 Broadmoor Criminal Lunatic Asylum, 1867.[98]

Moral therapy and the criminal lunatic facilities

The Victorian era was one of development in the asylum system and in medical treatment of insanity. Nationally, large county asylums were established, eventually becoming accepted as part of the local community.[99] The treatment regimens also evolved, encompassing principles of moral therapy as a more humanitarian system of care for the insane. Originally conceived in the early nineteenth century by Samuel Tuke of The Retreat in York, it was a treatment regime designed to give the mentally disordered time to recover from the stresses of their former lives. [100] Moral treatment of insanity was based on ideas of developing renewed self-esteem through keeping the mind and body occupied within a domestic environment, supported by good nutrition and exercise.[101] The therapy advocated a life modelled on the middle-class home, with minimum restraint. Patients and staff would eat and work together, recovery would be assisted by a mixture of praise and blame, reward and punishment, thereby enabling the mind to recover self-control.[102] There would be little medical intervention, with limited use of tranquilizers or hypnotic drugs and restraint. If restraint was deemed necessary, it was supposed to be restricted to use for the protection and safety of individuals, not punishment.[103] The premise was that, if mentally ill patients were treated with benevolence and compassionate regulation, then they would recover rational control over their minds and actions.[104]

An essential part of the moral therapy philosophy was that sympathetic personal interactions would induce patients 'to adopt orderly habits' and help patients recover mental stability and their sanity.[105] Environmental factors were also believed to play an important role in the aetiology of mental problems. Through creating the right atmosphere of calm and respect for patients in the asylums, moral therapy was believed to be the treatment with the most potential to 'cure' insanity. All the objectives of moral therapy as a treatment for the insane were well-intentioned. However, through some of the more paternalistic elements of its philosophy, moral therapy did have an underlying authoritarian aspect of control. In the opinion of Michel Foucault, moral therapy or rather moral management was a systematic process to coerce and control the insane members of society.[106] In her work about The Retreat, Anne Digby suggests that while some records from the Retreat show a genuine concern from the therapists for the patients' well-being, others indicate that a certain amount of control and domination was necessary to achieve the curative aims of the regime.[107] Foucault's interpretation of the purpose behind the use of moral management in the asylums was to control and shape the mentally ill into submission to a larger 'bourgeois' system of management.[108] Andrew Scull further suggests that moral treatment existed to transform asylum patients into 'a bourgeois ideal of the rational individual'.[109] He also points out that moral treatment was 'a superior way of managing patients'.[110] That being said, Scull accepts that the system was a more humane way of treating the insane than the prevalent methods of the eighteenth century. In many ways, Andrew Scull's and Michel Foucault's assertions that the asylums were disciplinary institutions and that moral therapy was a system of control are correct.[111]

When it comes to the criminal lunatic facilities, by the nature of some of the crimes committed and the people who had committed them, discipline and control were necessary for the safety of other patients and staff. This was particularly true of Bethlem and Broadmoor. The perception of Bethlem as a harsh, uncaring environment was due in part to its long history and to some past less-than-humane methods of treatment. In the case of Broadmoor, press reports of the behaviour, treatment and control of the patients who were considered to be from the feared criminal classes, added to its reputation. Certainly, in 1867, three years after Broadmoor was established, it was reported in the *Illustrated London News* that there was a separate block 'for the special security of violent and dangerous men'.[112] Contemporary press reports represented the convict lunatic patients as dangerous and manipulative, and that they could 'contaminate and offend … all the other patients'.[113] Twenty years later, in 1885, the *Globe* carried an article which also painted a less than positive view of the patients. Despite praising the environs of the asylum and the positivity of occupational treatment, there was still negativity when describing the patients, painting many of them as hopeless and lost cases. The writer was particularly harsh and unsympathetic about the women patients saying,

> While neither so savage nor ungovernable as the worst cases among the men, the mad women at Broadmoor form a spectacle painful in the extreme. Among their number every form of mania and hypochondria may found and … the result is frequently sufficiently terrible to be gladly avoided by all excepting those whose duty requires their attendance[114]

All such descriptions added to the popular, and lasting, reputation that Broadmoor was a horrific place in which to be confined.[115] A more positive portrait of the asylum was painted in 1903 by George C. Griffith-Jones (1857–1906). He was an author and wrote a number of books about prisons and prison life. He visited Broadmoor in 1902 and within his subsequent book wrote, 'The only likeness that Broadmoor bears to a prison consists in the fact that you can go nowhere without the unlocking and relocking of solid doors and iron gates; but within these there is no evidence of restraint.' Further on in the chapter, Griffiths commented on the environment of the asylum:

> there are the common rooms, recreation-rooms, theatre, and concert-rooms, which you would look for in vain in the most perfect of British prisons. In short, the main idea of the designers appears to have been to get as much fresh air and sunlight as possible, and they have certainly succeeded exceedingly well. In fact, take away the bars from the windows, the iron gratings at the ends of the corridors and at every entrance from the grounds, and you would have in Broadmoor a perfectly arranged sanatorium, situated amidst the most delightful surroundings[116]

Oppressive discipline and patriarchal control were more often an intention than a reality, particularly in criminal asylums. Humanitarian initiatives in treatment and interactions, such as gainful employment and basic education, were pursued at the same time as the perceived controlling elements. [117] These strategies and activities were an integral part of Samuel Tuke's ideas for treatment of the insane and practised by the criminal lunatic asylums.[118] Their influence and impact in the criminal lunatic asylums, particularly in regard to women patients, are examined in the chapters about life in the asylums. The tenets of moral treatment remained at the root of many aspects of life in the asylums and had an impact on the lives of all women patients, including the infanticidal and homicidal mothers. The discussions within scholarship, in particular the work about criminally insane women, generally agree that Victorian facilities for the criminally insane were not just places of containment but could also be places of redemption, rehabilitation and restitution.[119] As places of containment for the dangerously and criminally insane, the facilities were there to protect the public. Nonetheless, an essential part of their mission was to also protect the mentally vulnerable and treat them humanely and kindly, eventually returning them to their kith and kin as at least 'recovered' and, hopefully, cured.[120]

Methodology and sources

The foundation for this book is my PhD thesis and its core research, the lives and experiences of infanticidal or child homicidal mothers deemed to be criminally insane, in Victorian England and Wales. The database for my thesis contained 288 records and covered records for the years from 1835 to 1895. It was an extremely useful tool which helped to control the records pertaining to the women and their individual life histories, while also helping with the necessary analyses. The principal aim for this book is to examine the experiences of the same discrete set of women over the slightly longer time period of 1835 to 1901, thereby encompassing all the years of Queen Victoria's reign. Accordingly, the database grew and now contains records well over three hundred records. The database was built from a number of sources, including casebooks, correspondence, official and personal, official administrative documents and other primary and secondary sources. The women's lives, experiences and social backgrounds were examined using a micro-historical approach, and personal biographies of the women were created. Individual experiences and social background impacted on all aspects of their passage through the Victorian medico-legal system, as did ideas of respectability, of marital status and familial relationships. Through a close analytical focus on the unique dataset of women in a time of much social change, my work contributes to the wider historiography of medical and legal treatment of insanity in the institutional systems of Victorian England and Wales. Case books, case files, both official and personal correspondence, reports and medical notes from the institutions and asylums have been explored. Bringing these investigations together with extensive reading of secondary sources, the book will supplement and complement extant historiography about nineteenth-century female criminality and insanity.

The research for the book was carried out in the archives of Bethlem Royal Hospital, Fisherton House Asylum and Broadmoor Criminal Lunatic Asylum. Additionally, as a comparison to treatment in the state criminal lunatic facilities, the large and accessible archive of Lancashire County Asylum at Rainhill, near Liverpool, was also explored. If some form of insanity was believed to be a factor in a crime, then the medical superintendent of the local asylum could be requested to examine the defendant and, on occasion, be requested to admit the accused on remand. This frequently happened in Liverpool. After the metropolitan area of London, the highest number of court cases for maternal infanticide and child murder was the north-west of England, and Liverpool had more cases than other cities.[121] The official case book notes at Bethlem, Fisherton House and Rainhill were written for clinical and medical consumption. Unlike the other asylums we do not have access to the official casebooks at Broadmoor; however, there are individual case files for each patient which contain draft and amended official documentation and personal and official letters. As such they are a less formal and thereby a somewhat richer source. The casebooks in other asylums were for reference and use in the private and official domain of the asylum and were not intended as records of personal reaction to patients and their welfare.

Jonathan Andrews suggests that the case notes could be and probably were censored by the prudery and prejudice of the Victorian medical officers, especially in the reporting of the sexual language and behaviour of the patients. He emphasizes that such notes were not written for historians 'but for asylum medical staff and for administrators and officials who required to keep tabs on staff and patients'.[122] Hilary Marland has a different opinion of the value and content of case book notes, with regard to the relationships between patient and doctor. She found the case books a rich source of social history, in that 'they open up a world of direct interaction between the doctors and their patients ... and enable us to explore ... the relationship between women, doctors and mental disorder'.[123] The case books and case files examined for this book, support both these arguments. Life and treatments in the asylums are discussed at length in Chapters 4, 5 and 6. Despite Andrews' comments that such documents were written in daily practice for the medical staff's use and information not as a historical account of asylum life, the documents offer informative insights.[124] Once deciphered from the papers and books, they give perceptive and occasionally surprising views of the asylum experience of infanticidal and homicidal mothers.

The social and cultural environment, as well as the medical regimes in the institutions had an impact on the quality of the women's experiences. The size of the studied group could be said to be relatively small in terms of Victorian female criminality. In view of this, the circumstances of other, non-murderous female criminal lunatics have been investigated to clarify why cure, redemption and recovery were thought possible for them too. The cases studied in this respect are those where the offenders were deemed as insane at the time of their criminal act and so retained in a lunatic asylum 'until her Majesty's pleasure be known'. For all women patients, favourable opinion was gained through displaying qualities such as diligence, obedience and respect, traits associated with contemporary acceptable female behaviour. Eventually, tractability and good temper as well as perceived sane behaviour could have a profound impact on whether the women would be considered as recovered enough to warrant discussions about discharge and release.

The medical superintendents of Bethlem, Broadmoor and Fisherton House did not leave private papers, diaries or personal correspondence. However, between them they were all quite prolific in their contributions to professional medical associations in the form of journals and presentations to medical colleagues, local and national press, books and other published articles. They also were required to write annual reports for the Commissioners in Lunacy and other work for government committees. The archival records for Fisherton House and Broadmoor contain other correspondence and ephemera. Broadmoor's archive includes rough notes for and copies of official governmental reports to the Home Office, together with correspondence with patients and their families. For Fisherton House, the Finch's correspondence and papers on the subject of criminal lunatics and the asylum's case books all contain a modicum of personal commentary and opinion. All types of writing from reports, articles and talks to references in case book notes include indications of personal attitudes. Asylum doctors rarely commented frankly and personally about the difficulties before them.[125] The clinical notes in the case books and files can give an indication of the level of engagement with their patients and, occasionally, the medical superintendents' opinions of the patients' social position and respectability.

It has taken careful interpretive reading of casebook notes, official correspondence and administrative documents to obtain a picture of the infanticidal and homicidal mothers' personal and emotional lives and treatment within the asylum system. The Bethlem casebooks are formal, concerned with medical matters and written in a similar manner to the records described by Andrews. Fisherton House's records are slightly different. There the casebooks are both medically and personally descriptive but do not record a patient's individual experience. Correspondence between Fisherton's proprietor and Chief Medical Officer, Dr William Corbin Finch and Whitehall which, together with occasional letters from patients' kith and kin, form a rich source of social history. Personal agency and inter-personal relationships, both medical and social, were important to the well-being of the patients but so was patient confidentiality. This was as true for criminal patients as for any other patients, as Dr Charles Hood of Bethlem wrote, 'it would be indelicate and improper of me to expiate upon the peculiar features of any case under my charge in Bethlehem [sic]'.[126]

In 1985 Roy Porter wrote a paper which discussed the worth of studying the history of medicine 'from below' in an attempt to give a voice to the 'voiceless' patients.[127] Since that time there has been much excellent work and research undertaken by scholars which highlights patient experience and opinion.[128] Porter encouraged historians to use new narratives and place patients at the forefront of medical history scholarship. He advocated the idea that the history of illnesses and their treatments should be focused on not just celebrating medical men's achievements but on the whole range of patient experience: the history of care as well as that of cure. The shift in emphasis and perspective was taken up by historians and scholars as being viewed as particularly relevant to the history of madness and asylums.[129] In his subsequent book, *A Social History of Madness*, Porter stated that his aim was to see 'what mad people meant to say' not to turn them into martyrs suffering at the hands of the medical world.[130] In a thirty-year retrospective of Porter's original article, Alexandra Bacopoulos and Aude Fauvel suggest that the patient's voice should not be seen as just an addendum to the history of psychiatry but 'should be interactively included with other madness discourses'.[131]

When exploring the asylum experience from the patient's point of view, other scholars have highlighted the difficulties of obtaining individual testimony in the case of pauper patients.[132] All agree that the use of any sources of a patient's voice and opinion adds an important dimension to the history of asylums. Catharine Coleborne has written recently about using asylum archives and cases as stories.[133] She describes the study of the history of the experience of madness as a 'complicated process for historians and other scholars'.[134] Coleborne suggests that the use of asylum records alone carry an inherent problem because clinical and administrative records were produced about the patients.[135] She asserts that only by supplementing official records with accounts from the patients and their families themselves, can the historian 'round out the picture' and produce a meaningful dimension to the stories of 'institutionalized people'.[136]

Broadmoor's case files give a rare insight into asylum life and the patient experience; their documentary contents give some understanding of asylum life, particularly from the patients' viewpoint. The papers in the individual case files consist of draft and amended official and medical documentation as well as the personal and official letters occasionally handwritten annotations. The personal views and opinions about the patients and their progress add another dimension to observations on interactions between staff, patients and relatives. Letters held in the individual case files contain personal reactions from some Broadmoor patients and document the personal circumstances of the inmates and their families. Jade Shepherd writes that the ephemera and letters contained in the Broadmoor case files give a perspective on parenthood and family relationships from a working-class point of view, as well as a middle-class one.[137] It is not always obvious that the letters were written by the patients or dictated to a third party, or indeed whether they were sent to designated recipient. Letters from husbands and children to the asylum administration and medical staff tell us much about the emotional familial bonds, with surviving letters from some of the patients giving a different aspect to the women's character and lives.

Other sources of information for all aspects of the women's lives, particularly outside metropolitan London, were newspaper reports. Newspapers played a vital role in constructing the narratives of the women's experiences and journeys. Newspapers and periodicals were accessed through the *British Newspapers Online Archive* and the *Times Digital Archive 1785–2013*. For cases heard at the Central Criminal Courts, like many historians, the *Old Bailey Proceedings Online* website was invaluable. Joel Peter Eigen used the *Proceedings* transcripts in his extensive studies of Central Criminal Courts trials.[138] In one article, he describes them as offering 'not only the voice of the [...] specialist in mental medicine but also the language employed by the judge, attorney, lay witness and jurors who occasionally questioned the medical witness directly. In some trials, the most audible voice belongs to the prisoner himself'.[139] That being said, the transcripts are not full accounts of everything that was said during a trial; for instance, legal arguments were often omitted from the proceedings. The *British Newspapers* and the *Times* archives more than adequately covered this aspect of Old Bailey trials.

Emotion and sentimentality played an important role in popular culture throughout the Victorian period. Press reportage could be very descriptive and vivid and, on occasion proscriptive, about all protagonists' reactions. With regard to the courtroom, Martin Wiener argues that the press used gender as a method 'to draw sympathy for ... women, even though (or perhaps because) juries, bar and bench were all male'.[140] Wiener contends that Victorian newspapers and periodicals were vehicles for disseminating differing views. The newspaper research undertaken for this book has found Weiner's observation to be largely true. Depending on their audience, newspaper articles would highlight different aspects and attitudes towards this set of women and their crimes. Frequently press reports and editorials concerning class and gender, responsibility and punishment, would be aimed at mirroring the perceived opinions of the individual newspapers' target readership.[141]

The creation of the individual stories of all the women discussed in this book has shown that the use of microhistory as a method of study and analysis is particularly appropriate to writing about others' personal experiences. Microhistory has been defined as a historical method the aim of which is to isolate ideas, beliefs, practices and actions of individuals and groups. True microhistorical research chronicles the dealings of individuals and small sets of people to find concepts, principles and practices which impact upon their lives. John Brewer suggests that the impact and significance of such interactions could be lost or sidelined, if researched by more large-scale historical strategies.[142] The backgrounds to the women's court appearances, domestic situations and finally their lives in the institutions highlight contemporary Victorian views about the susceptibility of the female mind to madness. While this book is not unique nor, perhaps, original in using microhistorical case studies, the integration of genealogy and family history into the approach is a fresh innovation.

Genealogical websites have been important in building biographies for the women and their individual families. By gathering data in online genealogical sources the personal histories and social backgrounds of the case study subjects are enriched. Thus, numerous family trees were created for each of the members of the dataset and a library of individual files.[143] It also meant that contact was made with descendants of some of the subject women which added to a sense of personal involvement. While being aware of the dangers of bias when reading the sources, personal and emotional reactions to some cases have had some impact on my choice of case studies. This research into the personal biographies and circumstances adds a different perception of the history of female criminal insanity, the law and asylums. It also elucidates the influence of contemporary sociocultural ideals, thereby highlighting the impact of different social expectations and gender ideals on people's lives. As the subjects in this book were individuals in their own right and not just defined by their crime, the use of genealogy and family history methods to create personal profiles is a legitimate and important approach to the subject matter. Emily Brand writes that through family history 'networks of kinship … and the emotional texture of communities can be brought back to some semblance of life'.[144] By creating new narratives through a micro-historical approach, a genealogical exploration of the women's social environments and the circumstances of their crimes adds nuance to the reasons behind their legal and medical treatment. The pioneering usage of family history and genealogical methods for this book adds a different perspective to the historiography of infanticide and child homicide. While complementing the extant and extensive work of others, the book builds on current knowledge and understandings of infanticide and female criminal insanity.

2

'How criminal lunatics are made': Pathways to the asylum – Court cases, criminal responsibility, insanity defence and the power of medical evidence

The quotation in the title of this chapter is taken from a rather sardonic headline to the newspaper reports about the trial of Elizabeth Stapleton in 1898. On 12 August 1898, Elizabeth Stapleton, a twenty-year-old factory hand from Battersea, appeared at the County of London Sessions, accused of attempted suicide. She had pleaded not guilty to the charge, despite having drunk a quantity of carbolic acid. After much discussion, the jury first decided that she was not guilty; however the judge, Sir W. Quaile Jones, requested, in the light of the overwhelming evidence, that they reconsider. The second verdict was that she was 'guilty but at the time the prisoner was not responsible for her actions'.[1] *Lloyds Weekly Newspaper* reported that the second verdict highly amused 'all the court' and the judge himself said that 'there was not a tittle of evidence to support' the second part of the verdict.[2] Sir Quaile Jones was confused by the rider to the guilty verdict as it meant that 'all he could do now was to order her to be detained at her Majesty's pleasure ... sent to a criminal lunatic asylum'. If they had returned a simple guilty verdict, without a rider, he would have been able to order her detention until a suitable 'home' could be found for her – obviously not an asylum. Elizabeth Stapleton was admitted to Broadmoor where it would appear her 'insanity' was also questioned.[3] Her story will be revisited in later chapters but is quoted here as it appears that the slightly derisive title is a summation of a public attitude, that the making of a 'criminal lunatic' was a simple matter of one juries' decision on a case. The title does infer that there was a set route into the criminal lunatic facilities, but the actual process was never clear-cut. The truth is that the 'making of a criminal lunatic' was not simplistic or straightforward, and evolved over the Victorian period.

On their journeys into the various criminal lunatic facilities, the purportedly insane infanticidal and homicidal mothers faced appearances in various courts, from coroners' inquests and magistrates' courts to the assize courts. There was no doubt in any of the hearings that the accused women had committed the crime. Therefore, evidence was needed to confirm that, in legal and medical terms, the accused mothers were, indeed, insane. This meant that the women's lives and backgrounds were dissected for clues to the circumstances to their crimes. The testimonies and evidence given in the lower courts laid the foundations of public, medical and judicial opinions about the accused mothers. Both lay and professional witness testimonies impacted on the future lives and experiences of the women. Not unsurprisingly, attitudes and opinions about imprisonment of those adjudged insane changed over the nineteenth century. Shifts in official opinions and practices regarding the incarceration of all insane criminals impacted the lives of the criminally insane mother. Concepts of criminal responsibility and delusion not only affected the way in which homicidal mothers were perceived in court but could also influence official policies on what was conceived as the 'correct' place of incarceration for the insane mothers.

The coroner's court

The coroner's court and inquest proceedings were important in cases of maternal infanticide and child homicide. The inquest was often the first official procedure to be faced by the accused women. The proceedings and the ensuing verdicts had significant impact on the future course of their lives. In most cases, it was at this stage that the first questions about possible insanity arose and discussions about both personal and familial mental health issues began. Medical men and lay witnesses, who were frequently friends family and neighbours, would offer their views on the woman's state of mind, both before and after her crime. Not unsurprisingly, many of those testifying would mention or suggest any history of insanity amongst the accused's kith and kin. These opinions, they believed, would show that the accused must have leanings towards insanity and been mad at the time of the crime.[4]

An inquest was convened to investigate any sudden, suspect death and the role of the coroner was to investigate such unexpected and violent events.[5] The purpose of the proceedings was to determine the cause of a victim's death and, if this was at the hand of another, to produce an indictment to send the accused to the assizes or the Central Criminal Court, for a criminal trial. In Victorian England

and Wales, coroners' inquest juries were usually made up of between twelve and fifteen jurors. Inquest jurors did not require a professional qualification, although in some parts of the country, the jury became quasi-professional, with a regular foreman and jury members.[6] The role of a coroner was not to comment on or judge the 'moral compass' within the community but, by necessity, it was a diplomatic role. The coroner was usually a local professional man with either a legal or medical background and as such, would be well aware of any local prejudices and personalities. Officially, the task of the inquest jury was to decide and give an opinion on, 'who the deceased was and how, when and where the deceased came by his death.'[7] Inquest jurors were entitled to directly question witnesses and frequently did so. They could also add riders to their verdicts, although such additions were not strictly a relevant part of the verdict.[8] On many occasions, coroners had to remind their jurors that the state of the mother's mind when she committed the crime was not of their concern, while also ensuring that those very details were heard within the court. In the opinion of many members of the judiciary, inquest verdicts could be too lenient. As Mr Justice Day commented in 1885, 'a coroner's jury were very often led away by sympathy or some other cause to return a verdict ... without the slightest justification.'[9] Often in cases of maternal infanticide, particularly in smaller communities, the family of the victim and mother would be known to the jury members and that acquaintance could impact on the final verdict. The juries' riders were not part of the formal verdict and did not form part of the indictment at the assizes or Central Criminal Court. As Ian Burney writes in his book *Bodies of Evidence*, they occasionally apportioned blame or expressed disapproval giving 'extra-legal communal judgement regarding the conduct of individuals'.[10] The views and statements given in the coroner's court and the interactions between all parties laid the foundations for the treatment of the accused mothers throughout their passage through the Victorian medico-legal system.

The medical evidence given at an inquest would be recorded to be given at the subsequent court hearings. There, the same medical witnesses could be cross-examined by both the defence and prosecution advocates on the evidence given at the inquest. When parental child murder, particularly at the hands of a mother, was suspected, medical evidence could take two significant forms. As well as presenting details of the post-mortem appearance of the child victim and any autopsy results, the same medical witness often gave additional evidence on the supposed mental state of the woman at the time of her fateful act. The clinical evidence of the autopsy included accounts of the post-mortem appearance, descriptions of the wounds or internal injuries and chemical analysis results if poisoning was suspected. The reports and evidence were usually presented dispassionately, despite some details being disturbingly graphic for the lay audience. Although, officially, the mental health of the accused was of no concern to the inquest jury on occasion, a medical officer from the local asylum would be summoned. He would be expected to give a statement on the alleged insane mother's demeanour and mental state.[11]

Another type of opinion was the personal, potentially more emotional, evidence concerning the putative murderer. Potentially such additional evidence could carry more weight if it were given by a doctor who had been personally attending the woman and her family and so knew their medical history. The evidence could be given at the request of the coroner or jury or, as frequently happened, the doctor would give his unsolicited diagnosis of the woman's state of mind. As a diagnosis, it would come from personal observation and experience, despite a general lack of substantial knowledge about mental illness.[12] On 17 February 1896 in Sefton, near Liverpool, Dr Fitzpatrick was called to the house of Ida and William Baxter to view the bodies of three-year-old William and two-year-old Alexander Baxter. That morning after her husband had left the house, Ida, their mother, had cut their throats and attempted to cut her own throat. Fitzpatrick confirmed the deaths of the two boys and then spoke with Ida. According to his evidence, she was wandering in her mind, unaware of what she had done and did not recognize him. As he said regretfully, 'She had known me for six years past' and he had also attended her at the birth of her third child just three months previously.[13] He later told the assize court that it was at this time he had concluded that Ida Baxter was insane when she committed the murders.[14]

Dr McLoughlin of Aspull, Lancashire, had cared for the local France family on many occasions over the period preceding the death of three-year-old Ellen France, at the hands of her mother, Mary France. In his deposition and evidence, as well as showing sympathy and compassion, he also expressed self-blame for not being more aware of the possibility of violence in the France household. McLoughlin told the inquest that he 'knew her (Mary France) very well' having 'attended her some weeks before where her children were ill' when '[s]he was then suffering from want of rest and worry'.[15] He was discernibly concerned that he had misread Mary's 'state of nervousness' and he categorically said, 'in fact I now consider that she was then suffering from dementia.' In the statement, McLoughlin said that Mary France's previous maternal behaviour showed that her homicidal act was completely out of character, saying, 'she seemed an exceptionally good Mother, excessively fond of her children and nursed them very well.'[16] Retrospectively, McLoughlin appears to be regretting his inability to spot the signs of incipient insanity in Mary France's apparently obsessive parental behaviour.

The innocence of the child victims and the apparent vulnerability of their homicidal mothers as victims of circumstance could incite 'moral emotions' such as guilt and compassion in the coroners' courts. A jury member at the inquest into the death of William Thomas Beck became very upset at what he thought was unjust wording of the verdict of wilful murder: 'Mr Gunn said that by returning a verdict of wilful murder … it included the unhappy woman amongst the blackest of criminals.' When it was pointed out to him that his role was to consider only who had committed the act and not to take into account any evidence heard about her mental health, Gunn expostulated, 'It is for me to consider whether I shall be dragooned against my conscience … No, I will sit here until I rot first … wilful murder is the blackest verdict we could think of.' The other jury members remarked, 'that they wished to be as "charitable" as they could' and eventually were persuaded to agree to the wilful murder verdict, qualifying it with a rider expressing their opinion, 'that the said Mary Ann Elizabeth Beck was not at the time accountable for her actions.'[17]

On occasion, medical witnesses sought to distance themselves from the woman and her crime.[18] While acknowledging that their patient's disturbed mental state lay at the root of the homicidal actions, some would look to share the blame by suggesting that other parties were neglectful in their duties of care. This was evident at the enquiry into the drowning of Frederick Smyth by his mother Ada Smyth (nee Pulsford), in Barnstaple in 1889.[19] The personal doctor to the Pulsford family, Dr J. W. Cooke, gave a very sympathetic portrait of Ada Smyth. However, he went on to infer that that some responsibility for her actions should lie with her family for not following his instructions. He told the inquest that he had requested that her child, Frederick, be taken away from her at night and cared for by a nurse, as Ada was suffering from melancholia. Unfortunately, on the night Smyth killed her son, the nurse had not arrived and her mother-in-law decided not to stay with her; she was left alone.[20] By implication, this was a medical man apportioning the blame for the death to family members for not carrying out his instruction. In these situations, such blame-shifting by medical men can be construed as a defensive act. Apportionment of responsibility was a way of reconciling a moral dilemma about responsibility for the circumstances of a child's death when caused by a mother's mental state. It was also about professional self-preservation, a defence against potential censure by their social and professional peers.[21] Implicit too would be the desire to protect a personal reputation and a standing in the local community. A medical man subtly would be placing himself apart from any suggested critical public reactions, particularly if voiced by jury members or the coroner.[22] The social and moral conscience of the male coroners, the jurors and witnesses, could be eased by apportioning blame to someone or something else, rather than the accused women themselves.

Blame, as a social concept, has been described as a base for legal systems and as a means of reconciling moral dilemmas.[23] Coroners and juries would frequently take a 'moral' stance and suggest that the 'blame' for the mothers' madness and any subsequent violent and fatal actions should be apportioned to others. In witness testimonies at inquests and trials, comparisons were made with the woman's 'normal' behaviour to show that she had shown no incipient signs of insanity and, therefore, she was not watched or supervised. It is possible that because of this, strange or unusual behaviour could often be missed, or assigned to domestic worries.[24] Such statements were used to excuse any tacit lack of supervision by kin and neighbours.[25] Husbands were castigated for not watching over their wives who might have displayed signs of incipient mental distress. Time and again inference was made that the woman had clearly not been protected from danger when there was an intimation that she might commit some rash deed. In 1859, the inquest jury's verdict of 'Wilful Murder' against Martha Ann Lewis carried a rider censuring her husband for his negligent conduct.[26] It had been noted that William Lewis was much affected when he had himself given evidence to the inquest, which had taken place the day after his children had been drowned by his wife. He was reproached by the jury because they felt 'strong indignation ... against the husband for not taking proper care of his wife after she had attempted suicide' three days before the children's drowning.[27]

Burney describes a nineteenth-century inquest as an 'open tribunal ... with a lay jury and an elected official ... cast as a traditional check on authority by an active and watchful citizenry.'[28] Coroners have been described as 'magistrates of the poor', championing the ordinary man against authority with inquests as progressive platforms for social improvement.[29] Certainly many coroners did use their closing speeches in inquests, to rebuke other authoritative bodies.[30] This was apparent in the case of Sarah Lancastell, where the coroner was severely critical of the parish relieving officer. After the premature birth of her baby in September 1863, Lancastell's neighbours were concerned about her strange behaviour. Her attending doctor requested that the parish relieving-officer find a nurse to care for Lancastell, giving the reason that he felt she would harm the child. The help did not materialize and Lancastell killed her child. In his summing-up, the coroner partially placed the blame for the baby's death on the relieving officer, 'a very strange part of this sad affair is the conduct of the parish relieving officer, who … has indirectly allowed the occurrence to take place'.[31]

Likewise in the case of Sarah Bates in Northampton in 1880, the coroner made a categorical statement which did not strictly fall within the scope of the inquiry. He advised his jury that, although it 'did not fall within their province', they should be aware that the examining surgeon and the relieving officer had failed the Bates family by not telling them that Sarah Bates was out of her senses and by not taking correct due protective precautions. He said that it should be noted that, in his opinion, 'If proper precautions had been taken, this terrible catastrophe might have been prevented.' Inferences that the crime had been occasioned by a lack of supervision, negligence or irresponsible behaviour by family and kin of the accused mother passed the blame to others. The criticism of third-party institutions such as the local Poor Law Union was more removed from the emotional nature of the cases than, perhaps, that of the doctors.

Magistrates' courts

In general, the interactions and opinions shared in the lower courts by all parties partially laid foundations for future reactions and attitudes towards the women in the Victorian medico-legal system. The evidence given in the magistrate's courts could often be a repetition of that given at the inquest in the case of murder. However, where the child victim, or indeed any victim, did not die, accused perpetrator's first court appearance would be at the police or magistrates' courts. Here, the decisions about indictments and remand would be made before capital cases were passed to the higher courts. It was here too, that the magistrates could offer their opinion on the crime and the accused and make suggestions about their welfare. Susan Burfield appeared before magistrates at Aylesbury for the attempted murder of her three-year-old daughter in May 1885. When she was committed for trial at the Hertfordshire Summer Assizes, the bench recommended that the 'special attention' of the medical officer and the governor of the prison 'should be called to her condition'.[32]

In another example, a magistrate's knowledge and concern for someone from his personal social circle were the cause of a debate in legal circles. In November 1883, Mary Ann Morgan, wife of a much-respected local government officer and scientist in Swansea, drowned her two-year-old daughter, Alice Maud, in the bath.[33] Her admittance to Broadmoor followed the inquest into her daughter's death and an appearance at the local police court.[34] Immediately after hearing the case, the Stipendiary Magistrate for Swansea had written, in some consternation, to the Home Office on 22 November 1883. He wrote that the coroner had signed a warrant to commit Morgan to H.M.P. Swansea, but her doctor had suggested that such 'confinement & the alarm … [of it] … would probably intensify the Lunacy.'[35] As the local magistrate, he was seeking advice on how to proceed in order to protect this vulnerable mother. On the Home Office's instruction, two Visiting Magistrates and two doctors visited Mary Ann, who was duly certified as insane.[36] It was originally suggested that she should be sent to the county asylum of Carmarthenshire to await trial.[37] However, rather than that, she was sent directly to Broadmoor, committed on the warrant of the Home Secretary before a judicial trial could take place.[38] She remained there until her death in 1926.[39]

The direct action by the Home Office in the fate of Mary Ann Morgan was met with some dismay by the judge at the Swansea Assizes in February 1884.[40] The magistrate's decision to immediately involve the Home Office was viewed as one which exceeded his authority. Rather than raising objections to the accused mother's actual incarceration, the judge commented that he was trying to protect the offender's right to a trial by jury. However, under the terms of the 1840 *Insane Prisoners Act*, insane offenders awaiting trial could be transferred directly to an asylum on a Home Secretary's warrant signed by two justices of the peace and two doctors.[41] Strictly speaking, by the terms of the Act, a trial should take place; however, following such a committal, it rarely did.[42] The action was not viewed favourably by members of the judiciary, because it seemed to hand more power to local justices, medical men, and the Home Office.[43] The impact that this could have on the future lives of the criminally insane women is reviewed in the next chapter.

Criminal responsibility and the defence of insanity

The nineteenth century saw the development of medico-legal defences with the emergence of medical testimony and in the use of the insanity defence in the criminal courts. Any testimony about the mental state of the alleged murderer was significant to the judgements made in the higher courts. Criminal responsibility and the existence of unconscious impulse and delusion were central in the evolution the insanity defence.[44] Before accepting a defence of insanity, it was expected that evidence would be presented indicating that the defendant was deluded at the time of the crime.[45] Any signs of delusion and of irresponsibility in the accused women's behaviour were highly significant in convincing the juries and judges that they were, indeed, insane. From coroners' enquiries and magistrates' courts to the assize or crown courts, any evidence of delusional behaviour by the accused mothers, at the time they killed their children, was considered vital. The looked-for evidential 'proof' which was more often than not, circumstantial or speculative, was important at all tribunal levels. However, with a crime such as a mother killing her child, it was difficult to prove absolutely that she was acting under a delusion at the time of the crime as, in most cases, there were no witnesses to the actual murder. Medical observational evidence could only 'prove' the mother was insane by analysis of her reported and observed behaviour before and after the event.[46] By its nature, this evidence was circumstantial, if not hearsay and could not conclusively prove that she was mad or delusional at the time she killed her child.

The McNaughton Rules was a set of guidelines formulated in 1843 to assist in judicial decisions about the insanity or sanity of the accused. The premise on which the McNaughton Rules were built, was that, at the time a crime was committed, a perpetrator needed to be aware that the criminal action was wrong and be aware of the consequences of their illegal activities. The Rules state that defendants might be considered insane if it could be shown that they had acted under a delusion, or that they were both delusional and unaware. This was particularly true in cases of mothers accused of murdering an infant or child. In any trial for child murder, whether the specific subject of insanity was mooted or not, the question was frequently raised of whether the defendant was aware that her act was wrongful at the time and whether she had had the criminal resolve to damage her child. This particular point, of knowing right from wrong, was an important part of the McNaughton's Rules.[47] Not uncommonly, zealous and exaggerated religious behaviour was cited as a possible cause of strange conduct and mental breakdown. The Rules form a basis for the standard test of criminal liability in relation to potentially mentally ill defendants in common law to the present day.[48] In principle, when the tests set out by the Rules were satisfied, the accused could be adjudged insane and be sentenced to an indeterminate period of confinement and treatment in an asylum or similar secure hospital facility, instead of a punitive incarceration.[49]

Although the McNaughton Rules were formulated to bring some continuity to the legal interpretation of criminal responsibility, the issue was problematic. In practice, the Rules were rarely mentioned by name in court and their interpretation could be either loosely or rigorously applied by different advocates and judges.[50]

The differences in interpretation between the medical and legal professions could be a source of friction, particularly between the medical expert witnesses and the judges.[51] Dr Alfred Swaine Taylor was a leading Victorian authority on medical jurisprudence who had extensive experience within the legal system.[52] He was openly critical of prosecution or defence attorneys engaging medical, or scientific, witnesses to prove or disprove evidence. In *Medical Jurisprudence*, he wrote about insanity as a defence to criminal charges and the 'civil responsibility of lunatics'.[53] He discussed the various medical and legal definitions of the term, highlighting the question of responsibility and stating that 'the rule of law ... is that no man is responsible like a sane person for any act committed by him while in a state of insanity.' In his opinion, '[the] acts of the insane generally arise from motives based on delusion.'[54] He qualified this by stating that he believed that the presence of delusion at the time of the criminal act should not be taken as the sole sign of insanity but be one amongst others. He wrote that for a defence of insanity to be successful, '[the] insanity must be proved to have existed at the time of the perpetration of the act. Whether the prisoner is or is not insane when placed on his trial is immaterial in reference to the question of responsibility.'[55] Taylor was critical of the legal principle of responsibility and concluded that 'it has been abundantly proved that the test of responsibility ... is of a purely theoretical kind and cannot be carried into practice.'[56]

Dr William Orange, an expert in practical matters concerning delusion and criminal insanity, was critical of the legal reliance on the McNaughton Rules. He was the Deputy Medical Superintendent at Broadmoor Criminal Lunatic Asylum from its opening in 1863 becoming the Medical Superintendent in 1870, retiring in 1886. In 1884 in a report to the Home Office, he gave his opinions on the subject. He wrote that, 'there are certain forms, or rather stages of insanity in which there are no delusions.' He argued that individuals could be both insane and aware that their actions were wrongful, at the same time.[57] Orange highlighted some of the difficulties that medical witnesses faced when called upon to ascertain a defendant's fitness to plead and stand trial. The questions asked of the medical expert, to establish whether the accused 'is in a fit state of mind to plead to the indictment' were, in Orange's opinion, relatively straightforward and 'plainly intelligible'.[58] However, when a medical witness was asked in full trial whether the accused was insane at the time of the criminal act, Orange remarked that such questions were 'by no means simple or intelligible', because 'the questions [were] founded upon the answers returned by the judges in McNaughton's case.' In Orange's opinion, the Rules were wanting because of the uncertainties attached to their authority, scope and exact meaning. When asked to consider whether the accused was insane at the time the act was committed, a jury, he suggested, would be challenged to understand theoretical ideas about insanity and delusion. He suggested that questions should be simplified and made more understandable to ensure that, the 'point for consideration [be] freed from the puzzling metaphysics with which it is surrounded'. Fundamentally, Orange believed that the starting point for a court's, and thereby the jury's consideration, should be whether the accused was to be treated as 'an ordinary felon or as a criminal lunatic'. Orange stated that medical witnesses should not be bound 'by precise legal rules' and should be able 'to make a critical examination of the individual case, with a view to ascertaining whether Mental Disease does or does not exist'.[59]

Despite these expert opinions, confirmation of the defendant's lack of awareness and their subsequent criminal irresponsibility at the time of their crime remained as a vital strand in legal practice regarding insanity. In the court, submitted defence and prosecution evidence that the accused was delusional, or unaware of the criminality of their actions was expected. Medical evidence would point to physiological reasons and hereditary traits to support the diagnosis of insanity. Signs of delusion or unconscious impulses caused by intemperance, grief or exaggerated religious fervour were highlighted to explain any dramatic changes in conduct and behaviour. This was particularly noticeable in cases of maternal infanticide and child murder, where the killing of their own offspring fell far outside the norms of sane maternal behaviour. This 'proof' that the defendant had been displaying signs of mental derangement before their crime gave more weight to the argument that they were insane at the time. With such evidence 'proving' irresponsibility and delusion at the time of the crime, a defence of insanity would likely be accepted by the judge and jury.

The other extenuating circumstances given as underlying reasons for irrational actions outside the norms of morally acceptable behaviour and maternal conduct included insobriety. Despite having socially undesirable aspects, misuse of alcohol and excessive drinking was sometimes accepted as an explanation of irresponsible, rash and negligent behaviour. If the woman had been driven to drinking by domestic circumstances or a misfortunate life event, then insanity related to intemperance appears to have been tolerated. Female drinking habits differed from class to class and what was considered a reasonable level of consumption to middle-class society differed to that of working-class society.[60] To both groups, the ideal moderate level was governed by concepts of respectability. One explanation for the seemingly tolerant attitude to insanity brought on by alcohol misuse could lie in contemporary views of the female temperament. Contemporary observers suggested that middle-class women might drink through boredom and intellectual ennui.[61] Other doctors linked women's excessive drinking to an 'unstable nervous organization'.[62] Another assumption was that an inherent weakness in the female character was a lack of resolve in the face of adverse and life-damaging situations. Drinking to excess could be seen as taking a refuge from reality and therefore an inability to take responsibility for their actions. This was believed by some to be at the root of alcohol-induced insanity.

The apparent lack of responsibility caused by over-indulgence in alcoholic drink obviously was not just relevant to cases of maternal child homicide. Public and legal opinion would be influenced by individuals' reaction to women drinking. Women who were seen to drink alcohol to excess were held in low esteem and such local knowledge would be a black mark against their names.[63] This can be seen in the case of Elizabeth Platts. She was tried for the attempted murder of one of her mother's farm hands, who had actually rescued her from a vicious sexual assault some weeks earlier. Platts, it was shown, was suffering from delusions when she attacked him, which had been caused by the shock and shame associated with the earlier assault on her. Contemporary press reports infer that Elizabeth came from a respectable family who were considered to be decent people in the local area. The *Sheffield Daily Telegraph* suggested that Elizabeth was to be pitied rather than chastised, although the comments also noted her reliance on alcohol. The report was mildly sympathetic towards her stating that, 'For a time past Mrs Platts has unhappily been addicted to drink, and the present troubles are all directly the result of drink.'[64] Complainants in assault cases, whether rape or not, were themselves expected to conform to social standards, which included the level of alcohol consumed. The evidence of those who did not match the criteria was less likely to be believed and their credibility as witnesses doubted.[65] Elizabeth wrote to her mother from Broadmoor describing the circumstances of her crime and the earlier assault on her. She admitted that she had had 'a little drink' on the day of the attack on her but then qualified this, saying, 'I had bought that drink with my own husband's money'.[66] It would appear that Elizabeth believed that some members of her community attributed her drunkenness that night to her drinking at the expense of a third party. The accusation does not seem to have been levelled at her publicly, but if her drinking addiction was known to the local community then there would be those who thought she had been asking for trouble.

The evidence offered and accepted at the trial of Mary Lyons in Leeds in 1866 is an illustration of that the misuse or overindulgence in alcohol could be accepted as a factor in uncontrollable impulsive behaviour leading to unconscious actions. Lyons was accused of attempting to drown her four-year-old daughter in the River Aire in Leeds. She was described in court as having 'always been a quiet, peaceable and inoffensive woman until she took to this habit of drinking'. Her defence counsel suggested that she had been suffering from delirium tremens when she threw her daughter from a bridge into the river. In his summing-up, Justice Lush said that perhaps there were other causes which 'might have overpowered [Lyons'] reason … Those causes, aggravated by the influence of drink, might have brought on diseases of the mind.' Evidence had been given that Lyons was often intoxicated but it was also suggested that the 'fear of public disgrace and the reports being circulated about her' were enough to unbalance her mind.[67]

Religious fervour and grief were accepted as plausible causes of delusion and uncontrollable urges, which possibly resulted in a woman committing a crime such as child murder. At Liverpool Assizes in December 1876, the defence counsel for Agnes Martha Morris sought proof that she was delusional when she shot her children by highlighting her odd manner in the months preceding the crime.[68] Her husband had died suddenly in November 1875, from which time her behaviour had become increasingly eccentric. She believed that she was almost destitute and that her children were starving and badly fed. She had disagreements with friends and neighbours and accused all of conspiring behind her back. Morris was the widow of a bank manager, living in an affluent part of Liverpool and was relatively well-off. Her strange behaviour culminated in an abortive attempt to buy prussic acid and eventually she obtained a handgun on a false pretext.[69] Throughout her trial the defence counsel asked each witness, lay and medical, their thoughts on the state of her mind, despite the fact that she had obviously been planning some sort of violent act for a while. Dr Banks, the surgeon of Kirkdale Prison, said in his testimony, 'she probably thought she was doing a right act in sending her children to heaven. She was overcome by an irresistible impulse; that's what constitutes the form of mania of which I consider her the victim.' The judge, Mr Justice Lindley, asked Dr Banks to clarify exactly what he considered to be an 'irresistible impulse'. Banks replied, 'a sane man could control his passion even when in a towering passion [sic]; an insane man could not'.[70]

Medical evidence in criminal courtrooms

The art of advocacy in English and Welsh courts developed through the nineteenth century and, as the adversarial court changed, the use of more specialized defences, such as insanity, grew.[71] In 1836 the Trial for Felonies Act

('Prisoners' Counsel Act') gave defendants the right to have defence counsel.[72] From the implementation of the Act, barristers acting for the defence were able to access pre-trial statements, to address the jury directly, to cross-examine witnesses and make speeches on behalf of their clients.[73] Prior to 1879, the Home Office could direct the Treasury Solicitor to institute criminal proceedings and give advice on prosecutions in capital cases. In 1879, the 'Prosecution of Offences Act' created the Office of the Director of Public Prosecutions (DPP) and its attendant role of public prosecutor.[74] The Act stipulated that the DPP, through the Treasury Solicitor, would take charge of court case prosecutions which possibly involved capital charges. Under the Act and its subsequent amendments, the Treasury Solicitor was directed to require and employ medical men of experience and repute, to visit prisoners before their trial to examine them for potential insanity.[75] Medical evidence was vital in order to prosecute and defend a case. Once both the prosecution and defence were able to address the juries and conduct cross-examinations, the ability to deliver well-honed speeches became an essential part of a barrister's role.[76]

Defence counsel would aim to word their questions in cross-examination of medical witnesses in such a way as to draw out the most 'forensically friendly opinions'.[77] They used their cross-questioning skills to clarify medical evidence for the jury (and possibly the bench) in such a way that their particular desired outcome to the trial would be attained. They strategically managed the experts' answers in order to highlight the defendants' abnormal behaviour at the time of their criminal act. Compassionate treatment and acceptance of female insanity were reinforced by evidence, which suggested that the 'madness' had been caused by physiological forces, or that the defendants were delusional and unaware of their actions. The increased use of medical evidence in nineteenth-century trials brought theories about female madness to a wider audience. The notion that all stages of motherhood could lead to mental instability and, hence, to violence, became accepted as a commonplace explanation for female insanity.[78] In cases involving women accused of killing their children, proving insanity at the time of the execution of the crime was difficult. Attesting that the defendant was insane at the time of the trial or within the period between the inquest and the court case did not necessarily mean that she had been mad at the time of her act. In order to bring a verdict of insanity, medical evidence from doctors who had seen the accused around the time of the crime, coupled with possible corroboration from friends, family and other witnesses, was essential to the judge and jury.

During the Victorian era, there was some disquiet about the implications of any offender, man or woman, being found 'unfit to plead' and immediately incarcerated, without trial. This led to much contemporary inter-disciplinary debate about possible misuses of the verdict. Both Joel Peter Eigen and Arlie Loughnan have suggested that emerging medical specialisms, specifically in areas of mental illness and 'mad-doctoring', led to a consequential increase in the number of medical men giving evidence in whichever court.[79] The doctors and surgeons would all claim to have some knowledge of female insanity and its various causes and manifestations. In the nineteenth century, medical witnesses in court were drawn from all areas of medicine: hospital physicians and surgeons, visiting prison doctors, asylum medics and domestic medical attendants. Evidence from the medical specialists in insanity was essential in establishing a defendant's state of mind and fitness to plead. Exclusively female forms of mental illness, such as puerperal mania, were part of insanity discourse by the mid-century and often given as the diagnosis of insanity in cases of maternal child homicide.[80] Any medical evidence about the accused's mental state at the time of their crime was very pertinent to these discussions. This contemporary debate about 'unfit to plead' verdicts and their consequences are described and examined in detail within the next chapter.[81]

The medical men who had dealt with the defendant at the time of their crime were prison and police divisional surgeons, and local doctors and physicians.[82] They had seen, spoken to or examined the woman soon after the violent attacks had occurred. Often these particular medical men had already given evidence at an inquest or in a magistrate's court, so any personal emotion shown in their earlier evidence would be diluted by time. Although their evidence in the judicial court was mostly a reiteration of deposition statements, cross-examination by counsel could draw out more information about other background circumstances. The medical expert witnesses would be expected to deliver the testimonies in a factual and clinical manner, but cases of child death and murder carried with them an underlying emotional current. It is difficult to state categorically that this did not impact on the doctors. By presenting their evidence in an unemotional manner, their emotional engagement with a case could appear to be distant and clinical. Their personal opinions about the circumstances of the crime and of the defendant were not necessarily apparent but may only be given if they were sought in cross-questioning. In this manner, the medical men would be seen to maintain their professional integrity, even in the face of opposition from prosecution council and, occasionally, from the bench. Emotional involvement might not be apparent in the evidence of medical examiners appointed by the Treasury Solicitors but where the medical witnesses had been personal physicians to the accused or where they had been at the scene of the murder, it might have been more so.

There were differences in the type of expert medical opinion consulted in cases of maternal child homicide between London and the provinces.[83] The work of expert writers was occasionally referenced in the provincial courts but they themselves rarely appeared outside London. Recognized expert medical writers, such as Dr Forbes Benignus Winslow, were known to appear at the Old Bailey as were other practitioners in the field of psychological medicine, including medical superintendents from many asylums including Bethlem and Broadmoor.[84] Winslow wrote extensively on the medico-legal aspects of insanity as well as being actively involved in the care and management of psychiatric patients.[85] He promoted himself as an expert witness for cases involving the insanity plea. At the trial of Ann Cornish Vyse at the Old Bailey in 1862, the prosecution and defence counsels between them, called on seven different medical experts to give evidence. Anne Cornish Vyse had murdered two of her daughters and the defence lay in the supposition that, at the time of the killing, that she was unaware of her actions. Dr Augustus Merritt, one of the seven, said in his testimony, 'I entertain an opinion that she is from two to three months pregnant now, there are all the usual signs – I cannot attribute the event that has occurred to anything else than the signs – I believe she was in a state of mania at the time.'[86] Another, Dr Charles Hood, gave evidence that he believed she 'suffered from a painful sensation in the interior of the cranium,' as Vyse had told him that the sensation felt like 'perspiring of the brain'.[87] Despite the fact that he had not met or physically examined Vyse, Forbes Winslow took to the stand to validate the medical evidence already given.[88] His opinion was delivered with certainty and some pomposity: 'I have been in Court during the whole of the day and I have heard the evidence in this case ... the act was committed by the prisoner [when] she was suffering under ... paroxysmal insanity.' He continued, 'This is a kind of insanity perfectly well understood by medical men and is an acknowledged disease.'[89]

Despite not actually appearing at courts outside London, the appearances of specialized experts in court in the Capital did sometimes inform the course of trials. By adding to the knowledge of the legal fraternity in court, such information was disseminated on the circuits. In 1873 at the trial of Elizabeth Marchant, Mr Douglas Straight Q.C. quoted the case of Ann Vyse when cross-examining a local doctor. He suggested that the occurrence of homicidal mania was a 'momentary insanity ... which ... might create an irresistible impulse to commit such an act ... [as in] ... the case of Mrs Vyse, of Ludgate Hill'.[90] The doctor in question did not know the case but agreed that such mania could induce someone to 'suddenly commit a crime and shortly after be deeply penitent'.[91] At the 1866 Leeds Assizes trial of Mary Lyons, her defence counsel referenced a case of insanity, quoted by Dr Alfred Swaine Taylor, as 'illustration of his argument that a person labouring under Delirium Tremens was not criminally liable'.[92]

The most common medical witnesses to appear in court were prison and police surgeons, and local asylum doctors. In the metropolitan area of London and in provincial courts, these prison and police surgeons had become specialists in finding signs of insanity in prisoners under their care and this hands-on experience was accepted by the courts as expert knowledge.[93] Other expert medical witnesses at the local assizes were, on many occasions, the medical officers from the county and local asylums, an acknowledgement of their expertise in the treatment of insanity. Such asylum medical officers and superintendents would visit the defendant before the trial, usually in the initial place of confinement, to assess their mental state. At Liverpool Assizes in 1887, the prosecution counsel in the trial of Mary Anthony advised the jury that the prosecution had 'decided that it was important and proper to place before the jury such medical opinions so as would guide them in returning a verdict'.[94] Dr Thomas Lawes Rogers, medical superintendent of Rainhill County Lunatic Asylum, had been instructed to examine her before the trial and, in addition, there had been a thorough investigation of Anthony's family and medical background.[95] It was reported that 'the prosecution had also made enquiry as to the prisoner's former state of mind ... Inquiries had also been made into the antecedents of the prisoner and as to any hereditary symptoms of insanity in the family'. The results of the enquiries evidenced, in the opinion of the prosecution counsel, 'the prisoner's temporary insanity'.[96]

Occasionally the medical officers and superintendents of Broadmoor would be consulted. These consultations occurred more frequently after 1879, with changes in legislation and the appointment of medical experts by the Treasury Solicitor. The appointed medical experts would examine potentially insane prisoners before trial and then their reports would be presented in court. Dr Orange was appointed by the Treasury Solicitor as the medical expert to examine Sarah Ann Hanson, in Oxford Gaol, prior to her trial in 1885. He did not give evidence in court, but his written diagnosis of puerperal melancholia and homicidal mania was passed on by the governor of the prison.[97] If the evidence was given by, or written by, a recognized specialist, it would appear that the judges and juries would accept their advice about the manifestation and characteristics of insanity. The word 'specialist' was used to denote expertise in an area of medicine, such as an asylum affiliation. Occasionally, as if to underline their authority, medical experts would present their credentials as an expert witness.[98] Before giving his opinion about Annie Player at her trial at the Old Bailey, Orange began his evidence thus, 'I have been 14 years medical superintendent of Broadmoor Criminal Lunatic Asylum and connected with the asylum for 21 years.'[99] On his two visits to Player in Clerkenwell his companion was Dr Robert Mundy Gover who, in addition to his role as Medical Inspector of Prisons, had given evidence to the 1880 enquiry into criminal lunacy.[100] Again, their visits and examinations were by instruction from the Treasury Solicitor to establish whether Annie Player was mentally fit to stand trial.

In both London and the provinces, the prison surgeons continued to appear as experts in diagnosing madness, their knowledge having been gleaned from years of experience of dealing with criminal lunatics. Despite the 'turf wars' over expertise about insanity in criminals between asylum doctors and prison surgeons, these initial diagnoses were often accepted. Descriptions of the type and possible cause of madness were a starting point for treatment when the women were admitted into their institutions.[101] At a trial at the Cumberland Assizes, the judge, Baron Huddleston, closely questioned Dr McDougall, assistant prison surgeon at Carlisle Gaol on his experience of insanity and insane persons. Dr McDougall had stated that '[i]t sometimes occurs that prisoners, when charged with a serious offence, conducted themselves as if insane but this was a very marked case [of insanity].'[102] Huddleston responded, 'You have had persons "shamming" in your charge? Witness – Yes, at times but they are always found out. I don't think this prisoner is making a sham. She does not understand what you say to her.'[103] When a judge cast doubt on a doctor's professional opinion or status in court, he could undermine the medical evidence given to prove a woman's insanity. The provincial doctors were able to stand their ground and have confidence in their assessments of the accused women, even in the face of close questioning by the judges. As in London, provincial prison surgeons and doctors proved that they were experts in insanity. These prison medical men prided themselves on recognizing insanity and rightly claimed a specialist expertise in identifying genuinely insane prisoners.[104]

Medical men who had examined defendants prior to their court appearance to confirm that they were mentally fit to be tried would frequently be asked about defendants' possible mental state at the time of the commission of the crime.[105] This type of statement, even if it were given by an acknowledged specialist, could only be speculative in nature. Dr Orange's opinion on Annie Player, although informed, was related more to her mental state at the time of the trial than at the time of her crime.[106] In 1887, during the trial of Annie Cherry at the Old Bailey, Dr Henry Bastian examined Cherry twice while she was in custody and, in his opinion, she had 'no trace of unsoundness of the mind about her'.[107] He believed that, from her reported history, she must have been in the early stages of melancholy following a difficult birth which 'often [caused] homicidal and suicidal tendencies'.[108] She was found 'guilty of the act but insane at the time of its commission' and admitted to Broadmoor. She was only in Broadmoor for eighteen months, which would appear to bear out Bastian's opinion that by the time of her trial, she showed no signs of insanity.[109]

If the evidence of a woman's mind being weakened by specifically female 'problems' was given by a medical man, ordinary or specialist, it was frequently accepted as being sufficient to prove her insanity. There are numerous examples of medical testimony being taken as the most important evidence of a woman's irrationality. In the case of Harriet Rowe in 1866, Mr G. H. Furber, a local Maidstone surgeon, was called to see Rowe and to examine the body of her drowned baby at the crime scene. He stated that he was of the opinion that Rowe was not of a sound state of mind at that time. After further questioning he said that 'it was not an uncommon thing for women, when nursing ... to fall into a state in which they were not accountable for their actions.' After his evidence, the prosecution counsel suggested that the 'best interests of justice would be served ... by leaving the case in the hands of the jury'.[110]

Similarly, doctor's evidence swayed the trial outcome in the case of Sarah Grout, who had murdered two of her children at West Thurrock in August 1848. The local surgeon, Mr Robert Jordison, had been called in to examine the children's bodies and had also examined Grout. He suggested that, because she appeared unstable when he had seen her at his surgery the previous day, Sarah was not accountable for her actions when she later killed her children. He said that, 'she appeared vacant, dejected and gloomy' and that he had always considered her to be 'a person of very weak mind'. He also testified that when he had seen her a few hours after the crime she was in a most deplorable state of anxiety and stupidity ... most decidedly in an unsound state of mind. 'Jordison gave his firm opinion that 'she did not know what she was about when she killed the children.'[111] The evidence was accepted, despite the fact that he had not physically witnessed the killings and his evidence was speculation.

Witness evidence in all courts

The testimonies of the lay witnesses often convey a sense of sadness, as well as bewilderment and incomprehension at the nature of the events that had taken place. At a fundamental level, inquests could be scenes of palpable emotion as lay witness evidence was often a spontaneous expression of what they had seen and their subsequent reactions. This was due in part due to the relationship of the lay witnesses to the deceased child and its mother and in part to the rapidity with which the inquest took place. The tragic events would still be fresh in the minds of all witnesses and the proximity of the inquest venue to the crime scene would impact on all parties and their testimonies. Popular ideas about how insanity manifested itself or how certain behaviours could precipitate an 'attack' of insanity, came into the witnesses' interpretations of the tragic events.[112] These lay testimonies and depositions were given as definitive evidence of insanity, and were taken into account by all juries, coroners, magistrates and judges.[113] Press reports and deposition statements show and record the grief of family and friends on the violent death of a child. Edward Suckling's emotional reaction was commented upon in press reports of his son's inquest, perhaps to confirm that he was a good father and husband, 'the father who stated [that] the body viewed was that of his son Charles John James Suckling aged four years … he last saw "the little dear" alive … on Wednesday morning'.[114] In his account of the circumstance of his son's death to the inquest jury, Thomas Beck demonstrated that he was a caring father and that he was bewildered by his wife's act. He refers to his son as 'the dear child' and his reaction to the situation was to exclaim, 'oh dear, oh dear what shall I do?'[115]

In cases where the mother obviously was 'mad', the interrogation of witnesses would bring out other possible causes of madness, beyond medical opinion. Circumstances as marital difficulties, privation, poverty and domestic violence were reported, not as a justification for insane and homicidal behaviour, but as potential additional damaging factors to a woman's mental state. A mother's deadly actions being a consequence of her domestic environment. Respectability and compliance with social expectations were important factors in peer-group witness testimonies about the accused women and the circumstances of their crimes. In his book, *Reconstructing the Criminal*, Martin Wiener argues that, during the nineteenth century, judges and reformers participated in 'a discourse of moralization', disseminating essentially middle-class male ideals of respectability to the nation through the courtroom.[116] Judges have also been described as moral arbiters, protectors of contemporary moral values, who would respond to socio-legal problems with understanding.[117] Respectability of lifestyle and behaviour fitted the middle-class moral code of the time. Domestic violence by women against children was threatening to contemporary ideals of the home as a safe haven, with the mother at its centre. By creating a picture of a woman wronged and driven to dreadful acts, lawyers played to the emotional and social sensibilities of those in the courtroom.

If it were shown that the accused were ultimately 'respectable' women who had been led to violence by uncontrollable forces and unfortunate circumstances, they were treated with sympathy. In his opening address in the case of Elizabeth Marchant at Surrey Assizes in 1873, Mr Douglas Straight Q.C. 'argued that she was driven to despair by the ill-treatment she received from the man Fordham … The parties went to live together as man and wife but with no bond of the Church to compel the man to support her and her child. … [H]er affection for that child … [was] … as strong as anything in nature.'[118] Likewise, in his closing statement to the jury, Straight emphasized Marchant's vulnerability apportioning a large amount of blame to her partner. It was reported that, '[Straight] made a powerful appeal to the jury' stressing Marchant's ill-treatment at the hands of her lover and that her 'demeanour was like that of a person filled with mad despair'.[119]

Similarly, in 1852 Emma Lewis received a sympathetic hearing as a single mother who had suffered at the hands of a man, She stood trial before Lord Justice Coleridge at the Nottinghamshire Assizes in July 1852, where she was described as 'a person of respectable connexions'. Unhappily she had 'formed an intimacy with a man named Clark, the result of which was … an illegitimate child'. His 'refusal … to marry her had preyed upon her mind' thereby affecting Lewis's reason and driving her to murder.[120] Despite her status as an unmarried mother and a lowly milliner, her status of being respectably poor and an abandoned woman, her desperation gave special consideration as victim as well as a murderer.

To consider respectability as a purely middle-class creation obscures its importance to other levels of society.[121] The home life of the bereaved family was of interest to the courts and was frequently remarked on. A harmonious home was important as a sign of respectability, as was the relationship between husband and wife which should be congenial and supportive. Conversely, marriage breakdown could be taken in mitigation of the woman's act, as could a husband's violence or his not being a proper provider for a family. As the lay witnesses could be from the same social background as a defendant, their idea of respectability could impact upon proceedings in court.[122] In order to support the defence case, it was important to convey the impression that the defendant's home-life before the murder was respectable and that her criminal actions were out of character. The main overseers of a working woman's reputation were her friends and neighbours. A woman's household skills and parenting prowess were key components of respectability, recognized not only by her peers but also by outside social agencies and investigators and by the courts.[123] At an inquest in Northwich in 1871, Hannah Ryan was described by her neighbour as 'liv[ing] on the best of terms with her husband'. The same neighbour also said she was 'a kind, steady, respectable woman'.[124] Frequently in witness depositions and evidence, there would be such personal comments on the women themselves. This happened most often with those who knew the families and the victims. In attempts to emphasize the women's maternal virtues, the witnesses would often refer to their abilities as mothers, commenting on their good mothering skills and the relationships with the children. In Reading in 1883, at the inquest into the death of Alice Lawrence, 'the Foreman asked whether the woman [Hannah Lawrence] had always seemed kind to the child? The witness [Mrs Seward, a neighbour] replied in the affirmative.'[125]

Despite only knowing Annie Player for three weeks, her neighbour, Amelia Newby, described Annie as seeming 'an unhappy sort of woman' but 'very kind to [her] children'.[126] Jane Smart described Sarah Freeman as being distraught about possible destitution and her husband's continued unemployment through ill-health, she still emphasized that Freeman was 'an affectionate mother' and that she 'lived on good terms with her husband'.[127] In 1849 Mrs Emma Creek, the neighbour of Sarah Grout, who stood accused of murdering her son and daughter with a billhook, deposed that, 'She always seemed very kind to her children.' The witness continued that she had observed 'in May last and since then she had had very strange ways but latterly, she had seemed rather better. She seemed more like a woman deranged in her mind.' Another neighbour said that she had told him that she had suicidal thoughts but 'did not want to leave behind but her two children'.[128] Despite her known drinking problems, Mary Lyons' neighbours were keen to emphasize her virtues as a mother and her respectability. Her next-door neighbours told the court that 'she was a very good mother and always treated her child kindly', a point which was corroborated by Lyons' cousin who said that Lyons had been 'a kind mother'.[129]

The testimonies of the ordinary men and women who knew the accused helped the court and public observers to make sense of the seemingly inexplicable crimes. Their witness statements would describe the defendant's behaviour and demeanour before the crime and the events leading up to its commission. The eye-witness remarks of neighbours could be taken as the necessary 'proof' of a deranged mind around the time of the commission of the murder. For example, after cutting the throat of her baby, Sarah Freeman ran to the house of her neighbour, Jane Smart, who described her as being 'very wild about the eyes' and wearing a bloody apron.[130] Another witness, Abram Tun, a thatcher, went into the Freeman's cottage and took the knife from the frantic Freeman while another neighbour saw to the child. He also described Freeman as looking 'very queer and wild about her eyes'. To his evidence he added that he had known Freeman's brother, who had died in a lunatic asylum after two- or three-year confinement there.[131] This evidence of familial insanity added more weight to the suggestion that Freeman was insane at the time of the murder. Such evidence appealed to the common conceptions of insanity and its manifestations and, when heard in conjunction with the professional opinion of medical men, would leave no doubt in popular opinion that the defendant was indeed mad.

In the Victorian age, there was an expectation that men would also fulfil certain standards of respectable behaviour within the domestic sphere. In all social classes, a good husband and father would provide for his family economically and protect their welfare.[132] A neighbour of the Sanderson family described Thomas Sanderson as 'a kind father, prudent man and affectionate to the extreme to the accused herself – perhaps too much'.[133] This did not mean that the fathers of the child victims were not sometimes censured by their male superiors and peers by failing in a basic duty. In not protecting their wives and their children adequately they should take some blame for the ensuing calamitous events. An example of manliness became a behavioural code being policed by other men.[134] This type of criticism was more apparent at inquests when the inquest juries were made of up of men from the local community. In 1866 at the inquest on the death of Emma Kirby's baby, when returning their verdict of wilful murder, the jury added a rider expressing 'their opinion that the mother was insane'. The coroner advised that although this would bear no weight in the assize court, he also wished to add a comment of his own. In his opinion, 'although not the least blame rests upon the husband, who is in great distress at the misfortune which has happened to him, it is to be regretted that she was not more narrowly looked after'.[135]

The appearance and the demeanour of the defendants would have an impact on the reactions of the reading public to a case and, doubtless, on the jury too. Susan Burfield was reported as being 'a pleasant-looking woman'. However, the report continued that she was 'presenting all the appearances of a person mentally deranged … She appeared to be muttering something to herself and … [had] … a nervous twitching of her mouth'.[136] The report gave a complex message, that being pleasant-looking and respectable did not protect from maniacal episodes, nevertheless the poor defendant should be afforded some compassion. Martha Lewis was described as 'a good-looking woman and respectably-dressed woman of twenty-five years of age', which no doubt resonated with the jury at her trial in 1859.[137] The *Times*' description of Agnes Bradley left no doubt about how contrary and deplorable her crime was to her social status. 'The prisoner['s] … appearance denoted her superior position in life,' and 'the mother [Bradley] had always manifested the tenderest affection [to her children].'[138] Likewise, in 1876, Mary Ann Elizabeth Beck was also described as 'a good-looking and respectably dressed young woman' at her trial.[139] The form of words used by the media would convey a message to their readership that, although the crime was horrendous, it was out of the ordinary for respectable persons such as these women.

If the woman were seen to be grieving or disconcerted, or even unaware of her surroundings in court, sympathy would be gained for her plight. In 1891, the description of Emma Onions entering the courtroom paints a sad and somewhat pathetic portrait. She was described as 'spare in form, careworn in appearance and about the average height of womankind. She was dreadfully pale and walked slowly into the dock, … When seated nothing but the black hat and the white face of the prisoner could be seen.'[140] The provincial Victorian press was very keen on presenting the respectable aspects of court cases.[141] They discussed and disseminated opinion on personal guilt, criminal responsibility and how it related to the defendants in court. As the reading public's access to court proceedings was through the media, popular opinion would be impacted by the cultural biases of the journalists and correspondents.[142]

It was also important for the impression to be conveyed that the home life of the family before the murder was harmonious and that there was affection between the wife and her husband. All this evidence would be gleaned from the statements of neighbours and friends and was important to appeal to the judge and jury, in order that a verdict of insanity be brought. The newspaper accounts would emphasize the respectability of lifestyle, home and personal nature of the defendants, gleaned from courtroom statements from their peers. Much as Louise Jackson found in press court reports on child abuse, reports on maternal child murder would reinforce the connections between suitable social behaviour and respectability, no matter the background of the defendant.[143] The press emphasis on socially positive attributes of respectability, coupled with vulnerability of the accused women, was instrumental in engendering sympathy and compassion for them, across all aspects of their careers through the medico-legal system.[144]

Judge and juries

Although their role, in simple terms, was to interpret the evidence, control proceedings within the courtroom and explain the law to the jury, judges could influence the juries' verdicts at the trials. A judge's personal understanding of the defendant's situation in life, her family relationships and his understanding of the reported state of her mind would affect his decision on a trial's course. A judge was responsible for summing up the evidence for the jury. This came after both prosecution and defence had presented their cases and evidence or when the judge felt that enough evidence had been heard by the jurors for them to come to a decision. Judges were known to engage in emotive oratory in the courtroom, which would impact on the juries' decisions. The judiciary and barristers were in all likelihood highly educated and erudite, certainly their words would have some influence on juries' verdicts.[145] In much the same way as the defence and prosecution barristers could be said to use emotive language in 'managing' evidence to obtain a favourable verdict, judges would also manipulate juries. If he held strong personal beliefs on a topic, a judge could use persuasive language to encourage jurymen to arrive at a verdict in keeping with his personal views.

Sir Henry Hawkins did not like the idea of potentially lifelong incarceration in asylums and was known to ensure the jury returned a guilty verdict in order to avoid the sentence which would have followed an acquittal on the ground of insanity. He wrote in his *Reminiscences* that he would word his advice to the jury so that the death sentence could be passed, albeit with his full recommendation for mercy, to avoid the asylum. Commenting on a case of maternal homicide where he felt he had to 'discountenance' the proposed plea of insanity he said, '[I asked] the jury whether, 'without being insane in the ordinary sense, the woman might not have been at the time of committing the deed in so excited a state as to not know what she was doing'.[146] It was an ambiguously worded question, which had resulted in his desired verdict. As he reminisced, 'I obtained a verdict of guilty but that the woman at the time was not answerable for her conduct, together with a strong recommendation to mercy'.[147] In his opinion this was a verdict in keeping with justice, if not strictly the law.

Judges could, and did, doubt and undermine evidence, particularly medical evidence. In the case of Martha Prior in 1848, Justice Denman questioned Mr Bell's, the medical witness, judgment. When he addressed the jury, he disparaged the surgeon's explanation of Prior's mental state. Denman argued that Mr Bell's suggestion that Prior 'committed the act under an uncontrollable impulse, acting upon a mind previously diseased' was 'a rashly formed judgement of the medical gentleman', continuing, 'great danger … would prevail … if people were taught that a sudden impulse was an excuse for a crime'.[148] Denman's speech illustrates some of the differences of opinion on perceptions of insanity and criminal lunacy between the medical and legal worlds.[149] Judicial addresses to the court can give clues to a judges' personal beliefs and opinions on insanity and the worth of asylum incarceration for those deemed criminally insane.[150] As the century progressed, many judges began to accept that personal responsibility was inapplicable in cases where women had killed their infants and that a psychiatric view of such cases was more appropriate.[151] Differences in opinion remained about the efficacy of incarceration 'at her Majesty's pleasure' in an asylum.

Judges rarely publicly expressed dissatisfaction with the jurors and the relationship between the judge and the jury was, usually, one of mutual respect. In the case of Sarah Freeman in 1879, it was reported that 'in summing up [the judge] said the jury had imposed upon them a very solemn authority and one that would exercise their sound judgement as well as their good healthy sound feeling'.[152] In the Martha Prior case, Denman recognized the independence of the jury. In his summing-up, he acknowledged that his views on whether Prior was responsible or not for her criminal actions would not be popular with the jury and that he accepted that the jurors would 'no doubt … act upon the testimony of the medical gentleman'. He recognized that the jury would accept 'the medical gentleman['s]' evidence and act independently of his judicial direction, 'as they should as final decision makers'.[153] There were a few mid-century murder cases where the jury returned a lesser verdict than that preferred by the judge. This divergence was due to the jury having different ideas of what constituted mitigating circumstances for a killing, particularly where murder was motivated by passion rather than by calculation.[154]

Judges would suggest verdicts either for conviction or not and express clear opinions of the facts of the cases as they saw them, expecting the juries to follow their instructions. Despite this, a jury could still react in a contrary way to a judge's expectation by interpreting the evidence for themselves and then returning an unforeseen verdict. Although it was rare for a jury not to follow a judge's direction to find a woman insane, they might diverge from that direction and add recommendations to a guilty verdict. Mary Ann Parr, who would eventually be the first patient in Broadmoor, was accused of suffocating her week-old baby at Bingham Union Workhouse, Derbyshire in December 1852.[155] The jury returned a verdict of guilty with a very strong recommendation to mercy. Justice Jervis, while agreeing with the verdict, did not seem to harbour the same view on mercy describing the jury as 'indulgent', saying, 'Mercy does not rest with me, I shall ... forward to the proper quarter the recommendation ... from the indulgent jury ... and whatever is fit and right ... will be taken into consideration.'[156] Analysing the influence of the testimonies of medical men and the prejudices of counsel and judges on court cases is all very well but the final decisions on the outcome of the trial lay with the jury.[157]

It has been suggested that the intellectual interactions between juries, counsel and the judiciary are a demonstration that justice in the long nineteenth century could only be determined by men of the elite classes.[158] While partly agreeing with this, it is not quite accurate due to the varied social classes of jurymen in English and Welsh courts. At both the Central Criminal Court and in the assize courts, there were two different types of juries, the 'Grand Jury' and the 'Petty' or 'Petit' jury. The two juries had very different roles. In essence, at the start of the assizes, the grand jury would vet the indictments and statements, hear evidence from the prosecution and their witnesses but not evidence from the defence or defendant. If the evidence was believed to be sufficient to warrant a trial, the case was approved as a 'true bill' and the defendant put on trial. The petty jury or trial jury consisted of twelve jurors and this jury heard the evidence in a trial, deciding on the innocence or guilt of a defendant.[159] The grand juries in English and Welsh courts were made up of local gentry and middle-ranking professionals, such as merchants and wealthier tradesmen. The petty jury included the same men as well as ordinary local ratepayers. The social and cultural backgrounds of many jurors meant that the two bodies were considered to be stolidly reliable and able to arrive at a just verdict.[160] The juries at the Old Bailey have been described as 'stubbornly independent' men who would mix a 'healthy dose of folk knowledge' with the information gleaned from all testimonies both expert and lay to arrive at their verdicts.[161] This depiction can be equally applied to the juries in the assize courts up and down the country, where local knowledge and opinion often could impact upon their decisions.

For the most part, judges trusted the juries to reach correct and just verdicts although, on occasion, they would be surprised by a result which was contrary to what they believed was the right one. In 1866 Sir James Fitzjames Stephen noted to the Capital Punishment Commission that juries had become reluctant to convict in cases they did not consider to be real murder.[162] Having expressed clear opinions and instructions on the presented evidence in their summings-up, judges could be thwarted and irritated, by jury obduracy. These acts of independence give an indication of the nature of the jury members and their reactions to the circumstances of the cases before them. Unlike inquest juries, the juries in the high courts deliberated in camera.[163] For that reason, it is difficult to ascertain their emotional reactions to any case, not just infanticide and child homicide cases. However, the juries were made up of 'respectable and dependable citizens' who would make their decisions based on experience and common-sense as well as the given evidence on a case.[164]

One case where a jury's opinions and compassionate opinions were displayed was that of Martha Ellen Birkenhead at the Liverpool Assizes in 1876. Martha Birkenhead appeared before Mr Justice Lindley at the Winter Assizes, indicted on a charge of causing the death of her infant daughter by negligence.[165] The jury deliberated for many hours but were unable to agree on a verdict and clearly had doubts about the evidence in the case. They were twice called back into court by Lindley who failed to understand why they could not reach a verdict and enquired how he might clarify evidence.[166] Their main objection to reaching the suggested verdict of manslaughter was that some of the responsibility for the child's death should lie with the parish authorities. Birkenhead had handed the child to the parish authorities twelve days before it died. Some of the jury members suggested the child's underlying lack of strength, as well as the alleged neglect, could be said to exonerate Birkenhead and that they objected to the potentially lengthy prison sentence which would follow a guilty verdict. The jury members were exercising a degree of independent thinking and determination, which eventually led to their dismissal and the postponement of the case to the next assizes. 'His Lordship said ... they had been dwelling too much upon the law and too little upon the facts ... they ought not, in fairness to any judge ... distrust him in the exercise of ... discretion [in sentencing] ... that the law had imposed upon him.'[167] Newspaper reports of the case give a sense that this reaction by an assize jury was unusual and noteworthy. The *Liverpool Mercury* subtitled their article 'A Troublesome Jury' and the *Wigan Observer* subtitled their piece, 'Obstinate Jurymen'.[168]

Conclusion

Over the whole period, the criteria which defined criminal insanity evolved and these changes impacted on the future lives of the homicidal mothers and, potentially, on their future mental welfare. The reactions of the male authority figures who came into contact with the homicidal mothers on their life-journeys through the medico-legal systems could be coloured by their social and educational backgrounds. Doctors' evidence played an essential part in the trials and was likely to be more effective if delivered in a factual, unemotional manner. However, medical men would not wish to show professional vulnerability and overt displays of emotion could weaken a case. Barristers would emphasize the tragedy of the situation and seek compassionate understanding from the jury and judges, with their more emotive interpretation of the facts.[169] Judges might not necessarily agree with the medical experts when it came to their assessments of the mental state of an accused woman but they could see the tragedy in the circumstances of her crime, and accordingly influence the jury. Many had been brought up in the early Victorian period an era of 'pathos' within writing and literature. A society which accorded sentimental emotions considerable cultural significance.[170]

The hypothesis that personal values and social situations would influence emotional responses to female defendants may be an overly simple interpretation of the reality.[171] Accepted establishment ideals of femininity and a paternal benevolence towards female mental fragility and vulnerability, shaped the judgment of women. Any presumptions of moral strength and virtuous, temperate and dependable motherly behaviour were challenged when a mother killed her own child. In fact, the increase of medical understanding of mental illness influenced legal and bureaucratic procedures through the nineteenth century. Insanity was used to rationalize a socially objectionable crime, with an underlying acceptance that the women were not criminals but victims of mental incapacity. This incapacity, which led to them not being accountable for their actions, was hoped to be temporary and with the right care, they would recover and be restored to their families and friends. Rather than running counter to the course of justice, medical evidence of insanity was used to prove that the mother had acted unconsciously and out of character, as a consequence of her mental state at the time of the murder of her child. If the women were committed to an institution by law, then they would be ensured of receiving what the medical experts believed would be the correct care for recovery from mental derangement, rather than punishment for the crime.

3

'To be held until her Majesty's pleasure be known': Confinement – opinions, discussions and decisions

The lives of the three hundred or so women researched for this book, were affected and impacted by the developments in both asylum care and in official policies dealing with the incarceration of all insane criminals. Despite the growing acceptance of theories about the cause and effects of insanity in cases of maternal child murder, differences of opinion about the efficacy of asylum incarceration remained. The ongoing discussions between the judiciary and the medical profession, between judges and the Home Office and amongst judges themselves, were prejudiced by opinion and policy.[1] Roger Smith wrote that official and public opinion of the women were influenced by theories about criminal accountability and insanity.[2] Differing ideas about the effect of unconscious impulse and criminal responsibility were often the subjects of discussion in court cases. The medical assessments made while they were on remand or at the time they had committed the crime, were important to all discussions about their future confinement. The perceived lack of responsibility and delusional impulse were an important topics of discussion in decisions about the confinement of criminally insane women and their capacity for recovery. Official perceptions of the criminally insane mothers' potential for recovery and possible restitution were significant at this stage of their lives. Once the mothers arrived in the relevant institution, their potential for recovery was evaluated again. These evaluations were benchmarks by which the institutional medical staff measured the immediate severity of the women's illnesses and the future trajectories of recovery. The examinations and the opinions gathered both before and after the verdict, from medical men and others, including judges, to an extent, defined the destinies of these mothers.

In the years before Broadmoor's opening, from about 1835 to 1863, mothers who had murdered their own children and been found insane by judicial process, were held in a variety of establishments or simply discharged. At a time when there was a general expansion in institutional care for the insane, institutions from workhouses and prisons to asylums were used. All were deemed unsuitable and inadequate.[3] Before 1863, while county asylum medical superintendents might object to the presence of convict patients ('lunatic criminals') in their asylums, they generally did accept homicidal mothers as genuine patients. They seem to have agreed with Dr Charles Hood's opinion that such patients deserved sympathy and help.[4] After 1863, practically all cases were admitted to the new Broadmoor Criminal Lunatic Asylum. There the medical staff firmly believed that the infanticidal and homicidal mothers were mentally ill, fully deserving of and needing compassionate treatment. A mother who had killed her child while insane, was an object of pity and rightfully merited her place in a curative institution; she was a 'true criminal lunatic'.[5]

There were always differing official views of what the 'correct' place of incarceration should be for these insane mothers. There were many discussions about what should happen after the sentence 'to be detained until her Majesty's pleasure be known' was pronounced. The debate after the opening of Broadmoor centred more upon the efficacy of asylum care, with different opinions being voiced by doctors, the judiciary and government officials. Nonetheless, all officials, for the most part, showed sympathetic understanding towards infanticidal and homicidal mothers. This was despite the fact that the women's actions were far outside their (and society's) expectations of motherhood and 'natural' maternal behaviour. Medical theories that the female physiology could place strains on women's sanity, causing them to perform in a manner totally contrary to acceptable female behaviour, were increasingly accepted by society. Over the Victorian era, medical opinion was that infanticidal women who were shown to be mentally ill would be best served in a place leading to cure and rehabilitation. Broadmoor became acknowledged as the correct institution for these women, an acknowledgement which some members of the judiciary refused to accept. To them, Broadmoor was a place of indefinite imprisonment and they clung to the point of view that Broadmoor Asylum was a prison, not a place of cure. Sir Henry Hawkins was one such judge who objected to an infanticidal mother being incarcerated in an asylum. As shown earlier in this chapter, he would rather have accepted a guilty verdict and pass the subsequent death sentence with his approval for mercy and commutation than commit an infanticidal mother to an asylum. The different interpretations of Broadmoor's status, whether it was a place of punishment and imprisonment or an asylum and a place for cure, was one which continued through the late nineteenth, the twentieth and into the twenty-first centuries.

As a former Clinical Director of Broadmoor said in 2012, 'It cannot be stated too often that Broadmoor is a hospital, never a prison.'[6]

As Hilary Marland has demonstrated in her work on puerperal insanity, the view that homicidal mothers who had killed their children were to be treated with compassions was consistent in the Victorian period.[7] The nineteenth-century medical ideas that puerperal mania and related mental illnesses were potentially remediable conditions, became accepted in the medical world and increasingly by the public. This belief in the 'curability' of specifically female mental conditions was fundamental to asylum medical staff, who held that the sufferers would recover with the right treatment in the right conditions.[8] Evolving medical understandings and treatments of such conditions are discussed in detail in the next chapters about asylums and asylum care. It is, however, relevant to discussions here too. The deliberations and the decisions about the confinement of insane women were always taken with reference to medical opinions. The importance of medical evidence and opinion was as vital in shaping decisions about the value of detention in a dedicated institution, as it had been in influencing trial outcomes. Medical confidence in the curative environment of an asylum supported the doctors' view that incarceration in such institutions was the most suitable and humane solution for criminally insane mothers. In 1902, echoing Charles Hood's thoughts, John Baker wrote that the majority of women held in Broadmoor for the murder of their children had killed out of 'morbid and mistaken maternal solicitude' and had been 'acquitted on the plea that they were insane at the time such acts were committed ... therefore ... free from the taint of crime ... having been held irresponsible for the acts ... by the virtue of their affliction.'[9]

In his thesis and subsequent monograph, Roger Chadwick analysed the records of the Home Office between 1860 and 1890 to investigate principles and patterns of deliberation which drove the administrative decisions about the prerogative of mercy.[10] Through this, he found that attitudes and 'mercy' were very different in the first half of the nineteenth century to the second half. Decision making around judicial matters passed from the direct intervention of the Crown (via the Privy Council) to the Secretary of State at the Home Office.[11] As mentioned previously, the Insane Prisoners Act, was viewed by some as expanding the bureaucratic powers of the Home Secretary and the Home Office.[12] Chadwick suggests that the Home Office became even more involved with the fate of criminal lunatics in 1879 after the Prosecution of Offenders Act and the establishment of the Department for Public Prosecutions.[13] The Act allowed more official involvement in cases before they came to trial and led to an increased role for third-party medical experts within the medico-legal system.[14] External third-party medics appointed by government officials were consulted to verify whether the homicidal mothers showed signs of insanity before their trials and before admission to Broadmoor. The correlation between greater centralization of the criminal justice system and increasing Home Office involvement in decisions about the futures of criminally insane women, is most noticeable in evolving release protocols and procedures.[15] This point is expanded on later in the book but the value of expert opinion, particularly those medical men specializing in caring for the mentally deranged, constantly played an important role in all relevant decisions at the Home Office. Also, growing amounts of legislation increased the involvement of the Home Office in the movement of criminal lunatics.[16] Admission and discharge procedures evolved with mounting and changing numbers of bureaucratic protocols to be fulfilled. However, the important point to be remembered is once a defendant had been admitted to whichever institution as a criminal lunatic, their ultimate fate in the penal or asylum system came under the jurisdiction of the Home Office.

Before Broadmoor, 1835 to 1863

Despite the existence of Bethlem and from 1848, the criminal wards at Fisherton House in the three decades before Broadmoor's opening, there was no discernible, consistent pattern to where insane homicidal mothers might be incarcerated. As can be seen in the diagram at Figure 3.2, not all cases of criminal lunacy were routinely admitted into Bethlem. This was despite its official status as the state criminal lunatic facility in the first thirty-six years of the nineteenth century.[17] I have identified sixty-eight cases of maternal child homicide between 1835 and 1863 and of that number, forty were firstly admitted to Bethlem. An acquittal of a mother for the murder of her child by reason of insanity was not a direct instruction for her to be committed to an asylum. Despite a jury passing down a verdict of not guilty but insane and the judge sentencing the defendant to be held until her Majesty's pleasure be known, there was no automatic passage to an asylum from remand. In all cases, the authorization of a doctor, usually the holding prison's medical officer, was needed and his opinion on the woman's behaviour and mental state was of paramount importance. When the decision was made about the place of detention, the opinion of the trial judge was rarely sought. In the latter forty years of the nineteenth century and, once again, after the opening of Broadmoor, the emphasis of a judge's opinion changed and accordingly became almost as important as medical opinion in such matters.[18]

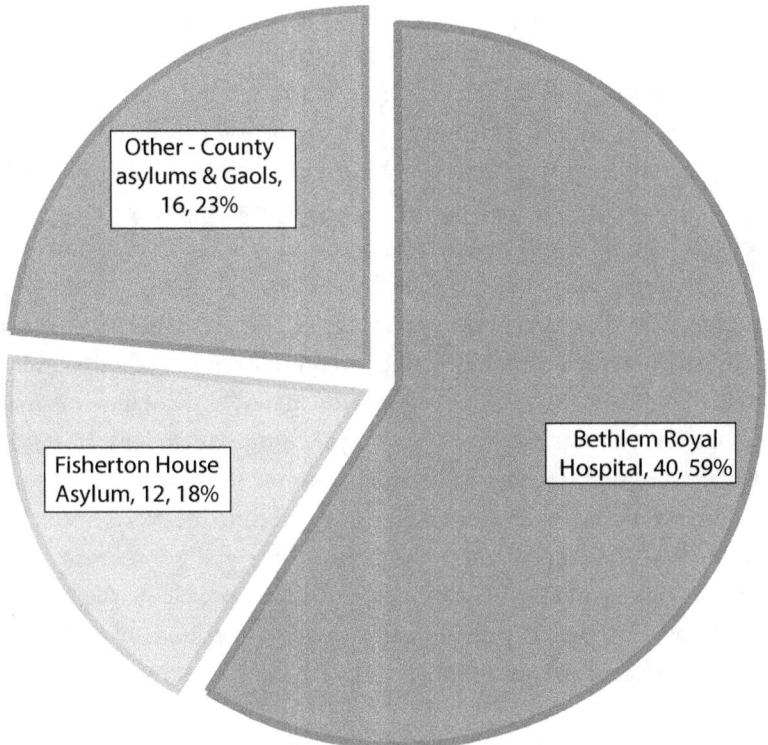

Chart 3.1 Initial place of incarceration for homicidal mothers deemed insane, 1835–63.[19]

The influence and importance of the prison surgeons' official opinion is illustrated by the cases of Ann Colley and Hannah Smith in 1837. Ann Colley was tried at the Stafford Summer Assizes in 1837 for the murder of three of her children and acquitted as insane. Despite the judge's direction, she was detained in Stafford gaol and not sent to the local asylum.[20] A petition was submitted in August 1837 to the Home Secretary from her husband who was acting on the advice that, 'the removal of his wife from the County Gaol of Stafford to the County Lunatic Asylum at Stafford … would be requisite as she was more fit to be an inmate of an asylum than that of a gaol.'[21] The surgeon to the prison, Mr Robert Hughes, vetoed the move, saying 'she is subject to attacks of nervous anxiety with palpitations … but very few medical men would venture to certify that she is insane' and that 'a certificate of insanity would be to no avail.'[22] Unfortunately, Ann Colley subsequently suffered another 'maniacal attack' and committed suicide in the prison in October 1837. At the inquest into her death, it was reported that Colley's husband had visited her and 'very incautiously gave her a locket containing portions of the hair of the murdered children.' This act was reported as having unhinged her mind and consequently Colley hanged herself 'with a silk handkerchief' in the prison privies. Despite Hughes reiterating his opinion that Colley had not displayed insane behaviour in the time leading up to her suicide, the inquest verdict was 'Insanity.'[23]

The case was notorious at the time and was widely reported in the press, including being the subject of at least two broadsides.[24] It is too speculative to say that Hughes was influenced by the recording of Colley's crime and court case but he would have been aware of the graphic and prolific reportage at the time.[25] The press accounts of her trial were quite respectful in tone and not uncompassionate towards Colley. She was the wife of an ex-police superintendent, referred to as 'Mrs Colley' and described as 'rather well educated for her station ... [and] ... a kind and affectionate wife and mother.'[26] Her mental breakdown was blamed on her husband's dismissal from the police force and subsequent domestic difficulties. This sympathy is less apparent after her suicide, when she was referred to as a 'wretched woman' and her death reported in an impersonal manner: 'the effect of strangulation on the brain was so great as to baffle medical skill.'[27]

Hannah Smith was also tried at Stafford, at the Lent Assizes of 1837, having been accused of wilfully murdering her youngest child by drowning. Like Ann Colley, she was acquitted as insane and sentenced to be detained at her Majesty's pleasure. Her conduct in gaol was described as 'that of an Insane Person' and her bodily health was 'Bad from refusing food.' Robert Hughes was once again the doctor involved in her case. Although there is no physical written record of his opinion on the state of Smith's mind, Hughes must have been convinced that her behaviour and demeanour were sufficiently insane to justify her transfer to an asylum. On 14 October 1837 she was 'prepared for removal to Bethlem,' where she was admitted on 7 November of that year.[28] As is noticeable from the cases of Colley and Smith, at this time early in the Victorian era, the authority of prison surgeons influenced the decisions about where a criminal lunatic should be held.

It is not clear from the available papers, why Smith was admitted to Bethlem, rather than Stafford County Asylum. She was not the sole such case. Before The Prison Act 1865, the role of prison surgeon was a part-time one and prison surgeons were only required to examine prisoners on an ad-hoc basis.[29] Infrequent medical examinations could explain why signs of insanity in inmates were occasionally missed. Other Bethlem casebook notes for criminal patients show that, if an accused woman's behaviour or demeanour while she was on remand in the local or county prisons showed signs of insanity, then the opinion of the prison surgeon was important. Potentially, this could lead to tensions arising between prison medical officers and asylum doctors, particularly in cases where a female prisoner had been improperly retained in gaol when she should have been removed to an asylum for treatment. After 1866 and the implementation of the 1865 Act, more frequent medical observations were arranged. This meant that the appointed prison medical officer would be the most likely person to detect incipient signs of mental derangement.[30] This aspect is expanded upon later in this chapter.

The absence of a cohesive policy on the detention of criminal lunatics meant that before 1862, places of confinement for criminally insane mothers varied from county to county. Sarah Grout, Martha Prior, Milicent Page and Esther Playle were four infanticidal mothers from Essex, who might have been candidates for Bethlem Royal Hospital at the time of their committals. Instead, their paths through institutional confinement followed a different route. In 1848, Martha Prior was found not guilty, on the grounds of insanity, of the murder of her thirteen-day-old daughter. She was sent to Essex County Gaol at Springfield as a criminal lunatic. A year later, in 1849, Sarah Grout was also committed to Springfield Gaol, after her trial for the murder of two of her children. Two years later, in March 1851, Milicent Page and Esther Playle each stood trial for murdering their children. Page had cut the throat of her month-old baby and Playle had violently assaulted her five-year-old daughter, before cutting the child's throat. Both women were acquitted on the ground of insanity to 'be kept in confinement, subject to the pleasure of her Majesty.'[31] They were admitted to Springfield Gaol, appearing in the 1851 Census alongside Prior and Grout and designated as 'Criminal Prisoner – acquitted as insane.'[32] Shortly afterwards, all four women were the subject of a successful application from the Visiting Magistrates to the Gaol, supported by the prison surgeons, for them to be transferred to a lunatic asylum. On 20 May 1851, the four were admitted to Hoxton House Asylum as criminal patients. Martha Prior was released as cured from Hoxton in August 1851, after successful formal petitioning by her husband.[33] Grout, Page and Playle were all transferred as 'ordinary lunatics' to Essex County Asylum and subsequently also released as recovered.[34]

Initially, it appears, Martha Prior and Sarah Grout were expected to serve some sort of custodial punishment for their crime, rather than receive specialized care for insanity. It was only after Esther Playle and Milicent Page were admitted to Springfield Gaol in March 1851, that the prison authorities felt that something else should be done for them. In May of that year two prison surgeons wrote that 'the Gaol is not a fit place for them' and suggested that all four women should be transferred to a more suitable environment. The surgeons' letter categorically stated that the women were 'now quiet and well-conducted' and would be better served in an asylum, as they needed 'useful employment' rather than close confinement.[35] The recommendation that they should still remain in some sort of safe custody was twofold in purpose. On one hand they would be protected from a recurrence of their insanity and on the other, public society would also be protected from them. The letter reads, 'We recommend that they be removed from the Gaol both on their own account and on public grounds.'[36] The request for the women's removal to an asylum was driven by the prison surgeons, another demonstration of the importance attached to the opinion of the medical men who had had contact with the women.

Another reason for the initial detentions in Springfield Gaol, rather than an asylum, appears to have been one of economy. Concerns about the costs involved with the retention and detention of criminal lunatics was a recurring one amongst Poor Law Unions and other local authorities. For instance, in 1852 Mary Ann Beveridge, a native of Portsmouth, was held in Winchester Gaol after her trial for the murder of two of her children. The town council of Portsmouth and the local Hampshire magistrates objected to having to support her as a criminal lunatic in Winchester Gaol. They believed that she would be better served in a dedicated, government facility. She was duly transferred to Bethlem, where she was 'maintained at the public expense'.[37] Financial considerations are noticeable in the change of institution for Grout, Page, Playle and Prior. When the four women were admitted into Hoxton House Asylum, there was no county asylum available in Essex and their maintenance was paid for by their respective Poor Law Unions.[38] In 1855, the Guardians for the Orsett Union wrote to Lord Palmerston as Secretary of State, requesting that Sarah Grout be transferred to the county asylum: 'The costs of maintenance of the Lunatic is now borne and paid by the Guardians of the Union and as the expenses are somewhat less in the [Essex] County Asylum, it is of course desirable that she should be moved to that establishment.'[39]

The choice of initial incarceration after trial may have been due, in part, to the fact the accused would have been held on remand in the county gaol before their trials but while there, had not shown signs of active or dangerous insanity. If an offender showed signs of being a danger to herself or others through madness while she was on remand, a prison surgeon or doctor could sanction her removal from the prison to the local asylum, to recover before her trial. This was the case with Agnes Bradley in 1856 and her trial was subsequently postponed for nearly two years. On Boxing Day in 1856, she poisoned her young son with an overdose of laudanum. In the first instance, she was taken to Kirkdale Gaol, Liverpool, where she spent three weeks.[40] While she was there, her behaviour and the evidence of her doctor persuaded the authorities that she should be transferred to the County Lunatic Asylum.[41] On 22 January 1857 she was admitted to Lancashire County Lunatic Asylum at Rainhill. Her case notes say that she described herself as 'a damned woman and ... too wicked to live' and that she had made two attempts at suicide.[42] Whether these attempts were made in Kirkdale is not noted but as no suicide attempts were given as evidence of her insanity at the inquest, it might be inferred that she had become suicidal in prison.[43]

Her admission into Rainhill meant that the trial was postponed and at this point Bradley was confined as an ordinary patient, not as a criminal lunatic. Her medical notes appear to show that her mental health improved slowly and it was not until March 1859, two years after the crime, that it was felt she was fit to face trial. Dr Rogers, the Medical Superintendent at Rainhill, said that, although there were 'peculiarities' about Bradley, he did not believe that they were 'sufficient to constitute insanity.' She went to trial on 26 March 1859 and 'bore the ordeal better than could have been expected'.[44] She was acquitted as insane and returned to Rainhill, designated as a 'criminal lunatic'. Despite there being two provisions for criminal lunatics in 1859, one at Bethlem and one at Fisherton House, she escaped being sent to either. After sanction from the Secretary of State at the Home Office and the direct intervention of trial judge, Lord Justice Willes, she was almost immediately discharged to the care of her husband. As a matter of speculation, had her trial happened five years later, Agnes Bradley might have been sent to Broadmoor. Later on in the century, judges attempting to actively influence where a female offender might be confined before and after her trial became a more common occurrence. Some saw it as part of their role as protectors of prisoners' rights and others acted from a sense of humane compassion. Further on in the chapter, the trend is examined in the light of its impact on the lives of the insane mothers.

All the mothers discussed earlier were sentenced to be held until her Majesty's pleasure be known, meaning that any petitions for removal to another place of detention, whether from prison to the asylum, or between the asylums, had to be made via the Home Office. They were then referred onward to the Crown in the form of the Privy Council.[45] Subsequent release warrants were signed by Queen Victoria herself and an unconditional discharge could be followed by a full Royal Pardon. The system changed in 1861 when the judiciary's and the Privy Council's powers of reprieve and commutation were transferred to the

Home Office. For a short time after Broadmoor opened, the protocols for release and discharge continued unchanged however once the dedicated asylum was fully functional, they changed again.

Broadmoor Criminal Lunatic Asylum, 1863 to 1901

> Broadmoor Prison [sic] ... a Government establishment intended ... solely to the reception of criminal lunatics', ... It is not yet completed and at present only a small number of females are confined in it ... when it is perfect it is understood that the Government intends to remove all criminal lunatics at present confined in Bedlam and other establishments to this prison which, by its construction and internal arrangements, is specially adapted for the reception of such persons[46]
>
> 'The Marylebone Murder', *The Era*, 6 December 1863.

The opening of the dedicated state criminal lunatic asylum, under the ultimate control of the government, put a different complexion on the detention of the criminally insane after 1863. After the mid-1870s, the nature of exchanges apropos the rationales behind the institutional confinement of the women criminal lunatics, between the judiciary, doctors and government officials, began to change. The increasing involvement of the Home Office with the fate of criminal lunatics led to prolonged negotiations and procedures concerning the destinies of Broadmoor patients. Such deliberations effectively allowed officials at the Home Office to exercise more bureaucratic control over decisions about incarceration of the criminally insane. As mentioned earlier in this chapter, the Prosecution of Offenders Act led to more official involvement of medical men notably early alienists and psychologists, both before and after trial. The governmental officials placed great reliance on the reports and opinions from consultations with third-party experts such as asylum superintendents.[47] Dr Orange and Dr Nicolson of Broadmoor in their positions as experts in and exponents of care for the mentally deranged are two important examples of men thus consulted. Their expert opinion was valuable to the decision-making processes of the Home Office. As the place of early psychiatric medicine, in the form of such specialist doctors, became more accepted by Home Office officials, the role of the prison doctors in decisions regarding the actual place of detention diminished. This did not mean that the diagnostic opinions of the prison surgeons were of any less importance in the system; however, the weighting given to those opinions was subtly changed.

It is clear that the observations, diagnoses and opinions of prison medical officers remained crucial to the asylum medical staff. Prison doctors and surgeons had had contact with the accused women from soon after the criminal act and during their time on remand. Observations about the women's behaviour, possible causes of their insanity, social background, as well as notes about their general state of health, were valuable to the asylum.[48] The 1865 Prisons Act brought in regular weekly medical inspections of prisoners by a qualified doctor in all places of detention, including centrally controlled prisons and local gaols. As prisoners on remand were usually held in local facilities, it was often the resident gaol surgeon who would observe any signs of insanity in a detainee. As mentioned in the previous chapter, many of these medical men claimed that, through experience, they had developed an expertise in diagnosing mental disorders and in recognizing cases of feigned mental illness. They believed they were well qualified to determine who was insane and who was not.[49] This knowledge resulted from close observation of individual cases while under confinement, rather than being based on the theories of asylum doctors and other medical men.

When a patient was admitted to Broadmoor, they were accompanied by proforma 'Schedule A – Statement respecting Criminal Lunatics'. This document was sent with each criminal lunatic on admittance to the Asylum from another institution, usually a prison.[50] It contained relevant information about the patient, including a supposed cause of the attack of insanity and whether they were suicidal or a danger to others. Obviously, the form was completed from observations by the staff at the previous place of incarceration, such as the prison surgeon but would give a putative diagnosis of insanity to the asylum staff which was invariably accepted and recorded in the asylum records.[51] The next chapter will discuss the diagnoses and the treatment in the asylums in detail. What is important here is that, despite the fact that the role of the prison doctors was apparently weakened by an increasing involvement of the Home Office and their appointed medical experts, within the medical profession there was general agreement about theories of the cause and effect of insanity, particularly in cases of maternal child murderers.

Unfit to plead, arraignment and direct admission

Any differences in legal and medical opinion about where the women should be incarcerated and treated were often apparent in 'unfit to plead' cases. Some women were admitted into an asylum without a full trial by jury, having been found insane on arraignment; in other words, they had been considered either unfit to plead or unable to understand the court proceedings. As shown in the table below (Table 3.1) 18 per cent of the dataset were admitted to Broadmoor this way. In such cases, the opinion of medical men was, once again, of paramount significance to the woman's fate. In other cases, the insanity of the charged homicidal mother was so obvious that it was deemed necessary to admit her directly to an asylum by way of a Home Secretary's warrant, thus by-passing a trial. Then there were the cases where it was suggested by some parties, both legal and medical, that just bringing the case to trial, would irreparably damage the physical and mental health of the accused mother. Some of the debate about the 'unfit to plead' verdict is well illustrated by the use of case studies. Their use in the rest of this chapter highlights the contemporary debate and unease amongst members of the judiciary concerning the range and the exercise of executive powers by the Home Office within the justice system.

Although there was a growing acceptance of theories concerning the cause and effects of insanity, particularly in cases of maternal child murder, differences of opinion still existed between the judiciary and the medical profession about the efficacy of asylum incarceration. On occasion, it was not unknown for a judge's views to override expert medical opinion. There was a continuing discussion about unconscious impulse and criminal responsibility between medical men and judges in relation to the destiny of these mothers.[52] Rather than running counter to the course of justice, medical evidence of insanity was used to prove that the mother had acted unconsciously and out of character, as a consequence of her mental state at the time of the murder of her child. If the women were committed to an institution by law, then they would be ensured of receiving what the medical experts believed would be the correct care for recovery from mental derangement, rather than punishment for the crime.

In his extensive works on crime and insanity Nigel Walker suggested that the implementation of the 1865 Act contributed to the increase in cases where the accused were found unfit to plead or insane on arraignment and were sent straight to Broadmoor without a full trial.[53] Although Walker was specifically referring to cases other than murder, it is worth assessing the numbers of homicidal mothers admitted to Broadmoor as unfit for trial, to see if there was a discernible increase as a result of closer medical attention. I have identified relatively few such mothers within my database. Table 3:1 shows that there were just seventy admissions out of two hundred and fifty-eight between 1863 and 1900. It is difficult to ascertain whether the number of 'unfit to plead cases'

Table 3.1 Women admitted for the killing of their own children. Broadmoor Criminal Lunatic Asylum, 1863 to 1900.[54]

Years admitted	Admissions 1863 to 1900				
	Verdict				
	Not tried	Arraigned	%age total	Tried & insane	Totals
1863–5	2	2	11	32	36
1866–9	2	2	18	18	22
1870–4	2	9	40	16	27
1875–9	1	10	34	21	23
1880–4	4	6	28	25	35
1885–9	-	11	32	23	34
1890–5	5	13	35	33	51
1896–1900	2	8	26	20	30
Totals 1863–1900	18	52	18	188	258

admitted to Broadmoor rose significantly after 1865, as the majority of the entries between 1863 and 1866 (when the Act was implemented) had been transferred from Bethlem or Fisherton House and records of the original court verdict were not necessarily transferred with the patients. After 1869, the number of cases found insane on arraignment remained more or less consistent with a reduction for the years between 1880 and 1884 when just 17 per cent of admissions were arraignment cases.

The provision that an accused person could be found insane on arraignment was contained in the 1800 Criminal Lunatics Act and was not a new phenomenon after 1863.[55] For a case to be arraigned, evidence of a person's unfitness to be tried had to be presented to a judge and a specifically empanelled jury. Evidence of the accused's mental incapacity was presented with testimony from medical expert witnesses such as prison surgeons or asylum superintendents.[56] In his opening address to the Hertfordshire Assizes, Watford, in August 1885, Mr Baron Huddleston commented on the upcoming case of Susan Burfield charged with the attempted murder of her three-year-old child. He said that although 'the prisoner was clearly not in her right mind', he recommended that the Grand Jury should find a true bill to answer, 'so that the matter might be investigated in the court below'. Burfield was duly brought to court before 'a jury ... sworn to determine the question whether she was in a fit state to plead'. It was reported that despite having a 'pleasing appearance' she was acting like 'a person mentally deranged ... muttering something to herself and ... [showed] ... the excitement under which she was labouring'. Burfield had been remanded in HMP St Albans since her magistrates' court appearance three months earlier. At the arraignment hearing, the prison medical officer, Dr J. T. N. Lipscomb, advised the court that in that time he had observed her constantly. He had come to the conclusion that she was 'labouring under a variety of delusions, there was no doubt she was insane'.[57] At Huddleston's direction, the jury found that Burfield was not in a fit state to plead. She was admitted to Broadmoor on 6 August 1885.[58] The arraignment proceedings acted as legal confirmation of the accused mother's mental derangement, so as such the outcomes did not always impact on where the accused woman would be incarcerated. Usually but not always that place of custody would be an asylum. Although occasionally in the years after 1863 there were criminal lunatic admissions to other asylums, the asylum of choice was usually Broadmoor. The process of arraignment, however, confirms that the knowledge and experience of medical men when dealing with insanity and its causes remained vitally important to the future life-path of mothers who murdered their children.

Martha Baines, the wife of a chemist and druggist from Kendal, murdered her five-month-old child on 5 November 1875 and had been admitted by direct warrant to Broadmoor in December 1875.[59] In his charge to the Grand Jury at the Westmorland Spring Assizes in 1876, Mr Justice Brett stated that he was doubtful about the legitimacy of direct admission to Broadmoor and about the legality of an offender being confined as a criminal lunatic without the case being brought to the assize court. He said, 'I know of no right that anyone has to confine her as if she were a criminal. ... [and] ... I know of no law by which she can be confined as a criminal lunatic without a bill being found by the Grand Jury.' His objection appeared to be that the Home Secretary's warrant circumvented the high court system. By being admitted to Broadmoor, Martha Baines had been designated a criminal without fair trial. Rather than suggesting that Baines had avoided trial, Brett was taking issue with the choice of institution, as an asylum for criminal lunatics. He understood and accepted that insane offenders could be admitted to asylums before trial saying, 'It may be that by certain certificates of medical men she may be confined in a county asylum ... [and] ... be treated with every consideration and kindness until, if it be so, she is cured.'[60] It would appear that to Brett, an admission into Broadmoor was a penal detention, ignoring the right of habeas corpus.[61] The Grand Jury did bring a true bill against Martha Baines, in her absence, but because she was already confined in Broadmoor, her trial was carried over to the following assizes. At those assizes, Mr Justice Lindley advised the Grand Jury that Baines remained in Broadmoor and still was not in a fit state to be tried.[62] Martha Baines never faced trial and, after a stay of two years, was discharged from Broadmoor to her husband's care, 'her sanity now ... re-established'.[63]

A similar action was taken in the case of Mary Ann Morgan in 1884, mentioned in the previous chapter. Once again, the action was not viewed favourably by the presiding judge at the assizes where Morgan was due to stand trial. At the Swansea Lent Assizes, Mr Justice Stephen made his opinions quite clear, when granting the prosecution's application for postponement of the trial on the grounds of Morgan's insanity. He said that 'persons accused of crime ... [are] ... entitled by various Acts to have their cases tried at the assizes' but by this action he did not see 'what there was to prevent a person ... from being shut up in a lunatic asylum for life without trial'.[64] He described such actions as a defect in the application of law. The outcome of this particular case has been described as a demonstration of the growing confidence of the Home Office in its authority on legal procedure.[65] The cases of Martha Baines and Mary Ann Morgan illustrate that members of the judiciary did not object to insane homicidal mothers being directly admitted to Broadmoor by Home Secretary's warrant, their objection was to a perceived undermining of judicial procedure. By defending a person's right to a trial before imprisonment, the judges were protecting the right of habeas corpus.[66] However, if a homicidal mother's insanity was so patently clear from medical examination and she was already confined in an asylum, it was plain that she would be unfit to plead and stand trial.[67] While the debate can be viewed as a judicial defence of the ancient right, it was also a dispute between bureaucracy in the guise of the Home Office and the legal authorities about the actual role of the criminal lunatic asylum.

Judges' opposition to the confinement of child murderers in Broadmoor was particularly noticeable in cases involving young, single mothers. Such reactions would appear to indicate that there was, for some, a struggle between paternalistic pity for the offender and the duty to follow the correct judicial procedure. Although it is a speculative point, conflicts of conscience may have stemmed from personal cultural belief. In their view, women, particularly the seemingly young and vulnerable, needed protection, nurturing and guidance, not confinement and punishment. In 1894, Emily Harriet Wilson was tried in Leeds before Mr Justice Gainsford Bruce for the murder of her illegitimate baby. In a letter to the Home Office, Bruce expressed his consternation that she might not be insane and therefore should not be in Broadmoor. 'The judge had great compassion for her sad case – he hopes for an early release.'[68] Wilson had been seduced by her stepfather, fell pregnant and killed her baby at birth. Bruce's intervention was the subject of a report in Wilson's Home Office file, the purpose of which was to ascertain how long similar cases remained in Broadmoor and whether their retention was justified in terms of their crime and insanity.[69]

Two other cases were referred to in this particular report, those of Annie Cherry and Matilda Wilcox, both of whom were in Broadmoor. There was no comment about the trial judges in the reference to Wilcox. However, the writer noted that the judge in the case of Cherry, Sir Henry Hawkins, 'wanted immediate release [of the accused] not go to the Asylum at all'.[70] In his *Reminiscences*, Hawkins wrote that he believed that 'in the case of poor creatures who make away with their ... offspring in the agony of their trouble and shame, there were always found very strong reasons for ... very limited periods of imprisonment'.[71] He also wrote that on such occasions, he would prefer to receive a guilty verdict with a full recommendation to mercy and pass the death sentence. His rationale in these situations was that a commuted death sentence with a limited period of penal servitude would be preferable to a potentially 'endless lifelong imprisonment' in an asylum.[72]

Periodically, legal opinion might lean towards the preference that a motion of 'nolle prosequi' be issued by the court but this was a rare occurrence.[73] Although no formal motion was issued in the case of Eliza Agar, it was suggested as a possibility in the discussions surrounding the case.[74] Her story also illustrates some of the differences in opinion between judges and medical experts in matters of criminal responsibility and incarceration. Agar's trial was postponed four times while the Home Office discussed the best course of action with Dr Orange, the superintendent of Broadmoor and the appointed judge, Henry Hawkins. In accordance with his firmly held belief in appropriate asylum care, Orange asserted that the correct place for women like Agar was in the protective atmosphere of an asylum. Hawkins, as previously shown, had an aversion to incarceration without a definitive end, whether curative or punitive.

In 1883, Eliza Agar, the wife of a warehouse manager, placed her four-week-old baby on the nursery fire. Despite a medical instruction that she was not to be alone with the child, the monthly nurse had left the room for a short while. Her doctor specifically stated that 'after ... confinement she [Eliza Agar] has suffered from Puerperal Mania' and that she was considered a risk to the child.[75] Agar appeared before magistrates at Barnet Police Court on 18 February 1883 and was committed for trial at the Old Bailey.[76] Agar was not remanded in prison but allowed to remain with friends and family, bailed against the surety of her husband and two brothers. Orange was instructed by the Treasury Solicitor to examine Agar, which examination he initially undertook on 16 May, concurring with her doctors that she was suffering from puerperal mania, which was still ongoing. He met with Agar again on 12 June, after which meeting, he sent his detailed report to the Home Office. Following his comments on criminal responsibility and awareness quoted in Chapter 2, Orange wrote that he believed Eliza Agar had known what she was doing when she killed her baby. The deposition evidence of the doctors tending her at the time pointed to the fact that she was in a state of puerperal insanity and that she found her infant child 'a bother to her', which, Orange suggested, could possibly be viewed by some as a malicious motive for murder.[77] That being said, he also thought that, from her demeanour when he visited her, she was more than likely to have also been suffering from puerperal melancholia at the time.

In these circumstances, if she were considered well enough to face trial, under the McNaughton Rules, then in Orange's opinion 'it might be quite possible, according to the law for the poor creature to be sentenced to death, a result too horrible to be seriously contemplated'.[78] In his report, Orange advised that in his opinion, Agar had improved in health enough to face arraignment or trial, possibly at the next Sessions at the Central Criminal Court. Despite the fact this suggestion could lead to the death sentence, Orange was still firm in his opinion that Agar had been insane when she assaulted her infant and that she would be better served by a stay in Broadmoor. However, after his report was submitted, there was a movement aimed at avoiding her admittance into the Asylum.

Hawkins was particularly against her removal to Broadmoor. In a letter to the Home Secretary, W. Vernon Harcourt, he categorically stated that because Agar was not responsible for her actions when she killed the child, she had not committed a crime. '[It is] beyond all doubt that at the time she caused the child's death she was not responsible ... She has been guilty of no crime.'[79] He had no doubt that she had killed her child but he did not believe she should be confined at all, certainly not within an asylum. In a somewhat extraordinary manner, Hawkins acted as defence, jury and judge in this case. The judge's stance caused a dilemma for the Home Office who consulted once again with Orange. Orange advised that he could do no more. In his opinion, if Agar had originally been admitted to Broadmoor instead of remaining at home, he would still say that she was in no fit state to be discharged.[80] It appears that Hawkins's opinion of Broadmoor was that it was a place of punishment and not a fit place for someone such as Eliza Agar. 'I believe that to commit her to a Criminal Lunatic Asylum ... would be absolutely destructive to her chances of recovery ... It is impossible to punish her for she has committed no crime and confinement ... would be destructive to her reason & worse than death to her.'[81] Despite the importance attached to Orange's medical opinion by the Home Office, Hawkins's view prevailed. The compromise was that Eliza Agar remained at home, with watchful nursing care and if she suffered any recurrence of her illness she would be confined in an asylum.[82]

The Agar case highlights the differences between medical and judicial opinions on criminal responsibility and incarceration. It is also a demonstration of how personal beliefs of men in authority could impact on a woman's life. Hawkins admitted that he had taken an unusual interest in the case and was 'anxious that the most humane course' should be taken with her future care.[83] This humane course in his view was not for her to admitted into an asylum and certainly not to Broadmoor. Orange, on the other hand, believed that the best place for Agar was in the safe confines of Broadmoor, where she would receive the appropriate care leading to her recovery. His reports and notes on the examination of Agar in the papers give an idea of his conviction in the appropriateness of confinement in an asylum in such cases. He believed that the regime in Broadmoor would help towards Agar's recovery from puerperal mania and potentially cure her insanity. On most occasions after 1863, if a homicidal mother was found to be unfit for trial or her insanity was defined by legal and medical opinion in court, she would be admitted to an asylum. Except for a few cases, that asylum was Broadmoor. While some judges might express their doubts about the efficacy of asylum treatment for some women, in the medical men's opinion confinement for possible cure in such places was the correct course of action.

The involvement of private opinions in judicial decisions is clearly demonstrated by Henry Hawkins's personal moral integrity and views. He appears to have taken a personal stance to protect a woman who he described as 'an object of sympathy and pity'.[84] Despite the fact that he said that all he wanted was what he saw as the right solution to the problem, his attitude can be seen as carrying an element of class bias. Eliza Agar came from a middle-class background with her husband employed in a managerial role and her own family were in respectable trades. From time to time, the personal and domestic circumstances of an accused woman had a discernible impact on the decisions made about her future. There were different reasons given for any diversion from the more usual courses of action, but the patients' standing on the social scale did appear to have bearing on where she would be detained.[85] The worry of the magistrate in the case of Mary Ann Morgan, that she would not survive in prison, came from his personal knowledge of her as being a fellow member of middle-class society in Swansea.[86]

In the case of Annie Florence Attree, the influence of connections is clear. Attree was charged with attempted murder in 1891, after she threw her infant son from the carriage of a train. She was 'found insane on arraignment by a jury empanelled for the purpose'.[87] In court she had been described as 'suffering from maniacal excitement, ... disposed to be violent, and presented symptoms of acute mania'.[88] At this point, she was removed to Bethel Hospital in Norwich.[89] Three days later she was moved to Holloway Sanatorium in Egham, Surrey, 'a high class establishment for insane patients'.[90] Although Holloway was a private asylum it did occasionally take middle-class criminal patients. The few that were admitted, had appeared to have recovered but still needed supervision and monitoring, which the families felt unable or unwilling to provide.[91] Attree remained there until October 1894 when she was transferred to Ipswich County Asylum. In 1896 a Home Office warrant transferred her back to Bethel, still as a criminal lunatic patient. She absconded from Bethel in September 1899 and was eventually found in Sussex in November of that year. This episode led to her final asylum admission in December 1899. She was admitted to Broadmoor on 21 December 1899, on the warrant of the Home Secretary.[92]

The complicated asylum career of Annie Florence Attree had its roots in her social background. A newspaper report, written at the time she absconded from Bethel in 1899, described her history as 'sad' and that her original detention in 1891, had 'created a great deal of sympathetic feeling at the time'.[93] The report continued, 'She is described as being connected with a good family, her uncle being the late Mr. Metcalfe, Q.C., Recorder of this city, and her husband and children reside at Carlton Colville.'[94] Her records at Broadmoor repeat the fact that she was related to William James Metcalf, and that she had other family connections which had assisted in where she was confined and resulted in a late admission into a specialized facility.[95] The influence of money and family networks on the procedures of confinement had complicated Annie's route into Broadmoor. She remained there until her death in 1915 however, during that time, she and her family never forgot their self-professed social superiority.[96] The perceived class and its associated ideas of criminal lunatic mothers also impacted on their lives once they were in the asylums. Interactions with medical and attendant staff became significant to the recovery and potential discharge from the asylum. The friendships and communications between the patients would also be impacted, with many slipping into their pre-asylum positions in life.[97] As social prejudice and class partisanship were elements which ran through the Victorian medico-legal system and officialdom, it is not surprising that they also had an impact in the asylums.

Conclusion

Establishment ideals of femininity shaped perceptions of women. Society's suppositions of moral motherly behaviour were challenged when mothers became the perpetrators of infanticide and child murder. In accepting that the female mind was unstable and vulnerable, there was an acceptance that mothers who killed their own babies and children were probably the victims of mental incapacity and aberration. Paternalistic compassion allowed that they were mentally weak through circumstance, which led to them not being accountable for their actions. They were not habitual criminals.

There was always a degree of disagreement about the best course of action for the insane mothers. Each party to the decision process would have had a personal opinion about the worth of asylum treatment which would play a part alongside any medical diagnoses of madness. Before the opening of Broadmoor, with the dearth of facilities devoted to the criminally insane, asylum care was not necessarily believed to be the best way to reach a cure and re-introduce the women into society. That being said, decisions about incarceration made between 1837 and 1863 were not so arbitrary as first appears. The opinion of the prison doctor was paramount and if he did not detect recognizable signs of insanity, then he would not suggest admission to an asylum. For those who did go into an asylum, they could be detained in a dedicated facility for the criminally insane, if there was space available, or in local asylums or prison if not. The cost of maintenance was a consideration to the local outside agencies and this seemed to have a bearing on the place of detention. The economic aspects of asylum care and their bearing on the welfare of the insane homicidal mothers, impacted upon the potential discharge or retention of patients.[98]

The discussions about incarceration and the debates about the future for the infanticidal mothers were the last dealings they would have with the justice system. The next stages on their journeys would be under the control of the medical world and of government bureaucracy. Their treatment in the institutions would be regulated by medical men and their potential discharges ultimately decided by the Home Office, albeit with medical advice. The remaining chapters of the book concentrate on their lives within the asylums, the people they came into contact with there and their future lives, whether inside or outside the institutions.

4

'God bless all hear [sic] for the good nursing I get now.' Dynamics of treatment and care in the asylums

In this chapter the asylum experiences of female criminal lunatics are examined. The main emphasis is on the lives of those women who had been admitted to an asylum to remain until her Majesty's pleasure be known. In Broadmoor parlance, those patients who had been admitted to await her Majesty's pleasure were referred to as 'Queen's pleasure patients'. Jade Shepherd found in her work on men in Broadmoor, for these 'pleasure patients' the main concern was to treat their mental illness, not to punish them.[1] This was true for the 'Queen's pleasure women' as it was for the men.[2] Both before and after 1863, as Hilary Marland writes, asylum doctors usually accepted and believed that infanticidal and homicidal mothers needed careful and understanding treatment, not punishment as criminals.[3] Despite having violently assaulted and murdered their children, their crimes became a side issue to the state of their mental welfare and illness. In the majority of cases, although asylum doctors were keen to ascertain and understand why the crime had been committed, only occasionally was it referred to after admission. Belief in the 'curability' of specifically female mental illnesses was fundamental to asylum medical staff, who believed sufferers would recover with the right treatment in the right conditions.[4] As Marland also finds, medical men including the clinical staff at the asylums recognized and understood that some of those conditions, such as puerperal mania, could disappear almost as rapidly as they appeared.[5] Indeed, in a few cases, the admitting doctors wrote that patients could arrive at the asylum not displaying any sign of insanity. Mothers who had killed their children through uncontrollable insanity were seen as deserving of their place in a therapeutic institution. Medical confidence in the curative environment of an asylum supported the views that incarceration in such institutions was the most suitable and humane solution for criminally insane mothers.

The remainder of the book is about treatment, relationships between staff, patients and their families and generally, about life in the asylums. In this chapter, the women's experiences of asylum life are reviewed in terms of their diagnoses of insanity and the subsequent treatment they received. Medical opinion was that all women, no matter what their background, were governed by their physiology. The strains of pregnancy, childbirth and early motherhood were understood to be difficult emotional experiences and these strains were particularly perilous to the balance of the female mind.[6] Mitigating social and environmental circumstances, together with the acceptance of female 'physical and mental fragility … agreed to be latent in all women', allowed for them to be treated compassionately.[7] After admission into an asylum, recommendations concerning continuing incarceration or possible release depended on the opinions of the staff, particularly those of the medical staff. As well as medical treatment, the interactions between the women and the staff were important to their asylum lives and their futures. As evidenced by the various records of the institutions, life in the asylums for the homicidal mothers was organized by the medical superintendent and his staff. The sociocultural environment, as well as the medical regimes in the institutions affected the quality of the women's experiences.

The asylums

Despite having some similarities, the three criminal lunatic facilities in Victorian England differed from one another. Before 1863, Bethlem Royal Hospital and Fisherton House Asylum were the only two asylums in England and Wales with official government status as specialist facilities for the criminally insane. There were many similarities in the administration and treatment regimens in the three criminal lunatic facilities or asylums but there were also significant differences. Bethlem and Broadmoor were public institutions but their designations as the state facilities for the criminally insane set them apart from the county asylums. Bethlem's uniqueness lay in having private wards, public and pauper wards and criminal lunatic wings. Broadmoor was always and remained a state institution with no private wards. As is described further on in the chapter, Fisherton House was unlike Bethlem and Broadmoor in terms of both ownership and organization.

Bethlem was very much a hybrid institution, which had grown organically over the many years since its foundation. In 1816, Bethlem had become the first institution in England to have specialist wards or wings for the criminally insane. These were maintained at the same time as the private wards and public or pauper wards. To begin with, the criminal patients were treated alongside the incurable patients and it was not always expected that they might recover from their insanity. Mechanical restraint was used alongside seclusion and purgatives, as would be meted out to all patients. In 1835, Dr Alexander Morison was appointed as one of two inspecting physicians to Bethlem. Morison was not totally in favour of moral management or treatment, and did not advocate the total abolition of mechanical restraint such as straitjackets. In 1852, this led to public controversy over the maltreatment of Bethlem patients and a Commission of Inquiry. In the wake of the publication of the damning report on Bethlem's regime, Morison retired from his post and was replaced by Charles Hood.[8] Hood was an ardent advocate of non-restraint and he took on the task of improving the medical administration and practice in the Hospital.[9] By his early death in 1870, he had introduced extensive reforms, successfully introducing non-restraint and basic occupational therapy. The changes owed a lot of their success to Hood's enthusiastic, hands-on approach.[10]

Fisherton House was a commercial enterprise and, despite a twenty-year commission as a criminal facility, many of the practices followed were more akin to those of a private asylum. As an institution, it was somewhat of an anomaly in the history of criminal lunatic asylums. Despite being managed by medical men, as a commercially run organization, the opinions and attitudes of the Finch family were proprietorial, as well as patriarchal. This is not to say that they were not caring towards their patients, in fact in some respects treatment in Fisherton was more personal and considerate than the bigger asylums. In 1857, Corbin Finch was quick to defend his institution's treatment of criminal patients, against complaints from a local magistrate, Rev. G. P. Lowther. Lowther had expressed concern about the relative freedom some criminal patients received, having observed some beyond the walls of the asylum. He was also concerned that the 'criminal lunatics [were]associating with pauper (not private) patients'.[11] In reply, Finch wrote to the Home Secretary defending his treatment and the practices of the asylum. He wrote that he saw no problem in such privileges which were mainly applied in the female ward. He justified this further by saying, 'the women to the most part being a better class of criminal'.[12] By not being government appointees, the management were not afraid to confront officialdom. William Corbin Finch, junior, was protective of the welfare and health of his patients as well as very sure of his own integrity and reputation. The smaller physical size of the asylum and the 'less dangerous' status of the criminal patients admitted had some impact on the experiences of the criminal mothers confined there.

By the mid-century, moral therapy or moral treatment formed the basis of the standard methods used to manage and treat the insane in all county and larger private asylums, such as Fisherton House.[13] By the mid-century, county asylums had grown in terms of population size, and some of the finer points of moral therapy had become diluted. Moral therapy had transformed into moral management, becoming a more controlling and coercive system. In its transformation into a patient management scheme, some of the more benevolent aspects of the therapy were lost.[14] In 1869, Dr Thomas Lawes Rogers of Lancashire County Lunatic Asylum at Rainhill commented on the lack of personal contact he had with patients. He bemoaned the fact that he could not know his patients saying, 'undoubtedly when in any establishment the number of patients exceeds 500, the Medical Superintendent cannot possess that intimate personal acquaintance with every individual case which is desirable for the patient's sake … they [the medical officers] simply do their best in existing circumstances'.[15] Rogers was writing at a time when treatment of the insane in the large county asylums was becoming less curative and more punitive. The 1860s and 1870s were a period when the earlier optimistic view of treatment in an asylum as a cure for madness abated.[16] The large asylums which had been previously lauded as places of cure through moral therapy were overfull and congested with patients, underfunded and were becoming materially dilapidated. 'Psychiatric pessimism' replaced curative optimism.[17]

In its time, Broadmoor, although run on lines more similar to county asylums, was set apart by its designation as the state criminal lunatic asylum. It was a separate, autonomous institution rather than an annex to an existing asylum, purely existing to hold and care for criminally insane men and women.[18] Jade Shepherd notes that at Broadmoor 'no definite shift towards pessimism [was] evident until … after 1896'.[19] In 1896 Dr Richard Brayn was appointed Medical Superintendent and after his appointment, changes were seen in the asylum's regime. The influence and opinions of the Broadmoor superintendents are discussed in detail in Chapter 6. The Victorian press repeatedly reported the idea that Broadmoor was a place of endless confinement, 'the ultimate prison, a place of life-in-death for its inmates'.[20] Despite what the press, popular and, occasionally, professional interpretations might have been and despite housing the criminally insane, Broadmoor was always conceived as a curative, not a penal institution.[21]

For women patients in any of the criminal lunatic facilities, the numbers on the women's wards remained manageable. In fact, in all three criminal lunatic facilities the female populations remained relatively low in number, particularly when compared with the number of female patients in the large county asylums, and even in comparison with the men's wards. In the Bethlem Physician's Report of 1847, it was reported that 'the male criminal wing is the most crowded and the female criminal wing the least of all the various departments of the Hospital'.[22] This may well have facilitated more personal interaction between individual patients and the medical and attendant staff in Bethlem, Fisherton House and Broadmoor. The patient–staff relationships are examined in this and in the next two chapters. In this chapter, they are reviewed as part of the curative and restorative process. The next chapter concentrates on the patient's perspective and Chapter 6 on the asylums' staffs' attitudes and duties of care towards the patients.

Treatments and change

The concept of moral therapy or treatment was intended as a humane regime to help restore mentally disturbed and restless patients to a calmer and their normal state of mind.[23] Early in the Victorian period, while the treatment was partly accepted, it was often supplemented with the use of other methods.[24] Medical treatments based on the methods used for physical ailments such as purging, bleeding and blistering, and the use of restraint and confinement were commonplace early in the century.[25] The records of Bethlem and of Fisherton House indicate that the favoured treatment method was a mixture of the 'old' methods and the 'new', perhaps gentler, methods.[26]

Eliza Pegg was a patient in Bethlem, Fisherton House and finally, in Broadmoor. She was seen as a source of trouble for the asylum authorities in Bethlem and Fisherton. In both institutions she attacked other patients, attendants and visitors.[27] In March 1847, Eliza Pegg had been found guilty of concealment at Norfolk Assizes and sentenced to four months imprisonment in the Wymondham Jail. At the time of her conviction, the prison medical officer was convinced that she was feigning insanity. After observing her over three months, he conceded that she was insane and she was admitted to Norfolk County Asylum. In February 1853, the resident physician, Dr A. D Foote, described her as 'one of the most violent patients in the house' and subsequently she was transferred to Bethlem in July 1853.[28] In Bethlem, her unpredictable behaviour continued and led to her being placed 'in a padded cell for some hours at a time'.[29] Despite the remit for Fisherton House being for less dangerous patients, Eliza Pegg was transferred there on 6 December 1853. On different occasions at Fisherton House, her head was shaved and 'a blister applied to the nape of the neck' in an effort to control her. She was given tepid baths which 'had the desired effect of tranquillizing her'.[30] However, Pegg did eventually calm down and was described in 1862 as continuing 'quiet & is constantly employed in the wash house … robust bodily health'.[31] The treatment she received at Bethlem and at Fisherton House appears to be quite severe, however it was noted by Foote in his report on her that 'she is not governed by kindness'.[32] Perhaps a case where moral treatment did not work. Eliza Pegg was transferred to Broadmoor in June 1863, where she was described as being capable of 'extreme violence' and 'demented'. Eventually, on 27 November 1867, she was transferred back to Norfolk County Asylum, not recovered from insanity but no longer a criminal patient.[33] She died there in June 1895, having spent forty years in one institution or other.[34]

Despite the recorded treatment given to Eliza Pegg, Finch was called to defend his use of bathing in the treatment of all patients in his asylum. He wrote to the Commissioners in Lunacy in 1856 stating that 'Baths, warm and cold, are in the first for the purposes of cleanliness and the latter as a sedative to subdue violence and excitement'. He went on saying that 'Warm Baths' were only with the authority of and supervised by a medical superintendent. He concluded, 'I have no Douche or Shower Baths – believing that the forcible administration of this kind of Bath is cruel.'[35] In 1857, Corbin Finch wrote to the Home Secretary once again defending his treatment and the practices of the Asylum.[36] Amongst other subjects, he stated categorically that, in Fisherton, there was 'an absence of all restraint'. He added, somewhat protectively, 'in seven years, the time the Criminal Patients have been under my care [there have been] no suicides'.[37] In an article written in 1861, Fisherton House was described as being 'remarkab[ly] quiet, more especially as no bodily restraint is used, nor is there any separation seclusion of any patient'. The writer added that 'there are no padded rooms for violent patients'.[38]

This was not the case at Broadmoor where the use of seclusion in particular was explained as being necessary for the safety of the patients. Orange wrote in 1875 that 'the use to a certain extent of individual separation … or seclusion as it is termed, is found to be unavoidable, especially during those portions of the day when the attendants are occupied with cleaning … and serving the meals'.[39] In all asylums, including Fisherton House, there was a wider use of newly developed drugs from the 1850s onwards. Tranquilisers and hypnotic drugs such as chloral hydrate and morphia were used to calm and sedate unruly patients, which would also have the effect of creating a more tranquil atmosphere in the asylums.[40]

In line with the arguments that the asylums utilized moral management to control their patient populations, there were many elements of patriarchal domination in the institutions. Originally a well-meant part of Samuel Tuke's philosophy as described in his 1813 monograph, *Description of the Retreat*, paternalism was an inherent part of patient care and welfare.[41] Over time, the elements of patriarchal rule and paternalistic discipline were incorporated into an overall ethos of 'social rehabilitation', impacting on patient's lives and managing their futures.[42] The need to conform to socially acceptable behaviour was a reflection of the expectations of outside society, not just a matter of control in the asylum.[43] Victorian society acknowledged that as criminal patients had been proven to be insane and irresponsible for their actions, then they should be treated in a suitable establishment to relieve and possibly cure their insanity. To this end, the patients needed some sort of treatment so they could be returned safely to their families and their expected place in the home. Moral treatment was arguably the most humane and ethical treatment when compared with earlier repressive and intrusive regimes. For Victorian society, it continued to be thought of as the most benevolent and compassionate way of achieving relief and redemption for the insane.[44]

Diagnosis and causes of insanity

On admission to an asylum, the majority of the homicidal mothers surveyed had their insanity attributed to mental disorders associated with female physiology (Chart 4:1). When broken down into the six separate decades, it can be seen that, on average, over one third of these admissions were specifically for those disorders associated with reproduction (Table 4:1).

In the sixty-three years of Victoria's reign, medical interpretations of the causes of female insanity laid more and more emphasis on the female reproductive function. Gynaecological causes of insanity were regarded as unpredictable and incomprehensible events which had the capacity to cause mental derangement and suffering to many women. Contemporary medical and cultural opinion accepted that the effect of childbirth was perilously uncertain on a woman's

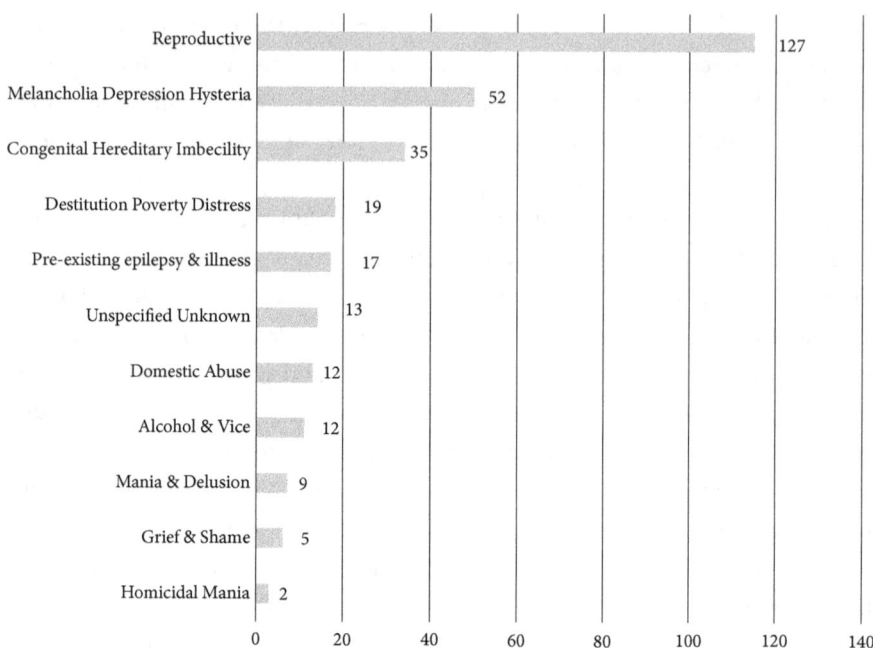

Chart 4.1 Recorded causes of insanity from asylum records, 1835 to 1900.

Table 4.1 Assigned causes of insanity, 1835 to 1900.

Years	No. of Asylum Admissions	Assigned cause – Reproductive	Percentage Admissions per decade
1835–44	8	3	38
1845–54	31	13	42
1855–64	41	8	20
1865–74	50	21	42
1875–84	68	31	46
1885–1900 (15 yrs)	104	51	49
Total	302	127	42

body and mind. Puerperal insanity or mania was one of many adverse medical disorders which could affect a woman after confinement. Charles Mercier, a prominent late-nineteenth-century alienist and medical superintendent, wrote that 'the homicidal act of an insane person is usually an isolated act, done in a mood of intense exasperation and not likely to be repeated'.[45] This description is certainly applicable to the homicidal and infanticidal women surveyed. Their criminal acts were perceived as having been committed because of mental breakdown caused by desperation, misguided feelings or delusion. It was widely accepted that particular disorders could cause a mother to harm herself, as well as making her violent towards her children and others.[46] Such conditions could cause violent criminal actions which were so contrary to proper maternal behaviour. In his 1901 survey, 'Female Criminal Lunatics', Dr John Baker wrote that this proper behaviour should be 'a function which exists for protection of the weak and [by which] a mother provides for her children by every means in her power'.[47]

Puerperal mania and related mental illnesses were viewed by the nineteenth-century medical world as potentially remediable conditions.[48] The contemporary medical belief was that, with the right treatment in the right conditions, women suffering from puerperal-related mental illness would recover.[49] In her rich scholarly study of puerperal mania, Hilary Marland points out that many Victorian doctors and midwives believed that treatment at home was best, if such conditions were caught early. Contrary to this, asylum doctors argued puerperal insanity was best treated within the confines of the asylum. Contemporary observers were shocked by the ferocity of the condition which defied the social standards of Victorian feminine behaviour and motherhood. Of all the causes of insanity recorded, puerperal insanity was met with perhaps the most sympathy and compassion its occurrence was classless and was generally considered to be a cruel turn of fate.[50] Many medical men viewed puerperal mania as an 'almost anticipated accompaniment of the process of giving birth'.[51] Although killing one's child constituted the antithesis of acceptable maternal behaviour, insanity and infanticide also were viewed as part of femininity and maternity, 'an intrinsic part of motherhood'.[52]

At the beginning of the nineteenth century medical interest in mental disorders associated with pregnancy, childbirth and lactation began to change and they began to recognized as distinct conditions.[53] Marland describes the early decades of the century as a time when the diagnosis of puerperal insanity became prominent in the medical canon. She attributes this to the growing professional medical interest in female disorders.[54] In 1820, Robert Gooch was the first British medical man to write a treatise on the subject. His *Observations on Puerperal Insanity* commanded much immediate attention and remained a prominent part of medical discourse on female insanity through the century.[55] Puerperal insanity as a diagnostic term covered both puerperal melancholia and puerperal mania, two distinct but related conditions. The actual root cause of the conditions could differ from case to case but the characteristic signs were 'depression of spirits', delusional beliefs, hallucinations and acute distress, particularly before and after childbirth.[56] Nineteenth-century doctors did not know what caused this category of insanity, although they believed that the onset of puerperal manias could be associated with a mother's and her family's medical history. When describing the condition, Victorian medical men noted that in diagnosed cases, attacks were frequently preceded by certain similar, recurring symptomatic behaviours.[57] In 1846, Dr John Conolly noted that, in his experience, in cases of postnatal mental illness, 'a quick pulse [was] an indicator of mischief ... together with want of rest and sleep, a ... quickness of manner and irritability'. Other 'premonitory symptoms' of the condition recorded by medical men noted that the condition could be accompanied by 'delusions', 'strong aversion to her child and husband', 'anger', 'vociferous and violent gesticulations', 'great excitability' and 'incessant talking'.[58]

According to Dr John Baker, in 1900 the majority of the infanticidal women in Broadmoor were suffering from mental disorders related to female physiology, specifically gynaecological and obstetrical causes.[59] He described these disorders as gestational and they were, namely insanity of pregnancy, puerperal insanity and insanity of lactation. He described insanity in pregnancy as the rarest and puerperal insanity as the most common; although he disputed where the differentiation should be made between puerperal insanity and lactational insanity.[60] He found that in his experience at Broadmoor, the latter two causes were frequently ascribed to 'puerperal mania'. He wrote that the term 'has become established by use ... but is a misnomer ... puerperal melancholia would be much more accurate'.[61] Baker believed that puerperal mania as a cause should only be assigned to those murders which occurred in the puerperal period 'within two months of parturition', otherwise they should be described as being caused by lactational insanity.[62] Baker described the effect of the strain of lactation thus: 'depression comes on, everything looks black and dismal, the idea takes possession of her that want and poverty are in store'.[63] The incidence of poverty and poor social conditions were believed to underlie many cases of child murder. This was particularly relevant to those cases which were specifically related to lactation.

Lactation was an exhausting process and many of the mothers were not in the best of health. The women were often described as being good mothers with respectable homes but they became weighed down with other domestic concerns which impacted on their mental stability. The strain of breastfeeding, caring for their families and overwork in running the household, when they themselves were depleted and exhausted, led to mental breakdown. In 1856, the Bethlem case notes for Mary McNeil state that she was suffering from 'Melancholia' and that 'at the time she committed the act she was suckling a child 11 months old and was much debilitated from suckling'.[64] Sarah Allen had attempted to drown her two children while suffering from 'delusional melancholia' caused by over-lactation. Maria Borley's insanity was originally attributed to ill-treatment at the hands of her husband. When she was in Bethlem, it was further noted that 'she was suckling her second child ... [and] ... she was actually starving for want of sustenance ... and in this weak state she drowned her infant'.[65] After her removal to Fisherton Asylum, the records state that her moods changed with catamenia (menstruation) which caused 'considerable languor' but not insanity.[66] Likewise, Ann Lacey's insanity was not only associated with lactation and possible family inclination to madness but also with menstruation; her relevant attack of insanity had occurred 'during the usual catamenial periods'.[67]

During the nineteenth century, the definitions and explanations of insanity evolved, with causes being attributed to many varied factors.[68] Explanations for insanity of pregnancy and puerperal mania differed and often the actual cause was attributed to some pre-existing circumstance or delusion which had triggered the sudden onset of mania. Frenetic delusional behaviour, epileptic-type fits and depression of spirits were often mentioned in concert with puerperal factors. For example, Mary Coleman attempted to strangle her two-month-old child in a fit of 'puerperal melancholia'. She had 'a melancholy view of her prospects of life and fear of her family coming to great want and distress'.[69] According to her case book notes from Bethlem, Elizabeth Thew suffered from epilepsy, or epileptic-type fits and this was cited as the main cause of her insanity. Up to the time of her crime she had shown no sign of insanity. Her 'fit' of violence was explained as being an 'epileptic seizure', brought on by childbirth and domestic disagreement.[70] Poverty, remorse after seduction and grief after the loss of a partner were cited, as were intemperance, domestic violence, distress and deprivation. Emily Lee drowned her three-year-old child, and the cause of her insanity was attributed to 'domestic trouble' after she had been 'deserted by her husband and left in distress'.[71] In many cases reviewed, insanities associated with female reproduction and maternity were not infrequently linked to destitution, hereditary tendencies and issues within family relationships.[72]

In the case of criminally insane infanticidal women who might be described as respectable in their habits and lifestyle, poverty and destitution were seen as acceptable mitigating circumstances for their insanity. They provided a possible scenario in which the violent attacks were committed. Although certain problems were thought to be prevalent amongst the poorest of society, others were recognized as occurring whatever the sufferer's background, circumstances and previous medical history. The doctors in an asylum always noted if there was an inherited propensity towards insanity within the patients' families. Their diagnoses would then be based not only on social and moral issues but also on hereditary factors.[73] Although Ann Lacey's insanity was seen as having been primarily caused by over-lactation, according to the case books at Fisherton House, there was existing insanity in her family. It was noted that 'there is an aunt in Leicester Asylum'.[74] The hereditary tendency to madness was classless and provided further explanation, beyond tangible medical reasons, for a 'decent' mother to kill her child. There were said to be cases of insanity in Mary Ann Morgan's middle-class family; it was noted that 'One of the brothers of her father died … in an asylum near London and a cousin of her father is now in the county asylum at Bridgend'.[75]

Respectability of the patient's domestic situation and her personal conduct within that domiciliary sphere were important considerations when possible reasons were being sought for her illness. It was important to establish that her murderous act had been contrary to her way of life and completely out of character. On her admission to Bethlem in 1856, Sarah Allen was described as having 'led a quiet and, it is said, exemplary life'.[76] In 1852, Maria Chitty was tried for the murder of one of her children and the attempted murder of another. Maria's behaviour was reported as having changed in the weeks leading up to her crime. She was said to be suffering from an 'impulsive mania'.[77] Despite being described as 'always evinc[ing] the greatest affection for her children' she had 'latterly neglected her duties'.[78] She was considered to have been neglectful in not only caring for her family and household but also in ignoring 'her religious duties'. She had attended 'religious meetings of a different denomination, Methodist meetings, at all hours'.[79] Maria Chitty's clinical notes indicate that her religious zeal was seen as an indicator of her insanity, although, her case notes attribute blame to 'her husband … the cause of her mental derangement'.[80] As shown in previous chapters, the diagnosis of insanity and its cause had, for the most part, been given by the medical men involved with the women before their incarceration in the asylums. The original assigned cause of insanity remained prominent in the women's records for the duration of their stay in the asylum, although over time the medical officers would add other factors and symptoms to the notes. In the casebooks from all the asylums, there are many patients with more than one cause of insanity listed.

Physical well-being and health

During their time in the asylums, the patients were routinely examined by the medical officers. These examinations of patient's physical health were an important factor in creating a relationship between the Victorian doctors and their patients. The main purpose of the meetings was to ensure that the patients were physically healthy but inevitably, medical staff would also listen to the patients talking about themselves. Not infrequently, the women would speak of the circumstances of their crime, their children and their previous lives. These regular observations would note any secondary issues which were believed to have played a role in causing the woman's insanity. The patients themselves could indicate other possible circumstances through discussion of their backgrounds and family-life. The notes made in these meetings not only are a source of contemporary medical practice but occasionally, record the patients' own words. Such observations and factors were duly noted in the records and were considered when discharge or release was mooted.

Any information gleaned in the meetings could provide more explanation for the patient's mental breakdown. The fragility of a patient's mind and her overall disposition was closely observed in the asylum as an indicator of insanity or, indeed, sanity. If a patient moved towards an improved 'cheerful' outlook and more amenable behaviour without delusions, it was taken as a sign that she was recovering from her mental illness. In 1871, on her admittance for her second stay in Fisherton House, Mary Ann Payne was described as 'very excited and agitated'. One month later she was 'more calm and somewhat stronger' and her final entry states that 'she is very considerably improved … being now quiet and industrious. Discharged'.[81] Likewise, in Broadmoor in 1873, Margery Nattress was reported as having had a calm and lucid conversation with Dr Orange. He wrote of her, 'she feels stronger and better than she used to be. She is grateful for the care and kindness received'.[82] She was subsequently recommended for discharge.

While the aim of the examinations was to assess the patients' physical health and to determine any signs of recovery from insanity, they also served another purpose. Jennifer Wallis suggests that physiological examinations were very important to Victorian alienists' research into the links between the physical body and the workings of the mind. These examinations were intended as medical checks to evaluate whether the woman could be considered as restored to mental normality and possibly cured. They were not seen as a treatment regime involving conversation with a patient about their thoughts, feelings and behaviour, although on occasion such subjects were discussed. As Wallis writes, doctors placed some reliance on the belief that the health of the physical body could offer explanations for a patient's mental state.[83] Throughout the nineteenth century and beyond, case book notes always recorded health issues and potential associated problems. The results recorded in the casebooks were not intended to be a full historical record of the patients' stays in the asylums but were aids to the patients' clinical management.[84] The notes are a source of contemporary medical practice and therefore from them, it is possible to get a sense of the evolution of treatment.[85]

Pregnancy and childbirth

Despite the fact that childbirth was seen as a danger to any woman's mental stability, most county and private asylums would prefer not to admit expectant mothers, as pregnant and lactating women would require extra nursing and attention. If they did accept cases, the asylum authorities would remove any babies born in their institution soon after birth, so passing on the responsibility to others.[86] The criminal lunatic facilities could not exercise any choice in their admissions, as they were legally bound to take those found to be insane by judicial process. If a pregnant and homicidal mother were adjudged as insane and incarcerated as a criminal lunatic, the child's birth would need to be dealt with in-house. Obviously as so many of the women under discussion here in this book had their mental illness attributed to manias connected to previous confinements, puerperal melancholia and, indeed, to pregnancy itself, they were considered to be at particular risk.[87] The crucial factor in all cases was that the women should be safeguarded against relapse and shielded from any possible opportunity to re-offend.

In 1878, in an article in the *Journal of Mental Science*, Dr David Nicolson, then Deputy Medical Superintendent of Broadmoor, wrote that, in his experience and opinion, if a woman had ever shown any inclination to depression or insanity in her life, she should never be left alone after 'the functional commotion' of childbirth. He wrote that alterations in her body, and also possibly in her domestic relationships, could give rise to anxiety which could 'drive her past herself and raise up in her mind terrible ideas and temptations'. She should have 'the companionship of some or any person, so that another "will" than her own may, by its presence, strengthen her resistance to the fearful suggestions of murder and self-destruction'.[88] Nicolson believed that protection of vulnerable women by outside parties would certainly lessen the number of maternal infanticides. His opinion was that 'puerperal cases of criminal lunacy … are so often due to positive neglect or unkindness in the nursing after childbirth'.[89] He believed in the efficacy of lying-in hospitals 'and of proper nursing, where the patient is not left to herself'.[90] Nicolson did admit that although his theory was that postnatal support, where available, might be efficacious for vulnerable mothers prone to insanity, his supposition was unproven.[91]

Normal practice for the Bethlem authorities appears to have been to send any patients, criminal or not, to another institution if they were believed to be pregnant.[92] In 1854, Catherine Savell was transferred out of Bethlem to Brixton Gaol as it was believed that she was about to give birth. In December 1854, she was 'removed to Brixton House of Correction for the purpose of her accouchement'. On 24 January 1855, she was returned to Bethlem because 'It has turned out that she was not pregnant. She had all the symptoms but was not.'[93] Dr Charles Hood wrote in her case book notes that the doctors and attendants had decided that Savell was pregnant, based on 'her own firm impression … founded on … experience of having given birth to seven children'.[94] Whether her 'pregnancy' was a phantom pregnancy, or an attention-seeking charade is not known, but whatever the reason, it was not seen as an insane or delusional act. Later, in 1861, the Bethlem authorities passed on responsibility for Harriet Salmon to Fisherton House. She had thrown herself and three children into a river where one perished although Harriet and two others survived. The Fisherton House case book notes that 'She has been removed from Bethlem Hospital to this asylum on account of her being pregnant.'[95] She had been in Bethlem after being found unfit to plead and as they no longer viewed their purpose to be for criminal patients, Bethlem sent her into Fisherton House.

Apart from Bethlem, the other criminal lunatic facilities dealt with childbirth in-house. In their dealings with pregnant patients, the medical and nursing staff at Fisherton House and Broadmoor treated the mothers with care, anxious to protect their and their babies' safety and well-being.[96] In Fisherton House, the expectant mothers received one-to-one nursing care and help, which would provide necessary close personal supervision. In 1864, Dr Finch wrote to Whitehall, justifying the costs involved in the confinements of Martha Hocken, Anne Cornish Vyse and Mary Ann Payne, each of whom had a baby in the Asylum. In the letter he stated, 'These patients had in each case destroyed their children and there was the great probability that without incessant care and watchfulness they might repeat the offence.'[97] Finch also commented that, in incurring the extra expenses, he was following a pattern set down in the earlier case of Harriet

Salmon. For her confinement in 1861, Harriet Salmon was given 'a separate room, an exclusive nurse, medical attention, … extra washing and a proper provision of child clothing'.[98] In all four cases, the infants stayed with their mothers for nearly a year, until weaned, which the Fisherton House management felt was the kindest treatment for both mother and child. As a policy, it would help the mother survive the more dangerous period when post-natal problems could set in.

While Broadmoor accepted and cared for pregnant women through their confinements, they tended to follow the same principle as other asylums and remove the babies from their mothers and the asylum as soon as humanely possible after birth. Catherine Dawson was the first patient to give birth in Broadmoor; her son was born on 26 December 1866.[99] After her husband declined to take the child and after negotiations with her local Poor Law Union in Lancashire, the baby was sent to Chorley Union Workhouse on 25 February 1867.[100] The Broadmoor superintendents took a view on the mother's state of mind before deciding to remove her child. In 1885, it was reported that 'A woman who was admitted in July … gave birth to a child in the following month, which she nursed for five weeks after which she became too restless to be any longer trusted with it'.[101]

The authorities did try, for the most part, to protect the child's welfare.[102] By removal from the Asylum, the child would be protected from potential harm from its mother, despite the careful watch taken by the nursing staff. Catherine Dawson had actually tried to make her son Stephen stand and walk before the nurses rapidly intervened.[103] Other patients who appeared to be reasonably sane were allowed to nurse their children for the first few months of their lives.[104] As Anna Shepherd found at Brookwood Asylum, sometimes it was decided the child would be safer with its family, preferably its father.[105] As reported in the Annual Report for 1888, 'L. O., who was admitted on the 10th of February, gave birth to a son on 2nd of April … At the husband's request, the child was transferred to the care of his wife's relations.'[106] If, as happened on occasion, family or kin were unwilling to take the baby, it would be entrusted to the care of the mother's local Poor Law Union or an orphanage. Sarah Dobbin's son was sent to St Alban's Home in Worcester when he was ten weeks old. While this may appear to be heartless, the medical superintendents were firmly of the opinion that Broadmoor was not a place for a young child and that the mother's welfare came first. There was a belief that, if the mother was separated from her child, she may recover more rapidly. As Orange commented on Sarah Dobbins after the baby's departure, '[she] gradually recovered, and is now tranquil, although often very depressed and melancholic'.[107]

Broadmoor exercised the same care and treatment of expectant mothers, their childbirth and their newborns whether the mother was a Queen's pleasure patient or a convict patient. This is well demonstrated by the case of Margaret Crimmings, a convict prisoner. Margaret Crimmings was a repeat petty offender and had been in and out of prison for ten years before her admission to Broadmoor. She had also had two other children; both were born while she was serving a prison sentence. Each time, she had been taken to Hanwell Asylum to give birth where each child died soon after they were born.[108] It would seem that she was practised in shamming insanity to get out of prison, probably with the intention of giving birth in what probably was a more pleasant environment than gaol. Her history aroused the suspicions of the staff at Broadmoor, nevertheless Margaret remained in Broadmoor for the birth.[109] Her daughter was born on 8 June and was christened Margaret Julia by the visiting Roman Catholic chaplain.[110] To begin with Margaret was allowed to nurse the baby, her case file notes state that she did so in an 'affectionate manner'. Then 'three days afterwards' as reported in the 1871 Annual Report, 'she was attacked with acute mania from which she gradually recovered'. Margaret's recovery was too late, Margaret Julia was 'removed to the nursery for the parish of Marylebone at Southall'.[111] There, two months later aged just seven weeks, Margaret Julia died from what was recorded as 'debility', very possibly some congenital cause, such as syphilis.[112] Margaret senior remained at Broadmoor, despite the fact she was ostensibly still a convict criminal, not a pleasure patient. Her genuine attack of insanity in the form of puerperal mania meant that the Broadmoor authorities did not advise a return to penal custody. She was eventually released in February 1876 and went to lodge with her brother in Marylebone.[113]

Chronic and terminal illness

The medical remit in the institutions was to alleviate and cure mental infirmities, not necessarily to cure bodily illnesses. Nonetheless, in situations where the patient was seen to be suffering from an incurable condition or terminal illness, medical and pastoral treatment changed. Symptoms such as a 'coated tongue' or 'a weak and irregular pulse' were noted as indications of physical illnesses such as consumption which could affect the mind.[114] While it is a dangerous practice to apply modern diagnoses to historical illnesses, it is possible to see that diseases such as tuberculosis (phthisis) and brain disease could have damaged some patients' mental states. Once in the asylum, the woman's crime and insanity were put to one side and their treatment was more focused on comfort and end of life treatment. In cases where it was clear that the woman's insanity had been caused by an underlying medical condition and that there was no hope of recovery, the asylum became a hospital.

Elizabeth Goddard was physically quite well when she arrived in Bethlem in April 1850. She had been found not guilty but insane at Kingston Assizes in March 1849 of the murder of her three-year-old child. From the start she was described as 'never shew[ing] any symptom of insanity … never alludes to her crime'. Elizabeth worked cheerfully in Bethlem but was known for having a 'hasty temper'. In July 1855 she caught typhus and her symptoms were described as 'severe with febrile disturbance'. She was admitted to the infirmary ward of Bethlem where she was dosed heavily with different sedatives, nourishing broths and wine and brandy. It was noted that she was restless, weak and in fact did not take nourishment well. The last entry on 22 July 1850, reads, 'There seems no hope of recovery. She is slowly sinking but still conscious … taken a little wine and brandy.' Elizabeth Goddard died at 6 am on 23 July.[115]

Bethlem had a policy, in later years, of not taking 'incurables', however that did not impact upon existing patients if they became infirm in the hospital.[116] Mary Ann Beveridge's case notes carry an air of compassion and sympathy due to the fact that she was blind. On 30 May 1863, the day that all the other criminally insane female patients were transferred from Bethlem to the newly opened Broadmoor, it was noted that 'in consequence of her blindness … the Government have allowed her to remain here [Bethlem] as she is … accustomed to find her way about'.[117] According to records, Mary Ann did not display any symptoms of insanity, her disability was her blindness and, in reality, she could have been discharged. She became an 'incurable patient' and notes in the 'Incurable Casebook' categorically state that she was no longer insane. In 1864, she was described as being 'quite sane, gentle in her behaviour and very grateful for all that is done for her'.[118] Her retention as an incurable patient appears to have been for humane reasons. It was suspected that the main reason for her insanity, at the time of her crimes, was the physical and mental abuse she suffered at the hands of her husband.[119] The medical officers and government officials allowed her to remain in Bethlem, because they were presumably reluctant to return her to a potentially dangerous situation.[120]

On 22 September 1862, Adelaide Cole was tried for the wilful murder of her fifteen-month-old son, Charles. At her Old Bailey trial, her personal doctor, Dr John Rogers, testified that while he was attending her 'for spitting of blood', noticed 'nothing particular in her state of mind … once or twice there was a wild expression about her eyes'.[121] He confirmed that he was attending her for 'consumption and spitting of blood, which', he noted, 'would produce a low state of body which would act upon the mind'.[122] Adelaide Cole was admitted into Fisherton House Asylum on 11 November 1862.[123] She was not sent to Broadmoor in 1863 with the other women, probably due to the fact that, at that point, the infirmary wards in Broadmoor had not been fully established. A brief comment on her case book notes reads, 'Lives with the private patients'.[124] No reason is given for this treatment beyond saying that she 'does not exhibit any delusions and answers questions rationally'.[125]

The medical officers in Fisherton House treated Cole with sympathetic care. They frequently remark on her quietness or disinclination to talk and that her demeanour was melancholic. There was no specific medical treatment for tuberculosis, but any sign that Cole was in better bodily health was noted. She was able to 'walk a short distance beyond the walls of the asylum' and she was 'occasionally visited by her husband'.[126] The final entry on her casebook page reads 'for the last few weeks this patient has been sinking from phthisis. She died this morning at 11.30'.[127] The ability to give close personal care would appear to be an attribute of Fisherton House, there was an element of humanity here in that she was sent to Fisherton to have a good end of life care in a small environment. Along with Adelaide Cole, there were other women sent to Fisherton House if it were perceived that their bodily health had impacted on their minds.

On 18 September Esther Lack was tried at the Old Bailey charged with the murder of three of her children. From the transcript of her trial, it becomes clear that she was suffering from some sort of debilitating condition. Her eldest surviving son was asked, 'Has your poor mother always been a kind affectionate mother to you and your brother and sisters?' to which he answered, 'Yes – for the last seven years she has been nearly blind, and within the last twelve months a cripple, scarcely able to walk.'[128] Other witnesses testified that she had suffered from headaches and fits and her demeanour had changed over recent years. The case of Esther Lack was a subject of great public interest and speculation over the cause of her homicidal madness. This interest has continued, her case was the subject of a BBC radio programme and podcast as recently as 2022 when it was suggested that Esther Lack may have had a brain tumour.[129] Whatever the cause, even to Victorian eyes it was accepted that she was obviously very ill. She was transferred from Horsemongers Lane Gaol to Fisherton House after her trial and admitted there on 11 October 1865.[130] By that year an admission to Fisherton House was unusual, normally women such as Lack would be admitted to Broadmoor as a pleasure patient. The annual report for Broadmoor for that year shows the asylum had ninety-nine female patients at the time, so with a maximum capacity of a hundred women, was on the cusp of being full. This would mean that there would not be enough care and attention available to deal with a potentially terminally ill patient.

From the start, Esther was confined to her bed and given what was considered to be the best sustenance for the sick, 'has taken wine, eggs, beef tea &c'.[131] It was noted that she seldom spoke, appeared very melancholic, could barely see and slept most of the day. The final entry on her casebook notes was, 'Esther Lack abt 41, died November 25, 1865, in the presence of Nurse – the cause of death being sequelae conditions.'[132] The medical staff could not cure her, nor did they know what her continuing condition might be. It was suggested in court that it was epilepsy, but the evidence given by her family was that Esther had been going blind as well as having seizures. Whatever the cause, despite the limited medical knowledge, the medical and nursing staff at Fisherton House, appear to have made her as comfortable as possible in her last days.[133]

Sarah Patey was admitted to Broadmoor from Fisherton House in 1863 and for the next twenty-seven years there was regular correspondence between the asylum and her husband Richard, who wrote each year asking the same question: 'I am very anxious to know of any change in my wife by this time.'[134] By 1883 she was described as 'very much deranged' and as having 'a frail heart'; her family was advised that it had been agreed that they 'may visit at any time'.[135] In February 1898 Richard Patey was advised that 'mentally she is demented, knows nobody and is unable to hold any conversation so she would not appreciate a visit'.[136] By June 1900 he was advised that 'your wife's health is declining ... there is, I fear, little hope of her recovery'.[137] Sarah Patey died in September 1900 and the final letter from Richard reads, 'I regret I will not be able to attend the funeral as I am now in very poor health ... I can only thank you and all at the Asylum for your care for my wife.'[138]

The asylum medical superintendents and their medical officers had autonomous control of the criminal lunatic patients in death; they could act in what they were believed were the best interests of their patients without reference to the Home Office. The paternalistic, interventionalist attitude applied to the families of the dying too. Families were actively encouraged to visit and communicate with their dying relative, as comfort to both parties.[139] As mentioned earlier, Adelaide Coles's husband occasionally visited her in Fisherton House. When Bridget Myles was seriously ill in Broadmoor, her sister and surviving daughters were encouraged to visit and correspond with her.

This correspondence continued until her death in 1909.[140] In 1885, Dr Nicolson wrote to Ann Goring's husband saying, '[she] is seriously ill with an attack of inflammation of the lungs and thereby she may be visited at any time'.[141] On many occasions, families finally accepted that they would not be able to care for or even see their errant member again. Catherine David was discharged to the care of her husband in October 1877 but she requested to return to Broadmoor just one month later. Her husband wrote to Orange in December 1877 in despairing terms saying, 'I do intrude upon your patience ... [but] ... I simply want to know how is my wife? ... I have bidden her farewell for life ... [but] ... I should like to know how she is ... and that is all.'[142]

Conclusion

Moral treatment was originally based on creating a cooperative relationship between the doctors and their patients. Compliance and communication with all the asylum staff would ideally result in mutually beneficial outcomes; release and cure on one side and satisfaction of having restored minds and recovered patients on the other. The aim of asylum care was supposed to build-up patients' confidence, self-worth and hopefully help them to recover. The Victorian cultural ideals of respectability which were thought necessary for a well-ordered, controlled and civilized society are evident in the asylum papers. Respectable behaviour, both before and after admission to the asylum, together with respectability of domestic and social circumstances mattered to the asylum staff.[143]

The close scrutinization of family and their circumstances was significant to all discussions about the women and their journeys through the Victorian legal and asylum systems. Even in death, the asylum authorities had control of the ensuing proceedings regarding funerals and burials. This is reviewed in greater detail in Chapter 7. On that subject, as with other discussions about the interactions with the families, kin and other authorities, the focus is on Broadmoor. As Broadmoor's records are made up of individual case files, there is a variety of relevant information and ephemera. The casebook notes from Bethlem and Fisherton are more heavily medical in nature, with little personal or family information. The interdependent relationships of medical superintendents and the attendant staff with the criminally insane mothers were important. Their impact on the interactions and relationships in the asylums is covered in greater detail in the next two chapters.

5

'They should be ... happy and comfortable.' Patient life in the asylums and the impact of behaviour and relationships

In an address to a professional meeting in 1883, Dr Lawes Rogers of Rainhill Asylum commented, 'people are sent to asylums ... kept there against their will' that they 'should be made ... happy and comfortable'.[1] A year earlier, in September 1882, Elizabeth Platts, wrote a letter to her mother from Broadmoor, in which she declared, 'When I look around and see and feel the comforts of this place ... I think it is one of the grandest places God ever caused to be made.' She continued, 'I think in all my life I have never been better or eaten better or spent a more happy time.'[2] On the other hand, Annie Florence Attree wrote in a letter to her husband that 'Broadmoor is a dreadful place, you little know how I fare in it'. She also believed that she was unreasonably detained as she had not killed her child and others who had were already released. She described it as a 'monstrous injustice' and 'clemency is only extended to some'.[3] Their words highlight very differing patient opinions on their incarceration. They also perhaps, reflect how patients from different social backgrounds reacted to the control and ambience of the asylum. Elizabeth Platts was from the mining community in Chesterfield and Annie Attree from the professional classes in Norfolk. Class expectations of treatment, both pastoral and medical, impacted upon at patients' responses to the quality of their incarceration.

The length of one woman's incarceration in the criminal lunatic asylums would always be different from another's. The reasons differed from case to case and the involved protocols developed and altered over time. Patients could recover or improve rapidly and possibly would be released after a short stay. Others could be retained for many years, and some for the rest of their lives. This chapter is a review of life in the criminal facilities at the three asylums. Notwithstanding that many of the admissions were mentally unwell, the authorities of the institutions expected certain levels of decent and correct

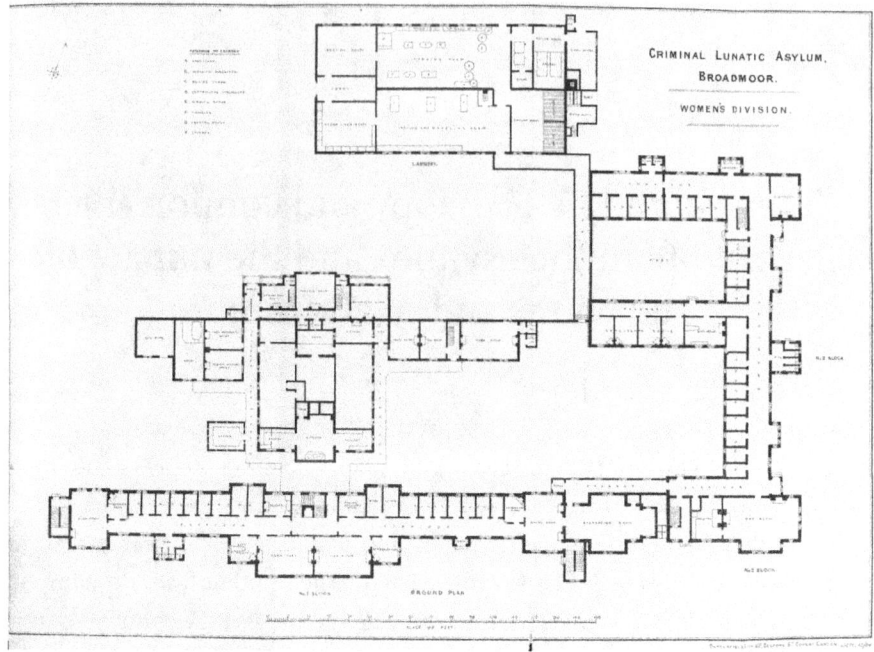

Image 5.1 Plan of Women's Division Broadmoor, 1885.[4]

behaviour. The asylum doctors and staffs' views of patients were coloured by how the women complied with their treatment and how they conducted themselves on a daily basis. For the patients' part, by being compliant, or non-compliant, with asylum procedures and rules, they could possibly gain a modicum of agency over their institutional lives. Small acts of rebellion, such as refusals to work or to socialize with other patients, can be read as possible signs of patient agency, taking some little control of their own lives.[5] Eventually, even those women who 'rebelled' against the system were only discharged once they behaved in a respectable and sane manner, as defined by the asylum authorities.

Social status, privileges and class

In their work on nineteenth-century asylums, Anna Shepherd and Lorraine Walsh, separately, assert that certain socially acceptable behaviours by patients, were important determinants of management and treatment.[6] Any patient, whatever their class, would command favourable attention if they were seen to be respectable in habits. For many differing reasons, the patients' respectability, domestic and personal, was important to the medical officers.[7] This, together with where the patients were perceived to be on the social scale, mattered and could have an influence on the asylums' staffs' attitudes, when dealing with criminal lunatic mothers.[8] It was considered important to note that has been said that most 'pleasure patients' who had committed homicide, neither had a history of criminality, nor displayed the behavioural traits of the criminal classes.[9] Therefore, it was deemed important to show that they were not habitual offenders nor belonged to the so-called criminal class. In the early years of the Victorian period, Bethlem held all classes of patient but in 1857, it was reported that Dr Charles Hood had a vision for the Royal Hospital. He was reported as suggesting that it should be 'an institution for the reception and cure of no person who is a proper object for admission to a county asylum'.[10] In other words, not paupers but the 'educated working class' and members of the 'impoverished middle class', such as clerks, bookkeepers, governesses and respectable people who had 'broken down ... checked by sudden failing of the mind'.[11] Hood's aim of only helping 'the poor, though educated and the insane of the middle class', was assisted by the opening of Broadmoor and the complete removal of criminal patients by the end of 1864.[12]

Broadmoor was created to hold just criminal lunatics, irrespective of background, as Deputy Medical Superintendent Dr David Nicolson described them, in an 1878 article, '*The patients at Broadmoor certainly do not belong to what are commonly called the criminal classes.* [Nicolson's italics]. To suppose that they do is a common error.'[13] He continued that in his experience Broadmoor's 'pleasure patients, ... do not belong to the higher or middle classes of the community; nor (before their offence) do they belong to the lower or pauper classes ... insanity spares not the rich or the poor." While Nicolson was describing the patients in his care, his words do underline the fact that anyone could be admitted to Broadmoor regardless of their social background. There are instances in all the asylums which show bias towards a perceived social status. Those who were seen to be better educated, possibly from the 'respectable' lower classes and middle classes, seem to be treated more favourably. Familial social circumstances of the female patients could have an effect on the manner and circumstances of their incarceration. The attitudes of authorities towards the women patients' families also changed when they were seen to be better educated and engaged with the asylum. This became apparent when discharge and release were discussed, when family financial and domestic circumstances were important. This subject is covered in detail later in Chapter 7.

Social concepts of proper female respectability were quite apparent in the casebooks at Fisherton House. Corbin Finch appears to have had what are called Victorian views about class and how different classes should behave. In June 1859, he wrote about Sarah Price saying:

> There is something about this young woman in her better moods that would indicate her to have belonged to an order something above the working classes. She has then a pleasing manner and speaks well. She has a very nice voice in singing, on one or two occasions she has been to the weekly meetings in the 'Recreation Room' and conducted herself with propriety.[14]

Whether or not such concepts of respectable female manners influenced other asylums' decisions, may be conjecture. However, it does seem that class bias could have an impact on the lives of the patients. Martha Baines was the wife of a chemist from Kendal who had poisoned her five-month-old baby with bleach.[15] Her eighteen-month stay in Broadmoor, from December 1875 to August 1877, was relatively short. The doctor's report recommending her release suggest that, in his opinion, Martha Baines's future safety appeared to be assured because she was 'in a respectable position in life & her husband is able & willing to provide for her'.[16] Catherine Savell, whose story was quoted in the previous chapter, was the wife of a linen draper, living in Shoreditch. As her spirits were so low after the birth of her baby, 'her husband had been strongly recommended to place her in some asylum'.[17] Instead, he had arranged for their servant and Catherine's grandmother to stay with her and their other children. The inference being that her family background appeared to be a respectable one and that she was from a comfortable home.[18] It appears that Bethlem's medical staff view of her social status as a respectable wife and mother impacted on her treatment. She was described as 'a quiet well-conducted woman' and as being 'well and cheerful'.[19] Catherine Savell had a relatively short stay in Bethlem of just eighteen months, on 23 July 1856, she received a royal pardon and was released to the care of her husband.[20]

In the main, whatever their crime, the majority of female patients in the criminal lunatic facilities were from the lower-middle and working classes.[21] Although a patient's social position did not influence the medical treatment she received, it could influence her material life in the asylum. Patients with family influence and available funds were rewarded by concessions and a certain amount of free movement. In December 1865, Valentine Vyse, the husband of Ann Cornish Vyse, wrote a letter of complaint to the Home Secretary about her treatment in Fisherton House. Corbin Finch replied somewhat indignantly, listing the privileges that were afforded to her, all permitted by the Home Office with an agreed subsidy from Vyse. Finch wrote, 'this patient resides with the private patients' and that she had 'two rooms to herself, the sanction [of] Secretary of State having been obtained by the Husband'. It was also noted that she had 'daily walks with an attendant beyond the limits of the Asylum' and had 'separate meals inclusive of wine and spirits'.[22] There does not appear to have been an obligation for Ann Vyse to undertake employment, in essence, she was allowed a lifestyle in keeping with her social status. However, Finch's final paragraph says, 'I respectfully submit ... that Mr Vyse has not the slightest ground of complaint ... of any treatments or of the charge of three guineas a week ... but not yet paid'.[23] Despite appearing to be a respected businessman in the City of London, Valentine Vyse was not fulfilling his obligations.

In Broadmoor, as well as being allowed personal possessions, the patients were allowed extra comforts if they, or their relatives, could afford them. This was relatively common on the men's side of the asylum, where there were a number of patients from the professional classes. It was more unusual on the female side, where there were few patients from the more privileged backgrounds. Before Agnes Morris's arrival in 1878, her family solicitor wrote to Orange stating that she had 'about £100 per annum at her disposal and with this sum ... we are anxious to procure for her such ... comforts as can be given'.[24] Orange replied that 'there are in the asylum ... several inmates whose social position was ... equal and superior to that which would appear to have been held by this lady ... and from the opening of the asylum the practice of ... allowing ... reasonable extra comforts supplied out of funds ... supplied by relatives or in their own right ... has been fully regarded'. In the same letter, Orange stated that 'the inmates who are allowed to receive extra comforts are not thereby removed out of the category of ordinary criminal lunatic'.[25] In other words, money and privilege might make confinement in an asylum more tolerable but it would not buy a way out of the fact that the patient was still officially criminally insane.

Alongside the women admitted 'to be held until her Majesty's pleasure be known', there were the other criminal patients, those admitted from prison after conviction. So often the so-called convict lunatic women were viewed with more disdain at times by the staff through the nature of their habits, personal and criminal.[26] As noted in Chapter 1, Dr Orange and Dr Nicolson from Broadmoor were of the belief that the pleasure patients would be 'contaminated by the degraded habits and conversation of the criminal class'.[27] In the other two asylums, there was a seemingly less tolerant attitude towards the patients admitted from penal custody and a certain amount of commentary on their bad habits and personal conduct. The convict patients could be more difficult to handle than the 'pleasure patients' and controlling them was more problematic.[28] For the majority, incarceration in the asylum was finite. Any noticeable recovery or 'relief' from symptoms of insanity could lead to a return to prison. On the other hand, if they were not seen as recovered by the time their penal sentence came to an end, they would be admitted to a pauper asylum in the vicinity of their home.

Others, like Margaret Crimmings, whose story was described in the previous chapter, may have started out as 'convict lunatics' but circumstances could change their asylum status. Her previous experiences in getting out of prison to give birth by feigning insanity may well have backfired in this instance. She probably did not expect to be removed to Broadmoor thereby earning herself the status of a lunatic criminal.[29] Notes and letters in her case file suggest that she had faked her insanity in order to be transferred to the asylum as she showed no signs of madness once in Broadmoor.[30] As previously noted after the birth of her baby, Crimmings suffered from puerperal depression, and so became a genuine patient, but not a pleasure patient.

For one patient, Ann Hurst, the fact that she was not from the criminal classes facilitated her transfer from Brixton Prison to Fisherton House as a criminal lunatic. She had been imprisoned for three years, after being found guilty at York Assizes, of stealing a letter.[31] The medical officer at Brixton wrote that she 'had never been convicted' and that she was 'very quiet, harmless & timid'. Ann was suffering from 'severe mental depression', evidenced by her refusing 'use her books in Chapel and … refusing to attend school'. He continued: 'I consider it an almost invariable rule that a woman who, as this instance, has never before been in a penitentiary will suffer much more in mind from the imprisonment, than would a woman who has been repeatedly convicted.'[32] Ann Hurst was admitted to Fisherton House in September 1862 and released, recovered, in June 1864.[33] There were similar cases throughout the country. It was thought by medical officers, like Dr Rendle of Brixton Prison, that the regimes of prisons were not in themselves to blame. It was supposed that the strains of incarceration brought on depression and previously undetected unsoundness of mind[34].

Family relationships

For all asylum patients, criminal or not, it would appear that family and background, in themselves, could be seen as possible factors in causing a patient's mental distress. Asylum authorities believed that the familial relationships had a significant effect on the mental state of all patients. Sometimes they were cited as the cause of mental illness but on the other hand, it was accepted that families' presence in a patients' life was necessary to ensure a good recovery and potential release back into society.[35] Many medical superintendents believed that husbands should shoulder some of the responsibility for the patient's mental disorder. While recognizing that there was always a threat of domestic violence in the homes of some of their patients, nevertheless, the preference was that husbands remain in touch with their wives.[36] The institutions wished for spouses to be involved on some level and indeed, they could find themselves rebuked if it were felt that they were neglecting their spousal duties. The quality of these relationships became of more importance when discharge and release were discussed.[37]

Maria Chitty was admitted into Bethlem in 1852, for the murder of her child.[38] At the time, Dr Hood laid the blame for her mental state on 'her husband's conduct [which] was to some extent the cause of her mental derangement'.[39] William Chitty had regularly been admitted to Bethlem himself, so the Hospital medical staff were well aware of his character and state of health. On his first admission in 1851, he was described as 'a very dangerous lunatic'. His insanity was ascribed to 'Hereditary indisposition, intemperance & general indulgence of the passions'. Chitty had reportedly 'threatened his wife & son – he bought a large, pointed knife and has been using firearms in idle sport'.[40] Charles Hood referred to this insane conduct in Maria Chitty's own case notes, although there is no direct reference to William's stays in the Hospital.[41]

On William's next admission in 1853, the case book notes do refer to Maria stating that she was 'in the Criminal Dept. [sic] … for destroying her child'.[42] William Chitty was re-admitted in 1860 and once again in 1867, each time at the request of their surviving children. There was obvious disharmony in the household caused by the insanity of both parents and this was noted in detail by the medical staff at Bethlem. It was explicitly stated on William's 1860 admission, that he and Maria had lived together 'quite comfortably' for a while, after she had received her free pardon. Early in 1860, she had shown 'some signs of mental disorder' and this had caused him to drink and 'his mental symptoms [to] appear'.[43] Maria died in 1863 and, in April 1867, William was once again admitted to Bethlem. He returned home in December of that year.[44] William appeared to have lived with his son Henry and his family from that date forwards, until his death in 1878.[45]

On her admission to Bethlem, it was noted that Elizabeth Goddard had told the admitting doctor that 'Her husband and she quarrelled about the child who he said was always crying'. This is followed by the statement that 'The Husband has doubts that this child being his'.[46] A suggestion, perhaps, that the Goddards' marital relationship and domestic situation lay at the root of Elizabeth's mental state. The notion that husbands were at the root of their wives' mental problems could also be fed by the women themselves. Some women treated their spouses with repugnance, believing them to be the cause of their troubles. Mary Ann Taylor was in Rainhill suffering from puerperal mania after the birth of her second child. She appeared 'very fond of her baby' but she had attempted to throw her eldest child out of the window. She also 'had taken an aversion to her husband who she called an assassin'. After six months of treatment her bodily and mental health improved but despite this, it was noted 'she still has the same aversion to her poor husband'.[47]

Whole families could be blamed for a mother's mental collapse, as in the case of Rebecca Loveridge, admitted to Broadmoor in 1884. She had drowned her youngest child and attempted suicide, after being worn down by family and domestic problems. On her admittance, the cause of her insanity was attributed to 'hereditary & domestic trouble (husband drank & ill-treated her)'.[48] Rebecca had been treated very badly by her whole family. In an early report, Orange wrote 'her elder children have been the source of much worry to her ... the two eldest boys instead of doing the work ... would play ... she would do the work for them in addition to her own housework ... her eldest daughter [was] often saucy to her'.[49] Rebecca Loveridge's family all had treated her disrespectfully and were seen to have partly caused her mental deterioration.[50] In 1885 a memorandum to the Home Office stated, 'her husband promises well now but it was his unkind treatment of her that she went mad & drowned her baby ... too soon for discharge'.[51] During her time in Broadmoor, George Loveridge was described as being 'most attentive' and he 'promise[d] well ... and ... quite prepared to sign an undertaking' to care for her, if Rebecca were to be released to his guardianship.

Intemperance and insobriety in women were considered to be unacceptable traits and seen as potential factors in any female violent behaviour. Rebecca Turton who was admitted to Broadmoor from Fisherton House in 1863, had murdered her husband, Thomas, in 1855. At her trial at the Old Bailey, witnesses testified that she was, like him, was extremely intoxicated when she attacked him.[52] Thomas and Rebecca Turton were known to be heavy drinkers and when drunk, would argue incessantly. In particular, she was described as being, 'very noisy by herself, and disturbed everybody in the neighbourhood'.[53] Even in these situations, however, some blame was laid on the husband. According to

Rebecca's version when she was in Broadmoor, Thomas had mocked her for being Irish and threatened to lock her in an asylum.[54]

As a failing, overindulgence in alcohol was classless and could affect anyone. Middle-class Mary Lyons 'had some disputes with her husband and had been drinking for some time … seemed careless of the value of her own life & her child's … intemperate at times for 3 or 4 years past'.[55] Ann Amess was described as having 'led a previously quarrelsome life with her husband & her other relations and … she, with them, was intemperate in her habits'.[56] Conversely, if it were discovered that an infanticidal mother had been driven to drink by domestic circumstances or mistreatment, then intemperance could be accepted as a mitigating reason for her madness. When she was in Rainhill, Bridget Myles was diagnosed as suffering from 'Melancholia after murdering her child', and 'it appears she has latterly taken to drinking'.[57] After her transfer to Broadmoor, it was discovered that she had been 'beaten by her drunk husband and in consequence had turned to drink herself'.

Employment and occupation

Work and useful employment were important aspects of moral treatment and were considered essential in assisting any patient's recovery from mental disorder. In his treatise, Samuel Tuke wrote that 'of all modes by which patients may be induced to restrain themselves, regular employment is perhaps the most efficacious'.[58] Work within the asylum has been described as coercive and it has been suggested that the different types of employment were designed to fit patients into stereotypical roles.[59] In the asylums the term 'employment' did not necessarily mean that the patient was working for reward or remuneration, but rather that they were occupying their time by doing something beneficial to their mental and physical well-being. In all the asylums, various entertainments were laid on for the patients, along with the opportunities for leisure. The 1866 annual report for Broadmoor reports that 'there is a good library – books periodicals and newspapers are distributed throughout the wards to all that are capable of using them'.[60] Social entertainments were put on for the benefit of patients and classes for 'elementary education and for singing' were seen as necessary regular occasions. George Griffiths described everyday life in the female wing;

> [I]n the female wing there are women sitting about the corridors, knitting and doing lacework or embroidery, or sitting in their common rooms reading or

talking, or also thinking those strange thoughts. In another room you will find one at a grand piano, playing, it may be, some standard piece of music, or it may be some weird creation of her own, and others sitting about on the chairs and lounges listening to her.[61]

A patient's employment was calculated to match their physical and mental capabilities, which often meant that the choices were very limited for women patients.[62] In line with his interpretation of moral treatment, Scull suggests that the occupations undertaken were part of the overall plan to transform asylum patients into 'a bourgeois ideal of the rational individual'.[63] This viewpoint, while being in part true, disregards the nuance in the purpose of employment as a part of moral therapy.[64] As well as being a method of keeping the patients busy, work and occupation in the asylum was also believed to be an important part of restoring self-esteem. In 1865, Dr John Meyer wrote in the Annual Report for 1864, the first full year of Broadmoor's operations, that 'Patients are employed in the wards, in the laundries, the garden, the shoemakers', tailors' and mattress makers' shops. A large amount of needlework has been done by the female patients.'[65] Employment was believed to be a way to bolster a patient's confidence in themselves and thereby return their minds to some sort of rationality. The patients were not forced into employment as Griffiths described in 1903, 'The life of the patients at Broadmoor is occupied by gardening, farm work ... keeping the place tidy, and just wandering about the beautiful grounds ..., or, as I have said, more frequently dreaming or carrying on conversations with imaginary hearers, which to the student of psychology would no doubt be most deeply interesting'.[66]

A table (Table 5.1) from Annual Report for 1875 shows the occupations for the patients were allocated in line with contemporary gender opinions on male and female employment. A rider under the table in the Annual Report reads, 'Many patients are employed in more than one description of work and the total of the foregoing figures would be, therefore, in excess of the number of patients employed at any one time. The actual number of patients usefully employed in 1875 was 165 men and 71 women.'[67]

In his 1857 report to the Home Secretary Dr Corbin Finch described the employment practices in Fisherton House, particularly with regard to the employment of female criminal patients. He advised that they were indeed employed 'at Needlework, in the Laundry, in the Kitchen and even in my own nursery'.[68] His reason for the seeming lenient treatment was that he believed that these particular women were 'a better class of criminals'. He further justified the

Table 5.1 Employment extract from Annual Report 1875.

From the Broadmoor Annual Report for 1875			
Showing the types of Industrial Occupation in which patients were employed during the year 1875			
Occupation	M	F	Tot
Making clothes for patients and attendants	9	50	59
Shoemaking	11		11
Making and repairing bedding	8		8
Making and repairing furniture	5		5
Repairing linen	31	6	36
Whitesmith	1		1
Printer	1		1
In the garden, on the terraces and farm	24		24
In kitchen bakehouse and stores	8	2	10
In laundry		25	25
In cleaning the wards	82	48	130
Coaling	11		11
Totals	191	131	322

situation saying, 'I have yet to discover what evils have come from this practice (a practice too pursued, I believe, in every Asylum in England – excepting Bethlehem [sic] Hospital).'[69]

Finch's assertions about Bethlem's policy were not quite correct however, employment there was more akin to patient control than to rehabilitation. When she was in Bethlem, Eliza Clark was described as 'rarely if ever occupy[ing] herself in any hospital work'. Her refusal did not endear her to the staff, especially when it was observed that she would occupy herself with tasks which satisfied her. The case notes record that 'whenever she has the opportunity [she] works at lacemaking, at which she is adept'.[70] She was transferred to Fisherton House in 1860 where it was reported that 'her time has been employed in fancy work and lace-making'.[71] The 1847 Physicians' report states, with reference to the criminal wings, 'The patients in this department ... partake of active exercises,' although it does not expand on what those exercises might be.[72]

For released patients, having worked within the asylums, gave them confidence to seek employment in the outside world, as in the case of Amelia Burt.[73] As her personal petition for release in 1870 stated, if she were released, she 'would endeavour to earn my living as a machinist or domestic servant'.[74]

Sarah Dickenson, admitted to Fisherton House in February 1854 from Bethlem, was singled out by Dr Corbin Finch as an example of how employment could help the future lives of criminal patients.[75] Sarah received her discharge on 27 October 1857 when Corbin Finch took her into his family's service as their private cook. She remained with them 'for many months discharging her duties in a most exemplary manner'. Corbin Finch continued on to say that he had 'recommended her to a family at Lymington, where she is still living, respected and esteemed by her employers'.[76] He also emphasized that her new employers were well aware of her 'antecedents' and previous circumstances. An indication, perhaps, that he had confidence in Sarah Dickinson's trustworthiness and confidence.

Conduct and agency

Samuel Tuke conceived that to be successful as a morally therapeutic establishment, an asylum's population should be a quasi-familial unit.[77] The medical superintendent was the patriarch and father of the house with the matron as a mother figure guiding the patients to rationality of mind and a calmer nature. Stretching the analogy further, the attendant staff could be seen as other relations such as older siblings or aunts and uncles, subordinate to the parental figures but still sympathetically corrective and caring towards the patients, the children. In the casebooks and case files, patients' behaviour and conduct were often described as juvenile so a parental type of discipline was considered to be necessary to control the more childish elements of behaviour.[78] The figurative concept of the asylum population as a family unit shaped other aspects of nineteenth-century views of the insane.[79] Homicidal mothers who failed in their maternal roles were now viewed almost as children themselves. In 1877, William Orange wrote 'the discipline of the insane in an asylum ... is very much like the discipline of the nursery'.[80] As late as 1910, Claybury Asylum was described as a 'huge and ... very refractory nursery'.[81] A patient in Rainhill, Bridget Doyle, was described as being 'passionate [and] quarrelsome' although she could be 'pulled up and brought to reason with a little management', just as a father might manage a recalcitrant child.[82] Patients were frequently described in terms associated with childish behaviour. Jane Gerrard, admitted to Rainhill suffering from puerperal mania, was 'quarrelsome and mischievous'.[83] In Broadmoor Lucy Keary was described as 'troublesome' and 'sullen', she 'will go days without speaking – sometimes taking food and at others, refusing … meals'.[84] Maria Borley's behaviour on admittance to Fisherton House was described as 'vivacious' but it was also 'mischievous, not inclined to violence but is likely to be troublesome'.[85]

On occasion patients would rebel and use resistance to work as an act of defiance against the authority of the asylum.[86] It was noted on several occasions that Eliza Pegg refused to work in the laundry at Fisherton House, due to 'quarrelling with the Laundress' who was an employee not a patient in the asylum. She was then put to work on the wards where she was described as 'very noisy & abusive'. Pegg 'steadily … refused to be again employed in the laundry' and continued to remain on the wards 'where she scrubs and cleans'.[87] Eventually, however, even some women who 'rebelled' against the system were discharged if they behaved in a respectable and sane manner, as defined by the asylum authorities. Once Eliza Clark arrived in Fisherton House, her reported behaviour and demeanour changed and she was described as 'very orderly and industrious' and she was happy to work at tasks that pleased her. Eliza was discharged from Fisherton just four months after her arrival from Bethlem as she was 'in every aspect perfectly convalescent, exhibiting no delusion whatever [and] cheerful'.[88]

Good behaviour and conduct could be rewarded by concessions and a certain amount of free movement within the institutions. Fisherton House regularly allowed well-behaved patients to walk beyond the asylum's walls, accompanied by a nurse and to attend the weekly balls in the Recreation Room.[89] However, allowed freedoms could also have unforeseen circumstances. In 1857, Maria Borley, a former Bethlem patient now in Fisherton House, was described as 'intelligent, quiet very well-behaved. She is also very industrious making herself useful in the kitchen … and assisting the upper servants'. By May 1858 she was allowed to go on errands into Salisbury and she was described as 'very well trusted'.[90] She was allowed to accompany some ladies on a month's visit to the Isle of Wight as well as attend Salisbury theatre with other patients. The trip was in accordance with the 1860 Criminal Lunatics Act which allowed for a leave of absence from an asylum for recovered patients.[91] In the case of Maria Borley, it would appear that her leave of absence was to act as a servant to assist the ladies from the private wards and their attendants. It was this trust and relative liberty which led to eventual problems. Borley was discharged as 'recovered' in November 1859. However, the asylum was subsequently advised that she was pregnant and the putative father was a gardener at Fisherton House.⁹² This was a unique occurrence amongst the cases studied, an extreme consequence of the trust that could be built up between the asylum staff and patients.

The 1871 Broadmoor Superintendent's Report records that 'well-conducted female patients have taken drives into the neighbouring country'.⁹³ In 1884, it was reported that 'weekly parties of 12 [were] selected from among the working women [to] walk on asylum estate, outside the airing courts'.⁹⁴ In 1901, about 13 per cent of the patient population (presumably men and women) were 'allowed to take exercise under supervision beyond the airing courts … and … sent for the occasional drives'.⁹⁵ The addendum note to the printed version of the table from Broadmoor's 1875 annual report finished by stating that, in addition to the 238 patients usefully employed, there were 'a large number employed in reading, writing, and in music and other pursuits'.⁹⁶ In 1885 the Lunacy Commissioners noted that 'supply of books, papers, and indoor games appears to be liberal'.⁹⁷ Again noted in 1885, for the 'usefully employed' patients there were regular 'amusements' provided in the large central hall, which, 'were severally attended by from 170 to 200 patients of both sexes'.⁹⁸

The ultimate reward for good, respectable behaviour was discharge and release from the asylum. Requests for release or discharge were more likely to be favourably considered and recommended for those patients who had worked hard, without trouble and complaint such as Elizabeth Thew. Elizabeth appeared to be a model patient in Bethlem, for she was 'cheerful and well-behaved, industrious and obliging'.¹⁰⁰ In 1861 she was transferred to Fisherton House from Bethlem, where her casebook notes described her as 'well-conducted' and 'industrious', often 'cheerful' or 'tranquil'. She received a Royal Pardon in 1862 and was released.¹⁰¹ Likewise, twenty-four-year-old Martha Lewis, the wife of a respectable artisan, William Lewis, a master shoemaker, was admitted to Bethlem

Image 5.2 Dancing on female airing court, 1867.⁹⁹

in 1860. She was described as being 'educated', 'in good health', 'industrious' and 'very well-conducted'.[102] Martha was not a middle-class patient but she was certainly from the respectable educated working class. Despite her designation as a criminal lunatic, her background fitted in well with Bethlem's preferred patient profile. By 1881, nineteen years after receiving a Royal Pardon, Martha and William were working at Warwickshire County Lunatic Asylum, where Martha herself was the Head Attendant and William the Head Storekeeper.[103] Martha possibly utilizing her experience from helping on the wards and of the personal treatment she received.[104]

Appearance

Physical appearance seemed to have an effect on the staff's perceptions of the women. In each of the asylums reviewed, the case notes always contained a physical description of the woman, usually without further comment. In Bethlem, Martha Lewis was described as 'a prepossessing young woman in appearance and manner' with an 'amiable appearance'.[105] When Sarah Allen was admitted to Bethlem in 1856, she was noted as being 'An interesting and amiable looking woman'.[106] Women were described as 'well-conducted' and 'industrious' their demeanours as 'cheerful' or 'tranquil'. Catherine Savell was described as being 'improved in appearance ... being now stout and healthy' and 'her manner has been uniformily [sic] cheerful'.[107] On the other hand, a woman's appearance could count against her. Ann Byrom was described in the Bethlem casebook notes as being 'of rude habits' and 'of a coarse description'.[108] Her description from Fisherton House is more detailed, 'she has dark grey hair, a florid countenance ... has lost the sight in one eye, the vision in the other is imperfect ... abusive & violent lunatic'.[109] Byrom went on to be transferred to Broadmoor where she was died in 1871.[110]

The notes at Fisherton House are much the same with the words 'industrious', well-behaved', and 'well-conducted' appearing in many patients' entries. In the occasional entry hint at a different type of observation of a patient's demeanour. It would appear that the medical officers there believed that physical appearance might be a reflection of the women's characters and histories. Eliza Clark was described as having a 'countenance [which] indicates intelligence and kindness of disposition which is confirmed by conversation'.[111] A suggestion, perhaps, that she might be an unlikely person to commit murder. This supposition was firmly stated in the case of Sarah Dickenson. 'She has an intelligent expression ... appears generally dejected but kind and benevolent. She probably would be one of the last who could be suspected of having committed any heinous crime.'[112]

Friendships and companionship

Amongst themselves, the women in asylums formed friendships which could sometimes last beyond the asylum. These friendships came from the ability to mingle with other patients whether when working or taking part in other forms of employment. Despite the best efforts of the asylum staff to encourage families and kin to visit the women, many of the women did not receive visitors. A lack of contact with familiar faces and a quieter living environment than many were used to, probably gave them a real sense of isolation. By forming bonds with other women, whether from similar backgrounds or maybe very different homes, the women's lives became more socially tolerable. There were many opportunities for interdependent friendships and relationships to grow. Broadmoor's female wings had a dayroom where patients could go and perhaps sew or read or just talk to each other. There those who slept in dormitories, and of course, many worked alongside each other in the laundries or female workshops. The smaller wards in Bethlem and Fisherton House could double up as dayrooms if necessary but in both, as noted earlier, the criminal female patients could mix in with other patients when they were working.

There is evidence of kindly mutual support from some patients towards those perceived as less-fortunate than themselves. On her removal to the Incurables Ward at Bethlem in 1864, Mary Ann Beveridge was described as being 'gentle in her behaviour' and 'grateful for all that is done for her'. However, by April 1873 there was more exasperation in the comment that Mary Ann had 'had an inveterate habit of "cadging" from other patients'.[113] In May 1879, Ellen Oldman's husband wrote to the Matron at Broadmoor asking permission to bring in 'some Tea, sugar Bacon and marmalade so that she can make a nice tea party as some of the patients have been so kind to her'.[114] Alongside the peaceful companionships, there were also patients who kept themselves to themselves. It was always noted in the casebooks if the woman was too quiet and reserved and efforts were made to get her to socialize. Maria Clarke was described as being "very quiet and subdued" but attempts by the Fisherton House staff to involve her on the ward met with "threats to the nurses" lives.[115] From the nature of some patients' mental illness and to some extent their natural temperaments, threatening behaviour and fights were not unknown. These were always reported and dealt with in as calm a manner as the staff could muster, but would result in withdrawal of privileges and in the worse cases, seclusion.

The friendships made in Broadmoor could last beyond the years women's incarceration. Lucy Thompson had been admitted to Broadmoor from Warwick Gaol on 30 December 1864.[116] Elizabeth Pryce arrived on 17 March 1865 just three months later. They had much in common, Lucy was 21, Elizabeth 23, they were both single and both had had killed their illegitimate babies. Each of them had been abandoned by the putative fathers of their children and had killed their babies in 'fits of despair' and 'deep distress'.[117] Elizabeth had been a pupil teacher whereas Lucy had been a bridle-stitcher from Birmingham and was noted as being poorly educated. Whether Elizabeth took Lucy under her wing or whether they were drawn together because of their similar circumstances, is not known, but three years after her discharge, Elizabeth wrote to Dr Orange about Lucy Thompson. She wrote that she 'had a sisterly regard' for Lucy and enquired whether she was still in the asylum and whether she was well.[118] Elizabeth continued, 'will you give me some hope of her liberty. I have long neglected her, but now I have a home of my own and most freely will I share it with her'. Elizabeth had married and her husband was also willing to give a home to her friend.[119]

Although her case file does not include Dr Orange's reply, it does include a second letter, from which it would appear that he had dissuaded Elizabeth from the idea of giving Lucy a home. In fact, Lucy Thompson had herself been discharged on 27 February 1874, ironically the same day as Elizabeth wrote her first letter. From the exchange of letters, it seems appear that while friendships in the asylum were considered good for the patients' well-being, association once discharged was not always agreeable to the asylum attendants and staff. Orange had told Elizabeth about Lucy's discharge but had not given any other details. She requested his permission to write to Lucy but is careful to say, 'I will in no way interfere with your plans for I'm sure it will be to her interest to comply with your plans'.[120] A similar reluctance for ex-patients to have anything to do with each other or with patients still in Broadmoor can be seen in other correspondence. In 1903 Lucille Dudley wrote to Mary Cornford saying she was going to visit her, which Mary did not want. Richard Brayn wrote in a memorandum that 'Mrs Cornford does not desire to see Mrs Dudley … she is somewhat afraid of her'.[121] Lucille Dudley said to be highly intelligent but was also was known to be very domineering. Mary Cornford was described as quiet and reserved. On her admittance her insanity had been put down to imbecility and Brayn suggested that 'she would be completely dominated by her (Dudley)'. Dudley had been finally discharged in 1901 after two abortive attempts by the Salvation Army to take care of her.[122] The visit did not seem to go ahead, the reason given being that Dr Brayn felt that it was not suitable for an ex-criminal lunatic such as Lucille Dudley, to go into the wards.[123]

Repercussions of former lives

In all the asylums there were patients who were seen as having brought their situation on themselves and had opened themselves to the possibility of mental disorder. Sometimes this was seen as coming from careless living and drink but also from a lifestyle at the other of the scale, sometimes by the opposite, overzealous religious belief and practice. If a woman had been driven to drinking by a catastrophic life event or domestic situations, her intemperance and insobriety were mitigated by circumstance. Ironically, at the end of the nineteenth century alcohol was still valued for medicinal purposes. Stout was viewed as important in rebuilding strength in a convalescent and brandy was given as a calming agent and for shock. The difference would be that the dosage given to a patient would be rationed and controlled. Such usage did decline towards the end of the century in the face of some disquiet in medical circles about the efficacy of alcohol as a therapeutic treatment.[124]

Elizabeth Platts was admitted to Broadmoor as a 'Class 2' patient on 18 August 1881. Her medical history and mental state was clearly described in her casebook notes:

> A woman of respectable appearance ... she had been assaulted & stripped naked & grossly insulted by ... eleven young men ... She never recovered from the shock this gave to her mind and she became restless.'[125]

Later, in 1884, in medical report to the Home Office, Orange further clarified the background to her insanity. He wrote, 'her mind was unhinged after an outrageous criminal assault & was under the influence of delusions when she stabbed one of her mother's labourers'.[126] Her casebook notes state that there were five possible factors causing her 'attack' of insanity. They were, 'Hereditary; Shock & Intemperance. Maternal Uncle insane. Father drank'. Despite the latter two factors, the medical examiner described Elizabeth as 'naturally simple-minded but of a kindly & industrious nature'.[127] It was well known in her local area that Elizabeth had a reliance on alcohol and from reading various records and reports about her case, it is likely that she was an alcoholic. Her short stay in Broadmoor meant she was away from easy access to alcoholic drink and any temptation to overindulge, which no doubt aided her recovery. The doctors' principal aim was to ensure that their patients were calmer, more rational and ostensibly cured of mental disturbance. If rationality was restored, they could be safely released back to their community. When the underlying causes of insanity were conditions such as alcoholism, time spent in the asylum would alleviate any symptoms of madness. The discharge of such patients would be considered as tenable in the hope that there would not be a future relapse.

Religious mania featured alongside physical disease, poverty and destitution as root causes of the damage to the women's minds.[128] In asylum records, doctors would frequently refer to excessive and exaggerated religious behaviour as an indicator and a cause of insanity. The belief that mental disorders could be were linked to religious fervour persisted though the Victorian period. There was always a debate about whether those classed as religiously mad were actually predisposed to some sort of melancholia.[129] Daniel Hack Tuke believed that 'religious delusions of melancholia', though perhaps 'deep-seated', were not hopeless of cure.[130] While mental disorders, physical disease, poverty and destitution were viewed as root causes of the damage to the women's minds and reason, the idea that such causes were exacerbated by religion continued through the century.[131] Writing in 1913 sometime after his retirement from Broadmoor, Dr David Nicolson attributed 'the great frequency at which ... infanticides occur' to the mother having 'an insanely exaggerated extension of religiousness and foreboding, accompanied by an overwhelming sense of personal unworthiness and unfitness to live'. He continued that in murdering her child, the mother sought to protect it from a 'horrible life as pictured by her anguished mind'.[132]

The moral and spiritual health of asylum patients was deemed to be important with religious practice and regular worship was part of everyday life in any Victorian lunatic asylum.[133] Worship in all county asylums, in Bethlem, Broadmoor, Fisherton House and many private asylums, was focused on the rites of the Church of England.[134] From the Fisherton House records, attendance at services was viewed favourably. Regular chapel attendance and religious observation were noted in records as positive signs of progressive, good recovery. Mary Ann Saville was commended on her weekly attendance at chapel in Fisherton House in 1863, as was Sarah Price who was said to 'conduct herself with propriety … attended chapel'.[135] Any child born in the asylum was christened in the local parish church or in the dedicated chapel after it was built in 1859.[136] In 1885, the Commissioners in Lunacy inspection report for 1884 recorded that in Broadmoor, 'on the Sunday preceding our visit about 70 men and 35 women attended Divine Service in the morning, and about as many in the afternoon'.[137] The Anglican services were supposedly the only formally provided forms of worship in the state institutions; however, provision was always made for other faiths.[138]. The Commissioners' report continued, '17 patients had attended the last Roman Catholic Service, and an equal number the last Wesleyan Service.'[139]

The main contacts many patients would have with religion would be with the assigned chaplain to the asylum. He could be responsible for the education of patients, both religious and secular, and ostensibly for their moral welfare. In the next chapter his role is examined in much closer detail to gain some impression on the influence of religious practice on the female asylum population. The patient population in all asylums came from many different religious backgrounds, including non-conformists, Roman Catholics and the Jewish faith. Provision was made for Roman Catholic chaplains and local non-conformist minsters to conduct services within the asylums. The Jewish patients in Broadmoor benefitted from the occasional visits from a representative of the United Synagogues in London. At the end of the period, religious organizations, such as the Salvation Army, and other philanthropic societies played a small part in some patients' rehabilitation and release. These interventions took the form of training and were significant in the rehabilitation of certain patients. Finally, in the case of funerals and burials various allowances were made for different beliefs. Both this and the philanthropic interventions are examined in detail in Chapter 7.

Conclusion

While they were in the asylums, medical superintendents and all their staff reigned supreme over the patients' lives. The routines of life under a moral therapy regime were loosely structured on Victorian, essentially middle-class, ideals of domesticity. The medical superintendent acted as the father of the house, the matron the mother figure, the attendant staff perhaps older siblings or extended family members and the patients viewed as the children.[140] Through the tenets of moral therapy, the medical superintendents and his staff replaced husbands, parents and other family members in looking after the women's welfare. The notion was that mental distress might be eased and normality restored by creating kind and tolerant staff relationships with the patients. Such asylum patient–staff relationships carried many elements of discipline and control which would have a direct impact on institutional patient life. This supervision over the asylum populations somewhat controlled patients' lives, present and future.[141]

Life in the asylum for the homicidal mothers was organized by the authorities, and sporadically, patients would react against that control. In all asylums, the conduct and language of the female patients were taken as indicators of various levels of restored sanity. Nonetheless, there would always be patients who acted in a way which ran contrary to the expectations of the asylum staff. They could refuse to behave in an acceptable manner, refuse to engage with the asylum's medical staff and, when it came to work and employment, refuse to take on any occupation. These small acts of rebellion, refusals to engage or to socialize with other patients, possibly were small of attempts to take back a little control of their own lives. Unfortunately, such conduct was invariably viewed negatively and would be more likely to lengthen, rather shorten, their incarceration.[142] So, despite the acts of patient opposition, it was well known that those patients who became more rational and calmer were more likely to be viewed favourably by those in charge. By behaving and acting in an acceptable manner, they would duly receive reward for their conduct, ultimately their discharge. The asylums' raisons d'etre was to cure and help the patients to return to as normal, pre-crime, pre-asylum life as possible. If that were achieved through a protective, somewhat patronizing, system of care, then the asylum staff would be satisfied.

Image 5.3 Female dormitory, 1867.[143]

6

'The paramount importance of gentleness and kindness to all patients.' Therapeutic agency – medical men, chaplains and attendant staff in the asylums

To function successfully and efficiently, any nineteenth-century asylum needed to have a responsible, caring staff from the most senior to the lowest post. The ultimate aim of medical superintendents and other medical officers was to restore rationality and peace to the women's mental states so that they could return to their normal lives, once released. In this endeavour they were assisted by the attendants, whose day-to-day contact and nursing care were necessary to ensure the patients' welfare.[1] All the staff were also accountable for the physical and mental safety of criminally insane women, until that responsibility could be passed on to husbands or other trustworthy family members. Generally, the asylum medical men and the attendant staff seem to hold the contemporary social belief that a woman's place was in the home, at the heart of her family. Certainly, various commentaries contained in files and asylum records reinforce this belief with statements such as, 'it is a sad thing for a wife and mother to be separated from her family' and that 'she is capable of attending to her domestic affairs at home'.[2] The professed wish of the asylums' authorities was that the women should be able to return to stable and safe home lives, albeit that their position within those homes would be different. A mother who had murdered her child had offended against the accepted criteria of respectability amongst their peer group and against society in general. Rather than being capable of managing the household and nurturing the family, they would now need to be managed and looked after themselves, to ensure that there would be no relapse into insanity. If the homicidal mothers were discharged, it would be more than

---

TNA, HO 45/9572/79056, *Rules for the Guidance of Officers, Attendants and Servants of Broadmoor Criminal Lunatic Asylum* (London: Her Majesty's Stationery Office, 1869), p. 4.

likely that they would not be seen as capable of returning to life as they knew it before incarceration. They would be more closely watched by their family and kin for signs of incipient insanity, as the reality was that they were never believed to be totally cured.

Moral treatment was originally based on a cooperative relationship between the doctors and their patients and an important part of the philosophy behind the therapy was that the medical men should adopt a benign didactic approach to their patients. This approach would help to alleviate the patients' psychological suffering and build-up their self-worth; in effect the doctor should act as a benevolent father figure.[3] Writing in 1882, Dr Daniel Hack Tuke, son of Samuel Tuke, described the then contemporary care of the mad as an enlightened progression, where compassion and sympathetic behaviour had replaced superstition, ignorance, cruelty and general barbaric behaviour.[4] He propounded that such treatments highlighted Victorian society's modern progressive attitudes towards insanity.[5] Daniel Tuke's high Victorian idealism was challenged by Michel Foucault and Andrew Scull as imperialistic.[6] Foucault described the therapeutic, moral treatments as coercive, a way to systematically control the insane who were considered as social outcasts.[7] He described Tuke's therapy as a scheme of treatment as one which replaced the fear of madness with the 'anguish of responsibility'.[8] Foucault linked nineteenth-century treatments for madness with punishment and a desire for regulated behaviour, submitting that they were aimed at imposing contemporary moral standards on the insane.[9] Scull took this point further describing Victorian alienists as 'moral entrepreneurs', men who coupled moral therapy with non-restraint to create a regime which could only be administered by medical practitioners. He called it professional imperialism, created for and by doctors' self-interest.[10]

The reality is more nuanced. Thomas Dixon argues that moral treatment could be viewed as humane and ethical compared with earlier repressive and intrusive regimes.[11] Moral therapy was generally accepted as the treatment which had the potential to alleviate symptoms of madness through calming the patients' own emotions.[12] Anne Digby countered the argument, saying that the discursive medical regime in which moral therapy ultimately operated, tended to have the effect of repressive control. She suggests that nature of the regime, be it benevolent or suppressive, was determined by an interactive combination of the character and condition of the patient and the ability and compassion of the medical man or therapist.[13] Moral therapy, as a treatment given in asylums, was originally developed with a well-intentioned purpose of providing meaningful care.[14] While the enduring image of an asylum doctor is one of a dominant patriarch, controlling a despotic regime within the asylum, it is simplistic to assert that the main impetus for Victorian mental health practitioners stemmed from an imperialistic desire for control of the vulnerable.[15]

The role of the medical men in charge of the asylums is more complex than has often been allowed. A medical superintendent was the head of his institution, the man in charge and by its nature, his position was expected to command respect. Any emotional engagement between him and his patients would be patriarchal in nature and not one of social equality. His compassion often came from a middle-class understanding of life and relationships and from his experiences in working with the insane. By virtue of being the 'men at the top' of the institution's hierarchy, the medical superintendents were responsible for the welfare of everyone in the asylum, including the well-being and safety of the whole staff.[16] All roles, particularly the medical roles, held their own significance in the dynamics of the asylum. The 'paternal' responsibility of the medical superintendent and having a sympathetic connection with their patients' physical and mental welfare, was seen as vital to successful treatment.[17] The interactions between all parties were intricate and multifaceted, open to more than one interpretation, varying between doctors and patients. Paternalism and patriarchy were not simply about oppression and control. As a protective, somewhat patronizing, component of asylum care, it did influence and affect the experiences of the criminally insane mothers, once they were in the asylum.[18]

The nineteenth century was a period when all medical men were constructing new professional identities. The development of the asylum system had led to the emergence of the new cadres of psychology and alienism.[19] Within the three criminal lunatic asylums, the medical superintendents were working in difficult, potentially dangerous, environments where their professional and personal backgrounds would have an impact upon the experience of homicidal mothers.[20] By virtue of their position as the men at the top, their personal beliefs and qualities would influence the day-to-day running of the institution and the delivery of the therapeutic regime. As Anna Shepherd comments, a long tenure at the head of the asylum would also give stability to the whole population, staff and patients.[21] The medical superintendents of Bethlem and Broadmoor had terms of office ranging from seven years to sixteen years whereas Fisherton House, as always, was different by being a privately owned by one family.

In this chapter, the relationships between the senior medical staff and the attendants in the three asylums and the infanticidal and homicidal mothers are explored. The investigations have been conducted through a nuanced reading of the casebook notes and other relevant papers. As previously mentioned, casebook notes were intended to document the medical and recovery progress of the patients, nonetheless, there are occasional hints of the writer's personal and perhaps emotional reactions to the case before them. To a greater or lesser degree, these books and other papers offer an insight into the extent to which personal circumstances could influence interpersonal encounters between the asylum staff and the insane patients. The investigations for this chapter have relied heavily upon the patient case files from Broadmoor. Unfortunately, the existence of similar correspondence and ephemera from Bethlem and Fisherton is very sparse, if there is any at all. For that reason, an exploration of the relationships between patients, families and all asylum staff are somewhat biased towards Broadmoor.

As described in preceding chapters, the concept of respectability in the Victorian period was a cultural ideal of a well-ordered, controlled and civilized society. Discernible 'respectable' behaviour from patients, both before and after admission to the asylum was important. The compassion and understanding shown by all the asylum staff to the homicidal mothers could be said to stem from their personal ideals of what they believed to be 'decent' and acceptable behaviour.[22] Whether motivated by paternalism, benevolence or professional probity, the medical superintendents' reactions to and relationships with the patient population would have far-reaching consequences on the future lives of the homicidal mothers. This could be said to also apply to the personal opinions of all authoritative figures in the asylums. The views and beliefs of all asylum doctors and staff were, in turn, informed by contemporary constructions of gender, by expectations of respectability and personal experience.[23]

Medical superintendents and other medical officers

A potent attribute for Victorian medical men, whatever their metier, was to be sympathetically attuned to their patients.[24] Understanding and interpreting any seemingly emotionally driven behaviour was a part of a successful doctor–patient relationship.[25] Dr John Bucknill argued that insanity could often be caused by an emotional disorder rather than by a physical or intellectual problem.[26] The institutional view of the patients could be driven by resistance to or compliance with treatment and care and by their responses towards the medical staff. Reading a patient's behaviour, if it seemed to have been driven by her emotional state, was essential in the treatment of certain forms of insanity. Certainly, in the case of the medical superintendents and other staff within the asylums, symbiotic emotional relations were vital to successful treatment. Through such interactions, mutually beneficial outcomes of release and cure on one side, and satisfaction in curing disordered minds and having recovered patients on the other. After admission into an asylum, recommendations concerning continuing incarceration or possible release depended on the opinions of the staff, particularly those of the medical staff.[27]

The senior and arguably the most important person on the asylum staff was the medical superintendent. The role has been described as sui generis, 'in a class of its own', and their individual, professional styles could define the character of the institution.[28] In 1894, Charles Mercier described the ideal Medical Superintendent as someone 'who combines the two qualifications of high scientific attainments and high administrative capacity'.[29] Mercier continued, 'For his patients he should have a depth of sympathy and a breadth of charity such that he places ... without effort or self-consciousness their interests, their comfort, their welfare in the foremost front of his endeavour.'[30] In other words, the perfect superintendent should combine such qualities as compassion and understanding with his professional achievements. As a medical superintendent himself, Mercier's words could be interpreted as a validation of the function he and his colleagues served. Alternatively, it could be a description of the aspirations of highly professional medical men. The ideal personal emotional temperament of a medical man was said to encompass important assets of 'cool, philosophical composure' and control of temper.[31] A powerful quality for Victorian doctors was the ability to have an emotional rapport of some kind with their patients, whatever their medical specialism.[32]

An important factor in the creation of gravitas and professionalism for Victorian medical practitioners was the control of emotion and the control of emotional involvement with their patients.[33] That being said, in general, the Victorian attitude to the role of emotion in medicine was ambivalent.[34] The ability to show compassion in their patient care was valued as an indication of accomplishment and success in practice. Sympathetic involvement with their patients was regarded by Victorian doctors as an important part of their medical arsenal, playing an essential part in diagnosis and treatment of illness.[35] While being able to master unnecessary emotional attachment was considered as a key skill for medical practitioners, it did not mean that a doctor should be unapproachable or unsympathetic. To be able to create some such connection with their patients, was of fundamental significance in the field of nineteenth century 'mental science'.[36]

All the medical men in the asylums had each trained and started their careers in general medicine and surgery. Their subsequent vocational career paths were through various institutions, asylums and penal institutions. Their expertise in treating insanity was acquired from working with and observing insane populations in institutional care, and their attention and attitudes, no doubt, coloured by those past careers and experiences. Charles Hood started his career, after qualifying, as resident physician to a private asylum, Fiddington House, Devizes, then he became the first medical superintendent of Colney Hatch before moving to Bethlem Hospital.[37] The doctors in the Finch family came from a medical dynasty, which had specialized in caring for the insane since the eighteenth century. Dr John Meyer had been medical supervisor of the Hospital and Convict Lunatic Asylum at New Norfolk, Tasmania, chief resident physician at the Surrey County Lunatic Asylum before being appointed as the first Medical Superintendent of Broadmoor.[38] Dr Orange started his career in 'mental science' as an Assistant Medical Superintendent of the Surrey County Lunatic Asylum at Springfield, Tooting, before his appointment as Deputy Superintendent to Meyer at Broadmoor.[39] Dr David Nicolson, was a Scottish Presbyterian with experience of working in prisons and asylums, including HMP Portland.

The last Medical Superintendent of Broadmoor in the nineteenth century was Dr Richard Brayn, who seemed to view himself as a custodian rather than as a friend or father. Treatment in Broadmoor up to 1896 under Drs Meyer, Nicolson and Orange, was been more or less in line with the tenets of moral therapy. Dr Brayn had previously been the medical officer at Aylesbury, then Woking prisons and, although fully medically qualified, he had not previously had any experience of working in an asylum. Ralph Partridge, in his account of Broadmoor, written in 1952, commented about Richard Brayn's appointment, that 'The inmates of Broadmoor were to remember that in the future that they were criminals by nature and proclivity and lunatics only by act of providence'.[40] It is apparent that Brayn was of a harsher school of thought and his term in office was described as one of 'rigid routine and inflexible discipline'.[41] With his appointment, the paternalistic elements of asylum management began to disappear which can be partly explained by the broader changes in therapeutic environments in other asylums from optimistic to psychiatric pessimism. As Jade Shepherd writes, Broadmoor's regime took thirty years to succumb to these changes.[42] Brayn contended that Broadmoor was a prison first and a hospital second, which was contrary to its original purpose and an opinion 'which would earn a sharp rebuke from modern medical directors of the institution'.[43] Although he was a well-respected leader at Broadmoor, he was not as affectionately regarded as his predecessors. His staff remembered him as being 'strict but fair' and that he ran 'a tight ship'.[44]

In 1901 Brayn discussed one of the problems he foresaw regarding the younger mothers in his charge. In a presentation written for the Medico-Psychological Association, he touched on the subject of sterilization of women who killed while suffering from an attack of puerperal insanity, as a way to prevent them from killing again. He commented, 'There cannot be any difference of opinion as to the undesirability of these [married women who killed their children] having any more children; but the difficulty is how are you to prevent it?' He continued, 'she can hardly be detained ... until past the childbearing age and public opinion is not yet educated up to the idea of having her sterilised.'[45] Brayn gave the presentation in 1901 at a time when eugenic theories were being considered in relation to treatment of the mentally ill. The suggestion of sterilization may have been an acknowledgement of Galton's beliefs. In particular, the idea that active population control could prevent those prone to mental problems from having children and thereby reduce the hereditary element of mental illness.[46] This drastic suggested solution of sterilization was never implemented at Broadmoor. Jade Shepherd notes that away from the wards for violent and less tractable criminal lunatics, Brayn's regime continued to follow existing therapeutic methods to successfully treat insanity. In other words, the Queen's pleasure patients continued to be treated by the regime in line with moral therapeutic ideals while the convict classes were subjected to more prison-like treatments. Shepherd suggests that Richard Brayn would not have viewed himself as a strict custodian and that evidence suggests even under his stewardship, many found Broadmoor a place of safety, comfort and respite.[47]

By the 1845 County Asylums Act, on-site residency became compulsory for supervisory physicians and doctors in all public asylums.[48] This residency brought the day-to-day contact with the patients nearer to medical superintendents, giving them the chance to observe their charges on a more personal level. An important consequence of the required residency of the medical superintendent was that his presence would lead to a continuous senior medical attendance on site. It also led to increased chances of personal interaction between the superintendent and the patients, which in turn propagated the quasi-familial environment so intrinsic in moral therapy.[49] The medical superintendent was the father figure, on hand to administer stability and security by his presence and the asylum population was his family.

The idealistic models of domestic harmony for the asylums were obvious in a literal sense too. At Fisherton, the extended Finch family lived in Fisherton House, or in houses in the grounds of the asylum, for the whole of the nineteenth century and into the early twentieth century. The idea of having the home of the superintendent in close proximity to his charges could act as a moral model of family to the asylum community, giving a sense of normality to the campus. Hood raised a young family at Bethlem and his two younger children were born there. Dr John Meyer arrived at Broadmoor with his wife and relatively young family, his children ranged from 12 years to 7 years old at the time. Orange and Nicolson at Broadmoor were all single on their original appointments to their respective asylums, marrying while in office and raising young families on the site of the asylum. In an 1857 article in Charles Dickens's *Household Words*, journalist Henry Morley commented upon the fact that he had observed Dr Charles Hood's children playing with some of the Bethlem patients in the gardens. 'They [the children of Dr Hood] are trusted freely among the patients ... sufferers feel that surely they are not cut off from fellowship ... not objects of harsh distrust – when little children ... play with them and prattle confidently in their ears.' In his lay opinion, he continued somewhat fulsomely, that the presence of 'the resident physician's family' was an 'embodiment of the good spirit that had found its way into the hospital'.[50]

Inversely, on-site residency could be detrimental to the personal welfare of the superintendents. With a potential inability to escape from asylum affairs, to have 'no hour in which he can occasionally get out of sight of his charges', the men could suffer profound effects on their well-being, causing damage to their fitness for office and health.[51] Charles Hood died of pleurisy in 1870 at the relatively young age of 52, his 'naturally robust and vigorous constitution' was said to have been compromised by 'incessant work'.[52] The first three superintendents of Broadmoor all suffered from ill-health caused by physical attacks in the asylum. In 1870, Dr John Meyer died suddenly in office from apoplexy; he had never fully recovered from an attack from a patient in 1866. William Orange was assaulted in 1882 by Henry Dodwell and it was suggested that this incident led to his resignation four years later, in 1886. His successor, David Nicolson, was the only superintendent to be attacked twice, once in 1884 and a second time in 1889.[53] It was after this attack that an inspecting Commissioner in Lunacy described the position of the role of the Broadmoor medical superintendent as being an 'anxious, dangerous task'.[54]

Charles Hood apparently treated his patient charges with 'wise thoughtfulness' and was himself 'at once thoughtful and energetic'.[55] William Corbin Finch, senior, was described by contemporaries as being 'well-known ... for kindness and humanity'.[56] On his resignation from Broadmoor in 1886, Orange's style of management was described as being 'characterised by a judicious firmness, combined with ... kindly consideration for ... the unfortunate patients ... under his care'.[57] David Nicolson wrote of Orange, that he was 'ever sympathetic with those in trouble and ready to help when appealed to'.[58] Nicolson, himself, was lauded as 'honourable, caring independent and fearless'.[59] While these observations are quoted from newspaper articles, citations or obituaries which are somewhat laudatory and favourable towards their subject, they are an indication of the qualities expected of senior medical figures in the institutions.

Ultimately, the most desirable outcome for most of the doctors was cure. A wish for the restoration of their patients' minds to a rational and sane state, as defined by nineteenth-century standards.[60] All medical men, not just asylum doctors, found satisfaction in treating particular insanities which were viewed as highly curable. Puerperal mania and melancholia were seen as such and success in curing these disorders could boost a professional reputation.[61] In alleviating such specific female conditions, medical men would also be fulfilling another social and cultural objective, to restore the woman to the heart of her family and home, her 'rightful place'.[62] Within the asylums, doctors treating insanity were working in an environment where their own concerns and emotions could impact upon the lives of their patients.[63] Attitudes, compassionate or critical, could be tempered by individual doctors' views of the respectability of a female patients' demeanour, family and behaviour.[64] The influence of their own backgrounds impacted on their emotional responses towards the infanticidal mothers in their care and possibly stemmed from middle-class ideals of what they believed to be 'decent', acceptable behaviour. For the most part, the medical men were from the conventional professional class and enjoyed stable, middle-class domestic circumstances. As the chief medical and executive officers of their respective institutions, they represented the asylum to the outside world and commanded some social standing. In their professional capacity, all the medical superintendents were expected to be paternally caring and benign.

Contemporary comments about the medical superintendents of the criminal lunatic asylums, emphasized their calm authority and sympathetic demeanour. Some patients viewed the medical superintendent as a kindly father figure, others saw him more as a protective benefactor. The medical superintendent's role was one which would be expected to command respect, rather than filial devotion. The medical officers' views on the women patients under their care would be coloured by the women's behaviour as previously noted, but the men's personal demeanour and attitude also influenced the giving of respectful regard. Elizabeth Platts found that conversation with William Orange was comforting and of therapeutic value, writing, 'I want to ask ... Dr Orange if he could ever get to the root of crime without great kindness ... I think I could talk to that man a whole day.' She suggests that others might benefit from similar treatment, 'the men and women of this place ... [should] ... tell thare [sic] tales of crime to a man like Orange ... they would soon know why they are kept hear [sic] so long'.[65]

Correspondence in the Broadmoor files from discharged patients and from those hoping for discharge, demonstrate that many of Broadmoor's patients seem to have had warmth and respect for the medical superintendents. Elizabeth Pryce was an intelligent, personable young lady who entered Broadmoor in 1865. She was allowed to socialize, widely creating friendships with other patients, as mentioned in the previous chapter, and having relaxed connections with the staff.[66] Orange interacted with her in a paternalistic manner. He appeared to appreciate that she was one of the better educated women in his care and, perhaps because of her relative youth and the distressing circumstances of her crime, he took a quasi-parental interest in her. He introduced her to his family and was active in securing her release from the institution.[67] After her discharge she wrote to him in a personal but deferential manner saying, 'Will you kindly remember me to ... your Lady and family?'[68] In another letter she wrote, 'your unbounded kindness to me, has made an impression ... I was and am still, ... grateful to you for all the kind consideration you bestowed upon me'.[69]

The role of the medical superintendent as a protector and benevolent mentor is clearly apparent in the case of Elizabeth Harris.[70] In March 1872, she was released from Broadmoor but by the middle of April she was writing to Orange asking for help. 'I think you would not say coming home had improved me ... for truly I am not nearly as well as I felt when I left Broadmoor. I cannot tell why for I use every means in my power to keep well.' In the same letter, Elizabeth said, 'I am sometimes so weary of myself ... I should be right glad to be sent away anywhere.'[71] It was arranged for Elizabeth to spend some time with a community of Anglican sisters in their 'House of Mercy' at Clewer near Windsor from May 1872.[72] The aim was to gradually prepare her for return to her home by undertaking gentle household tasks, without too much interference from her husband. The medical officers, led by Orange, believed that active and protective intervention was needed to maintain her sanity and stop her sliding into melancholy depression.

After her eventual return to her family in 1873, Elizabeth Harris stayed in correspondence with Orange, who regularly assisted the family with small financial donations and practical help.[73] Within other casefiles, there is evidence that Orange would often oblige his ex-patients with small grants or practical help in times of difficulty, much as a benevolent father might do. Rebecca Turton wrote from her sister's home in Ireland asking for money, to which request Dr

Orange sent her five stamps.[74] Many of Orange's released patients gave indication of the genuine warmth and respect they felt for him. As Elizabeth Harris wrote to Orange in 1872, saying, 'I cannot find the words as I could wish to thank you for your great kindness to me.'[75] In her request for discharge to 'Dear Husband & Darling Children', Sarah Bates wrote, 'What I will know you carnt [sic] do all for me but you kindly do what you can.'[76] A similar regard can be seen in later letters to the superintendents of Broadmoor both in ex-patients' letters and those from family and kin. Such correspondence arrived even after the death of their family member. In 1916 Alfred Freeman, son of Sarah Freeman, wrote, 'To the Superintendent. Dear Sir, I am taking the liberty to write to thank you … for the great kindness that was shown to my Mother … through her illness and her long stay … I felt it my duty to write has [sic] we could not come again [to Broadmoor].'[77]

On the other side to this, were those who could not or would not appreciate the medical officers' position, taking incarceration as a personal insult. Some believed that, despite their crime, all the medical officers were part of a conspiracy to deny them freedom. The actual reasons for their incarceration, the murder or attempted murder of their child, were forgotten. Mary Bennett, wrote directly to Orange, 'I see you as the sole fault of my being here … a lifetime you have had out of me … I do blame you that I am not at my house.'[78] Another patient who came under Orange's care was Sarah Bull who ultimately committed suicide in Broadmoor. In her suicide note she wrote, 'It seems as if Dr Orange has quite made up his mind to keep us here for life … I fear I shall never get out of this living tomb.'[79] This note apportioned some of the blame for her depression to the refusal of the medical staff to consider her fit for discharge. As Orange wrote in the subsequent Annual Report for 1884, 'it would appear that no amount of precaution is capable of guarding entirely against accidents of this nature.'[80] A reflection of a sense of failure on his and his staff's behalf for not protecting their mentally fragile patients. Later in 1901, Annie Attree was convinced that the asylum and government officials were deliberately keeping her in Broadmoor, to rob her of her money.[81] The Medical Superintendent by this time was Dr Richard Brayn and the Master of Lunacy overseeing in her case was David Nicolson, his immediate predecessor. In a letter to her husband she wrote, 'That old fool, Nicolson, when I saw him, he quoted at me what I had … said, that I did not want my money polluted … I tried hard not to get Broadmoor paid.'[82]

Families would also express dissatisfaction with the treatment their wives and mothers received in the asylums. Richard Harris wrote to Dr Orange in 1873 during his wife Elizabeth's stay, expressing his dissatisfaction with the situation.

He demanded her return, saying, 'I was willing for my wife to have 3 months holliday [sic] to recruit [sic] her health and I must say ... that would be quite sufficient.'[83] Others would doubt the diagnoses of the medical officers, even to the extent of offering the medical opinions of their own medical attendants or contacts. Dr John Isaacs, a senior medical officer at Broadmoor, was challenged by the husband of Mary Ann Reynolds in 1890. Reynolds wrote, 'The principal reason for my belief that it was only a temporary attack of mania was the very emphatic opinion of Mr Smith of Argyle Square, Kings Cross.'[84] Reynolds signed off his letter in a somewhat condescending manner saying, 'kindly allow me to disclaim any intention ... to influence your opinion in anyway ... if you find from a medical point view it will be necessary to detain her ... I should be extremely glad to inform me ... whenever you have the leisure to do so'.[85] In 1913, Annie Attree's sister went to the extent of bringing her personal doctor to Broadmoor to examine her sister to counter the then medical superintendent, Dr John Baker. Mrs Bromwich was insistent that her sister should be transferred to a private asylum. The attempt was not successful, in Baker's own words, 'I told her plainly that I did not think that a transfer to a private asylum would benefit the patient.'[86] These two examples also show a difference in the manner in which friends and family would address the senior medical men of the asylums, depending on their perceived positions in society. It is clear from the tone of the letters that both William Reynolds and Mrs Clara Bromwich believed themselves to be social equals with the professional medical staff in Broadmoor.

Chaplains

Notwithstanding the possibility that religious delusion had intensified mental disorder in patients, religious observance in the form of daily prayers and chapel attendance was believed to be of comfort and assist moral recovery.[87] It was thought that behaviour at services was seen as an indication of recovery, if patients could be decorous and self-controlled.[88] Fisherton House's patients, who were deemed well enough, went to the local parish church until 1859 when a chapel was built and consecrated. It appears that the local rector in Fisherton Anger acted as chaplain to the asylum, taking weekly services as well as baptisms of the babies born in the asylum and the funerals of those patients who died. Services in the chapel at Fisherton House were described as fulfilling the purpose of calming patients; 'The offices of prayer and praise were not such would tend to excite, but were of a calm and peaceful character.'[89] They were also open to local people to attend if they so wished. Dr William Corbin Finch believed that patients' attendance in the chapel was another way to assimilate them back into society and restore self-confidence. 'Dr Finch ... observed that his principal reason for making the services public ... was in order his patients might feel that they were under the same ecclesiastical control and religious agencies as their ... brethren'.[90]

In the administrative hierarchy of the county asylums, the chaplain was viewed as the second most senior figure. When Broadmoor opened in 1863, the decision was taken that it too would have a resident chaplain in line not only with county asylums but also with the prisons of the day. The hospital or asylum chaplain had to be an ordained minister of the Church of England, 'licensed by the Bishop of the diocese'.[91] The chaplain at Broadmoor was 'provided, rent-free, with a detached house about 250 yards distant from the Asylum'. It was a sizable property which was needed because 'Mr Burt has a large family'.[92] At that time, he had a salary of £350 per annum, the same as the Deputy Medical Superintendent, William Orange.

Reverend John Burt was the first chaplain at Broadmoor where he remained for nearly eighteen years until 1881, when he was replaced by Reverend Thomas Ashe. Ashe was in post for the next ten years when, in turn, he was replaced by Reverend Hugh Wood. The three men came from very different career backgrounds and John Burt was the only one who had been in the asylum and the prison service. Thomas Ashe had been a naval chaplain, while Hugh Wood had been an Assistant Master at nearby Wellington College.[93] While it is difficult to fully understand what, if any, influence religion and religious instruction had on the patients' lives, it is almost as hard to gauge the chaplain's opinions of the patients. From the reports written by the chaplains in the asylum annual reports, John Burt appears to have been more articulate in describing the asylum and his impressions of the patients, than his two successors. The later reports just referred to the numbers of patients attending services, the elementary school in the grounds of the asylum for the children of staff and progress on the use of the library. It is not to say that Ashe and Wood did not take part in caring for the patients' spiritual welfare or neglect their pastoral duties. It may be more of an indication that patterns and routines introduced in Broadmoor's early years were continuing to add to the stability of the administration as a whole.

In Burt's annual report for 1864, he wrote that he believed that 'moral and religious improvement is ... aimed at ... by the ministrations of the chaplain'. He had quite firm views about his role. It was to get the patients in Broadmoor to see and accept the errors of their previous lives and look forward to a more moral life in the future. Later in the same report he described the effect of his interventions on the female patients. He had 'continued to observe among [female patients] signs of Christian faith and the workings of Christian charity'. Burt believed that 'moral and religious improvement' was often assisted 'by the unceasing influence of the attendants alongside the chaplain's work'.[94] He continued on saying that he had observed 'among the worst class of the women a marked decrease in violence'. Burt did not necessarily put this down to his influence but instead to their previous incarceration in Bethlem. 'I should be inclined to attribute ... [this] ... to an influence exerted upon some of the women ... from Bethlem Hospital by one attendant of earnest piety. I venture to report ... this influence .... as a testimony to the excellence of that person.'[95]

The chaplain had other roles alongside his clerical duties which were categorically laid out in the official Broadmoor staff rule book. The chaplain was expected to 'form reading classes ... organize and superintend a system of elementary instruction for the patients'. He was also to 'pay special attention to the sick and dying' and 'to those patients whose mental conditions would ... advantage [from] his ministrations'.[96] As a potential comforter, confidante and educator to everyone in the hospital, his position was seen as an important part of asylum life.[97] As far as the patients were concerned, he was a source of secular and religious instruction and fixture in pastoral matters. He was part of the senior administrative staff where his daily pastoral duties included liaising with patients' kith and kin and monitoring patients' correspondence, as well as looking after the 'spiritual' well-being of all, including the staff.[98] The chaplain figured large in the lives of the attendants inside and outside the asylum walls. He was responsible for the education of their children and, as in his opinion the attendants and nursing staff exerted some influence over the patients, 'providing every measure to promote morals and religion among the servants'.[99]

Attendants

The attendants had always been viewed as an essential part in the successful care and treatment of the insane. In the 1847 Bethlem Physicians' report it was stated that 'The same uniform spirit of gentleness and attention which has so often adverted to on former occasions has continued to influence the nurses and attendants'. The report continued, 'There is no sphere where more patience and forbearance are requisite than within the walls of a Lunatic Hospital.'[100]

This view of the attitudes and place of the attendants was echoed in a pamphlet for Broadmoor staff entitled *Rules for the Guidance of Officers, Attendants and Servants*.[101] The opening paragraph states that 'kindness and forbearance [are] the first principles in the care and management of persons of an unsound mind'. In the annual report for 1885, Dr Orange wrote, 'I am very glad to speak very highly of the careful, considerate, and attentive manner in which they (the attendants) discharge their duties.'[102] Apart from the medical officers, the staff who dealt directly with the women were always female. They came under the overall charge of the Matron, who was in charge of female patients' day-to-day welfare. It was laid down in the Broadmoor Rules that she would see all the female patients at least twice a day, 'enforcing kindly but firmly the observance of all rules made ... for the guidance of attendants ... in the care and treatment of the patients'.[103]

Female Division

The Matron has under her at present a Head, and 12 Ordinary Attendants, the latter of whom are distributed as follows.
No1 Ward. 5, No.2 Ward 3., No. 3 Ward 4.
The duty of taking charge of the Patients in the airing ground, is assigned to the Ward Attendants in rotation during stated hours. Viz.

> *From   9.30 to 10.45, 3 Attendants one from each ward*
> *-do- 11.45 to 12.25 2 Attendants from 2&3 Wards*
> *-do   2.25 to 3.15, 3 attendants one from each Ward.*

Similar arrangements are made as respects the daily service in chapel, Bathing, Evening duty from 8 to 10pm, and night duty from 10 pm to 6.10 am.
The above assignment of duties is reported to work very satisfactorily.

Taken from a handwritten copy of Report of the Commissioners in Lunacy Medical Superintendents' Letter books[104]

The Matron was another point of contact for the patients' families, and it could possibly be surmised that some felt her more approachable due to her gender. It was to her that they would address their requests regarding bringing in small comforts for their family member and on occasion, their worries about a patient's well-being after discharge. Rebecca Bell was discharged from Broadmoor to the care of her sister, a nurse and midwife, in Farnham.[105] In August 1900 her sister wrote to the matron at Broadmoor to say that Rebecca was suffering from depression, and had begun to believe about people talking about her in the street. Her sister was asking for advice about Rebecca's possible return.[106] The sister also mentioned Rebecca's 'change of life', a subject which she perhaps more comfortable discussing with another woman.[107] Other family members would ensure that the matron's part in a woman's recovery should be acknowledged, along with her attendants. In 1878 Richard Nicholls wrote to Orange saying, 'I … thank Matron for the attention and kindness she has shown to my wife and also the attendants under whose immediate care my wife was placed.'[108]

Many patients, as well as having made friends amongst their peers, were on good terms with the Broadmoor staff.[109] However, sadly, there were also incidents of threatening behaviour and attacks on the attendant staff were not unknown. These would be dealt with as calmly as possible, but would produce tension in the asylum. It should be noted, however, that it was frequently difficult for the medical superintendents to find suitable and trustworthy attendant staff. In 1865, John Meyer remarked that it was difficult to find 'attendants and servants able to meet the various requirements of service'.[110] He blamed, in part, the isolated position of the asylum, however similar complaints had been made by William Finch at Fisherton and Charles Hood at Bethlem, both of whose asylums were less isolated than Broadmoor. In a later report, Meyer listed the reasons why female staff members had resigned during over the years since Broadmoor opened:

'1 female attendant was discharged for drunkenness
2 ditto for gross misconduct.
4 ditto unsuited for work.
1 ditto certificate refuse by Civil Service Commissioner
20 ditto resigned of their own accord.'[111]

Other ancillary workers were also dismissed for inefficiency, drunkenness and dishonesty. Meyer wrote that he had had difficulty in securing 'the services of efficient and respectable female attendants only two have been here since the opening of the asylum'.[112]

The recruitment of mainly single staff members led to personnel issues. Some of the problems began to be resolved with improvements in staff accommodation. Eventually, Broadmoor evolved into a sizeable community in the area. In the female divisions there was a recurring problem when female staff married. As Orange wrote in his 1876 report, 'The changes in female staff are … more numerous … as in their case, marriage, in the majority of instances, leads to their retirement.' He also noted, 'The number of married male attendants at the end of the year (1876) is 48.'[113] These men were more than likely to have married other attendants if not the daughters of colleagues. In time, the Broadmoor attendant staff was made up of a number of members from the same families, related by marriage, and in later years, paternity. The daughter of Chief Attendant Charles Coleman wrote, 'When a patient gets their liberty from Broadmoor, they have a "Certificate of Sanity" ... to prove they are sane – which is more than can be said for you or I.'[114] Life in Broadmoor was all-compassing for everyone from patients through the staff to the families living on the estate.

Conclusion

The medical superintendents were all-powerful in their institutions and their influence permeated through life in the asylums.[115] Their belief in the possible curability of their patients' insanity, or at least holding a medical hope that they could alleviate the mental suffering, would be a stimulus in their dealings with patients. The final decisions about patients' physical, medical and mental treatment lay with him, whether they were criminally insane homicidal mothers or 'ordinary' mentally ill patients.[116] In day-to-day medical and pastoral matters, they were supported by assistant medical officers, chaplains and the asylum attendants.[117] Any emotional engagement between them and their patients would be patriarchal in nature and not one of social equality. Their perception of the men and women under their care was influenced by experiences gained from working within asylums tempered by middle-class perceptions of domestic life and relationships.[118]

As quoted earlier in this chapter, Charles Mercier's description of a medical superintendent was an ideal that many would strive for. For the medical staff within the asylums, having a sympathetic connection with their patients' physical and mental welfare was vital to successful treatment. The cultivation of good interpersonal skills was a powerful addition to any doctor's armoury but in the field of mental health care it was of vital importance. The medical superintendents and other medical staff could be said to encapsulate the Victorian middle-class ideals of professionalism and masculine virtues of rationality, ethical firmness and compassion. Asylum medical officers were not just involved in healing bodily illnesses but they were also attempting to alleviate and cure mental infirmities, in an emotionally challenging environment.

The Victorian cultural ideals of respectability which were thought necessary for a well-ordered, controlled and civilized society are evident in the asylum. A mother who had murdered her child had offended against the accepted criteria of respectability in their peer group and in society in general. The relationships and interactions between the asylum staff both medical and pastoral, and the criminal lunatic mothers, were important factors in effecting recovery, coloured by contemporary behavioural expectations of gender and social status. Such expectations also were in evidence in the procedures surrounding discharge. While the opinions and recommendations of the medical superintendents had a profound effect on the decisions, those opinions would be supplemented with the opinions of other asylum staff. The institutional careers of the criminal lunatic mothers were influenced by contemporary gender construct, by expectations of respectability and by personal experience.[119] This was apparent in discussions surrounding female patients and, in particular, for the infanticidal and homicidal mothers. The medical superintendents were accountable for their welfare until that care could be passed on to husbands or other trustworthy family members. The medical superintendents' opinions about a homicidal mother were an important factor in the relationship between him and his patients. In its turn, that doctor–patient relationship played an essential part in securing the mothers' futures, whether in an institution or in the community. The criminal lunatic asylums were duty-bound to pass their obligation for the future welfare of their discharges and the safety of the public, on to other responsible parties. The circumstances of future guardians would need to be acceptable in order that the discharged patient would be safe from harm, and from harming others. That transference of responsibility was of paramount importance in consideration of any discharge or release, which subject is covered in greater detail in the next chapter.

7

'She might, without unwarrantable risk, be discharged': Release or retention and the protocols of discharge

On 8 March 1859, an official at the Home Office wrote to the Governors of Bethlem Hospital informing them that, Sir Thomas Sotheron-Estcourt, the Home Secretary, was 'disposed to advise [the] restoration to liberty' of Sarah Jackson, a criminal patient, if she had friends 'able and willing to take charge of [her]'.[1] Dr Hood replied saying that, as she had 'been quite sane since 1852', he could see no reason for her retention.[2] After discussion with her family and local Parish Union, Sarah Jackson was released on 11 July 1859 and it was noted in the relevant casebook that 'she has received the Royal Pardon and left the Hospital with her sister [to] reside in Enfield'.[3]

Twenty-one years later, on 10th February 1880, Sarah Bates was admitted to Broadmoor after being tried for the murder of her six-month-old daughter, Florence.[4] She had been found not guilty but insane and was to be detained until her Majesty's pleasure be known. Her insanity was attributed to severe melancholia brought on by over-lactation.[5] In February 1881, her husband, James Bates, began enquiring about the worth of petitioning for release, eventually receiving a positive answer in 1884.[6] Sarah was discharged from Broadmoor in June 1886 but returned after her husband asked for help.[7] For the next fourteen years the family and Sarah herself sought permission for another release. In 1904, she was discharged to the care of her daughter and son-in-law and, at her own request, later transferred to the care of her husband.[8] Following another bout of depression and an attempt at suicide, she returned to Broadmoor in 1905, where she then remained until her death in 1911.[9] These two differing cases highlight and are illustrations of the changes in the protocols and system for the discharge of criminal lunatics from an asylum between 1835 and 1900. The deliberations which took place about potential discharge and the comments made about the women, are important in building the complete story of the mothers' experiences on their journeys through the system.

Throughout the Victorian era criminal lunatics could only be released by order of the Secretary of State at the Home Office. However, over time, the procedures involved in obtaining a discharge evolved, becoming more stringent and formal.[10] Not only did the wording and terms of the discharge warrants alter but so did the officials' expectations of the patients, their families and lives. For the years between 1835 and the 1860s, the procedure for discharge of the criminally insane was similar to the asylum discharge practice for any insane patients.[11] Official approaches concerning release would come from petitions and requests to the Crown, through the medium of the Home Office.[12] There does not seem to have been any official enquiry into the ability of family and friends to care for the released patient, just a confirmation of their preparedness to take in the dischargee. In this respect, the discharge of a criminal lunatic followed similar lines to that of pauper lunatics from public asylums. The decision relied not only on medical evaluations of whether the criminal patient was now sane and recovered from insanity, but also on the willingness of family and friends to accept the woman back into the household.[13] In the early part of the period, protection of the woman's future mental health was viewed as a duty of friends and family but it was not a prerequisite of discharge. This changed over time and the criteria altered.

In later years, the history of domestic troubles, abuse and familial economic circumstances became important to the asylum authorities when a patient's discharge was being considered. These circumstances appear to have been quite critical to decisions made at Broadmoor.[14] Within those decisions it was important to establish that the future guardians should be emotionally and economically capable of caring for a vulnerable patient and able to protect and shield them from potential relapse. These evaluations cast a light on the authorities' perceptions of the patients' social circumstances. By getting assurances that there would be suitable supervisory care and support for released patients, the asylum authorities were seeking to safeguard the future lives of their charges. If the safeguards were seen to be too weak or unworkable, then the female patients would be retained in asylum care.

David Nicolson believed that society in general, as well as family and kin should shoulder some responsibility for the care of criminal lunatics, irrespective of social status. He argued that, if society accepted that 'some portion of our criminal lunacy is preventable', then it should be a 'practical responsibility of society ... to prevent the performance of criminal acts by insane ... members of the community'.[15] Nicolson believed that society had a responsibility to be watchful over its mentally vulnerable members. 'If we were to tot up the amount of crime committed by lunatics under such circumstances [intentional or unintentional neglect], ... we would speedily realize ... how grave the *duty* of society becomes, in regard ... to the proper care of the insane.'[16] In the context of potential discharges from asylum care, issues of social responsibility towards the criminally insane mothers were often discussed. In many cases, perceptions of social responsibility informed the official discussions and decisions about their release.

This chapter falls into two sections. The first examines the discharges of homicidal mothers from various asylums in the years before Broadmoor's opening. It explores what investigations took place and seeks to ascertain whether the medical officers and physicians had any influence on release decisions. The second part is an analysis of the discharges from Broadmoor, highlighting family involvement, changing official protocols and procedures. Once Broadmoor was firmly established, the Asylum's medical staff and Home Office officials believed they had a lasting duty of care to protect the future sanity of the discharged women and that they also had a duty to ensure public safety. Orange wrote in 1885, 'no persons [...] are set at liberty under such circumstances as to render it reasonably probable that they will not again prove a danger to the community'.[17] The decision-making process changed both at the Asylum and at the Home Office over the time span of the pre- and post- Broadmoor years. The protocols of asylum discharge procedures impacted on the future lives of all incarcerated criminally insane homicidal mothers.

There were cases where the attempts by family and friends to secure a woman's discharge were unsuccessful. In the final section, the circumstances of those women who were not released but who died in the asylum are discussed. Some were discharged but returned and then remained in the institutions until their deaths. Others were never discharged. The interactions between the asylum authorities, the Home Office and the families and friends are interesting in all cases, successful and unsuccessful. The unsuccessful discharge requests and the communications about those who were never considered suitable for discharge show a quasi-paternalistic concern by the asylum staff towards the patients. At Broadmoor, the families and kin groups were encouraged to remain in touch with the patients throughout their incarceration. In return, the asylum medical staff kept the families informed of the health and welfare of their family member.

The discussions contained within all casebooks and case files contain valuable material about interpersonal relationships and family life, perhaps reflecting contemporary cultural attitudes towards the women and their kith and kin. The growing involvement of bureaucracy in areas of public health and ideas of protective domesticity were central to Victorian, mainly middle-class, ideals of the home.[18] The recurring factor of respectability seemed, once again, to be central to the authorities' decisions. Recent studies have highlighted the part that family and kin groups played in the admission and discharge of patients in county asylums.[19] As all the women who are the subjects of this book were admitted into asylum care by legal process, their families had no influence over their entry into the institutions. However, even if it was not their decision, families could have a role in the discharge process. As with concepts of respectability, there were class differences in the perception and cultural expectations of the family unit.[20] Social and economic factors, together with concerns over intellectual capability and respectability, were as important as medical reports in the process to discharge mothers who had murdered their children, from asylum care. The chapter is illustrated with some brief resumés of the lives of the women after discharge from an asylum, when request and petitions were successful.

Discharge from the asylum

The correspondence between the Home Office and the asylums, as well as procedural medical reports, highlights cultural attitudes towards criminal lunatic mothers. As the women had, after all, committed a violent crime, the authorities placed some emphasis on issues of public safety. Procedure and protocols changed over the years, as did the criteria for release and the different methods by which discharge decisions were made. Between 1835 and the mid-1860s, patronage, third-party interest and the economic circumstance of a patient's family played a different part in the authorities' discharge decisions compared with those made in the later decades. With regard to the criminal lunatic patients themselves, what was meant by a 'conditional discharge' also changed. The definition went from one where the patient herself agreed to the conditions of her release, to one where another party took on the responsibility for the fulfilment of attached conditions. Up to the late 1860s, the possibility of unconditional discharge and pardon existed. Where a discharge was conditional, there was an obligation on the patient herself to accept the terms of her release, thereby expecting her to be able to understand the terms of her release. This expectation of personal responsibility had an impact on the future lives of released patients and their status in their social communities. They were never fully considered as cured and the consequences of this is discussed later in this chapter.

Criminal lunatic patients were always under the control of the State. The implications of a 'conditional discharge' at any point in the period was that, effectively, the woman remained 'under her Majesty's pleasure' and could be recalled to an asylum at any time, if she were considered to be at risk of harming herself or others. An essential point which should be remembered is that incarcerations 'at her Majesty's pleasure' were by their nature unfixed, indeterminate sentences. Legally, they would last for as long as the offender was considered to be unfit to be at large, a danger to themselves or others and for as long as they were thought to be insane, unable to take care of themselves, or be cared for by others.[21] In 1883, the Trial of Lunatics Act changed the wording to be used in court from 'not guilty but insane' to 'guilty but insane'. This appears to have had an influence on the status of criminal lunatics; by being found guilty rather than acquitted, they became convicted offenders.[22] The following year, 1884, saw the implementation of the Criminal Lunatics Act, by which the conditions and obligations of discharge changed.[23] Under the previous acts, the protocols around release and discharge of patients appear to have been concentrated upon those lunatic criminals who had been found insane after sentencing, or in prison.

Before 1883, the discharge of criminal lunatics, such as the subject women and any enquiries about their well-being after discharge, was ad hoc and sporadic. The change of legal status brought about by the 1883 Act appears to have made life after discharge more confined. The 1884 Criminal Lunatics Act formalized reporting procedures for both the asylum and the guardians of discharged patients. The superintendent of any asylum was obliged to report on the condition of any criminal lunatic in his care at least once a year and, in his turn and at least every three years, the Home Secretary would consider 'the condition, history and circumstances of such lunatic and determine whether he ought to be discharged'.[24] In the same section of the Act, it was laid down that reports on the condition of the discharged criminal lunatic 'shall be made to a Secretary of State by such persons at such times and containing particulars as may be required by the warrant of discharge'.[25] In the future, their lives, whether in the asylum or at large, were now closely monitored by the State.

Figures 7:1 is a graphical representation of the outcomes for the women of my sample group. The numbers were taken from the various asylum discharge registers which, in cases of conditional discharge, also recorded the name of the patient's future guardian. As can be seen, the numbers of women released compared relatively closely with the numbers of those who died in the asylum.

144   *Mothers, Criminal Insanity and the Asylum in Victorian England*

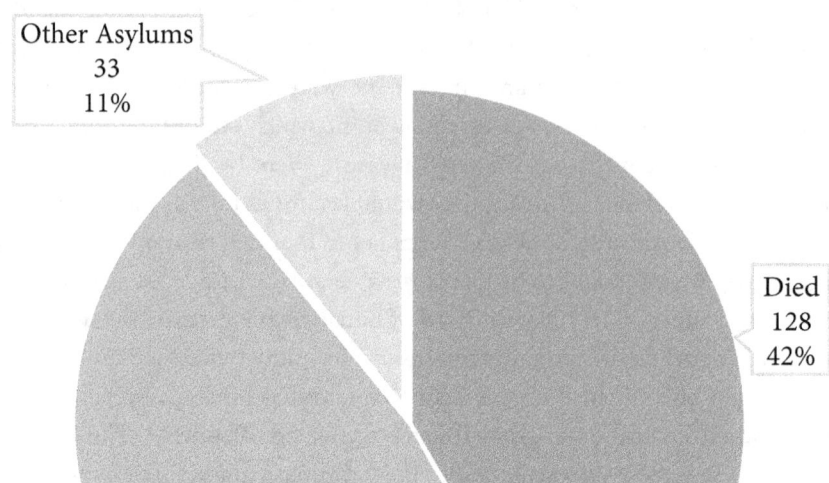

Chart 7.1 Discharges of 302 women admitted between 1835–1900.

Over the sixty-five years, a slightly higher proportion of women were not discharged, 42 per cent, remained in the respective asylums until death and 11 per cent were transferred to other asylums and institutions. When the women were transferred to other asylums, their official status changed from criminal lunatic to pauper or 'ordinary' lunatic. In all probability these thirty-three women remained in institutional care for the rest of their lives.[26]

The patterns of the discharged women's lives after incarceration seemed to depend on how and where they were viewed in general society. A review of the cases of single women who murdered their children indicates a social bias in the authorities' attitudes towards them, and that unmarried mothers were more likely to be transferred to another asylum rather than be released. It is difficult to categorically link this with social attitude without a thorough examination of each case. There is potential in researching the outcomes for all those women who were transferred, as part of an exploration of nineteenth-century asylum experiences. However, as this chapter examines the circumstances of discharge

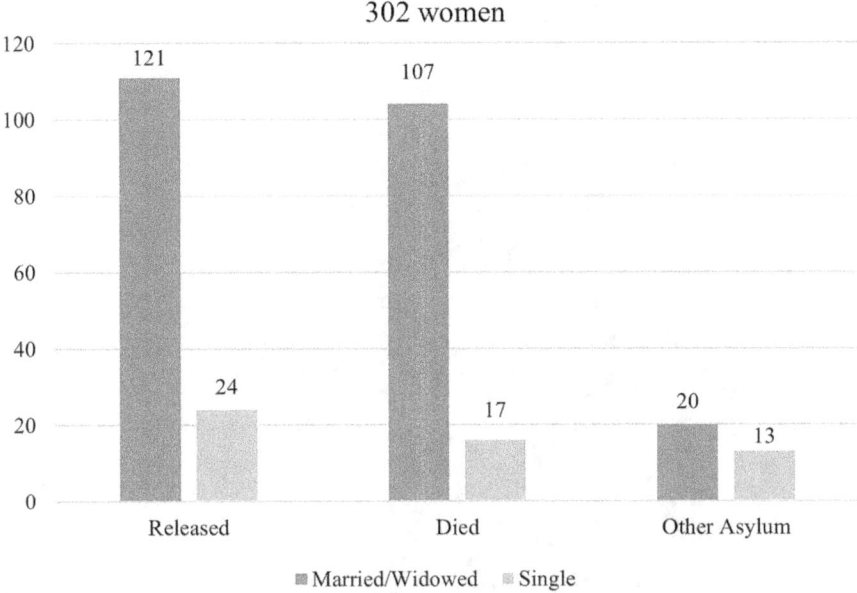

Chart 7.2 Discharges by marital status (admissions between 1835 and 1900).[27]

and death of those, mainly married, mothers who remained designated as criminal lunatics, a detailed examination of the transfer cases was not undertaken.

Leaving the asylum before 1867

The chart below (7:3), shows thirty-seven cases where the homicidal mother was admitted to an asylum as a criminal lunatic from 1835, then subsequently released or died before 1867. These are the women who did not go into Broadmoor. Of this number five died while in the institution, one woman was transferred to a county asylum and the majority, thirty-one (86 per cent), were released. Depending on when they were released, they could receive a Royal Pardon, be conditionally discharged on a Home Secretary's warrant, or be released back to their friends and family as recovered.

Anyone, patients' families, friends, the asylum authorities, or other third parties could make the initial approach about possible release before the 1860 and 1867 Criminal Lunatics Acts. At that time, decisions regarding the discharge of criminal lunatics were taken at the Privy Council level on the recommendation of the Secretary of State and discharge warrants were

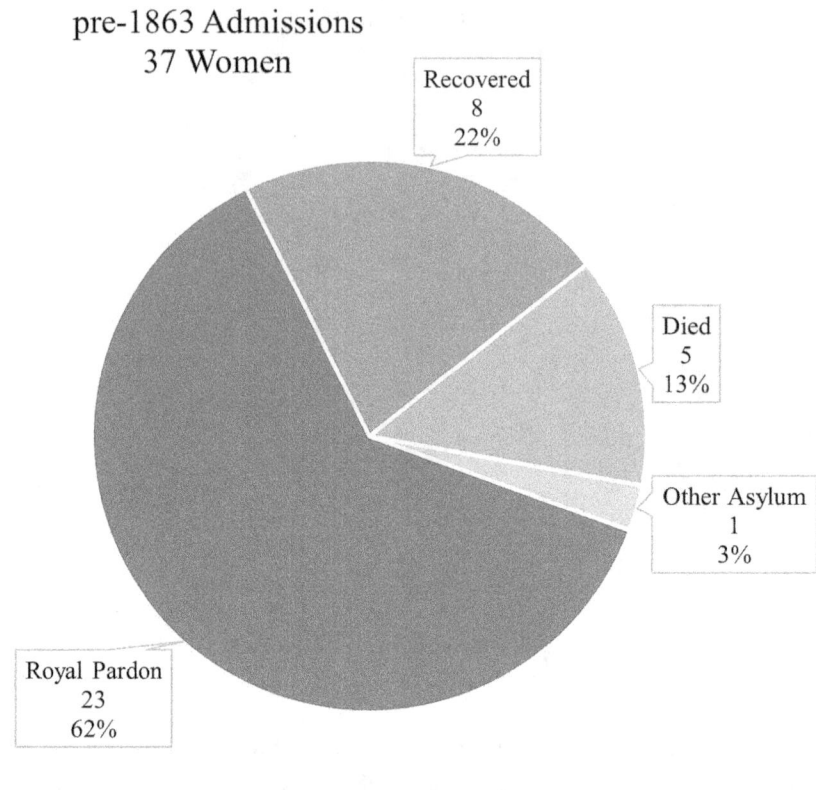

Chart 7.3 Discharges of pre-1863 Admissions (not Broadmoor) with destination.

personally signed by Queen Victoria.[28] As such, it would seem from records that these warrants were regarded as 'Royal Pardons' which apparently carried with them an indication of absolute discharge. The 1860 Act had made provision for the so-called 'convict lunatics' or 'lunatic criminals' once they had reached the end of their term of imprisonment. If it were certified that they were now 'of sound Mind [sic]', they would receive their discharge; if not they would be admitted to a County Asylum as pauper lunatics.[29] After 1867, the Secretary of State at the Home Office was 'empower[ed] … to discharge, absolutely or conditionally, any Criminal Lunatic'.[30] The opinions and recommendations of the asylum authorities were merely advisory and only the Home Office or Privy Council could sanction the actual release of patients. Under the terms of the 1853 Lunatic Asylum Act, the Secretary of State had the power to allow 'a Lunatic to be absent from the State Asylum on trial'.[31] The 1860 Act also allowed for absences from the asylum on a trial basis, with the permission of the Secretary of State.[32]

The Commissioners in Lunacy stated in their 1867 report to Parliament that these powers had been extended to cases of 'Criminal Lunatics generally, in whatever Asylums or places of confinement they may be'. The report specifically states that this had been allowed for 'Criminal Lunatics at Fisherton House and elsewhere who were not dangerous to themselves or others'.[33] The criminal patients in Fisherton House had been sent there because they were regarded as 'less dangerous' and were regularly given a measure of pre-discharge freedom and worked alongside the pauper patients. The provision fell away in later years, although it was still in use in the early days of Broadmoor. In July 1864, Mary Ann Harris was granted a leave of absence 'with an Allowance of Ten shillings per week during the time she shall so remain at large upon trial'.[34] Again, in September 1866, Ann Wilson was given a trial leave of absence 'on a conditional License' as she was 'now of sound mind'.[35]

The formal discharge papers issued in accordance with the 1860 and 1867 Acts indicate that, as the discharged patient herself signed her agreement to the terms, the authorities expected her to have an understanding of her responsibilities. The only condition contained within the document was that the discharged patient would immediately return to custody, if required to by the Home Secretary. This policy placed some responsibility for the outcome of her future life on to the discharged woman herself. Such a return would occur if the dischargee was adjudged to be 'a person unfit to be at large'.[36] The wording of the warrant continued to be used for early discharges from Broadmoor and such warrants were still signed by the released patient. In November 1867, in response to the provisions in the Criminal Lunatics Act, the last remaining female criminal lunatic patients were moved from Fisherton House Asylum.[37] Within the group of twenty women were five mothers who had murdered their children, Ann Lacey, Harriet Goodliffe, Harriet Salmon, Sarah Lancastell and Eliza Kirby. Ann Lacey was initially discharged in 1868 but was readmitted and remained until her death in 1884. Lancastell and Salmon were eventually conditionally discharged to their families but Kirby and Goodliffe did not recover sufficiently to allow the medical men to support their release.[38] Eliza Kirby died in Broadmoor in 1887 and Harriet Goodliffe in 1920.[39]

Broadmoor discharges

Between 1863 and 1900, there were 266 mothers admitted to Broadmoor for murdering or violently assaulting their children. Of that number, 145 were discharged and 117 died in the asylum. From 145 patients who left Broadmoor, 32 were admitted to other asylums with the rest being released to the care of family members or to that of employers. These numbers contained are broken down further in Table 7.1, and from these it can be seen that family involvement in the Broadmoor discharge process was considered to be important. Additionally, the table also highlights the fact that the majority of women remained in an asylum, although not necessarily Broadmoor, until their deaths.[40] Twenty-one women, however, were initially discharged, returned to Broadmoor and died there; this point is addressed in greater detail later in the chapter.[41]

The discharge process at Broadmoor changed after its opening in 1863 from a system similar to that of Bethlem and Fisherton House, to one which became more stringent and controlled. One of the first female patients to be discharged was Mary Ann Harris, who had been admitted to Fisherton House in August 1862 for the attempted murder of her child. She was transferred to Broadmoor in June 1863, along with forty-nine other women who were to help fill the first

Table 7.1 'Discharges, Removals & Deaths': admissions between 1863 and 1900.[42]

Discharges from Broadmoor					
To the care of:	Single	Married/ Widow	Total	%age of total	%age of discharges
Husband		44	50		34
Siblings	7	13	20		14
Parents	6	14	20		12
Children (adult)	1	9	10		8
Other Relatives	1	5	6		4
Total to Family care	12	84	96		72
Other Asylums	15	24	30		23
Employers	5	2	7		5
Discharges – total	28	106	134	55	100
Died in Asylum (exc. readmissions)	14	93	107	45	
Total: 'Discharges Removals & Deaths'	42	199	242	100	

hundred places in the new criminal lunatic asylum.[43] In January 1864, George Harris, Mary Ann's husband, enquired of the Home Secretary whether his wife might be considered well enough for release.[44] After enquiries into the facts about Mary Ann's case and into the state of her mind, Harris was advised that 'Sir George Grey has felt warranted in authorizing the Superintendent of Broadmoor ... to grant her leave of absence upon trial.'[45] As previously noted, Mary Ann Harris duly left Broadmoor with a parole warrant and an allowance of ten shillings a week, which lasted until her full discharge was granted in September 1864.[46] Only four women of the group, including Mary Ann Harris, were released before 1867. All four discharges were treated in the same manner; the women returned to their homes and families with an allowance and an unconditional discharge.[47] The early Broadmoor release criteria were a hybrid of prison and asylum procedures, followed by the Home Office to sanction releases from county prisons and asylums.

After 1867, when the provisions of the Criminal Lunatics Act added formal conditions to the warrants of discharge, the release processes began to change. In the early years of Broadmoor's history, the authorities at the Home Office appear to have regarded the Broadmoor's population as prisoners first and as patients second. Whitehall letters would refer to the patients as prisoners and the wording of the warrants would suggest that their incarceration was custodial rather than medical. Although the Home Office required a medical certificate from the asylum doctors regarding the patient's state of mind, there is no mention within the release document of this fact. As an example, the wording on the warrant for Ann Lacey states, 'Ann Lacey accepts her discharge out of Custody on the condition that she return into the same or other Custody whenever required to do so by an Order in writing under the hand of one of her Majesty's Principal Secretaries of State.'[48] The warrant was signed by Lacey on 21 September 1868, the day of her release. The officials were not unaware of the risks attached to releasing the seemingly recovered patients and even in the early days of Broadmoor, advice was given to husbands about treatment of their wives on release.

Orange became Medical Superintendent in 1870 and, during his tenure, medical opinion became more significant and official requirements grew. Orange always believed in the importance of the curative nature of Broadmoor and when he was Deputy Superintendent the lack of medical input in his duties frustrated him.[49] In 1868 Dr Meyer, the then Medical Superintendent, recorded in his official journal that Orange had protested, 'I am not doing my duty

I am not doctoring the patients.'[50] Details of a patient's physical and mental health were considered necessary to discharge discussions and, increasingly, so were examinations of her family background and potential future living circumstances.[51] Also, from this time there evidence suggests that there were changes in what was expected of the patients themselves. As shown in early conditional discharges, the discharged woman signed that she personally accepted the conditions of her discharge from the asylum, thereby having some say in her future life. This began to change from the early 1870s and eventually such confirmations disappeared from discharge documents. The warrant issued for the discharge of Sarah Allen in August 1872 was similarly worded to that of Ann Lacey and it bore Allen's signature. There is, however, a further clause attached to the document which reads, 'We most readily enter into agreement jointly and severally to take all proper care of Sarah Allen and ... should there be any tendency to relapse or should she leave without consent ... we will write to you [Secretary of State for the Home Department].'[52] This was signed by her brother-in-law and proposed guardian on behalf of himself and his wife, Ann.

The role of the superintendent in the discharge procedure was not formalized until 1884 and the implementation of the Criminal Lunatics Act. The Act stipulated that 'it shall be the duty of the superintendent ... to take all reasonable means for his [the criminal lunatic] being placed under the care of some relation or friend'.[53] This did not mean, however, that the superintendent had gained any more autonomy in deciding who should be discharged. The Home Secretary and the Home Office remained as the ultimate decision-makers, informed by the annual reports about patients from the asylum and by the research undertaken to ensure a safe future for patients, as stipulated in the Act. As time went on, conditions placed on the guardian became even more regulatory and protective. They tended to be aimed at keeping the discharged woman from relapse into insanity by placing restrictions on her living arrangements and movements. Conditional discharges increasingly meant that former patients were supposed to spend every night at the address to which they had been discharged. Guardians were obliged to get permission for ex-patients to spend even one night away from that address, a condition which was not always fulfilled.[54] The discharged patient, consequently, lost some control over decisions about her life; in effect, she would be treated as she had been in the asylum, more like a child than an adult.

The role of family

The women's crime and subsequent incarceration, had a social impact on the families and friends of the homicidal mothers, with long-term confinement potentially profoundly impacting family dynamics.[55] In many cases, although not understanding the reasons behind the women's criminal acts, relatives would support their errant family members.[56] In his study of county asylum releases, David Wright demonstrates that patient discharge was not dependent solely on medical evaluation, nor was it age or gender specific. That being said as with county asylums, more women were discharged from Broadmoor than men. Jade Shepherd found in her study of men in Broadmoor between 1863 and 1900, 23 per cent of all women patients and just 7 per cent of men were discharged.[57] This is, in part, explained by cultural perceptions of gender roles within family and kin groups. In his Annual Report for 1885 Orange wrote that it was easier to find care for female discharges than it was for men. In his opinion, relatives and friends were more willing to offer a home and more able to supervise women ex-patients than they were men. Orange wrote that the conditions and the circumstances of discharge were set in order 'to render it reasonably probable that they [the discharged] will not prove a danger to the community'. He continued, 'it is more difficult to ensure these conditions in the case of men than in the case of women'.[58]

Despite the women having committed a violent crime, it was considered that they would be 'easier' to manage by their new guardians, because, culturally, they were thought to be more naturally passive. In the same report, Orange also attributed the higher proportion of female discharges to biological reasons, writing, 'A considerable number of the women have been sent to this asylum in consequence of having killed their children ... the mere lapse of time removes ... the risk of repetition of this offence.'[59] There was not an official policy of retaining mothers who had murdered their children beyond their child-bearing years but, unofficially, such reasoning does appear to have been a factor in delaying discharges.[60] In some cases women remained in Broadmoor into their forties and fifties towards the onset of the menopause. Retention in Broadmoor until this point in a woman's biological cycle would be an effective quarantine policy against pregnancy as it would forestall a recurrence of puerperal insanity. Such a policy, however, would mean a long and potentially unnecessary stay in the asylum, a situation which was recognized by the medical authorities. The dilemma was highlighted in the file of Hannah Ryan who had been admitted in 1871 suffering from puerperal insanity. Orange wrote in 1873 'considering her age, the years of her detention before the time of her naturally not being subjected to the chances of relapse would necessitate a term of separation which appears ... cruelly long'.[61] She was then thirty-five years of age.

The desire and the ability of a patient's family and friends to take them back into the domestic sphere was an important consideration in the process.[62] In the first half of the period, up to the late 1860s, the concern for the patient's future welfare centred more upon financial abilities of the family to care for the dischargee than their social and domestic circumstances. In the case of Sarah Jackson described at the beginning of the chapter, her friends and family were, initially, quoted as not being 'willing to take charge of her', although the guardians of the parish union at Enfield agreed to maintain her but in the local workhouse. Eventually, after discussions with the Home Office, Jackson's sister agreed to take responsibility for her. The Home Office duly sent a discharge warrant to the governors of Bethlem, advising them that 'Sec. [sic] Sir George Lewis ... received from the prisoner's sister ... assurance that if released she will be properly taken care of by her friends'.[63] Sarah Jackson was released from Bethlem to the care of her sister and remained living in Enfield until her death in 1889.[64] Jackson's husband had been a gunsmith at the Royal Small Arms Factory in Enfield, as were her sons and other family members. In the thirty years after she left Bethlem, Jackson lived with various different members of her extended family, including her surviving children. All belonged to the community of workers at the Royal Enfield factory and all lived in the same road, a demonstration of an extended family caring for one of its members.[65]

At Broadmoor, there seemed to be some confusion amongst relatives about how to approach the question of release with the authorities. Discharge procedures were not routinely explained to interested parties and appear to have been given on a 'need to know' basis. In county lunatic asylums, families could make a direct request to the superintendent for the release of a relative.[66] Although, like their counterparts in the state criminal facilities, county asylum medical superintendents had little say in who was admitted to the asylum, they had more influence over who was discharged, the ultimate discharge decisions lay in their hands.[67] Perhaps, because they regarded the medical superintendent at Broadmoor as all-powerful in such matters, there were cases of relatives appealing directly to him, thereby following the 'normal' route for discharge. These demands and requests were invariably answered by the medical officers with a reminder to the relatives that the decision was not theirs to make and that Whitehall must be petitioned. Despite this, many families persisted in their direct hounding of the medical superintendent, using different strategies. The family of Mary Bennett frequently requested that she be released and that they would come and collect her when the Medical Superintendent of Broadmoor gave them a time.[68] Orange reminded them on each occasion that only the Home Office could sanction her release. There is a sense of exasperation in Orange's reply that 'it is only right that I tell you ... to save you needless trouble ... the question of liberation of persons from this asylum ... rests solely with the Secretary of State for the Home Dept'.[69]

Issues of social status and respectability, as well as the perceived capability of family and friends to adequately support and care for a discharged patient, played a part in the discharge decisions.[70] These, of course, were not impartial criteria, being highly prone to cultural biases. In their observations of the domestic circumstances of the patients, both the asylum medical officers and Home Office officials seem to adhere to the contemporary, arguably middle-class, cultural ideals.[71] A fundamental view in Victorian society was that a woman's place was in the home caring for her family and spouse. Sometimes medical men were critical of relatives, not necessarily understanding their ways of life, and viewed family interventions as damaging to the patient's welfare. For Ann Amess, 'the character of her domestic relations' did not 'warrant a favourable consideration' for release.[72] Her family requested her discharge on four separate occasions between 1881 and 1886; each time Orange recommended that the petition be refused. Amess's family were described as 'thoroughly disreputable' and their circumstances as 'woeful'.[73] Amess was never discharged; she died in 1899 and was buried in the Broadmoor Burial Ground.[74]

For some, insanity was viewed as a shameful stain on a family's reputation and the stigma, or shame, of a family member being in an asylum was hard for many families to bear.[75] Agnes Morris's family and friends distanced themselves from her after she was admitted to Broadmoor in 1877. Having the funds for a comfortable life, she convinced herself that she would be better in a private asylum, nearer her home in Liverpool.[76] This move was vigorously opposed by her family and friends, ostensibly to protect her other children. It was noted in her case file that 'her own family [do not] make any move about her release'.[77] The guardian of her surviving children requested that her communications to them be monitored, as the children had been greatly disturbed by her letters.[78] This aspect of families distancing themselves from the asylum is relevant when considering the reasons for nearly half of the women of the group remaining in the asylum until their deaths. Later in this chapter, the interactions between the families and friends of the mothers and the asylum authorities in the cases of these long-term patients are considered in more detail.

Joseph Melling and Bill Forsythe suggest that 'intense anxiety' existed amongst the friends and family of pauper patients regarding their treatment in asylums.[79] However, Cara Dobbing in her more recent work on families and inmates of Garlands Asylum, Carlisle, finds that not all members of the public feared the asylum, once they had come into contact with it.[80] Jade Shepherd finds, much as has been suggested in this book, that much of the correspondence from family and kin suggests that Broadmoor was seen as a place of recuperation and recovery.[81] The asylum was regarded as somewhere for their wife, daughter or mother to regain her sanity and, consequently, lead to her release. She would then be able to resume her place in the heart of the family. The daughter of Eliza Kirby wrote to Orange:

> [M]y Father and self will yield to every wish of yours as regards the care of my mother ... After this long time, we miss her more and more each day. I am often overcome with emotion to know that I have one [a mother] with much love in her heart towards us ... I assure you that nothing shall be left unturned for her happiness and comfort.[82]

Alongside the moral and social conditions of the families, the educational levels of the proposed guardians and their ability to understand the needs of the women on their release featured amongst the important considerations for the authorities. Despite the best of intentions from the family and friends, sometimes their intellectual abilities and economic circumstances were viewed as a potential risk to the woman's future welfare. Jonathan Andrews attributes this to a lack of understanding of the nuances and mores of working-class society by the, mainly, middle-class officials and doctors.[83] When the women were admitted to the asylums, their levels of literacy were recorded and played a part in the assessment of suitability for discharge.[84] Similarly, the literacy level and intelligence of their husbands and extended families appeared to be of significance in the authorities' decisions about the relatives' capabilities as potential guardians.[85]

The case of Emma Luke is an illustration of the judgmental attitude of officials both at the Home Office and Broadmoor.[86] Applications for Emma Luke's release began within a few months of her admission but met with little success.[87] Thomas Luke, her husband, was a nail caster and they lived in a poor area of Aston, Birmingham.[88] Despite the humble state of their home life, the couple were regarded as respectable people in the local community, and Emma was described as having 'a character amongst her neighbours for industry and respectability'.[89]

Thomas Luke was described as a 'hardworking respectable man' but it was noted that he was rather short of employment at the time of the murder.[90] Dr John Isaacs, Assistant Medical Officer at Broadmoor, doubted Luke's ability to protect Emma and guard against potential relapse. In 1876, he wrote disparagingly that 'her husband does not ... possess the necessary degree of intelligence which would enable him to have his wife properly taken care of'. The report also said that Luke did 'not appear to be in sufficiently good circumstances ... to prevent the future possibility of violence on her part to herself or to others'.[91]

Emma was discharged in 1878 into the care of friends, not Thomas, although she did return to her husband sometime before 1881.[92] They had five more children after her release, with no apparent need for Emma to return to an asylum following the births.[93] The Luke household was regarded as respectable by their local community and Emma was described as a fond mother and good housewife, both important social virtues. While the officials at Broadmoor and the Home Office may have had doubts about the Luke's, their friends and neighbours did not. The support of their peers helped in securing a quick release. As noted in the Introduction and as has been shown by other scholars, this case acts as an illustration of the sociocultural the role of kin and community in the poorer sections of Victorian society.[94]

There are signs that the patient's opinion could be taken into account when discharge was discussed. It was noted in Eliza Kirby's file that she refused to write to her husband and that 'she herself says, in her insane way, she will not go to her husband'.[95] Elizabeth Williams was admitted from Bethlem in 1863. In 1858, she drowned her two children and attempted suicide in the sea at Clevedon, Somerset. She was described as a very respectable and loving mother but had been subject to manic episodes, when there 'was almost a wildness in her love for her husband and children'.[96] Dated from 1871 to about 1880, there is a series of letters between Elizabeth's sister-in-law, Alice, and the asylum, which caused Dr Orange to say, 'I should be glad to know whether there is any property associated with this application.'[97] He may have had suspicions about Alice's motives, despite her writing that Elizabeth 'has been cruelly wronged'. In 1881, Orange wrote about Elizabeth that 'She herself ... states that she would prefer staying in the Asylum to accepting the offer ... made by her sister-in-law'.[98]

Expectations of spouses

It is discernible that all through the sixty-five years, the authorities expected that the husbands of the homicidal mothers would be active in seeking their wives' discharge. They were expected to take responsibility for the patient's mental and physical welfare after her discharge. On release, there was often a proviso that the men should guard against creating a situation where there was a possibility of relapse, which, in the case of many, was another pregnancy. Dr Hood agreed to the release of Emma Sanderson from Bethlem in order that she could join her husband in Tennessee but he took 'care ... to mention the circumstance of the liability of a return of mania were she again in the same condition [pregnancy]'.[99] Hood also believed that Thomas Sanderson had made a great effort to provide a safe and secure future for his wife and family. He had emigrated to the United States and set up a business: 'I have emigrated to this State ... with a view of making a home for my Wife where her misfortune is unknown.'[100]

The Medical Superintendents of Broadmoor would also request compliance from the spouses for patients they discharged. An 1867 letter from the Home Office about Ann Wilson sent to a petitioner for her release advised that the Home Secretary, Gathorne Hardy, agreed to Wilson's conditional discharge.[101] The letter continued, 'her husband [is] to be informed that ... it is the opinion of the Medical Officers that when insanity has occurred at the time of childbirth ... as in the present case, there must always be a risk of a recurrence of the insanity at the birth of subsequent children.'[102] Annie Howell was described as being 'not at all unlikely to relapse into insanity more especially in the event of her becoming pregnant'. It was advised that her husband, Captain James Howell, 'should be clearly informed of the risk of the occurrence of a relapse into insanity and that suitable provision should be made for taking necessary steps to avert danger.'[103] John Ashley wrote, 'it is our desire that she [his wife Louisa] be restored to us ... there is little probability of her having more children, she would be free from those cares which were the cause of her mind giving way'.[104]

The medical men's preference that the husbands should be involved and remain in touch with their wives did not mean that there was a lack of awareness of the threat of domestic violence in the homes of some of their patients.[105] As described in Chapter 6, the asylum medical staff recognized that domestic disharmony and violence could have devastating effects on a woman's mental state.[106] When Sarah Beagley was admitted to Broadmoor in 1882 after strangling her child, her attack of insanity was attributed to 'Lactation and domestic trouble'.[107] In her case file, a draft medical report for the Home Office noted that '[her] husband was unfaithful ... acknowledged being with other women'.[108] She appears to have 'lived very unhappily with her husband ... was a wife and mother at 14, [in Canada] 1st husband dead, married to 2nd husband

13 years ... has always suffered from headaches; both husbands have struck her about the head'.[109] This was a possible acknowledgement by the medical staff that her treatment by her spouses and her domestic circumstances, lay at the root of her mental illness. In 1890, Sarah Beagley's husband applied for her release but his request was refused. Dr Nicolson had received a letter from her son that accused his father of drinking to excess and of being the cause of all the family problems.[110] Eventually, in 1895, Sarah was released to the care of another of her sons, who was accepted as a worthy guardian as he was 'respectably employed as a bricklayer' and 'always a teetotaller'.[111]

When a mother was missing from a home, her key cultural roles in the domestic sphere of everyday management and childcare caused problems within a household. Sometimes family needs seemed to override potential domestic problems for a discharged patient and pragmatic motivation played a part in release decisions.[112] Rebecca Loveridge's case, as told in Chapter 5, is a demonstration of some of the inconsistencies which could occur in discharge decisions. After her return to the family home in Kingsteignton, Devon, in November 1885, all seemed to be well.[113] She did not have any more children and she remained with George Loveridge, with no recorded instances of relapse, until her death in 1922.[114] This was an occasion where the asylum authorities appeared prepared to take a risk, believing that the need for the mother to return to run the home and family should be prioritized over the discharged patient's welfare. The asylum doctors would seem to have taken a risky decision but decided it was a choice worth taking. It also highlights a belief that the safest place for a mother was in her own home, in the care of her kith and kin, whatever the previous circumstance.[115]

That being said, discharge decisions and release would not be agreed for the vulnerable women, irrespective of the domestic situation and, as far as possible, assurances were sought to protect them. Blame was often laid on husbands for their wives' mental deterioration through not fulfilling their expected masculine role of faithful provider and carer.[116] Elizabeth Hillier was admitted to Broadmoor in 1875 and by 1877 she was described as sane and as having shown no sign of relapse. It was noted that her husband had regularly visited her for two years but then had ceased his visits. It was reported that he had 'found connexion with another woman by whom ... he has now two children'.[117] The doctors at Broadmoor believed that Elizabeth should be allowed to leave to the care of her brother as she was well and would be able to contribute to her own maintenance. Orange wrote that his concern was that her mind would not be 'strong enough to bear up against troubles consequent upon her husband's misconduct' and, therefore, he requested that the Home Office 'take steps for effecting some settlement with respect to her marital position'.[118]

Despite the authorities' preference that a released mother should return to her marital home and the care of her husband, some spouses decided that they could not be responsible for a mentally fragile wife. Charles Oldman was an attentive husband, regularly visiting and writing to his wife Ellen after her admission into Broadmoor in 1878. Although initially he seemed willing to take responsibility for her on discharge, in 1882 when the final decision came to be made, he admitted that he felt unable to cope with her care.[119] Ellen Oldman's stepfather had written to Orange in April 1880 offering to look after his wife's daughter, an offer which was accepted after the Asylum received Charles Oldman's refusal.[120] William Allen, husband of Bethlem transferee Sarah Allen, steadfastly refused to write to or visit her after her transfer to Broadmoor in 1863.[121] Dr Meyer wrote to him, 'it appears that it is 8 years since you last saw her and you might find that during that long period a considerable improvement … in her mental condition'.[122] He rejected all attempts to make him communicate with her and, despite pressure from the Broadmoor authorities, would not consider taking her home.[123] When eventually her release was agreed, he still did not want anything to do with her. Orange wrote to inform him that she would be discharged to the care of her sister and he replied, 'I sincerely hope that the arrangements … add to her [Sarah's] comfort and still more to the friends whose … feeling has urged them to take upon themselves so serious a responsibility'.[124]

Patronage and references

In many cases of discharge throughout the Victorian period, the intervention and patronage of third-party agencies added weight to any discharge applications for patients. After the trial of Agnes Bradley in 1859 for the murder of her baby son, the direct intervention of the trial judge led to her unconditional discharge as a criminal lunatic and release from Rainhill.[125] Bradley was acquitted as insane for the murder of her son on 25 March 1859, Lord Justice Willes wrote to the Home Secretary on 27 March and he received an almost immediate reply. A letter dated 8 April from the permanent undersecretary at the Home Office, Horatio Waddington, confirmed 'that under all circumstances Mr Estcourt has felt warranted in advising her Majesty to authorize this woman's release from further confinement'.[126] Bradley was duly released to the care of her husband. It was obviously felt it would serve no further purpose to retain her in the asylum, as to all intents and purposes she appeared cured. The more knowledgeable middle-classes would use their social connections to enlist the help of well-known political figures to assist in their petitioning for their relatives' release. Their social background was recognizable to the officials at the Home Office and would aid their cause. For instance, in 1852, Thomas Sanderson, a well-known bookseller in the City of London, petitioned Lord Palmerston about the possible release of his wife, Emma, from Bethlem. Palmerston personally took the case to Privy Council and put forward Sanderson's plea.[127]

These pathways were also available to ordinary working-class families. They sought help from their local MPs, magistrates, church ministers and other local dignitaries, which interventions often spurred the Home Office into action. In 1893, a sub-headline in *Coventry Evening Telegraph* announced (in capital letters) that, in 'IN THE CASE OF MRS. ONIONS' Mr. W.H. Ballantine, M.P., was 'TRYING TO SECURE HER RELEASE'.[128] Emma Onions had been accused of manslaughter and attempted suicide in 1891. Despite appearances at the inquest into her daughter's death and at the magistrate's court, her case had not proceeded to the assize court for trial by jury. Her disturbed state of mind and the cause of her suicidal and homicidal actions had been attributed to 'puerperal melancholia'.[129] On the advice of the medical officer at Warwick Gaol, supported by the medical superintendent of Hatton Asylum, Emma Onions had been admitted to Broadmoor on the warrant of the Home Secretary.[130] Her case was something of a cause celebre and her plight stirred up feelings of compassion amongst the population. The *Evening Telegraph* stated that the local MP for Coventry, William Ballantine, had 'been in communication with the Home Secretary with the view of securing the woman's release'.[131] His intervention was unsuccessful but he still believed it necessary to have the Home Office's reply publicly printed. Whether this was a political move to show he was a caring MP or a genuine philanthropic gesture to use his position for his constituents is a moot point. Nonetheless, it is a demonstration that two years after the crime, the case of Emma Onions was in public memory and that there was a wish to restore her to her home. She was conditionally discharged to the care of her husband in 1902, readmitted in 1903, discharged and readmitted in 1914 before being finally released in 1920, always into the care of her husband, Joseph.[132] She died in 1927 in her hometown of Coventry.[133]

The campaign for Sarah Bates's release was backed by local community leaders and her husband's employer. A local Wesleyan minister wrote of James Bates that 'the man has conducted himself so as to gain true esteem … his life is free from reproach and the children always appearing clean and neat and comfortable'.[134] Bates's employer wrote 'I have always found him to be a very industrious & honest man' adding that 'they always lived very happily together' and that the 'home was a very comfortable one'.[135] In 1886, when writing to the Home Office in support of Sarah's release, Orange advised that 'her husband and father are ... in a position to give her a good home and their respectability is testified by the Mayor of Northampton'.[136] Favourable third-party confirmation of a family's capacity to be responsible for the wife and of the quality of the circumstances of family and home was considered desirable by all officials.

On occasion, references could go against the family. In 1886, Mary Coleman's proposed discharge to the care of her son was aborted after a local doctor, Dr Henry Ormerod, wrote to the Medical Superintendent. He advised that the son was illiterate and although working, the family circumstances were poor and Ormerod questioned whether it was realistic to expect the son to be able to look after his mother.[137] Despite the favourable medical report from the asylum medical staff, Ormerod's letter sounded a note of caution and Mary Coleman was not discharged. She died in 1902, still in Broadmoor.[138]

As well as third parties being involved, former employers would also take an interest in the potential discharge and future of the patients. Between 1875 and 1883, Sarah Fletcher's former mistress, Mrs Annie Litton, a rector's wife and Fletcher's husband's employer, R. Coxwell Rogers, unsuccessfully sought to help in obtaining her release.[139] The exchange of correspondence between Orange and the two separate employers is an illustration of a contemporary assumption of the correspondents that they had a lasting moral duty to look after their staff. Despite their assurance that her husband was 'willing and anxious to take the poor woman home', Orange did not recommend her release.[140]

In 1871 Hannah Ryan was admitted to Broadmoor for the murder of her daughter Lizzie. At the time of the murder, Hannah's husband Isaac was coachman to a Mrs Brocklehurst of Butley Hall in Prestbury, Cheshire.[141] Mrs Brocklehurst was the wife of William Brocklehurst who served as MP for Macclesfield between 1868 and 1880. In 1872 Mrs Brocklehurst wrote to Orange enquiring how she should proceed in helping to get Hannah discharged and he advised petitioning the Home Secretary. Hannah was discharged in August 1875, ostensibly to her husband's care but Mrs Brocklehurst did take her into her personal service. It was Mrs Brocklehurst who gave the asylum the assurance that she would take care to protect Hannah from any potential relapse into insanity.[142] Similarly, Elizabeth White was supported on her discharge by her husband's employers, Mr George Dunn and his mother, Mrs Dunn, of Wooley Hall, White Waltham, Berkshire.[143] In 1893 it was noted although 'she was progressing very satisfactorily' and that she had 'good bodily health [but] it is too soon to discharge at present'.[144] Her eventual release in September 1894 came about because her husband was considered to be 'a very respectable man' and his employers, the Dunn's, 'promise[d] to look after her welfare'.[145] Such social interventions highlight cultural interactions in Victorian society. The cases quoted here are examples which support Susie Steinbach's suggestion that there were those in the middle and upper classes who believed that they had a moral duty and social responsibility to look after the welfare of their staff and their families.[146] That is not to say that were not many employers who had no sense of responsibility towards their former employees and would abandon their mentally-ill staff. Notwithstanding this, the quoted cases illustrate that the opinions of employers could be significant to the lives of the patients.

Trustworthy third-party opinion mattered throughout the Victorian period. Employers, local dignitaries as well as national figures of authority could influence the futures of patients in the criminal lunatic facilities. The referees were usually from a similar social and professional background to the officials at both the Home Office and the institutions. The appraisals by doctors and officials into the dependability and the respectability of the patients' families, friends and their general social circle were often contingent on the opinions of local officials and both the patients and their spouses' employers. As such people were of similar backgrounds to the medical men and officials, their judgements of the domestic situations of the families were accepted as reliable and believable assessments. Their advice would be very influential on the decision to discharge or retain the women.[147]

Philanthropy and charitable intent

Although charitable intent and patronage usually came through the efforts of the patients' families, their local people of influence and communities, there were those who did not have family willing or able to help assimilate them back into society. As previously mentioned, Dr Corbin Finch actively helped and supported dischargees from Fisherton House, helping them to find permanent positions in service once released. Reverend John Burt, chaplain of Broadmoor, would help through his connections with the Discharged Prisoners' Aid Society. There were a number of small Discharged Prisoners' Aid Societies set up in England in the mid-century. Before being appointed to Broadmoor, Burt had been the prison chaplain at Birmingham Borough Gaol. In a published sermon delivered to the local DPAS, he advocated the establishment of such societies as 'a duty binding on us as Christians'.[148] There was an agreement that a local DPAS could apply to the Chaplain at Broadmoor hospital for a grant of 40/- to aid released inmates, or as then styled 'prisoners', in need. Lucy Thompson was originally discharged to live with her brother in Birmingham but due to violent family disagreements she moved out. The local DPAS wrote, on Lucy's behalf, to Reverend Burt at Broadmoor asking for financial help, which was provided by the Society through his offices.[149]

Towards the end of the century, the Broadmoor discharge registers show outside charitable patronage or philanthropic agencies were becoming involved with the futures of Broadmoor patients. Graham Mooney notes that there was a perception in the nineteenth century that the 'better-off' classes had a responsibility for both the moral and physical welfare of the poorer sections of society.[150] The reactions and scrutiny of the authorities in the later years of the period reflect increasing social intervention fuelled by middle-class philanthropic ideals. While such interactions appear to reflect good intentions, there is an element of control and moral reformation behind such philanthropic interventions. There is evidence in Broadmoor's records that this type of philanthropic involvement was present even in a criminal lunatic facility. In 1894, Emily Wilson was discharged into the care of Miss Henrietta Smith of Reading, to be trained in service, and in 1898 Elizabeth Keating was discharged to the care of Mrs Lewis, a police court missionary in Hulme in Manchester.[151]

During this time, the Salvation Army, as well as the Anglican Sisters of Mercy, started to play a small part in rehabilitation by attempting to retrain selected patients to what they considered socially and morally acceptable roles in life.[152] Much Victorian philanthropy and typically the women's refuges offered moral and religious guidance underpinned by stereotypical female work and domestic chores as a way to rehabilitation. Helen Johnstone and Jo Turner suggest that the aim for women released from penal institutions was to 'rescue' women from a life of perceived depravity and fit them for a subjugated place in society.[153] A single or widowed woman who had attempted suicide or a single mother who had murdered her child was not morally depraved, but was mentally ill and Broadmoor patients were, as often said, not of the criminal class. Yet from the Salvation Army's own records, it is stated that the aims of their refuges did not differ to other charitable organizations in trying to reform and retrain women released from institutional care.[154] The Salvation Army would take likely candidates into one of their receiving homes or a rescue home for 'rehabilitation' and training, with the intention of helping them to find positions.[155] The Salvation

Army's purpose in establishing their rescue homes was to remove women from their previous lives which the Army perceived as ungodly. Although the inmates would be taught skills to help them find work after leaving the home, the main concern was to spiritually save the women. 'Spiritual improvement was seen as paramount, with an emphasis on the women gaining salvation.'[156]

The intentions of the two organizations were not necessarily charitable nor religious nor altruistic as both communities expected to receive remuneration from the Home Office covering the keep of their discharges. They viewed themselves as standing *in loco* for the asylum in caring for and supporting the women they took for retraining and in their efforts in finding them a life after Broadmoor. There were the sixty-five admissions between 1890 and 1900, of which seven women left Broadmoor in the care of the two agencies. Of that seven, four returned to Broadmoor as 'unsuitable' for assistance. What is noticeable is that the women discharged to the two organizations were, in the main, widowed or single. The Broadmoor authorities appear to have taken the view that young unmarried mothers or young women who had tried to commit suicide needed the guidance of outside people and organizations. This was particularly apparent if they did not appear to have any family or extended family willing to take on responsibility for their futures. Both Emily Wilson and Elizabeth Keating mentioned earlier were single and alone. Similarly, widowed patients without family or kin would find a place with the Salvation Army or the Sisters of Mercy.

Following the Oxford Movement spiritual revival in the Church of England, a number of Anglican religious communities were founded, the first such orders since the Dissolution. Popularly known collectively as Sisters of Mercy, the communities were in fact separate foundations within the Anglican Church. The Sisters ran orphanages, schools, convalescent hospitals, homes for 'fallen women and girls' and a church needlework business. The three sisterhoods which featured in the Broadmoor discharge register in the 1890s were the Community of St John Baptist at Clewer, near Windsor, the Community of St Mary the Virgin at Wantage and the Sisterhood of St Peter at Horbury, near Wakefield. As mentioned in the case of Elizabeth Harris, the Sisters at Clewer near Windsor had an existing relationship with Broadmoor, due perhaps to its geographical proximity.[157] Elizabeth Stapleton, whose story opened Chapter 2, was admitted to Broadmoor in 1898. At her trial, the judge, Sir Quaile Jones was reported as saying that she needed a suitable home, not Broadmoor. In September 1900, Elizabeth was discharged to St Helena's Home at Drayton Green, West Ealing. St Helena's Home was managed by Sisters from the Anglican Community of St Mary the Virgin, Wantage. The home was founded to house and reform 'unfallen' female prisoners, after their discharge from Millbank and other prisons. A payment of £5 was expected; or for unconvicted cases sent privately, 5s. per week. By 1897, the Home had about fifty girls, aged from 15 to 30, they were expected to remain for one year. The residents were occupied mostly in needlework and laundry work. Elizabeth Stapleton was returned to Broadmoor in 1903 and subsequently re-released in 1914.[158]

The Salvation Army would take the women into their hostels or homes, give them employment and a protected environment in which to live. The Booth family would stand as guardian under the terms of the conditional release.[159] The initial requests or enquiries about the possibility of conditional discharge to their care seem to have come from various sources. In 1896 Mrs Constance Booth wrote to Dr Brayn enquiring whether a petition from the Salvation Army would facilitate Sarah Fletcher's discharge to their care. The exchange of letters appears to have been triggered by Sarah herself. The request was refused; it was felt that Sarah had never totally recovered and would easily relapse once again into insanity.[160] Sarah remained in Broadmoor until her death two years later. The discharge of Eva Lonnon was relatively more successful. Eva Lonnon was conditionally discharged from Broadmoor in 1895 to the care of a Mrs F. H. Lawrence and the Salvation Army.[161] It was, however, not all plain sailing. Initial attempts by the Army to retrain or save Eva appeared to have failed. Later in 1895, she was returned to Broadmoor. She was discharged again, in 1900 to the care of Mrs Florence Bramwell Booth, this time with success. By the 1901 Census she is recorded as living in Penge, with members of the Salvation Army and her occupation is recorded as 'S.A. Servt [sic]', and her status as 'Inmate of S.A. Home'.[162] By 1911, she was a cook in the household of a retired Royal Naval Lieutenant Commander, in Fareham.[163]

Relapse and return

At the beginning of the sixty-five years under discussion, a release was not dependent on whether or not the family could safeguard the patient's mental state. The asylum authorities were expected to advise the Home Office whether the patient was sane and recovered from the insanity which had caused her crime. Family and friends were approached as carers for the dischargee's physical welfare, rather than as guardians of her mental state. This is demonstrated in an 1868 letter from the Home Office to Broadmoor about a potential release: 'I am directed to request that … [you] … will endeavour to ascertain whether the prisoner's [sic] family are in a position to take care of her and whether they are willing to do so in the event of her release.'[164] If family and friends did not provide a home, a discharged criminally insane woman would become the responsibility of her parish union and possibly go into a workhouse. The implication in Whitehall communications was that the officials at the Home Office were concerned that a discharged criminal lunatic patient should no longer be the responsibility of the state but would be sufficiently looked after by family or parish unions. The conditional clause in the discharge warrant only obligated the woman to return to custody on the Secretary of State's warranty if she should relapse into insanity or was considered to be unfit to be at large. Of the thirty-seven non-Broadmoor cases, only one returned to her original place of incarceration and it is not clear from the records whether her second stay was financed by the Home Office.

Mary Ann Payne was discharged on a conditional warrant from Fisherton House to her family home in Marylebone on 7 August 1867.[165] On the 11 October 1871, in accordance with the terms of her discharge warrant, she was readmitted to Fisherton suffering from 'religious fancies and ... she conceives she must destroy her friends and herself'. Her casebook notes suggest that, unlike her previous admission when her insanity had been attributed to her pregnancy, this time her mental state was related to drinking: 'this woman has some of the symptoms of delirium tremens'. Payne was given treatment and rest. By 1 November 1871 she was recorded as being quiet and industrious.[166] Other research shows that prior to her admission in 1871, Mary Ann had been living in London apart from her husband who was living in Wantage, Berkshire.[167] Nowhere in her notes is there an indication that she returned because of an official request; nor does it appear that the Home Office was aware of her readmittance. Therefore, unlike later cases in Broadmoor, there was no obligation for Payne to remain in Fisherton House while another official enquiry into her re-release was conducted. She was released from Fisherton House as recovered on 18 January 1872 and joined the rest of her family in Wantage, where she remained until her death.[168]

Most of those women discharged from Fisherton House or Bethlem were unconditionally released with a Royal Pardon; No record of any returning to either asylum as a criminal lunatic was found in their records. It is possible that some returned to non-criminal asylum care at some point in their lives, but an exploration of this is outside the scope of the present investigation. In later years and particularly with Broadmoor patients, great care was exercised in trying to ensure that the future situation of discharged homicidal mothers would be appropriate; all officials involved in assessing suitability for discharge were conscious of the risk of relapse.[169] In a letter written in 1885, Orange spelled out his personal thoughts about releasing patients. He wrote, '[I] enclose these few lines to say ... It is one of the most painful parts of [my] duty to have to listen to piteous appeals for discharge from the unfortunate inmates and at the same time to know that it would not be right to grant what is asked for.'[170] This was particularly relevant to those women who had been diagnosed as suffering from puerperal insanity and other manias related to childbearing.[171] As noted previously in this chapter with regard to husbands, prevention would become the responsibility of the guardians to whom the woman was released. One of the doctors' prime anxieties was the potential risk attached to any future pregnancy. Former patients were readmitted but, amongst the cases reviewed, none of the relapses were caused by childbearing.

Following the passing of the 1884 Criminal Lunatics Act, the pro-forma *Warrant of Conditional Discharge* specifically stated that 'if any of the conditions of discharge appear to be broken ... the Secretary of State may by warrant direct ... [the Criminal Lunatic] ... to be taken into custody and to be conveyed to some Asylum'.[172] The main condition of discharge was that the guardian should submit periodic reports to Broadmoor on the progress of the former patient, countersigned by a person of authority such as a local doctor or minister. In most cases the discharged patients and in later years their guardians, complied with any conditions laid down in their release documentation. Sarah Lancestell's son regularly submitted Annual Reports about his mother's welfare from her release in February 1886 until her death in January 1891.[173]

There were those who wished to distance themselves from the stigma of Broadmoor and deliberately moved away. In 1892 Charles Barrow wrote to Dr Nicolson requesting that the conditions of his wife's discharge be dropped as he felt 'it is not necessary for our new society to be aware of our circumstances'.[174] The request was formally declined but Barrow gave up furnishing the reports anyway. Without informing Broadmoor, he moved his family to Birmingham which action culminated in a police search. Eventually, their whereabouts and circumstances were reported to Broadmoor by the Chief Constable of Birmingham Police. He wrote explaining that 'Mr Barrow is in a terrible state of anxiety ... he appeared to think that Mrs Barrow should not be obliged to return to Broadmoor if she lost her reason again.'[175] From the lack of further papers in her case file, it would appear Barrow's explanation was satisfactory to the Asylum and Home Office authorities. Kate Barrow remained with her husband and family without any further reference to Broadmoor.[176]

Patients could be readmitted because their guardians felt they were no longer able to manage their charge. In 1885 Sarah Newman was discharged to the guardianship of her husband, Daniel but in 1900 he wrote to Broadmoor saying, 'I can no longer be answerable for my wife's safety or my own as I live in fear of my life ... her threats and behaviour are past all bounds, she cannot be restrained.'[177] Others were readmitted because the women themselves admitted to their guardians that they felt vulnerable and unable to cope with life outside the asylum. On 11 January 1897 Rebecca Bell was discharged from Broadmoor to the care of her sister in Farnham, with whom she lived 'well and happy' for three years.[178] In August 1900 her sister wrote to the matron at Broadmoor to say that Rebecca was suffering from depression, could not sleep at night and would not eat properly. She had also become very nervous of others and had 'asked me to send her back'; Rebecca Bell returned on 16 August.[179]

Caroline Gardiner was admitted into Broadmoor in 1887 and discharged to the care of her husband in December 1897.[180] He regularly sent the requisite reports to the authorities and she appeared to be in good spirits and health. In November 1905 the Medical Superintendent, Dr Brayn, received an unsigned letter from her home in Dover saying that Caroline 'should be sent for at once'. He wrote to the Chief Constable of Kent advising him that 'An anonymous note believed to be from Mrs Gardiner has been received at this Asylum' and requesting that 'quiet inquiry [be made] respecting the present mental state of Mrs Caroline Gardiner'.[181] A visit from a local doctor confirmed that Caroline was 'furtive & suspicious' and wandering in her mind but, he wrote, there was 'no evidence of suicidal or destructive tendency'.[182] Nevertheless, Caroline was returned to Broadmoor and her Warrant of Conditional Discharge was revoked on 5 November 1905.

Whatever the circumstances were surrounding readmission, a patient could be re-released if their physical and mental states were considered suitable. The domestic circumstances and capabilities of the 'new' guardians were once again reviewed and assessed to ensure a safe discharge. Not only were the discharged patients effectively policed and watched for the rest of their lives, so were the families and kin who had accepted responsibility for them.[183] Sarah Newman, whose story opened this chapter, was re-discharged to the care of her son with whom she lived until her death in 1905. Despite what was viewed as thorough investigation and assessment by the asylum authorities and government officials, unfortunately not every subsequent discharge was successful. Sarah Bates's release to her daughter in July 1904, only lasted six months and she returned in January 1905.[184] In fact, twenty-one of the 106 women discharged were readmitted and then remained in Broadmoor for the rest of their lives. Amongst these were Rebecca Bell, Sarah Bates and Caroline Gardiner who died in 1905, 1911 and 1918, respectively.[185]

Image 7.1 Dayroom for infirm female patients, c. 1910.[186]

Death in the asylum

There were many women for whom discharge and release were never considered. Alongside them were those whose families unsuccessfully campaigned for release and who died in Broadmoor.[187] The fragility of a patient's mind and her overall disposition was closely observed in the asylum as an indicator of insanity or, indeed, sanity. If a patient moved towards an improved 'cheerful' outlook and more amenable behaviour without delusions, it was taken as a sign that she was recovering from her mental illness. The one common factor for those women retained in the asylum, therefore, may be the lack of these traits. In 1871, on her admittance for her second stay in Fisherton House, Mary Ann Payne was described as 'very excited and agitated'. One month later she was 'more calm and somewhat stronger' and her final entry states that 'she is very considerably improved … being now quiet and industrious. Discharged.'[188] In contrast, Mary Bennett's medical reports in Broadmoor consistently say that she was not improved in mind and that she was 'petulant and troublesome'.[189] She was admitted in 1866. In 1875 Orange wrote that she 'was not improved in mind' and in 1880, she was described as 'irascible and very much depressed'.[190] Bennett was never released and died in 1884 of phthisis and meningitis.[191]

Some of the women who had been incarcerated between 1835 and 1863 in Bethlem or Fisherton House were transferred into Broadmoor and therefore either died there or were discharged. Table 7.2 shows the percentage of the women of the group admitted between 1835 and 1900 who died in incarceration, broken down by admission pattern. Although 47 per cent of the sample group died in the asylum, it is difficult to ascertain one common factor which determined their retention. Some of the women who had been incarcerated between 1835 and 1863 in Bethlem or Fisherton House were transferred into Broadmoor and therefore either died there or were discharged.

Table 7.3 is a breakdown of the causes of death for those who died in Broadmoor, including twenty-one women who were discharged and returned. The table has been compiled from the open case books, open personal case files and newspaper reports.

Table 7.2 Deaths in the asylums; admissions between 1835 and 1895.[192]

Admissions 1835 to 1895		Died	%
Non-Broadmoor	37	5	14
Transferred from Bethlem & Fisherton House to Broadmoor	31	21	68
Broadmoor only	220	109	50
Total	288	135	47

Table 7.3 Cause of death in incarceration, 1835 to 1895.

Cause of death in incarceration 1835 to 1895				
	Non-Broadmoor	Transferees	Broadmoor	Total
Apoplexy	1		2	3
Cancer		4	18	22
Cardiac		5	5	10
Cerebral disease	1	2	4	6
Chest disease	1		3	4
Chronic conditions			3	3
Consumption & phthisis	1		7	8
GPI (syphilis)		1	4	5
Kidney disease		3	4	7
Meningitis			2	2
Senile decay/ dementia		3	5	8
Suicide	1		1	2
Typhus	1			1
Ulceration of gut			2	2
Unknown (not available post-1919 deaths)		5	50	53
Totals	6	21	109	136

All deaths in Broadmoor were the subject of a county coroner's inquest and a number of these inquests were reported in the local Berkshire newspapers. What is apparent is that, amongst the women of my sample group, there were only two deaths from general paralysis of the insane (GPI or syphilis) and none from causes directly stemming from childbearing. As mentioned in Chapter 5, insanity had, in some cases, been caused by underlying medical conditions and that diseases such as tuberculosis, and cardiac and cerebral diseases. Hilary Marland has analysed the deaths of women who suffered from puerperal insanity. She highlights the association of the perceived trauma of childbirth and its aftermath with patients' fear of impending mortality and damnation, suicidal impulses and depression.[193]

There were two suicides amongst the group, the first was that of Anne Colley in Stafford Gaol mentioned in an earlier chapter and just one within an asylum, that of Sarah Bull in Broadmoor. As Sarah York indicates in her extensive work, even if asylum records described the patient as suicidal on entry into the asylum, suicides within asylums were rare.[194] Her research echoes and endorses that of Olive Anderson, Anne Shepherd and David Wright.[195] The reasons for this probably lay in the preventative methods used, which consisted of strict surveillance and on occasion, sedation. Dr Orange's report on Sarah Bull's case indicates that observation was not always enough and that some responsibility should lie with the patient.[196] In the four years of her incarceration prior to her death, her husband, George Bull, had made numerous enquiries about possible discharge and visited regularly. Despite being favourably viewed by the staff as coming from a respectable and educated home, George Bull was a Schools Board Inspector, the asylum medical men did not believe that Sarah Bull was in a fit mental state to be released. As a medical report in 1883 stated, 'she has been comparatively tranquil yet her mental health is by no means re-established ... her release ... would be attended with a considerable risk of relapse into a state of active insanity'.[197] The last refusal for release was one week before her suicide and would appear to have preyed on her mind, as demonstrated in the wording of her suicide note, 'I have felt dreadful strange for some days ... What good am I here? ... What anxiety for my husband. It is far better for him to be relieved of such a burden.'[198]

Orange's 1884 report on the case to the Commissioners in Lunacy gives a sense that he believed that the asylum was not at fault for missing the signs that Bull might harm herself. Her case demonstrates that the attendants and medical staff had also relied on patients articulating how they were actually feeling. Orange wrote:

> ... No change was observed in her condition until she was found ... at 6.30 am ... The fact that was stated by her that she 'felt dreadful strange' had been concealed by her and not observed otherwise it is unlikely to say that she would not have been removed to another ward and placed under suitable supervision ...[199]

At the inquest into her death, the attendant who had seen her at bedtime said that she had said good night 'in the usual way' and that there was no reason to visit her during the night because she had 'always seemed very cheerful'. Her husband's evidence supported that of the Broadmoor staff saying 'she appeared to be in her usual good health and spirits' when he had last seen her on the Tuesday before.[200] Where it might seem that Orange was justifying the non-action of the asylum staff in protecting a patient from self-harm, there is also a sense of disappointment and failure. The asylum existed to safeguard the patients from harm and they had failed to do so.

As mentioned earlier in the chapter, it has been suggested that the asylum medical men seem to favour keeping the women in the asylum until menopause as a preventative measure against future pregnancies.[201] There is evidence in the case files that to an extent this was a consideration, although the menopause itself was thought to hold an inherent risk to the female mind. As Orange wrote in Eliza Kirby's notes in 1877:

> ... She has not yet passed that period of life when with the ... cessation of the female functions of the generative organs there comes to those who are subjects of insanity of a chronic even comparatively mild description, a considerable liability to the accession of attacks of mania, more active and more acute ...[202]

It was felt that, in Kirby's case, her mind would never be settled enough to ensure a 'safe' discharge. Despite persistent and sustained attempts by her family for her discharge, her release was always resisted by the authorities. Eliza Kirby died of heart disease in February 1887, having spent twenty years in Broadmoor.[203]

It is difficult to ascertain from Bethlem and Fisherton House records what negotiations and contact took place with families when a patient died. The Broadmoor case files contain much correspondence and other papers which detail the interactions between the asylum and patients' kith and kin.

Therefore, the following observations about what happened after a death in the asylum, once again, rely on the Broadmoor archival records. Although the casebook notes are available for the other asylums, they contain medical commentary rather than information on interactions with the families or other authorities.

As with workhouse deaths, responsibility for funerals and burials lay with the asylums. Julie-Marie Strange writes that workhouse and pauper burials were popularly viewed as 'undignified interments'. That view does not appear to have been taken by the families of the Broadmoor patients.[204] In the case of Broadmoor, family members would gratefully accept the Asylum's authority at this time, writing letters of gratitude for the care their family member had received before and after death. The families were invited to attend the funeral and burial at Broadmoor but their presence was not considered essential. The burial of patients at Broadmoor was also a matter of practicality. The costs of transportation of a body and of a funeral would be beyond the economic capability of many of the patients' families. As the deceased remained a responsibility of the Crown all costs were borne by Broadmoor.[205] In all cases after the death, the asylum authorities afforded the deceased patient's dignity in death in accordance with their creed, whatever their social background.[206] On occasion the deceased's family claimed the body for private burial, which was readily accepted by the hospital authorities. In the case of Jewish patients, the Broadmoor authorities had a connection with the Burial Society of the United Synagogue in St James Place, Aldgate, who would collect the deceased for interment in the Jewish cemetery in east London.[207]

If the funeral and burial did take place at Broadmoor, it was considered respectable and acceptable, unlike pauper burials which Strange described as being viewed as an offence to the dignity of the dead and the bereaved.[208] This meant that, in most cases, the dead family member would then be interred away from their community, although it would appear that the whereabouts of the grave was of less importance than knowing that their family member had been 'decently' buried. The families and kin would remember the deceased mother in different contexts without necessarily visiting the cemetery or burial ground in question.[209] The asylum authorities were willing to allow families to visit and personalize the burial site if they so wished. In 1879, William Greenwood requested that he and his surviving children be allowed to visit the grave of his wife, Emma, in order to plant shrubs in her memory, which request was granted.[210]

Image 7.2 Site of old burial ground, Broadmoor Hospital, Crowthorne, March 2020.[211]

Conclusion

Family involvement and the integrity of a family and home were always a consideration in decisions made about releasing the mothers from the custody of an asylum. The existence of good social bonds and strong extended family units, such as those of Sarah Jackson (1859) and Sarah Newman (1885 and 1900), led to positive responses from the authorities to discharge requests. Family and friends were always examined to confirm that they were willing and able to provide a home for the discharged woman. The economic condition and to a lesser extent the respectability of a family was always significant to the Home Office officials. Prior to Broadmoor's opening, the importance of respectability to the discharge procedure was less evident. Records from Fisherton House and Bethlem indicate that the social status of a patient's family had an influence on release decisions. The opening of Broadmoor as an asylum dedicated to the treatment of criminal lunatics was a major contributor to the changes in discharge procedures and protocols between 1835 and 1900. In the thirty-seven years after Broadmoor opened, family domestic and economic social circumstances were increasingly subject to close examination, to ensure that the proposed care would safeguard vulnerable patients.

The majority of the mothers who had murdered their children were from a working-class background and social status played a part in the way the women and their home circumstances were perceived. Occasionally, the educational background of the family and husband was questioned and references from employers and other community figures were required, to confirm the family's suitability to be carers. Officials at the Home Office sought reassurances that the respectability and moral circumstances of families and friends were suitable to ensure a safe future for the discharged patient. The concepts of acceptable social behaviour differed between classes but respectability was always a shared point of reference. A strong element of middle-class culture was a belief in an obligation to look after the welfare of the 'less fortunate' members of society. This perceived paternalistic responsibility is demonstrated by interplay in the discharge procedure between the asylum medical men the personal referees for the guardians and the officials at the Home Office.

Although the medical officers at Broadmoor placed a value on the emotional bonds of a family, there could be an absence of comprehension about the domestic situations of poorer families. As with the discharge arrangements for ordinary lunatics, the authorities were concerned with the quality of the homes to which the discharged mothers would return.[212] Increasingly, particular emphasis was placed on the future comfort and welfare of the discharged patient rather than on a return to her former role. For women whose crimes had been closely related to familial and gynaecological problems, the capability of family and kin to provide a reputable, comfortable home was a key factor in evaluating release from an asylum. If it were shown that the husband and the patient's extended family were offering a respectable domestic environment, together with caring companionship, discharge would be recommended.

For the women who remained in the dedicated criminal lunatic facilities for the rest of their lives, families were only involved with them as visitors and correspondents and in their deaths at the behest of the asylum authorities. Whatever happened to the women, whether they were released or died in the asylum, control over their futures lay in the hands of the Home Office and the asylum authorities, and that control grew over the Victorian era. From the 1830s up to the early 1870s, if the women received a Royal Pardon, then their lives no longer fell under the purview of the Home Office. This was particularly true of the releases from Bethlem. Royal Pardons fell from use and, gradually the releases became conditional. Conditions of discharge became more formal and stringent until, by the end of the nineteenth century, the discharged patient remained ostensibly always a responsibility of the Crown, wherever they were. None of the women, including those who remained in Broadmoor until their deaths, lost the status of being held at her Majesty's pleasure as criminal lunatics.

8

'A depth of sympathy and a breadth of charity': Conclusion

For a mother to commit infanticide, in its broader definition, represented a total rejection of the culturally accepted maternal bonds, feelings and duties. To Victorian society, the idea that a woman's mental state and capacity was determined by her biological make-up was a common factor in medical and lay debates.[1] Medical explanations for married mothers murdering their children were influenced by gender expectations. These views were grounded in a recognition that because women had supposedly weaker physical and mental states, childbearing and motherhood could put immense strain on their bodies, constitution and minds.[2] In this final chapter, the various arguments of the preceding chapters are drawn together with the intention of, potentially, finding to answers to the questions asked in my introduction; what made these women so different? It could be argued that by focusing research on a singular set of three hundred or so cases spread over sixty years of the nineteenth century, the findings are not representative of female criminality or child homicide as a whole. Nonetheless, despite the size of the studied group my contention remains that social judgements and views held by all sections of society were key elements in determining the quality of the treatment and future of female criminal lunatics. Common patterns of experience, not only in legal and medical contexts, but also in social and environmental circumstances impacted on the life-journeys of infanticidal (in its widest definition) mothers and other women who were deemed to be criminally insane.

The profile of the 'typical' case of a mother had killed or violently attacked one or more of her children, could be said to fit the following description. The mother would be married, aged between thirty and forty years, living in an urban conurbation or the metropolitan area of London and classed as being from the unskilled lower working class. Her child victim would be female, aged between newborn and twelve months old and an only child. The attack would have occurred in the family home, with a household object as the weapon. An implement such as a knife, a razor or another sharp implement would be used, or if the death was by drowning, the bath or copper. There was not, however, one archetypal or standard case; each woman's case history in the diverse group studied was unique.

There were many similarities in their diagnoses, treatments and social circumstances, as there were in the responses of medical and legal authorities, families, the press and, through their offices, the general public. But equally, there were many differences. A bald reading of such statistics does not allow for any extenuating circumstances which might have lain behind the mother's violence. Mitigating factors were often reported in the courts, in newspaper reports and then further recorded in asylum and institutional records. Teenage cases were afforded compassion because the young women had been seduced and abandoned. Seduction along with domestic abuse was seen as an offence against a cultural moral code of behaviour towards women. Likewise, poverty and privation, as underlying aspects, could engender similar sympathies. Women who were the victims of illness, grief and other factors beyond their control were also met with compassion. It was, in many cases, these other causes which were emphasized to create sympathetic consideration, both in the courtroom and in the public domain. The reasons for this can also be attributed to other factors, such as views on social behaviours and respectability, inter-class relationships and identifications and evolving medical knowledge of insanity and its perceived causes.

Respectability of behaviour and backgrounds impacted on the professional and personal relationships. It was important to the way they were viewed by their own society, by the medical fraternity and the asylum community. Analysis of the social background of all parties, including the women, their families and kin and the men of authority, highlights this importance. To be seen as 'well-thought-of' and decent or to always act in an appropriate manner was a dominant cultural and social aspiration for most levels of society. Despite holding differing views and an occasional apparent lack of understanding about life for poorer families, the middle-class medical and governmental officials accepted many of the domestic values of lower classes, as 'respectable'. In the main, women within the dataset were not viewed as morally deviant or degenerate. Their lives and characters might have been medically, and publicly, scrutinized, but so often they were described as respectable women in all aspects and frequently as loving, fond mothers. A plausible explanation of their violent, out of character, behaviour lay in mental illness. Victorian society and medical opinion began to accept that certain gynaecological and obstetric issues could cause, what was hoped to be temporary, psychotic behaviour and mental illness. Mothers who were so afflicted were seen as fully deserving of sympathetic and careful treatment.

It is important to consider the individual class concepts of 'proper' behaviour, when reviewing and analysing any historical familial information. Middle-class ideals of the home and family relationships informed the opinions of the male authority figures and, at times, would colour their views of a working-class household. One factor which was common to all classes was the belief that a home and family needed a mother at its centre. A good wife and mother should have good housekeeping skills, manage the family economy and be a fond and protective mother.[3] The women were rarely described as 'bad' mothers, and the lack of interest in caring for the home and for her children was sometimes given as evidence of insanity. If such evidence was given, it was as 'proof' of abnormal behaviour, not as a criticism of the accused's abilities as a home-maker. Offence against such criteria was frequently accepted in mitigation of the mother's crime. The idea of the infanticidal mother being found insane offered an acceptable explanation to the essentially middle-class male authorities.[4]

Diagnoses and suggestions of insanity were often attributed to interruptions in the normal patterns of life and conduct, which the mainly middle-class male authorities would expect of women. The home-lives and relationships of working-class women were dissected by men from the professional middle class, by the press and by the public. Domestic circumstances were commented on and sometimes found wanting. Despite this, within newspaper reports and indeed within case book records, authors also would go to great lengths to emphasize the decency and propriety of the household. The larger part of the 302 women researched, came from the lower income brackets but rarely were they designated as being of the criminal class. They were seen as victims of misfortune, rather than being members of a felonious underclass. Within all levels of society, the Victorian ideal of home was considered to be a female-dominated space, a place which should provide safety and some security, to the family.[5] The fact that the attacks, both serious and fatal, happened within the domestic sphere would be another factor in proving that the woman must have been mentally deranged to kill.

Through exploring the women's lives, it is apparent that individual experiences and social background impacted on all aspects of their passage through the Victorian medico-legal systems. The discrete group of mothers who had killed their children were not necessarily condemned by the male-led medical and legal authorities, nor by Victorian society. This would appear to run contrary to present-day understanding of nineteenth-century concepts of motherhood, respectability and female violence. The perpetration of the crime of child homicide by a mother was an act which did not fit into any conventional portrayal of a Victorian woman, let alone one of Victorian parenthood.[6] A diagnosis or a suggestion of puerperal mania gave the medico-legal world a viable rationalization for an inexplicable crime, whether the mother was single or married.

In 1885, in his last annual report, Dr William Orange, Medical Superintendent of Broadmoor, wrote about infanticidal mothers who were discharged from the asylum during his tenure. He commented:

> It must not be supposed that those women who are discharged consist only, or indeed chiefly, of those who have taken the lives of new-born infants. The number of women discharged in 1885 was seven; and of these, five had killed their children, and in four cases out of the five the ages of the children were above one year, the average age, indeed, having been four years.[7]

The age of the child victim was immaterial to medical men. There was an accepted belief that puerperally-related insanities could manifest themselves at any post-partum stage. This was reiterated by Dr John Baker who wrote that, by 1902 the majority of patients in the Women's Division at Broadmoor were infanticidal mothers and that they had not all killed newborn children.[8]

The majority of asylum admissions discussed in this book were said to be suffering from insanity, classified as puerperal in origin. In accepting that the puerperal state could have a drastic impact on a woman's mental health, the medico-legal world and the general public conceded that maternal child murders committed under its influence deserved special consideration. This attitude is also apparent when those causes were allied with feminine medical issues of pregnancy, childbirth and lactation, menstruation, miscarriage or menopause. The prevalence of causes connected with female reproduction confirms that contemporary medical theories believed there were connections between the female body and mind. The idea that the female mind was vulnerable to any biological bodily change, which caused the woman to behave in an extraordinary and violent manner, became an acknowledged motivation for her subsequent vicious actions. Admissions to county and private asylums, together with those into criminal lunatic facilities, show that puerperal mania did not just happen amongst the poorer mothers in society; it could affect anyone.[9]

Other women were described as suffering from conditions associated with their previous lives, families and other stages of their life-cycles and physiology.

Such reasons were presented as having the ability to have a profound effect upon a woman's behaviour, even pushing her to the destruction of her child. Witness statements, in all courts, would frequently contain phrases to the effect that the accused woman was a good and caring mother, until she went through some catastrophic personal event. Amongst the women admitted to the criminal lunatic facilities, there were a number whose insanity was attributed to a grief-driven fear of destitution, rather than its actual occurrence. The single mothers considered to be insane, received the same sympathy for such circumstances, together with the added suggestion of mental derangement caused by their physical health. All occurrences of insanity could not necessarily be attributed to 'hereditary degeneracy' either. Despite such degeneracy being believed to prevalent in the lower classes, any incidence of any historical insanity within a family was relevant to the legal and medical authorities, whatever the woman's social status.

Much of the discussion in this book has been about how the women were viewed by various authorities, outside agencies and their families. These differing views of the women, coloured by concepts of 'correct' social behaviour and respectability, can hide the individual experiences of the women. One aim has been to contextualize the women and their lives, to assign some distinctiveness to each of them, before they became cogs in the wheels of the medico-legal system. From the research for this book as a whole, it has become evident that different principles of behaviour and respectability played a significant part in determining the quality of the women's passages through judicial and medical processes. It is apparent that inter- and intra-class perceptions of respectability played a powerful role in the dynamics of the mothers' life-journeys. They also impacted upon the emotional engagements and relationships between the women and all men in authority. Some ideas of behaviour and outlook were entrenched in class perceptions. Others were more nuanced, depending on situation and persons involved. The authorities' reactions were impacted by their cultural perceptions of other classes' expectations of respectable domestic and personal behaviour.

The mothers' individual histories contribute to the wider histories of medical and legal treatment of insanity under the law and in the institutional systems of nineteenth-century England and Wales. In taking a micro-historical, narrative approach to the researched material and sources, I have analysed the experiences of the dataset of women, to explain the circumstances of the women and their crime and for the legal and medical treatment they received. Research into the personal biographies illustrates, and sometimes, clarifies the impact of contemporary ideals. Victorian expectations of motherhood coupled with social class ideas of respectability influenced decisions made about all maternal child homicides. These ideals of motherhood were rooted in one basic premise that a mother should always look after and care for her children. This was nuanced across the different class cultures. From the middle-class ideal of the 'angel in the house' to the industrious housewife and working mothers of the lower classes, all were expected to nurture their children to the best of their abilities.

When writing this book, one subject which has come to the fore, is the role of emotion. It is ascertainable that the lives of the criminally insane mothers were influenced by emotionally driven responses from all parties. Although this book is not a study within the field of the history of emotions, the existence of emotional influences on the life-journeys of the three hundred women must be recognized. Emotional language engendered sympathy for both the woman and her family in court. Barristers, expert witnesses and judges would openly express their personal reactions to cases, which impacted directly on a woman's future. The interactions between the criminally insane mothers and their families and kin, while they were in the asylums, demonstrate the emotions existing within a familial unit. Letters and other ephemera illustrating dealings between the families and the asylum staff reveal some aspects of the emotional relationships between the infanticidal and homicidal mothers and their families. Close and extended family played a very important part in the women's lives. Their support and continuing contact could ensure the women's futures outside institutional life and assist with their comfort within the asylum, if discharge was thought inappropriate. Familial disapprobation and estrangement equally, although more negatively, could impact the women's lives.

The death of a child carries with it an inherent poignancy and a raft of different emotional reactions. When that death is a violent one at the hands of the child's mother or father, the emotional responses to the case, at any level, whether legal, medical, family or public, are varied and mixed. This is as true in the present day as it was in Victorian Britain. The women were not necessarily condemned by society, despite committing an abhorrent crime. Rather than punishment, compassionate solutions were ultimately sought for their situation. Considerations of social background, and emotional experience of all parties, lend weight to the theory that there was a level of sympathetic humanity present, not only in the interactions with the male-led authorities but also in Victorian society in general. This led to a willingness to reintegrate and accept 'cured' women to their place in their social and familial environment, albeit possibly a different role or standing therein.

During my research, I have come across cases where it is quite obvious to modern eyes that the patient was bi-polar or that a puerperally insane mother had postnatal psychosis. In the case of Esther Lack, for instance, a modern-day forensic psychiatrist put forward the plausible theory that Esther Lack may have suffered from an aggressive brain disease such as a cancer or tumour.[10] Although it can be quite compelling, retrospective diagnosis is a dangerous pastime. That being said, I have been drawn to examining the experiences of postnatal psychiatric conditions in present-day sufferers, to briefly compare them with those of Victorian mothers. In her 2002 chapter, 'Nothing in between', Julie Wheelwright states that contemporary cases of women who kill their children should be and are rightly first dealt with by the criminal justice system, because they have committed a criminal act. She submits that such crime needs sympathy, not condemnation, which compassion is afforded by present-day tolerant society. This modern social tolerance accepts that postpartum mental instability can cause devastating despair in mothers, which can lead to child murder. She suggests this consideration understands that the impaired judgement and reasoning of mothers suffering from psychological illnesses and psychoses can be mentally overwhelming and, thereby, their 'fragile sense of humanity' can be broken.[11] The research carried out for this book shows that similar sympathetic and compassionate views existed within Victorian society and it is not a phenomenon confined to the present day.

Definitive reasons for the occurrence of puerperal (as it still can be designated) or postpartum psychosis remain an enigma in the medical world. Research points to biological, probably hormonal, factors related to pregnancy and childbirth, but many other factors are likely to be involved.[12] As the charity Action on Postpartum Psychosis states, 'it is accepted that it can take six to twelve months, or more, to recover from postpartum psychosis' and further states that there is no absolute cure for the condition. While the condition can recur with subsequent pregnancies and childbirth, much like Victorian doctors such as David Nicolson, current medical advice emphasizes that support from family and friends is still essential, both in prevention and in recovery.[13] In 2012, Felicia Boots suffocated her two children, aged fourteen months and ten weeks. Psychiatric reports prepared for her trial at the Old Bailey said of her that she 'knew what she had done, but did not understand why she had done it'.[14] A plea of manslaughter on grounds of diminished responsibility was accepted and the judge, Mr Justice Fulford, described the case as indescribably sad' and that her actions were a result of 'psychological and biological causes beyond her control'.[15] Her detention order was issued without a time restriction, which meant that Felicia Boots was able to return home in May 2014, having undergone psychiatric treatment.[16]

The facts, the legal and medical reactions and, indeed, the reporting of the case are remarkably similar to the nineteenth-century cases studied for this book. There are differences in diagnostic terminology and ideological societal principles, but it is still accepted today, as it was then, that, for some women, insanities occur around childbirth. In the worse cases, the effects of those conditions can lead to maternal child murder and suicide. By a brief comparison with modern-day accounts of mothers' experiences of twenty-first-century psychiatric medicine, the reasons for the onset of psychotic episodes in certain women and not others are still as unpredictable today as they were in Victorian Britain, one hundred and fifty years ago. Like their Victorian counterparts, modern psychiatrists, and legal bodies, still accept that childbirth and its after-effects can have a devastating impact on a woman's mental state.

Image 8.1 Female Airing Court, Broadmoor, c.1910.[17]

Notes

Chapter 1

1. The National Archives, Kew (hereafter TNA), HO18/350 Criminal Petitions: Series II, Amelia Burt. 'Letter to Secretary of State at the Home Office 28 February 1870'.
2. Old Bailey Proceedings Online (hereafter OBP) January 1884, Trial of Amelia Elizabeth Burt (30) (t18521213-149).
3. 'Murder of an Infant', *Lady's Own Paper* (27 November 1852), p. 3, col. 2.
4. TNA, HO18/350, Criminal Petitions, II, 'Application for Removal to Bethlem 27 December 1870'.
5. Bethlem Museum of the Mind, Bethlem Royal Hospital Archive ((hereafter BMM) CBC-03 Criminal Patient Casebooks 1850–1857, Amelia Elizabeth Burt f. 50.
6. BMM, CBC-03 Criminal Patient Casebooks 1850–1857, Amelia Elizabeth Burt f. 50.
7. Berkshire Record Office, Broadmoor Hospital Archive, (hereafter BCLA-BRO), D/H14/D2/2/2/11, Case File: Amelia Elizabeth Burt.
8. TNA, HO18/350, Criminal Petitions, II, 'Letter to Secretary of State at the Home Office 28 February 1870'.
9. TNA, HO18/350, Criminal Petitions, II, 'Medical Certificate, 7 March 1870'.
10. TNA, HO18/350, Criminal Petitions, II, 'Letter, 15 March 1870'.
11. BCLA-BRO, D/H14/D2/2/2/11, Burt.
12. TNA, 1871 England Census. Class: RG10; Piece: 628; Folio: 123; Page: 25.
13. OBP, January 1884, Burt; BMM, CBC-03 Burt f. 50; BCLA-BRO, D/H14/D2/2/2/11, Burt.
14. TNA, HO18/350, Criminal Petitions, II, Amelia Elizabeth Burt.
15. Susie L. Steinbach, *Understanding the Victorians. Politics, Culture and Society in Nineteenth-Century Britain* (Abingdon: Routledge, 2012), p. 125.
16. David Cannadine, *Class in Britain* (London: Penguin Books, 1998), pp. 90–1.
17. Ibid., p. 92.
18. Ibid.; Dror Wahrman, *Imagining the Middle Class. The Political Representation of Class in Britain c.1740–1840* (Cambridge: Cambridge University Press, 1995).
19. Daniel J. R. Grey, '"No Crime to Kill a Bastard–Child": Stereotypes of Infanticide in Nineteenth-Century England and Wales', in Barbara Leonardi (ed.), *Intersections of Gender, Class, and Race in the Long Nineteenth Century and beyond* (Cham: Palgrave Macmillan, 2018), pp. 41–66, p. 42.

20 Lucia Zedner, 'Women, Crime and Penal Responses: A Historical Account', *Crime and Justice*, vol. 14 (1991), pp. 307–62, p. 308.
21 Idem., *Women, Crime and Custody in Victorian England* (Oxford: Clarendon Press, 1991), pp. 29–30.
22 A. James Hammerton, *Cruelty and Companionship. Conflict in Nineteenth-Century Married Life* (London: Routledge, 1995), pp. 71–2.
23 Hammerton, *Cruelty and Companionship*, p. 2.
24 See amongst others: Ann Digby, 'Victorian Values and Women in Private and Public', *Proceedings of the British Academy*, vol. 78 (1990), pp. 195–215; John Tosh, *A Man's Place: Masculinity and the Middle-Class Home* (New Haven, CT & London: Yale University Press, 1999).
25 David Cannadine, *Victorious Century: The United Kingdom, 1800–1906* (London: Penguin Random House, 2017), p. 331.
26 Joanne Begiato, *Manliness in Britain, 1760–1900. Bodies, Emotion and Material Culture* (Manchester: Manchester University Press, 2020), pp. 153 & 160.
27 Joanne Bailey, *Parenting in England 1760–1830: Emotion, Identity and Generation* (Oxford: Oxford University Press, 2012), pp. 12–13.
28 Jonathan Andrews, 'The boundaries of Her Majesty's Pleasure: Discharging Child Murderers from Broadmoor and Perth Criminal Lunatic Department, c. 1860–1920', in Mark Jackson (ed.), *Infanticide: Historical Perspectives on Child Murder and Concealment, 1550 – 2000* (Aldershot: Ashgate, 2002), pp. 216–48, p. 236.
29 For example: Carol Beardmore, Cara Dobbing & Steven King (eds.), *Family Life in Britain, 1650–1910* (Basingstoke: Palgrave Macmillan, 2019); Leonore Davidoff and Catherine Hall, *Family Fortunes: Men and Women of the English Middle Class,1780–1850* (London & New York: Routledge, 1987, 3rd edition 2019); Ellen Ross, *Love and Toil: Motherhood in Outcast London, 1870–1918* (Oxford: Oxford University Press, 1993).
30 Ross, *Love and Toil*, pp. 131–2.
31 Ibid., pp. 128–65.
32 Steinbach, *Understanding the Victorians*, pp. 130–4.
33 Steven J. Taylor, 'Conceptualising the "Perfect Family" in Late Nineteenth Century Philanthropic Institutions', in Carol Beardmore, Cara Dobbing & Steven King (eds.), *Family Life in Britain, 1650–1910* (Basingstoke: Palgrave Macmillan, 2019), pp. 155–78, p. 170.
34 For example: Beardmore, Dobbing & King, *Family Life in Britain*; Emma Griffin, 'The Emotions of Motherhood: Love, Culture and Poverty in Victorian Britain', *The American Historical Review*, vol. 123, no. 1 (2018), pp. 60–85; James Marten, 'Family Relationships', in Colin Heywood (ed.), *In the Age of Empire. A Cultural History of Childhood and Family* (London: Bloomsbury, 2014), pp. 19–38; Julie-Marie Strange, *Death, Grief and Poverty, 1870–1914* (Cambridge: Cambridge University Press, 2005).

35 Emma Cuming, *Housing, Class and Gender in Modern British Writing, 1880–2012* (Cambridge: Cambridge University Press, 2016), pp. 28–30.
36 Taylor, 'Conceptualising the "Perfect Family"', p. 156.
37 Marten, 'Family Relationships', p. 19.
38 Taylor, 'Conceptualising the "Perfect Family"', p. 158.
39 Ibid., p. 170.
40 Strange, *Death, Grief and Poverty*, p. 251.
41 Ibid., pp. 15–16.
42 Joanne Bailey, 'Think Wot a Mother Must Feel: Parenting in English Pauper Letters c.1760–1834', *Family and Community History*, vol. 13, no. 1 (2010), pp. 5–19.
43 Griffin, 'The Emotions of Motherhood', p. 72.
44 Ibid., p. 64.
45 Anne Higginbotham, 'Sin of the Age: Infanticide and Illegitimacy in Victorian London', *Victorian Studies*, vol. 32, no. 3 (1989), pp. 319–37, p. 320.
46 George K. Behlmer, 'Deadly Motherhood: Infanticide and Medical Opinion in Mid-Victorian England', *Journal of the History of Medicine and Allied Sciences*, vol. 34, no. 4 (1979), pp. 403–27, p. 414.
47 Mark Jackson, 'The Trial of Harriet Vooght: Continuity and Change in the History of Infanticide', in Mark Jackson (ed.), *Infanticide: Historical Perspectives on Child Murder and Concealment, 1550–2000* (Aldershot: Ashgate, 2002), pp. 1–17, p. 10.
48 Daniel J. R. Grey, 'Women's Policy Networks and the Infanticide Act 1922', *20th Century British History*, vol. 21, no. 4 (2010), pp. 441–63. doi: 10.1093/tcbh/hwq024.
49 *Daily Telegraph* (13 September 1865) quoted in Tony Ward, 'Legislating for Human Nature: Legal Responses to Infanticide, 1860–1938', in Jackson (ed.), *Infanticide*, pp. 249–69, p. 253.
50 Margaret L. Arnot, 'Understanding Women Committing New-born Child Murder', in Shani D'Cruze (ed.), *Everyday Violence in Britain, 1850–1950* (Edinburgh: Pearson Education Ltd, 2000), p. 59.
51 For example: Margaret L. Arnot, 'Gender in Focus: Infanticide in England 1840–1880' (unpublished PhD Thesis, University of Essex, 1994); Daniel J. R. Grey, 'Discourses of Infanticide in England, 1880–1922' (unpublished PhD Thesis, University of Roehampton, 2008); Aeron Hunt, 'Calculations and Concealments', *Victorian Literature and Culture*, vol. 34, no. 1 (2006), pp. 71–94; Hilary Marland, *Dangerous Motherhood. Insanity and Childbirth in Victorian Britain* (Basingstoke: Palgrave Macmillan, 2004).
52 'Seduction' would often be used as a euphemism for rape. Barry Godfrey & Paul Lawrence, *Crime and Justice since 1850* (Abingdon: Routledge, 2015), pp. 98–9, p. 58.
53 Higginbotham, 'Sin of the Age', p. 319.

54 'By Far the Most Serious Feature …', *Times* (18 March 1846), issue 19187, p. 4, col. 5.
55 Margaret L. Arnot, 'Perceptions of Parental Child Homicide in English Popular Visual Culture 1800–1850', *Law, Crime and History*, vol. 1 (2017), pp. 16–74, p. 33.
56 Lionel Rose, *Massacre of the Innocents. Infanticide in Great Britain, 1800–1939* (London: Routledge & Kegan Paul, 1986), p. 187.
57 Anne Marie Kilday, *A History of Infanticide in Britain c1600 to the Present*, (Basingstoke: Palgrave Macmillan, 2013), p. 163.
58 Ibid., p. 172–8.
59 Grey, 'No Crime to Kill a Bastard–Child', p. 42.
60 Ibid., pp. 42–3.
61 Katherine D. Watson, *Medicine and Justice: Medico-Legal Practice in England and Wales, 1700–1914* (London & New York: Routledge, 2020), p. 163.
62 Joel Peter Eigen, *Witnessing Insanity: Madness and Mad-Doctors in the English Court* (New Haven & London: Yale University Press, 1995); Idem., *Unconscious Crime: Mental Absence and Criminal Responsibility in Victorian London* (Baltimore: The Johns Hopkins University Press, 2003); Idem., *Mad-Doctors in the Dock. Defending the Diagnosis, 1760–1913* (Baltimore: The Johns Hopkins University Press, 2016); Catherine L. Evans, *Unsound Empire. Civilization & Madness in Late-Victorian Law* (New Haven & London: Yale University Press, 2021); Hilary Marland, 'Getting away with Murder? Puerperal Insanity, Infanticide and the Defence Plea', in Jackson (ed.) *Infanticide*, pp. 168–92; Roger Smith, *Trial by Medicine. Insanity and Responsibility in Victorian Britain* (Edinburgh: Edinburgh University Press, 1982); Nigel Walker, *Crime and Insanity in England: Volume 1 the Historical Perspective* (Edinburgh: Edinburgh University Press, 1968); Nigel Walker & Sarah McCabe, *Crime & Insanity in England Vol 2 New Solutions & New Problems* (Edinburgh: Edinburgh University Press, 1973).
63 Zedner, *Women, Crime and Custody*, p. 90.
64 Walker, *Crime & Insanity*, vol. 1, p. 125; Smith, *Trial by Medicine*, p. 159.
65 Alison Pedley, 'The Emotional Reactions of Judges in Cases of Maternal Child Murder in England, 1840–1890', in James Gregory, Daniel J. R Grey & Annika Bautz (eds.), *Judgment in the Victorian Age* (Abingdon: Routledge, 2019), pp. 83–99; Smith, *Trial by Medicine*, pp. 143–50.
66 Smith, *Trial by Medicine*, p. 160.
67 Ibid., p. 154.
68 Examples of scholarship about the role of the insanity plea in trials, the role of doctors and medical evidence and medico-legal debate: Eigen, *Witnessing Insanity*; Idem., *Unconscious Crime*; Idem., *Mad-Doctors in the Dock*; Marland, 'Getting away with Murder?' pp. 168–92; Smith, *Trial by Medicine*.
69 Smith, *Trial by Medicine*, p. 154.
70 Wm. Charles Hood. M.D., *Suggestions for the Future Provision of Criminal Lunatics* (London: John Churchill, Soho, 1854).

71 Ibid., pp. 162–4.
72 Eigen, *Unconscious Crime*, p. 83; Martin J. Wiener, *Reconstructing the Criminal: Culture, Law and Policy in England, 1830–1914* (Cambridge: CUP, 1990), p. 269.
73 Arlie Loughnan, *Manifest Madness: Mental Incapacity in the Criminal Law* (Oxford: Oxford University Press, 2012), pp. 214–16.
74 BCLA, John Baker, M.D., Deputy Medical Superintendent. 1896–1902, Medical Superintendent, 1902–1912.
75 John Baker, 'Female Criminal Lunatics: A Sketch', *Journal of Mental Science*, vol. 48 (1902), pp. 13–28, p. 15.
76 TNA, HO144/579/A63301, ASSI13/32 R. v Worley. Letter dated 15 December 1902 from the Home Office to Lord Alverstone, L.J.
77 David Nicolson, 'A Chapter in the History of Criminal Lunacy in England', *Journal of Mental Science*, vol. 23 (July 1877), pp. 165–85.
78 Baker, 'Female Criminal Lunatics', p. 15.
79 Jade Shepherd, '"I am very glad and cheered when I hear the flute": The Treatment of Criminal Lunatics in Late Victorian Broadmoor', *Medical History*, vol. 60, no. 4 (2016), pp. 473–91. doi:10.1017/mdh.2016.56.
80 Idem., 'Feigning Insanity in Late-Victorian Britain', *Prison Service Journal*, no. 232 (July 2017), pp. 17–23.
81 Nicolson, 'A Chapter in the History of Criminal Lunacy', p. 168.
82 The Hospital of Bethlem [Bedlam], St George's Fields, Lambeth. Wood engraving, 1848. Wellcome Collection. Public Domain Mark. Creative Commons Attribution (CC BY 4.0).
83 Harvey Gordon, *Broadmoor* (London: Psychology News Press, 2012). Chapter 1.
84 Image: Fisherton House Asylum c. 2013. Richard Avery – licensed under the CCA-S 3.0.
85 William Ll. Parry-Jones, *The Trade in Lunacy. A Study of Private Madhouses in the Eighteenth and Nineteenth Centuries* (London: Routledge & Kegan Paul, 1972).
86 Ibid., p. 68.
87 'Public Health and Medical Services', in R. B. Pugh & Elizabeth Crittall (eds.), *A History of the County of Wiltshire*, vol. 5 (London, 1957), pp. 318–47. British History Online http://www.british-history.ac.uk/vch/wilts/vol5/pp318-347.
88 John Alfred Lush was a G.P. in Salisbury and became one of the proprietors of Fisherton House after his marriage to Sarah Martha Finch daughter of Dr Wm. Corbin Finch Snr, in May 1853. 'John Alfred Lush', *Munks Roll*, vol. 4, Royal College of Psychiatrists, p. 204.
89 Parry-Jones, *The Trade in Lunacy*.
90 Gordon, *Broadmoor*.
91 3 & 4 Vict., c.54. An Act for Making Further Provision for the Confinement and Maintenance of Insane Prisoners, 1840.

92 Catherine Cox & Hilary Marland, *Disorder Contained: Mental Breakdown and the Modern Prison in England and Ireland, 1840–1900* (Cambridge: Cambridge University Press, 2022), pp. 152–3.
93 Anthony Ashley-Cooper, 7th Earl of Shaftesbury Speech to the House of Lords, 1852, 'Criminal Lunatics' House of Lords Debate 18 May 1852 *Hansard 1803–2005* vol. 126 cc. 1230–1244.
94 Cox & Marland, *Disorder Contained*, pp. 161–2.
95 *Sixth Report of the Commissioners in Lunacy to the Lord Chancellor (pursuant to Acts 8 & 9 Vict., c. 100, s. 88)* (ordered by The House of Commons, to be printed 8 August 1851), p. 20.
96 Mark Stevens, *Broadmoor Revealed: Victorian Crime and the Lunatic Asylum*. (Barnsley: Pen & Sword Books Ltd., 2013), p. 7.
97 23 & 24 Vict., c.75. Criminal Lunatics Asylum Act 1860.
98 Engraving Broadmoor Criminal Lunatic Asylum, in 1867. *Illustrated London News*, 24 August 1867, image by kind permission, Mark Stevens, Berkshire Record Office, Reading, Berkshire.
99 Amongst many works on treatment and asylum development see: Anne Digby, *Madness, Morality and Medicine: A Study of the York Retreat, 1796–1914* (Cambridge: Cambridge University Press, 1985); Thomas Dixon, 'Patients and Passions: Languages of Medicine and Emotion, 1789–1850', in Fay Bound Alberti (ed.), *Medicine, Emotion and Disease, 1700–1950* (Basingstoke: Palgrave Macmillan, 2006), pp. 22–52; Louise Hide, *Gender and Class in English Asylums, 1890–1914* (Basingstoke: Palgrave Macmillan, 2014); Anna Shepherd, *Institutionalizing the Insane in Nineteenth-Century England* (London: Pickering & Chatto, 2014); Leonard D. Smith, *Cure, Comfort and Safe Custody: Public Lunatic Asylums in Early Nineteenth-Century England* (London: Leicester University Press, 1999).
100 Samuel Tuke, *Description of the Retreat, an Institution Near York, for Insane Persons of the Society of Friends* (York: W. Alexander, 1813).
101 Digby, *Madness, Morality and Medicine*, pp. 51–3.
102 Ibid.; Roy Porter, *Madness. A Short History* (Oxford: Oxford University Press, 2010), p. 104.
103 Digby, *Madness, Morality and Medicine*, p. 53.
104 Roy Porter, *Madness. A Brief History* (Oxford: Oxford University Press, 2002), p. 104–5.
105 Tuke, *Description of the Retreat*, pp. 90–1.
106 Michel Foucault, *Madness and Civilisation: A History of Insanity in the Age of Reason*, trans. Richard Howard (London: Routledge, 2001).
107 Digby, *Madness, Morality and Medicine*.
108 Foucault, *Madness and Civilisation*.

109 Andrew Scull, *Social Order/Mental Disorder. Anglo-American Psychiatry in Historical Perspective* (Berkeley & Los Angeles: University of California Press,1989), p. 89.
110 Andrew Scull, *The Most Solitary of Afflictions: Madness and Society in Britain, 1700–1900* (New Haven & London: Yale University Press, 1993), p. 170.
111 Foucault, *Madness and Civilisation*; Scull, *The Most Solitary of Afflictions*, pp. 169–74.
112 'Broadmoor Asylum', *Illustrated London News*, 24 August 1867, pp. 208–9.
113 'Criminal Lunatics and Lunatic Convicts', *British Medical Journal* (July 1874), quoted in Shepherd, 'I am very glad and cheered when I hear the flute'.
114 'A Visit to Broadmoor', *Globe* (1 April 1885), p. 6, col. 1.
115 Deborah E. Weiner, '"This coy and secluded dwelling" Broadmoor Asylum for the Criminally Insane', in Leslie Topp, James E. Moran & Jonathan Andews (eds.), *Madness, Architecture and the Built Environment* (Abingdon: Routledge, 2007), pp. 131–48, p. 142.
116 George Griffith, *Sidelights on Convict Life* (London: John Long, 1903). Chapter 5.
117 Rosalind Crone, *Illiterate Inmates: Educating Criminals in Nineteenth Century England* (Oxford: Oxford University Press, 2022) Kindle ed., Introduction.
118 Tuke, *Description of the Retreat*, p. 89.
119 Examples: Caroline A. Conley, *Certain Other Countries: Homicide, Gender and National Identity in Late Nineteenth-Century England, Ireland, Scotland and Wales* (Columbus, OH: Ohio State University Press, 2007); Shani D'Cruze & Louise Jackson, *Women, Crime and Justice in England since 1660* (Basingstoke: Palgrave Macmillan, 2009); Helen Johnston, *Crime in England, 1815–1880* (Abingdon: Routledge, 2015); Kilday, *A History of Infanticide in Britain*; Katherine D. Watson, *Poisoned Lives: English Poisoners and Their Victims* (London & New York: Hambledon, 2004); Idem., *Medicine and Justice*.
120 Alison C. Pedley, 'A Deed at which Humanity Shudders; Mad Mothers, the Law and the Asylum, 1835–1895' (unpublished PhD Thesis, University of Roehampton, 2020).
121 Ibid.
122 Jonathan Andrews, 'Case Notes, Case Histories and the Patient Experience of Insanity at Gartnaval Royal Asylum, Glasgow, in the Nineteenth Century', *Social History of Medicine*, vol. 11, no. 2 (1998), pp. 255–81, p. 256.
123 Hilary Marland, 'Disappointment and Desolation: Women, Doctors and Interpretations of Puerperal Insanity in the Nineteenth Century', *History of Psychiatry*, vol. 14, no. 3 (2003), pp. 303–20, p. 305.
124 Andrews, 'Case Notes, Case Histories', pp. 255–81.

125 Wiltshire & Swindon History Centre, Chippenham. (hereafter FHA-WHC) J7/131/1, Correspondence Criminal Lunatics and their maintenance at Fisherton by the Commissioners in Lunacy, 1854–1875. (4 bundles).
126 Hood, M.D., *Suggestions for the Future Provision of Criminal Lunatics*, p. 161.
127 Roy Porter, 'The Patients's View: Doing Medical History from Below', *Theory and Society*, vol. 4, no. 2 (1985), pp. 175–98.
128 Examples: Sarah Chaney, '"No 'Sane' Person Would Have Any Idea"; Patients' Involvement in Late Nineteenth-century British Asylum Psychiatry', *Medical History*, vol. 60, no. 1 (2016), pp. 37–53; Louise Hide, 'From Asylum to Mental Hospital: Gender, Space and the Patient Experience in London County Council Asylums, 1890–1910', in Jane Hamlett, Lesley Hoskins & Rebecca Preston (eds.), *Residential Institutions in Britain, 1725–1970* (London: Chatto & Pickering, 2013), pp. 51–64; Jade Shepherd, 'Life for the Families of the Victorian Criminally Insane', *The Historical Journal*, vol. 63, no. 3 (2019), pp. 603–32; Idem., 'I Am Very Glad and Cheered when I Hear the Flute', pp. 473–91.
129 For example: Cara Dobbing, 'Pauper Lunatics at Home in the Asylum', in Joseph Harley & Vicky Holmes (eds.), *The Working Class at Home, 1790–1940* (Cham: Palgrave Macmillan, 2022), pp. 193–211; Anne Shepherd, 'The Female Patient Experience in Two Late-Nineteenth Century Surrey Asylums', in Jonathan Andrews & Anne Digby (eds.), *Sex and Seclusion, Class & Custody in the History of British and Irish Psychiatry* (New York: Rodopi Clio, 2004), pp. 223–48; Leonard D. Smith, '"Your Very Thankful Inmate": Discovering the Patients of an Early County Lunatic Asylum', *Social History of Medicine*, vol. 221, no. 2 (2008), pp. 237–52.
130 Roy Porter, *A Social History of Madness: Stories of the Insane* (London: Phoenix, 1999), p. 6.
131 Alexandra Bacopolous-Viau & Aude Fauvel, 'The Patient's Turn. Roy Porter and Psychiatry's Tales, Thirty Years on', *Medical History*, vol. 60, no. 1 (2016), pp. 1–18, p. 14.
132 As examples this specific discussion: Andrews, 'Case Notes, Case Histories', pp. 255–81; Brendan D. Kelly, 'Searching for the patient's voice in the Irish asylums', *Medical Humanities*, vol. 42, no. 2 (2016), pp. 1–5; Marland, 'Disappointment and Desolation'; Smith, 'Your Very Thankful Inmate'.
133 Catharine Coleborne, *Why Talk About Madness? Bringing History into the Conversation* (Cham: Palgrave Macmillan, 2020).
134 Ibid., p. 15.
135 Ibid., p. 19.
136 Ibid., p. 19.
137 Shepherd, 'Life for the Families of the Victorian Criminally Insane', p. 607.

138   Eigen, *Witnessing Insanity*; Idem., *Unconscious Crime*; Idem., *Mad-Doctors in the Dock*.
139   Idem., '"Diagnosing Homicidal Mania": Forensic Psychiatry and the Purposeless Murder', *Medical History*, vol. 54, no. 4 (2010), pp. 433–56, p. 435.
140   Martin J. Wiener, 'Convicted Murderers and the Victorian Press: Condemnation vs. Sympathy', *Crime and Misdemeanours*, vol. 1, no. 2 (2007), pp. 110–25, p. 112.
141   Ibid., p. 111.
142   John Brewer, 'Microhistory and the Histories of Everyday Life', *Cultural and Social History*, vol. 7, no. 1 (2010), pp. 87–109, p. 90.
143   The genealogical websites used are www.ancestry.co.uk and www.findmypast.co.uk. Both sites also are sources of government and legal documents.
144   Emily Brand, 'Why Family History Matters', in Helen Carr & Suzannah Lipscomb (eds.), *What Is History, Now?* (London: Weidenfeld & Nicolson, 2021), pp. 213–29, p. 228.

Chapter 2

1   *Lloyds Weekly Newspaper* (15 August 1898), p. 2, col. 4.
2   Ibid.
3   BCLA-BRO, D/H14/D2/2/2/550. Case File: Elizabeth Stapleton.
4   Ian Burney, *Bodies of Evidence: Medicine and the Politics of the English Inquest, 1830–1926* (London: Routledge, 2000).
5   Margaret L. Arnot, 'Understanding Women Committing New-born Child Murder in Victorian England', in Shani D'Cruze (ed.), *Everyday Violence in Britain, 1850–1950* (Edinburgh: Pearson Education Ltd, 2000), pp. 55–69, p. 56.
6   In Newcastle upon Tyne the borough coroner, John Theodore Hoyle, repeatedly worked with the same twelve men but would summon others, in the expectation that some would not attend. Helen Rutherford, 'The Coroner in an Emerging Industrial Society: John Theodore Hoyle and Newcastle upon Tyne 1857–1885', (unpublished PhD Thesis, University of Newcastle, July 2021).
7   50 & 51 Vict., c.71. An Act to Consolidate the Law relating to Coroners, Coroners Act 1887.
8   Burney, *Bodies of Evidence*, p. 5.
9   'Central Criminal Court', *Morning Post* (28 October 1885), p. 3, col. 6.
10 Burney, *Bodies of Evidence*, p. 5.
11 Katherine D. Watson, *Medicine and Justice: Medico-Legal Practice in England and Wales, 1700–1914* (London & New York: Routledge, 2020), pp. 6–8, p. 121.
12 Victor Bailey, '*This Rash Act*': *Suicide, across the Life Cycle in the Victorian City* (Stanford: Stanford University Press, 1998), pp. 52–3.

13 'The Terrible Tragedy at Sefton', *Liverpool Mercury* (19 February 1896), p. 5. col. 6.
14 'The Sefton Murder Case', *Manchester Courier & Lancashire General Advertiser* (28 March 1896) p. 14, col. 7.
15 TNA, ASSI 52/9, Assize: Northern Circuit: Criminal Depositions and Case Papers, 1887. 'The Deposition Statement of Edward Percy Plantagenet McLoughlin'.
16 TNA, ASSI 52/9, 'Deposition Statement'.
17 'The Wardington Child Murder', *Banbury Advertiser* (9 March 1876), p. 3, col. 1.
18 Watson, *Medicine and Justice*, p. 150.
19 'The Murder of an Infant at Barnstaple', *Western Times* (25 May 1889), p. 5, col. 4.
20 *The Western Times* (17 May 1889), p. 5.
21 Ciara Breathnach & Eugene O'Halpin, 'Scripting Blame: Irish Coroner's Courts and Unnamed Infant Dead, 1916-32', *Social History*, vol. 39, no. 2 (2014), pp. 210-28, p. 211.
22 Ibid., p. 211.
23 Ibid., p. 212.
24 Hilary Marland, 'Languages and Landscapes of Emotion: Motherhood and Puerperal Insanity in the Nineteenth Century', in Fay Bound Alberti (ed.), *Medicine, Emotion and Disease, 1700-1950* (Basingstoke: Palgrave Macmillan, 2006), pp. 53-78, p. 68-9.
25 Ibid., p. 69.
26 'Murder of Two Children by Their Mother', *London Daily News* (20 August 1859), p. 3, col. 4.
27 'Murder of Two Children by Their Mother', *Sheffield Daily Telegraph* (22 August 1859), p. 4, col. 3.
28 Burney, *Bodies of Evidence*, p. 2.
29 Joe Sim & Tony Ward, 'The Magistrates of the Poor? Coroners and Deaths in Custody in Nineteenth-century England', in Michael Clark & Catherine Crawford (eds.), *Legal Medicine in History* (Cambridge: Cambridge University Press, 1994), pp. 245-68.
30 Hurren, 'Remaking the Medico-Legal Scene', p. 209.
31 'Child Murder at Llandaff', *Cardiff Times* (25 September 1863), p. 5, col. 6.
32 'A Mother Attempting to Drown Her Child: A Sad Case', *Herts Advertiser* (8 August 1885), p. 7, col. 3.
33 'The Tragedy at Swansea. Committal of Mrs. Morgan for Murder' M, *South Wales Daily News* (23 November 1883) p. 3, col. 8.
34 TNA, HO145, Criminal Lunacy Warrant and Entry Books, 1882-9. Warrant no. 131, Mary Ann Morgan, 28 November 1883.
35 TNA, HO144/128/A33589, Home Office Registered Papers, Home Office Memorandum. 'Lunacy: Proposed Acceptance of Bail Pending Murder Trial at Assizes. Criminal: Morgan, Marianne [sic]; Court: Swansea P.C.; Offence: Murder; Sentence: Criminal Lunatic. 1883-1884'.

36 TNA, HO144/128/A33589, 'Lunacy: Proposed Acceptance of Bail Pending Murder Trial at Assizes. Criminal: Morgan, Marianne [sic]; Court: Swansea P.C.; Offence: Murder; Sentence: Criminal Lunatic. 1883–1884'.
37 TNA, HO144/128/A33589: Morgan, Letter 22 November 1883.
38 TNA, /A33589, Memorandum: 22 November 1883.
39 BCLA-BRO, D/H14/D2/2/2/362, Case File: Mary Ann Morgan.
40 'Serious Defect in the Law', *Banbury Advertiser* (21 February 1884), p. 3, col. 4.
41 3 & 4 Vict., c.54. The Insane Prisoners Act 1840.
42 Roger Smith, *Trial by Medicine. Insanity and Responsibility in Victorian Britain* (Edinburgh: Edinburgh University Press, 1982), p. 21.
43 Ibid., p. 92.
44 Joel Peter Eigen, *Unconscious Crime: Mental Absence and Criminal Responsibility in Victorian London* (Baltimore: The Johns Hopkins University Press, 2003), p. 184.
45 Ibid.
46 Idem., *Mad-Doctors in the Dock. Defending the Diagnosis, 1760–1913* (Baltimore: Johns Hopkins University Press, 2016), p. 113.
47 UKHL J16 (19 June 1843), The Case of Daniel M'Naghten; 10 Cl & Fin 200: 8 ER 718. United Kingdom House of Lords Decisions. (1843) 'M'Naghten's Case'.
48 Daniel M'Naghten's Case Enquiry, 1843. United Kingdom House of Lords Decisions. (1843) M'Naghten's Case UKHL J16 (19 June 1843). Daniel J. R. Grey, 'Discourses of Infanticide in England, 1880–1922' (unpublished PhD Thesis, University of Roehampton, 2008), pp. 204–5.
49 Smith, *Trial by Medicine*, p. 19.
50 Eigen, *Unconscious Mind*, p. 66; Grey, 'Discourses of Infanticide in England', pp. 204–5.
51 Eigen, *Mad Doctors*, p. 142; Grey, 'Discourses of Infanticide', p. 205.
52 Dr Alfred Swaine Taylor (1806–1880), Professor of Medical Jurisprudence at Guys Hospital, 1831–1877. The acknowledged Victorian authority on medical jurisprudence, who published The Principles and Practice of Medical Jurisprudence. The book became the standard reference book for medical examiners and forensic pathologists. It ranged widely over the causes of death through foul play. Taylor frequently appeared as a witness for the Crown and his assistance was often sought in criminal investigations. Helen Barrell & Fatal Evidence, *Professor Alfred Swaine Taylor & the Dawn of Forensic Science* (Barnsley: Pen & Sword History, 2017).
53 A. S. Taylor, *The Principles and Practice of Medical Jurisprudence* (London: J. Churchill, 1861, 7th edition), pp. 660–1.
54 Ibid., p. 660.
55 Ibid., p. 661.
56 Ibid., p. 676.

57 TNA, HO144/129/A34007 Home Office Registered Papers: 'Criminal: AGAR, Elizabeth Matilda; Court: Central Criminal Court; Offence: Murder of Her One-month Old Child; Sentence: Criminal Lunatic'.
58 TNA, HO144/129/A34007 Case: Agar. 'Report of Dr Orange dated 17th June 1883'.
59 Ibid., 17 June 1883.
60 Thora Hands, *Drinking in Victorian and Edwardian Britain. Beyond the Spectre of the Drunkard* (Basingstoke (Open Access): Palgrave Macmillan, 2018), pp. 129–43.
61 Louise Hide, *Gender and Class in English Asylums, 1890–1914* (Basingstoke: Palgrave Macmillan, 2014), p. 35.
62 Ibid.
63 Hands, *Drinking in Victorian and Edwardian Britain*, 47.
64 *Sheffield Daily Telegraph,* 13 May 1881.
65 Kim Stevenson, 'Fulfilling Their Mission: The Intervention of Voluntary Societies in Cases of Sexual Assault in the Victorian Criminal Process', *Crime, History & Societies*, vol. 8, no. 1 (2004), pp. 93–110, p. 96.
66 BCLA-BRO, D/H14/D2/2/2/326/8.
67 'Attempted Murder in Leeds', *Leeds Mercury* (21 December 1866), p. 4, col. 1.
68 'The Domestic Tragedy at Great Crosby', *Liverpool Mercury*, 12 December 1876, p. 8, col. 4.
69 BCLA-BRO, D/H14/D2/2/2/261/6 Case File: Agnes Martha Morris. 'Schedule A: Statement Accompanying Criminal Lunatic' January 1877; Draft Report to Home Office.
70 *Liverpool Mercury* (12 December 1876), p. 8.
71 Cerian C. Griffiths, 'Advocacy in Criminal Trials', in Jo Turner, Paul Taylor, Sharon Morley, & Karen Corteen (eds.), *A Companion to the History of Crime & Criminal Justice* (Bristol: Policy Press, 2017), pp. 1–3, p. 2.
72 6 & 7 Will. IV. c.114. Trials for Felony Act 1836.
73 Griffiths, 'Advocacy in Criminal Trials', p. 2.
74 42 & 43 Vict., c.22. Prosecution of Offences Act 1879.
75 G. Roger Chadwick, 'Bureaucratic Mercy: The Home Office and the Treatment of Capital Cases in Victorian England' (unpublished PhD Thesis, Rice University, Houston Texas, 1989), p. 281.
76 See amongst others: Anne-Marie Kilday, *A History of Infanticide in Britain, c.1600 to the Present* (Basingstoke: Palgrave Macmillan, 2013); Hilary Marland, *Dangerous Motherhood. Insanity and Childbirth in Victorian Britain* (Basingstoke: Palgrave MacMillan, 2004); Nigel Walker, *Crime and Insanity in England: Volume One: The Historical Perspective* (Edinburgh: Edinburgh University Press. 1968); Lucia Zedner, *Women, Crime and Custody in Victorian England* (Oxford: Clarendon Press, 1991).
77 Eigen, *Unconscious Crime*, p. 159.

78 Ibid., p. 75; Hilary Marland, '"Destined to Perfect Recovery" The Confinement of Puerperal Insanity in the Nineteenth Century', in Joseph Melling & Bill Forsythe (eds.), *Insanity, Institutions and Society, 1800–1914* (Abingdon: Routledge, 2000), pp. 137–56, p. 140.
79 Eigen, *Unconscious Crime*; Idem., *Mad-Doctors*; Arlie Loughnan, *Manifest Madness: Mental Incapacity in Criminal Law* (Oxford: Oxford University Press, 2012); Smith, *Trial by Medicine*.
80 Arnot, 'Gender in Focus', p. 200; Loughnan, *Manifest Madness*, p. 210; Hilary Marland, 'Getting away with Murder? Puerperal Insanity, Infanticide and the Defence Plea', in Jackson (ed.) *Infanticide: Historical Perspectives*, pp. 168–92.
81 Chadwick, 'Bureaucratic Mercy'.
82 Watson, *Medicine and Justice*, p. 103.
83 Ibid., p. 97.
84 Eigen, *Mad-Doctors*, pp. 68–9.
85 Dr Benignus Forbes Winslow (1810–1874) published On Obscure Diseases of the Brain and Mind in 1860 which was considered a standard textbook for a period. He was instrumental in founding the *Journal of Psychological Medicine and Mental Pathology*. He was called as an expert witness in many trials and gave key evidence in the trial of Daniel M'Naghton. Jonathan Andrews; Forbes Benignus Winslow (1810–1874) *Oxford Dictionary of National Biography* (Oxford: Oxford University Press, 2004).
86 OBP. July 1862, trial of Ann Cornish Vyse (t18620707-746).
87 Smith, *Trial by Medicine*. p. 64.
88 OBP, Ann Cornish Vyse.
89 'The Murder on Ludgate Hill', *Times* (8 July 1862), p. 13, col. 3.
90 *Croydon Advertiser* (2 August 1873) p. 2.
91 Ibid., p. 2.
92 *Leeds Mercury* (21 December 1866), p. 4.
93 Catherine Cox & Hilary Marland, *Disorder Contained: Mental Breakdown and the Modern Prison in England and Ireland, 1840–1900* (Cambridge: Cambridge University Press, 2022), pp. 151–2.
94 'Shocking Murder by Mother', *Liverpool Mercury* (5 August 1887) p. 8, col. 8.
95 TNA, ASSI 52/9 Criminal depositions and case papers. Murder: Mary Anthony. 'Medical Report, Dr Thomas Lawes Rogers. 5 July 1887'.
96 *Liverpool Mercury* (5 August 1887), p. 8.
97 *Oxford Journal* (4 July1885), p. 2.
98 Watson, *Medicine and Justice*, p. 96.
99 OBP, January 1884, Trial of Annie Player (25) (t18840107-219).
100 'Gover', *Munks Roll*, p. 294.
101 Cox & Marland, *Disorder Contained*, p. 192–3.

102 'The Egremont Child Murder', *Carlisle Patriot* (23 February 1877), p. 6, col. 2.
103 *Carlisle Patriot* (23 February 1877), p. 6.
104 Catherine Cox & Hilary Marland, 'Broken Minds and Beaten Bodies: Cultures of Harm and the Management of Mental Illness in Late Nineteenth Century England and Irish Prisons', *Social History of Medicine*, vol. 31, no. 4 (2018), pp. 688–710, p. 689.
105 Watson, *Medicine and Justice*, p. 203.
106 'Central Criminal Court, Jan. 14', *Times* (15 January 1884), issue 31030, p. 12, col. 1.
107 OBP, May 1887, Trial of Annie Cherry (21) (t18870523-659).
108 OBP, May 1887, Cherry.
109 BCLA-BRO, D/H14/D2/2/2/411 Case File: Annie Cherry.
110 'The Alleged Murder in Maidstone', *Maidstone Journal and Kentish Advertiser* (24 December 1866), p. 9, col. 3.
111 'Murder of Two Children at West Thurrock', *Chelmsford Chronicle* (16 March 1849) p. 4, col. 5.
112 Watson, *Medicine and Justice,* p. 121.
113 Ibid., p. 122.
114 *East Anglian Daily Times* (20 May 1893), p. 7.
115 *Banbury Guardian* (9 March 1876), pp. 7–8.
116 Wiener, *Reconstructing the Criminal*, p. 269.
117 Craig Newbery-Jones, 'Judging the Judges: The Image of the Judge in the Popular Illustrated Press', in James Gregory, Daniel J. R. Grey and Annika Bautz (eds.), *Judgment in the Victorian Age* (Abingdon: Routledge, 2019), pp. 161–81, pp. 170–1.
118 'Murder at Epsom', *Croydon Advertiser & East Surrey Reporter* (2 August 1873), p. 2, col. 1.
119 Ibid., p. 2.
120 'Emma Lewis', *Globe* (17 July 1852), p. 4, col. 4.
121 Louise A. Jackson, *Child Sexual Abuse in Victorian England* (London & New York: Routledge, 2000), p. 108.
122 Shani D'Cruze, C*rimes of Outrage. Sex, Violence and Victorian Working Women*, (London: UCL Press, 1998), p. 190.
123 Ibid., p. 192.
124 *Northwich Guardian* (18 February 1871), p. 3.
125 *Reading Observer* (25 August 1883), p. 3.
126 OBP, January 1884, Player.
127 *Northampton Mercury* (26 April 1879), p. 7.
128 *Chelmsford Chronicle* (16 March 1849), p. 4.
129 *Leeds Mercury* (26 December 1866), p. 2.

130 'The Lavendon Child Murder', *Northampton Mercury* (26 April 1879), p. 7, col. 4.
131 *Northampton Mercury* (26 April 1879), p. 7.
132 Carol Beardmore, 'Balancing the Family: Edward Wrench, Baslow G.P., c1862–1890', in Carol Beardmore, Cara Dobbing & Steven King (eds.), *Family Life in Britain, 1650–1910* (Basingstoke: Palgrave Macmillan, 2019), pp. 113–34, p. 114.
133 'Infanticide and Attempted Suicide', *Kentish Independent* (13 April 1850), p. 2, col. 3.
134 John Tosh, 'Masculinities in an Industrializing Society: Britain, 1800–1914', *Journal of British Studies*, vol. 44, no. 2 (April 2005), pp. 330–42, p. 335.
135 *North Devon Journal* (12 July 1866), p. 8.
136 'A Mother Attempting to Drown Her Child: A Sad Case', *Herts Advertiser* (8 August 1885), p. 7, col. 1.
137 'The Murder of Two Children by Their Mother', *The Scotsman* (22 August 1859), p. 2, col. 3.
138 'Northern Circuit', *Times* (28 March 1859), issue 23265, p. 11, col. 5.
139 'Child Murder at Wardington', *Banbury Guardian* (9 March 1876), p. 7, col. 4.
140 'Alleged Child Murder At Coventry', *Coventry Evening Echo* (4 May 1891), p. 3.
141 D'Cruze, *Crimes of Outrage*, p. 188.
142 Martin J. Wiener, 'Convicted Murderers and the Victorian Press: Condemnation vs. Sympathy', *Crime and Misdemeanours*, vol. 1, no. 2 (2007), pp. 110–25, p. 111–2.
143 Jackson, *Child Sexual Abuse*, p. 126–7.
144 Rowbotham, et al., *Crime News in Modern Britain*.
145 Watson, *Medicine and Justice*, p. 83.
146 Hawkins, *Reminiscences*, pp. 226–7.
147 Ibid., p. 227.
148 *Morning Advertiser* (11 March 1848), p. 4.
149 Smith, *Trial by Medicine*, p. 109.
150 Anne Scwan, *Convict Voices: Women, Class and Writing about Prison in Nineteenth-Century England* (Durham, New Hampshire: University of New Hampshire Press, 2014), pp. 113–14.
151 Wiener, *Reconstructing the Criminal*, pp. 268–9.
152 *Northampton Mercury* (26 April 1879), p. 4.
153 'Lent Assizes. Home Circuit Chelmsford', *Morning Advertiser* (11 March 1848) p. 4, col. 3.
154 Martin J. Wiener, 'Judges v. Jurors: Courtroom Tensions in Murder Trials and the law of Criminal Responsibility in Nineteenth-Century England', *Law and History Review*, vol. 7, no. 3 (1999), pp. 467–506, p. 481.
155 BCLA-BRO, D/H14/D2/2/2/1 Case File: Mary Ann Parr.
156 'Infanticide at Bingham', *Nottinghamshire Guardian* (10 March 1853), p. 2, col. 2.
157 Eigen, *Mad-Doctors*, p. 174.

158 Katie Barclay, *Men on Trial. Performing Emotion, Embodiment and Identity in Ireland, 1800–45* (Manchester: Manchester University Press, 2019), p. 141.
159 Watson, *Medicine and Justice*, p. 8.
160 Ibid., p. 140.
161 Eigen, *Mad-Doctors*, p. 174.
162 Ibid., pp. 153–4.
163 Helen Rutherford, 'Unity or Disunity? The Trials of a Jury: R v John William Anderson: Newcastle Winter Assizes 1875', in James Gregory & Daniel J. R. Grey, (eds.), *Union and Disunion in the Nineteenth Century* (London & New York: Routledge, 2020), pp. 242–58, p. 243.
164 Phil Handler, 'Judges and the Criminal Law in England 1808–1861', in Paul Brand and Joshua Getzler (eds.), *Judges and Judging in the History of the Common Law and Civil Law; from Antiquity to Modern Times* (Cambridge: Cambridge University Press, 2012), pp. 138–74, p. 153.
165 'Alleged Starvation of a Child', *Liverpool Mercury* (18 December 1876), p. 6, col. 4.
166 'The Sankey Bridge Starvation Case', *Wigan Observer* (22 December 1876), p. 6, col. 3.
167 *Liverpool Mercury* (18 December 1876), p. 6.
168 Ibid.; *Wigan Observer* (22 December 1876), p. 6.
169 Katie Barclay, 'Narrative, Law and Emotion: Husband Killers in Early Nineteenth-Century Ireland', *The Journal of Legal History*, vol. 38, no. 2, (2017), pp. 203–27; Idem., *Men on Trial*.
170 Alison Pedley, 'The Emotional Reactions of Judges in Cases of Maternal Child Murder in England, 1840–1890', in James Gregory, Daniel J. R. Grey and Annika Bautz (eds.), *Judgment in the Victorian Age* (Abingdon: Routledge, 2019), pp. 90–4.
171 Smith, *Trial by Medicine*, p. 23.

Chapter 3

1 Alison Pedley, 'The Emotional Reactions of Judges in Cases of Maternal Child Murder in England, 1840–1890', in James Gregory, Daniel J. R. Grey and Annika Bautz (eds.), *Judgment in the Victorian Age* (Abingdon: Routledge, 2019), pp. 83–99, p. 90.
2 Roger Smith, *Trial by Medicine. Insanity and Responsibility in Victorian Britain* (Edinburgh: Edinburgh University Press, 1982), p. 23.
3 Catherine Cox & Hilary Marland (2022), *Disorder Contained: Mental Breakdown and the Modern Prison in England and Ireland, 1840–1900* (Cambridge: Cambridge University Press, 2022) pp. 152–3.

4   Wm. Charles Hood. M.D., *Suggestions for the Future Provision of Criminal Lunatics* (London: John Churchill, Soho, 1854), pp. 162–4.
5   John Baker, 'Female Criminal Lunatics: A Sketch', *Journal of Mental Science*, vol. 48 (1902), pp. 13–28, p. 16.
6   Dr Kevin Murray in Harvey Gordon, *Broadmoor* (London: Psychology News Press, 2012), p. xix.
7   Hilary Marland, 'Disappointment and Desolation: Women, Doctors and Interpretations of Puerperal Insanity in the Nineteenth Century', *History of Psychiatry*, vol. 14, no. 3, (2003) pp. 303–20.
8   Ibid., p. 306.
9   Baker, 'Female Criminal Lunatics', p. 13–4.
10 G. Roger Chadwick, 'Bureaucratic Mercy: The Home Office and the Treatment of Capital Cases in Victorian England' (unpublished PhD Thesis, Rice University, Houston Texas, 1989).
11 Ibid., p. 281.
12 3 & 4 Vict., c.54. The Insane Prisoners Act 1840.
13 42 & 43 Vict., c.22. Prosecution of Offences Act 1879.
14 Chadwick, 'Bureaucratic Mercy', p. 281.
15 Nigel Walker, *Crime and Insanity in England: Volume One: The Historical Perspective* (Edinburgh: Edinburgh University Press. 1968), pp. 226–9.
16 Ibid., p. 281.
17 Jonathan Andrews, Asa Briggs, Roy Porter, Penny Tucker & Kier Waddington, *The History of Bethlem* (London: Routledge, 1997).
18 Chadwick, 'Bureaucratic Mercy', p. 280.
19 Between 1835 and 1863, sixty-five cases have beenfound in various sources.
20 'Murder of Three Children by Their Mother', *Morning Chronicle* (24 July 1837) p. 6, col. 3.
21 TNA, HO17/106/TX40, H.O. Criminal Petitions: I, 'Petition of George Colley 12 August 1837'.
22 TNA, HO17/106/TX40, H.O. Criminal Petitions: I, 'Letter from Robt. Hughes, Surgeon. 6 August 1837'.
23 'Suicide of Ann Colley', *Globe* (10 October 1837) p. 4, col. 5.
24 'Dreadful murder of three children by their mother', Crime: Broadsides: Murder and Executions folder 5 (1), 1837, John Johnson Collection of Printed Ephemera (Oxford: Bodleian Library); 'Horrible Murder of Three Children by Their Mother' Broadside, 1837. Broadsides – England-19th Century Crime and Execution Broadsides (Cambridge, MA: Harvard Digital Collections Harvard Law School Library, Harvard University).
25 Anne Schwan, *Convict Voices: Women, Class and Writing about Prison in Nineteenth-Century England* (Durham, New Hampshire: University of New Hampshire Press, 2014), p. 35.

26 'Murder of Three Children by Their Mother', *Morning Chronicle* (24 July 1837) p. 6, col. 3.
27 *Globe* (10 October 1837) p. 4.
28 TNA, HO17/126/YX31, H.O. Criminal Petitions: I, 'List of Criminal Lunatics in the Gaol at Stafford'.
29 28 & 29 Vict., c. 126. Prison Act 1865.
30 Walker, *Crime and Insanity. Vol. 1*, pp. 226–9.
31 'The Child Murder at Chelmsford', *Chelmsford Chronicle* (7 March 1851), p. 1, col. 7.
32 TNA, HO17/1776/464/2, 1851 England and Wales Census, Springfield, Chelmsford, Essex, Schedule 1. Piece 1776. Folio 464. Page 2.
33 TNA, HO18/305, Home Office Criminal Petitions: Home Office Criminal Petitions: Series II. 'Petition of Charles Prior and Other Supporting Correspondence. 30 July 1851'.
34 TNA, MH94/3 to MH94/15 UK Lunacy Patients Admission Register, 1846–1912.
35 TNA, HO18/305, H.O. Criminal Petitions: II, 'Surgeons' Recommendation of Removal of Milicent Page, Sarah Grout, Martha Prior and Esther Playle from Springfield Gaol, Essex to an Asylum. 19 May 1850'.
36 TNA, HO18/305, H.O. Criminal Petitions: II, 'Surgeons' Recommendation of Removal of Milicent Page, Sarah Grout, Martha Prior and Esther Playle from Springfield Gaol, Essex to an Asylum. 19 May 1850'.
37 TNA, HO13/104/193, H.O. Correspondence and Warrants, Copy 'Letter to the Town Clerk of Portsmouth from Horatio Waddington. 10 December 1855'.
38 Essex County Lunatic Asylum opened at Brentwood in 1853.
39 TNA, HO18/305/31, H.O. Criminal Petitions: II, 'Letter from Orsett Union. 22 January 1855'.
40 'Coroners Court, Yesterday – Painful Case', *Liverpool Daily Post* (2 January 1857), p. 4, col. 3.
41 LRO, LCLAR, M614 RAI/8/3 Female Patient Case Book 1856–1859, Agnes Bradley.
42 LRO, M614 RAI/8/3, Bradley.
43 Ibid.
44 LRO, LCLAR, M614 RAI/8/3 Bradley.
45 TNA, HO18/305, H.O. Criminal Petitions: II, 'Petition of Charles Prior'. For Martha Prior's release was headed 'To the Queen's Most Excellent Majesty in Council'.
46 'The Marylebone Murder', *Era* (6 December 1863), p. 15, col. 4.
47 Walker, *Crime and Insanity. Vol. 1*, pp. 226–9.
48 Katherine D. Watson, *Medicine and Justice: Medico-Legal Practice in England and Wales, 1700–1914* (London & New York: Routledge, 2020), p. 162.
49 Catherine Cox & Hilary Marland, 'Broken Minds and Beaten Bodies: Cultures of Harm and the Management of Mental Illness in Late Nineteenth Century England and Irish Prisons', *Social History of Medicine*, vol. 31, no. 4 (2018), p. 175.

50 Schedule A was held for most admissions to Broadmoor. Full title – 'Statement respecting Criminal Lunatics to Be Filled and Transmitted to the Medical Superintendent with Every Criminal Lunatic'.
51 Cox & Marland, 'Broken Minds and Beaten Bodies', p. 176.
52 Pedley, 'The Emotional Reactions of Judges in Cases of Maternal Child Murder in England, 1840–1890', p. 90.
53 Walker, *Crime and Insanity. Vol. 1*, pp. 226–9.
54 Extracted from BCLA-BRO, D/H14/D1/1/1/1&2, Admission Registers, male & female vol. 1 1863–1871, Vol. 2 1868–1900.
55 39 & 40 Geo. 3, c.94, The Criminal Lunatics Act 1800. This Act was subtitled 'An Act for the Safe Custody of Insane Persons Charged with Offences'.
56 Watson, *Medicine and Justice*, p. 162.
57 'Herts Summer Assizes', *Herts Advertiser* (8 August 1885), p. 7, col. 3.
58 BCLA-BRO, D/H14/D2/2/2/385, Case File: Susan Burfield.
59 BCLA-BRO, D/H14/D2/2/2/251, Case File: Martha Baines.
60 'The Assizes – Westmorland. The Judge's Charge', *Kendal Mercury* (4 March 1876), p. 8, col. 2.
61 The writ of habeas corpus, often shortened to habeas corpus, is the requirement that an arrested person be brought before a judge or court before being detained or imprisoned. Smith, *Trial by Medicine*, p. 92.
62 'Maiden Assize for Westmorland', *Carlisle Express and Examiner* (8 July 1876), p. 4, col. 2.
63 BCLA-BRO, D/H14/D2/2/2/251, Case File: Martha Baines, 'Draft Report to Home Office', 24 July 1877.
64 'Serious Defect in the Law', *Banbury Advertiser* (21 February 1884), p. 3, col. 4.
65 Chadwick, 'Bureaucratic Mercy', pp. 62–3.
66 Smith, *Trial by Medicine*, p. 91.
67 Daniel. J. R. Grey, 'Discourses of Infanticide in England, 1880–1922' (unpublished PhD Thesis, University of Roehampton, 2009).
68 TNA, HO144/496/X42157/3, Home Office Registered Papers: Home Office Memorandum. 'Lunacy: Emily Harriet Wilson. Murder, Guilty but Insane. Conditional Discharge 1894–1899'.
69 TNA, HO144/496/X42157/3: Wilson. Undated annotation.
70 Ibid.
71 Baron Brampton Henry Hawkins, *The Reminiscences of Sir Henry Hawkins, Baron Brampton*, ed. Richard Harris K.C. (London: Thomas Nelson, 1904), p. 289.
72 Hawkins, *Reminiscences*, p. 227.
73 'Nolle prosequi' an entry made on the court record when the prosecutor in a criminal prosecution undertakes not to continue the action or the prosecution.
74 Grey, 'Discourses of Infanticide', p. 206.

75 TNA, HO144/129/A34007, Home Office Registered Papers. 'Criminal: Agar, Elizabeth Matilda; Court: Central Criminal Court; Offence: Murder of Her One-Month Old Child; Sentence: Criminal Lunatic. 1883–1884'.
76 TNA, HO144/129/A34007: Agar. Notes.
77 TNA, HO144/129/A34007: Agar. 'Report of Dr Orange dated 17th June 1883'.
78 Ibid.
79 TNA, HO144/129/A34007: Agar. 'Letter from Sir Henry Hawkins to W. Vernon Harcourt 10th July 1884'.
80 TNA, HO144/129/A34007: Agar. 'Report 17th June 1883'.
81 TNA, HO144/129/A34007: Agar. 'Letter 10th July 1884'.
82 TNA, HO144/129/A34007: Agar.
83 TNA, HO144/129/A34007: Agar. 'Letter from Mr E T E Beasley, Counsel, in case of Reg-v-Agar. 4th July 1884'.
84 TNA, HO144/129/A34007: Agar. 'Letter 10th July 1884'.
85 Anna Shepherd, *Institutionalizing the Insane in Nineteenth-Century England* (London: Pickering & Chatto, 2014), pp. 62–3.
86 TNA, HO144/128/A33589, Home Office Registered Papers, Home Office Memorandum. 'Lunacy: Proposed Acceptance of Bail Pending Murder Trial at Assizes. Criminal: Morgan, Marianne [sic]; Court: Swansea P.C.; Offence: Murder; Sentence: Criminal Lunatic. 1883–1884'.
87 TNA, HO/27: Home Office Registered Papers: Criminal Registers, England And Wales, 1805–1892. HO/40 Calendar of Prisoners, Norwich Assizes, 21 November 1891.
88 'The Disposal of a Baby', *Bury and Norwich Post* (1 December 1891) p. 7, col. 1.
89 BCLA-BRO, D/H14/D2/2/2/567 Case file Annie Florence Attree.
90 'Reported Escape from the Bethel Hospital', *Norfolk Chronicle* (23 September 1899), p. 4.
91 Anna Shepherd, *Institutionalizing the Insane*, p. 64.
92 BCLA-BRO, D/H14/D2/2/2/567, Attree.
93 'Reported Escape', *Norfolk Chronicle* (1899).
94 Ibid.
95 BCLA-BRO, D/H14/D2/2/2/567, Attree.
96 Ibid.
97 Anna Shepherd, *Institutionalizing the Insane*, p. 173.
98 Cox & Marland, 'Broken Minds and Beaten Bodies', p. 175.

Chapter 4

1. Jade Shepherd, '"I Am Very Glad and Cheered When I Hear the Flute": The Treatment of Criminal Lunatics in Late Victorian Broadmoor', *Medical History*, vol. 60, no. 4 (2016), pp. 473–91.
2. Ibid., p. 478.
3. Hilary Marland, 'Disappointment and Desolation: Women, Doctors and Interpretations of Puerperal Insanity in the Nineteenth Century', *History of Psychiatry*, vol. 14, no. 3 (2003), pp. 303–20.
4. Jade Shepherd, "I Am Very Glad and Cheered When I Hear the Flute', p. 474. Also idem., 'Victorian Madmen: Broadmoor, Masculinity and the Experiences of the Criminally Insane, 1863–1900' (unpublished PhD Thesis, Queen Mary University London, 2013), pp. 155–6.
5. Hilary Marland, *Dangerous Motherhood. Insanity and Childbirth in Victorian Britain* (Basingstoke: Palgrave Macmillan, 2004), p. 189.
6. Ibid., p. 73.
7. Ibid., p. 200.
8. *Biography – Alexander Morison*, www.museumofthemind.org.uk (Bethlem Royal Hospital).
9. Jonathan Andrews, Asa Briggs, Roy Porter, Penny Tucker & Keir Waddington, *The History of Bethlem* (Abingdon: Routledge, 1997), p. 484.
10. Colin Gale & Robert Howard, *Presumed Curable: An Illustrated Casebook of Victorian Psychiatric Patients in Bethlem Hospital* (Petersfield: Wrightson Biomedical Publishing Ltd, 2003).
11. FHA-WHC, J7/131/1, Correspondence: Letter to Home Secretary, 2 January 1854.
12. FHA-WHC, J7/131/1, Letter, 2 January 1854.
13. Andrews, 'The Rise of the Asylum', p. 300.
14. Anna Shepherd, *Institutionalizing the Insane in Nineteenth-Century England* (London: Pickering & Chatto, 2014), p. 127.
15. LRO, (Liverpool Record Office), M614 RAI 40/28/1, Thomas Lawes Rogers, 'Superintendent's Report to the Committee of Visitors for 1869', Annual Report on the County Lunatic Asylum at Rainhill 1869.
16. Jade Shepherd, 'I Am Very Glad and Cheered When I Hear the Flute', p. 474.
17. Phil Fennell, *Treatment without Consent: Law, Psychiatry and the Treatment of Mentally Disordered People since 1845* (London and New York: Routledge, 1996), p. 48. Shepherd, *Institutionalizing the Insane*, p. 127; Jade Shepherd, 'I Am Very Glad and Cheered When I Hear the Flute', p. 478.
18. Deborah E. Weiner, '"This Coy and Secluded Dwelling" Broadmoor Asylum for the Criminally Insane', in Leslie Topp, James E. Moran & Jonathan Andrews (eds.),

Madness, Architecture and the Built Environment, Psychiatric Spaces in Historical Context (Abingdon: Routledge, 2007), pp. 131–48, p. 145.
19. Shepherd, 'I Am Very Glad and Cheered when I Hear the Flute', p. 488.
20. Weiner, 'This Coy and Secluded Dwelling', p. 144.
21. Harvey Gordon, *Broadmoor*, p. xix.
22. WC, (Wellcome Collection), Edward Thos. Monro & Alexander Morison, *The Physicians' Report for the Year 1847: Ordered to Be Printed for the Use of Governors of The Royal Hospital of Bethlem* (London: G.J. Palmer, 1846), p. 11.
23. Alison C. Pedley, "A Deed at Which Humanity Shudders' Mad Mothers, the Law and the Asylum, c.1835–1895' (unpublished PhD Thesis, University of Roehampton, 2020).
24. Leonard D. Smith, *Cure, Comfort and Safe Custody: Public Lunatic Asylums in Early Nineteenth-Century England* (London & New York: Leicester University Press, 1999), p. 200.
25. Ibid., p. 201.
26. FHA-WHC, ARA-09 A11/3, Admission Register, 2 April 1841–31 December 1842: J7/190/1–9, Fisherton House Asylum Casebooks, 1854–1875.
27. BMM, CBC-03 Incurable & Criminal Patient Casebooks, 1778–1864, Criminal patient casebook, 1850–7, Eliza Pegg, f.67: FHA-WHC, J7/190/5, Eliza Pegg Patient no. 1223, f. 111.
28. BMM, CBC-03, Pegg.
29. Ibid.
30. FHA-WHC, J7/190/5, Pegg, f.111–12.
31. FHA-WHC, J7/190/5, Pegg, f.127.
32. BMM, CBC-03, Pegg. Quoted from Norfolk's casebook by admitting officer to Bethlem on casebook page.
33. BCLA-BRO, D/H14/D2/2/2/84, Case File: Eliza Pegg.
34. TNA, MH94/20/1867, Lunacy Patients Admission Registers.
35. FHA-WHC, J7/131/1, Letter, October 1856.
36. FHA-WHC, J7/131/1, Letter, 2 January 1854.
37. Ibid.
38. 'Opening of the New Chapel at Fisherton House Asylum', *Salisbury and Winchester Journal* (28 May 1859), p. 7, col. 3.
39. BCLA-BRO, D/H14/ A2/1/1/1, 'Annual Reports Broadmoor Criminal Lunatic Asylum for the Year 1875'.
40. Jonathan Andrews, 'The Rise of the Asylum in Britain', in Deborah Brunton (ed.), *Medicine Transformed: Health, Disease and Society in Europe, 1800–1930* (Manchester: Manchester University Press. Milton Keynes: The Open University, 2004), pp. 298–326, p. 321.

41 Samuel Tuke, *Description of the Retreat, an Institution Near York, for Insane Persons of the Society of Friends* (York: W. Alexander, 1813); Anne Digby, *Madness, Morality and Medicine. A Study of the York Retreat, 1796–1914* (Cambridge: Cambridge University Press, 1985), pp. 51–3.
42 David Black, *Broadmoor Interacts; Criminal Insanity Revisited* (Chicheter: Barry Rose Law Publishers, 2003), p. 132.
43 Anne Shepherd, 'The Female Patient Experience in Two Late-Nineteenth Century Surrey Asylums', in Jonathan Andrews & Anne Digby (eds.), *Sex and Seclusion, Class and Custody: Perspectives on Gender and Class in the History of British and Irish Psychiatry* (New York: Rodopi, 2004), pp. 223–48, p. 225.
44 Thomas Dixon, 'Patients and Passions: Languages of Medicine and Emotion 1789–1850', in Fay Bound Alberti (ed.), *Medicine, Emotion and Disease, 1700–1950* (Basingstoke: Palgrave Macmillan, 2006), pp. 22–52, p. 43.
45 Charles Mercier, *Criminal Responsibility* (Oxford: Clarendon Press, 1905), pp. 123–4.
46 Marland, *Dangerous Motherhood*, p. 173.
47 John Baker, 'Female Criminal Lunatics – A Sketch', *Journal of Mental Science*, vol. 48 (1902), pp. 13–28.
48 Marland, 'Languages and Landscapes', p. 73.
49 Marland, 'Disappointment and Desolation', pp. 303–20.
50 Idem., *Dangerous Motherhood*, p. 200.
51 Ibid., p. 5.
52 Ibid., p. 200.
53 Marland, 'Languages and Landscapes', p. 59.
54 Marland, *Dangerous Motherhood*, p. 26.
55 Ibid., p. 26.
56 Ibid., p. 54.
57 Ibid., pp. 29–31.
58 John Conolly, 'Description and Treatment of Puerperal Insanity', *Lancet*, 1 (28 March 1846), pp. 349–54, p. 354. Quoted Marland, *Dangerous Motherhood*, p. 38.
59 John Baker, 'Female Criminal Lunatics', pp. 13–28.
60 Ibid., p. 16.
61 Ibid.
62 Ibid., pp. 17–19.
63 Ibid., p. 21.
64 BMM, CBC-04 Incurable & Criminal Patient Casebook, 1857–1862, Mary McNeil f.199.
65 BMM, CBC-03 Maria Borley, f. 106.

66 FHA-WHC, J7/190/6, Fisherton House Asylum Casebooks 1855–1866, Maria Borley Patient 1367, f. 341.
67 FHA-WHC, J7/190/8, Fisherton House Asylum Casebooks 1855–1866, Ann Lacey Patient 1394, f. 153.
68 Andrews, 'The Rise of the Asylum in Britain', pp. 298–326. Louise Hide, *Gender and Class in English Asylums, 1890–1914* (Basingstoke: Palgrave Macmillan, 2014), p. 19; Joseph Melling & Bill Forsythe, *The Politics of Madness: The State, Insanity and Society in England, 1845–1914* (London: Routledge, 1996), pp. 46–7.
69 BCLA-BRO, D/H14/D2/2/2/123, Case File: Mary Coleman.
70 BMM, CBC-03 Incurable & Criminal Patient Casebook 1850–1857, Elizabeth Thew, f. 41.
71 BCLA-BRO, D/H14/D2/2/2/341, Case File: Emily Lee.
72 Hide, *Gender and Class*, p. 19; Melling & Forsythe, *Politics of Madness*, pp. 46–7.
73 Andrews, 'The Rise of the Asylum', p. 296.
74 FHA-WHC, J7/190/8, Casebooks: Fisherton House Asylum 1855–1866, Ann Lacey, Patient 1394, f. 153.
75 TNA, HO144/128/A33589, Home Office Registered Papers. 'LUNACY: Proposed Acceptance of Bail Pending Murder Trial at Assizes. Secretary of State Has Not Authority to Sanction This; CRIMINAL: MORGAN, Marianne [sic]; COURT: Swansea P.C.; OFFENCE: Murder; SENTENCE: Criminal Lunatic. 1883–1884'.
76 BMM, CBC-03, Sarah Allen, f. 166.
77 BMM, CBC-03, Maria Chitty, f. 38.
78 Ibid.
79 Ibid.
80 Ibid.
81 FHA-WHC, J7/190/12, Patient Casebook 1871–1875, Mary Ann Payne f. 177.
82 BCLA-BRO, D/H14/D2/2/2/157, Case File: Margery Nattrass.
83 Jennifer Wallis, *Investigating the Body in the Victorian Asylum. Doctors, Patients and Practices* (Basingstoke: Palgrave Macmillan, 2017), p. 87.
84 Jonathan Andrews, 'Case Notes, Case Histories and the Patients Experience of Insanity at Gartnaval Royal Asylum, Glasgow, in the Nineteenth Century', *Social History of Medicine*, vol. 11, no. 2 (1998), pp. 255–81, p. 256.
85 Wallis, *Investigating the Body*, p. 87.
86 Shepherd, *Institutionalizing the Insane*, p. 67.
87 Marland, *Dangerous Motherhood*, p. 130.
88 David Nicolson, 'The Measure of Individual and Social Responsibility in Criminal Cases', *British Journal of Psychiatry*, vol. 24 (1878), pp. 249–73, p. 264.
89 Ibid., p. 264.
90 Ibid.
91 Ibid., p. 265.

92 BMM, CBC-03, Ann Raven, f. 47; CBC-03 Catherine Savell, f. 105.
93 BMM, CBC-03, f. 105.
94 Ibid.
95 FHA-WHC, J7/190/5, Fisherton House Asylum Patient Case Book, Patient no. 1840, Harriet Salmon f. 228.
96 Shepherd, *Institutionalizing the Insane*, p. 65; Mark Stevens, *Broadmoor Revealed: Victorian Crime and the Lunatic Asylum* (Barnsley: Pen & Sword Books Ltd., 2013), p. 120.
97 FHA-WHC, J7/131/1, Correspondence: Criminal Lunatics, 'Letter to H. Waddington dated 28th September 1861'.
98 Ibid.
99 BCLA-BRO, D/H14/D2/2/2/113, Case File: Catherine Dawson.
100 Stevens, *Broadmoor Revealed*, p. 124.
101 William Orange, 'Twenty-Third Annual Report of the Medical Superintendent', *Annual Reports upon Broadmoor Criminal Lunatic Asylum with Statistical Tables, for the Year 1885* (London: Eyre & Spottiswood, 1886), p. 9.
102 Stevens, *Broadmoor Revealed*, p. 121.
103 Ibid., p. 124.
104 BCLA-BRO, D/H14/D2/2/2/146, Case File: Mary Meller; D/H14/D2/2/2/177, Case File: Margaret Cummings.
105 Anna Shepherd, *Institutionalizing the Insane*, p. 84.
106 David Nicolson, 'Twenty-Sixth Annual Report of the Medical Superintendent', *Annual Reports upon Broadmoor Criminal Lunatic Asylum with Statistical Tables, for the Year 1888* (London: Eyre & Spottiswood, 1890), p. 7.
107 BCLA-BRO, D/H14/D2/2/2/384, Case File: Sarah E. Dobbins.
108 TNA, MH 94/18 Lunacy Patients Admission Registers, 1846–1912. Piece 18 1861–1864.
109 BCLA-BRO, D/H14/D2/2/2/177, Case File: Margaret Cummings.
110 Ibid.
111 'Superintendent's Report for 1871', p. 7.
112 BCLA-BRO, D/H14/D2/2/2/177/15 Letter from John Paton, Master of Marylebone Schools at Southall.
113 BCLA-BRO, D/H14/D2/2/2/177, Case File: Margaret Cummings.
114 FHA-WHC, J7/190/6, Fisherton House Asylum Casebooks 1855–1866, Catherine Oliver Patient no. 1821, f. 193.
115 BRHA, CBC-02, Elizabeth Goddard, f.179.
116 Colin Gale & Robert Howard, *Presumed Curable: An Illustrated Casebook of Victorian Psychiatric Patients in Bethlem Hospital* (Petersfield: Wrightson Biomedical Publishing Ltd, 2003).
117 BRHA, CBC-03 Mary Ann Beveridge, f. 160.

118 CB-063 Incurable Patients Book 1805–1893, Mary Ann Beveridge, f. 123.
119 Roger Smith, *Trial by Medicine. Insanity and Responsibility in Victorian Trials* (Edinburgh: Edinburgh University Press, 1981), p. 153.
120 Alison C. Pedley, 'A Deed at Which Humanity Shudders' Mad Mothers, the Law and the Asylum, c.1835–1895' (unpublished PhD Thesis, University of Roehampton, 2020), pp. 9–10.
121 OBP, September 1862 Trial of Adelaide Cole (30), (t18620922-957).
122 OBP, September 1862, Cole.
123 FHA-WHC, J7/190/4, Fisherton House Asylum Patient Case Book. Adelaide Cole; patient no. 1940, f. 31.
124 FHA-WHC, J7/190/4, Cole; f. 31.
125 Ibid., 6 December 1862.
126 Ibid., 16 March 1863.
127 Ibid., 23 June 1864.
128 OBP, 18th September 1862 Trial of Esther Lack (41), (t18650918-915).
129 Esther Lack was the subject of Episode 10 of *Lady Killers with Lucy Worsley*, bbc.co.uk podcast, originally broadcast 28 April 2022. In the podcast, forensic psychiatrist Dr Gwen Adshead suggested that, based on the medical evidence, Lack might have had a brain tumour.
130 FHA-WHC, J7/190/4, Fisherton House Asylum Patient Case Book, Patient no. 2263, Esther Lack, f. 229.
131 FHA-WHC, J7/190/4, Esther Lack, 21 October 1865.
132 Ibid., 28 November 1865.
133 Esther Lack was the subject of Episode 10 of *Lady Killers with Lucy Worsley*, bbc.co.uk podcast, originally broadcast 28 April 2022. In the podcast, forensic psychiatrist Dr Gwen Adshead suggested that, based on the medical evidence, Lack might have had a brain tumour.
134 BCLA-BRO, D/H14/D2/2/2/71, Case File: Sarah Patey. Series of letters from Richard Patey.
135 BCLA-BRO, D/H14/D2/2/2/71, Patey, 'Letter from Dr Nicolson 20 April December 1883'.
136 BCLA-BRO, D/H14/D2/2/2/71, Patey, 'Letter from Dr Baker 14 February 1898'.
137 Ibid., 12 June 1900.
138 Ibid., 18 September 1900; BHFS, Berkshire Burial Records, 18 September 1900 St John the Baptist, Crowthorne, Sarah Patey (62).
139 Jade Shepherd, 'Life for the Families of the Criminally Insane', *The Historical Journal* (Cambridge University Press, 2019), pp. 1–30, p. 27.
140 BCLA-BRO, D/H14/D2/2/2/150, Case File Bridget Myles. 'Death Notice 3 March 1909'; BHFS, Berkshire Burial Records 8 March 1909 St John the Baptist, Crowthorne, Bridget Miles [sic] (76).

141 BCLA-BRO, D/H14/D2/2/2/318, Case File Ann Goring, 'Letter 21 January 1885'.
142 BCLA-BRO, D/H14/D2/2/2/220 Case File: Catherine David. 'Letter from John David 21 December 1877'.
143 Lorraine Walsh, 'A Class Apart? Admissions to the Dundee Royal Lunatic Asylum. 1890–1910', in Jonathan Andrews & Anne Digby (eds.), *Sex and Seclusion, Class and Custody: Perspectives on Gender and Class in the History of British and Irish Psychiatry* (Amsterdam & New York: Rodopi, 2004), pp. 249–70, p. 265.

Chapter 5

1 Thomas Lawes Rogers, 'An Address to the Section of Psychology of the British Medical Association in Liverpool', *British Medical Journal* (4 August 1883), p. 232.
2 BCLA-BRO, D/H14/D2/2/2/326/8, Case File: Elizabeth Platts, 'Letter 26 September 1882'.
3 BCLA-BRO, D/H14 2/2/2/567/29, Case File: Annie Florence Attree, 'Letter to Charles Attree 25th April 1901'.
4 Image from Reports upon Broadmoor Criminal Lunatic Asylum, with statistical tables, for the year 1885. Wellcome Collection Attribution 4.0 International (CC BY 4.0).
5 Cara Dobbing, 'The Circulation of the Insane: The Pauper Lunatic Experience of the Garlands Asylum, 1862–1913' (unpublished PhD Thesis, University of Leicester, 2019); Jade Shepherd, 'Victorian Madmen: Broadmoor, Masculinity and the Experiences of the Criminally Insane, 1863–1900' (unpublished PhD Thesis, Queen Mary University London, 2013), p. 158.
6 Anna Shepherd, *Institutionalizing the Insane in Nineteenth-Century England* (London: Pickering & Chatto, 2014), p. 173; Lorraine Walsh, 'A Class Apart? Admissions to the Dundee Royal Lunatic Asylum. 1890–1910', in Jonathan Andrews & Anne Digby (eds.), *Sex and Seclusion, Class and Custody: Perspectives on Gender and Class in the History of British and Irish Psychiatry* (Amsterdam & New York: Rodopi, 2004), pp. 249–70, p. 250.
7 Shepherd, *Institutionalizing the Insane*, p. 173.
8 Alison C. Pedley, '"A Deed at which Humanity Shudders" Mad Mothers, the Law and the Asylum, c.1835–1895' (unpublished PhD Thesis, University of Roehampton, 2020).
9 Jade Shepherd, '"I Am Very Glad and Cheered When I Hear the Flute": The Treatment of Criminal Lunatics in Late Victorian Broadmoor', *Medical History*, vol. 60, no. 4 (2016), 473–91. doi:10.1017/mdh.2016.56.

10 *Household Words* (15 August 1857), p. 149.
11 Colin Gale & Robert Howard, *Presumed Curable: An Illustrated Casebook of Victorian Psychiatric Patients in Bethlem Hospital* (Petersfield: Wrightson Biomedical Publishing Ltd, 2003).
12 Wm. Charles Hood, *Statistics of Insanity. A Decennial Report of Bethlem Hospital from 1846–1855* (London: Batten, 1856) quoted in Andrews et al. *History of Bethlem*, p. 496.
13 David Nicolson, 'The Measure of Individual and Social Responsibility in Criminal Cases', *Journal of Mental Science*, vol. 24 (July 1878), Part II, pp. 249–73, p. 272.
14 FHA-WHC, J7/190/6, Patient Case Book, Sarah Price, patient no. 1468, f. 281.
15 BCLA-BRO, D/H14/D2/2/2/251, Case File: Martha Baines.
16 BCLA-BRO, D/H14/D2/2/2/251/3, Baines, 'Report to Secretary of State at the Home Office (draft) 24 July1877'.
17 OBP, May 1854, trial of Catherine Savill [sic] (t18540508-682).
18 BMM, CBC-03, f. 105.
19 Ibid., f. 132.
20 Ibid.
21 Anna Shepherd, *Institutionalizing the Insane*, p. 42.
22 FHA-WHC, J7/131/4, Letter to Home Office re Vyse, 30 December 1865.
23 Ibid.
24 BCLA-BRO, D/H14 2/2/2/261/16, Case File: Agnes Martha Morris. 'Letter Dated 28 January 1878'.
25 BCLA-BRO, D/H14 2/2/2/261/18, Case File: Morris. 'Letter Dated 15 February 1878'.
26 Jade Shepherd, 'Victorian Madmen: Broadmoor', pp. 155–6.
27 Jade Shepherd, 'I Am Very Glad and Cheered When I Hear the Flute'.
28 Ibid.
29 'Superintendent's Report for 1871', in *Annual Reports upon Broadmoor Criminal Lunatic Asylum with Statistical Tables, for the Year 1871* (London: Eyre & Spottiswood, 1872), p. 7.
30 BCLA-BRO, D/H14/D2/2/2/177, Case File: Margaret Cummings.
31 TNA, Class: HO 27; England & Wales, Criminal Registers, 1791–1892; Piece: 127; p. 256.
32 FHA-WHC, J7/131/4 Letter from J. D. Rendle, Medical Officer, Brixton, 12 September 1862.
33 TNA, Lunacy Patients Admission Registers; Class: MH 94; Piece: 10.
34 Rachel Bennett, '"Bad for the Health of the Body, Worse for the Health of the Mind": Female Responses to Imprisonment in England, 1853–1869', *Social History of Medicine*, vol. 34, no. 2 (May 2021), pp. 532–52.
35 Dobbing, 'The Family and Insanity', pp. 144–8.

36 Shani D'Cruze, *Crimes of Outrage: Sex, Violence and Victorian Working Women* (London: UCL Press, 1998).
37 Alison Pedley, 'Family Union and the Discharge of Infanticidal Married Mothers from Broadmoor Criminal Lunatic Asylum, 1863–1895', in James Gregory & Daniel J. R. Grey (eds.), *Union and Disunion in the Nineteenth Century* (Abingdon: Routledge, 2020), pp. 223–41, p. 230.
38 BMM, CBC-03 Maria Chitty, f. 38.
39 Ibid.
40 BMM, CB-052, Male Patient Case book 1851–52, William Chitty, f. 44.
41 BMM, CBC-03, Maria Chitty, f. 38.
42 BMM, CB-060, Male Patient Case book 1853, William Chitty, f. 52.
43 BMM, CB-076, Male Patient Case book 1860, William Chitty, f. 15.
44 BMM, CB-090, Male Patient Case book 1867, William Chitty, f. 28.
45 TNA, 1871 England Wales & Scotland Census. RG10; Piece: 8122; Folio: 13; Page: 18.
46 BRHA, CBC-02, Elizabeth Goddard, f.179.
47 LRO, LCLAR, M614 RAI/8/1, Case books: Female Patients, Mary Ann Taylor, ff. 109–112.
48 BCLA-BRO, D/H14/D2/2/2/365, Case File: Rebecca Loveridge, 'Schedule A'.
49 BCLA-BRO, D/H14/D2/2/2/365, Loveridge, 'Report August 1884'.
50 BCLA-BRO, D/H14/D2/2/2/365, Case File: Rebecca Loveridge.
51 BCLA-BRO, D/H14/D2/2/2/365, Loveridge, 'Memorandum to Home Office Signed WO and DN, 10 February 1885'.
52 OBP August 1855, trial of REBECCA TURTON (t18550820-768). (www.oldbaileyonline.org, version 8.0, 17 June 2022).
53 OBP August 1855, trial of REBECCA TURTON.
54 Kim Thomas, *Broadmoor Women: Tales from Britain's First Criminal Lunatic Asylum* (Barnsley: Pen & Sword History, 2022): BCLA-BRO D/H14/D2/2/2/21, Case file: Rebecca Turton.
55 BCLA-BRO, D/H14/D2/2/2/119, Case File: Mary Lyons.
56 BCLA-BRO, D/H14/D2/2/2/276, Case File: Ann Amess.
57 Liverpool Record Office, LCLAR, M614 RAI/8/4, Casebook: Female Patients 1860–1865, Bridget Myles.
58 Samuel Tuke, *Description of the Retreat, an Institution Near York, for Insane Persons of the Society of Friends* (York: W. Alexander, 1813), p. 89.
59 Hide, *Gender and Class*, p. 104.
60 BCLA-BRO. D/H14/A2/1/1/1 *Reports of the Superintendent and Chaplain of Broadmoor Criminal Lunatic Asylum for the Year 1866 with Statistical Tables*. Berkshire Record Office.
61 George Griffith, *Sidelights on Convict Life* (London: John Long, 1903), Ch. 5.

62 Andrews, 'The Rise of the Asylum', p. 300.
63 Andrew Scull, *Social Order/Mental Disorder. Anglo-American Psychiatry in Historical Perspective* (Berkeley & Los Angeles: University of California Press,1989), p. 89.
64 Anne Digby, *Madness, Morality and Medicine: A Study of the York Retreat, 1796–1914* (Cambridge: Cambridge University Press, 1985), p. 63; Jade Shepherd. 'Victorian Madmen: Broadmoor', pp. 155–8.
65 BCLA-BRO, D/H14/A2/1/1/1 *Reports of the Superintendent and Chaplain of Broadmoor Criminal Lunatic Asylum for the Years 1864 with Statistical Tables*. Berkshire Record Office.
66 Griffith, *Sidelights on Convict Life*, Ch. 5.
67 *Annual Reports of the Superintendent and Chaplain of Broadmoor Criminal Lunatic Asylum with Statistical Tables, for the Year 1875* (London: George E. Eyre and William Spottiswoode, 1876), p. 37. Wellcome Collection.
68 FHA-WHC, J7/131/1, Correspondence: Criminal Lunatics, 'Letter Dated 2 January 1854 to H. Waddington, Under Secretary of State signed Wm. Corbin Finch'.
69 FHA-WHC, J7/131/1, Letter, 2 January 1854.
70 BMM, CBC-02 Incurable & Criminal Patient Casebook, 1816–1850, Eliza Clark, f. 103.
71 FHA-WHC, J7/190/5, Fisherton House Asylum Patient Case Book, Eliza Clark Patient no. 1240, f. 44.
72 WC: *The Physicians' Report for the year 1847 ordered to be printed for the use of the Governors of The Royal Hospital of Bethlem*. Public Domain Mark.
73 Hide, *Gender and Class*, p. 102.
74 TNA, HO18/350, Criminal Petitions, II, 'Letter 28 February 1870'.
75 FHA-WHC, J7/190/5, Fisherton House Asylum Casebooks, 1855–1866, Sarah Dickenson Patient no 1239, f. 142.
76 FHA-WHC, J7/131/1 bundle 2, 'Letter 2 January 1857'.
77 Samuel Tuke, *Description of the Retreat, an Institution Near York, for Insane Persons of the Society of Friends* (York: W. Alexander, 1813).
78 Dobbing, 'The Family and Insanity', pp. 144–8.
79 Hide, *Gender and Class*, p. 92.
80 William Orange, 'An Address on the Present Relation of Insanity to the Criminal Law of England', *The British Medical Journal* (13 October 1877), p. 510.
81 Dr Robert Jones, Medical Superintendent, Claybury Asylum quoted in Hide, *Gender and Class*, p. 92.
82 LRO, LCLAR, M614 RAI/8/1, Casebook: Female Patients 1851, Bridget Doyle, Admission no.174.
83 LRO, LCLAR, M614 RAI/8/2, Casebook: Female Patients 1851, Jane Gerrard, Admission no. 141.

84 BCLA-BRO, D2/2/2/284, Case File: Lucy Keary, Handwritten note by William Orange, October 1878.
85 FHA-WHC, J7/190/6, Maria Borley Patient no. 1367, f. 341.
86 Ibid., p. 103.
87 FHA-WHC, J7/190/5, Eliza Pegg Patient no. 1223, f. 121.
88 FHA-WHC, J7/190/5, Patient Case Book, Eliza Clark Patient no. 1240, f. 44.
89 FHA-WHC J7/190/6, Patient Casebook, Mary Ann Savill alias Day, Patient no. 1964, f.61.
90 FHA-WHC, J7/190/5, Patient Casebook Maria Borley Patient 1367, f. 341.
91 23 & 24 Vict., c. 75. Criminal Lunatics Asylum Act 1860. The act was specifically amended to include Fisherton House.
92 FHA-WHC, J7/131/1, Correspondence Criminal Lunatics and their maintenance at Fisherton by the Commissioners in Lunacy 1854–1875. 'Letter from the Office of Commissioners in Lunacy to Dr Corbin Finch, Fisherton House Asylum'.
93 *Superintendents Report for 1871, Annual Reports of the Superintendent and Chaplain of Broadmoor Criminal Lunatic Asylum with Statistical Tables, for the Year 1871* (London: Eyre & Spottiswood, 1872), p. 7. Wellcome Collection.
94 *Reports of the Superintendent and Chaplain of Broadmoor Criminal Lunatic Asylum for the Year 1885* (London: George E. Eyre and William Spottiswoode, 1887), p. 17.
95 *Reports upon Broadmoor Criminal Lunatic Asylum with Statistical Tables, for the Year 1901* (London: for HMSO Darling & Son, 1902), p. 10.
96 *Annual Reports Broadmoor Criminal Lunatic Asylum 1875.* p. 37. Wellcome Collection.
97 Report of the Commissioners in Lunacy, *Annual Reports of the Superintendent and Chaplain for the Year 1885 Broadmoor Criminal Lunatic Asylum.*
98 Ibid., p. 16–17.
99 'The Airing Court', *Illustrated London News*, 24 August 1867, image by kind permission, Mark Stevens, Berkshire Record Office, Reading, Berkshire.
100 BMM, CBC-03, Elizabeth Thew, f. 41.
101 FHA-WHC, J7/190/5, Elizabeth Thew, Patient no. 1225, f. 34.
102 BMM, CBC-04, Martha Lewis. f. 132.
103 TNA, 1881 England Census. Class: RG11; Piece: 3090; Folio: 108; Page: 2.
104 BMM, CBC-04, f. 132.
105 Ibid., 132.
106 BMM, CBC-03, Sarah Allen, f. 166.
107 BMM, CBC-03, Catherine Savell, f. 105.
108 BMM, CBC-02 Ann Byrom, f. 44; BCLA-BRO, D/H14/D2/2/2/38, Case File: Ann Byrom.
109 FHA-WHC, J7/190/5, Ann Byrom Patient no. 1238, f. 140.

110 BCLA, D/H14/D2/2/2/38, Byrom.
111 FHA-WHC, J7/190/5, Eliza Clark f. 44.
112 FHA-WHC, J7/190/5, Sarah Dickenson Patient no. 1239, f. 142.
113 BRHA, CBC-03 Mary Ann Beveridge, f. 160.
114 BCLA-BRO, D/H14/D2/2/2/274, Case File: Ellen Oldman, Letter, April 1879.
115 FHA-WHC, J7/190/7 Maria Clarke, patient no. 1964, f. 26–8.
116 BCLA-BRO, D/H/14/D2/2/2/105, Case file Lucy Thompson.
117 *Aris's Birmingham Gazette*, 27 August 1864: *North Wales Chronicle*, 18 March 1865.
118 BCLA-BRO, D/H14/D2/2/2/107/5, Case file: Elizabeth Pryce. Letter dated 27 February 1874. No. 326.
119 BCLA-BRO, D/H14/D2/2/2/107/5, Pryce.
120 BCLA-BRO, D/H14/D2/2/2/107/6, Pryce. Letter dated 11 March 1874.
121 BCLA-BRO, D/H14/D2/2/2/321, Case file, May or Mary Cornford.
122 BCLA-BRO, D/H/D/2/2/2/457&528, Case Files, Lucille Dudley.
123 HO 144/567/A62310, LUNACY, Case of Lucille Dudley continued from A32014, 1896–1903. Memo RB dated 16 July 1903.
124 Thora Hands, *Drinking in Victorian and Edwardian Britain. Beyond the Spectre of the Drunkard* (Basingstoke: Palgrave Macmillan, 2018), pp. 95–7.
125 BCLA-BRO, D/H14/D2/1/2/2, Casebook: Females Admitted 1879–1901. No. 326.
126 BRO, D/H14/D2/2/2/326/13, draft medical report by Dr William Orange, 25 June 1884.
127 BCLA-BRO, D/H14/D2/1/2/2, Casebook: Females Admitted 1879–1901. Reg. No. 326.
128 Hilary Marland, 'Disappointment and Desolation: Women, Doctors and Interpretations of Puerperal Insanity in the Nineteenth Century', *History of Psychiatry*, vol. 14, no. 3, (2003), pp. 303–20, p. 306.
129 Ute Oswald, *'God, the Great Physician': Religious Activities in Nineteenth-Century British Asylums*, European Association for the History of Medicine and Health (EAHMH), Leuven (Belgium), 7–10 September 2021. Clarify that this is a conference presentation?
130 Ibid., Dr Daniel Hack Tuke quoted.
131 Marland, 'Disappointment and Desolation', p. 306.
132 David Nicolson, 'An Address on Mind and Motive: Some Notes on Criminal Lunacy', *The Lancet*, vol. 182, no. 4698 (1913), pp. 783–850, p. 847–8.
133 Diana Peschier, *Lost Souls. Women, Religion and Mental Illness in the Victorian Asylum* (London: Bloomsbury Academic, 2020), p. 169.
134 Rosemary Golding, *Music and Moral Management in the Nineteenth-Century English Lunatic Asylum* (Cham: Palgrave Macmillan, 2021), p. 78.
135 FHA-WHC, J7/190/7 Mary Ann Saville: J7/190/6 Sarah Price, patient no. 1468, f. 281.

136 'Opening of the New Chapel at Fisherton House Asylum', *Salisbury and Winchester Journal* (28 May 1859), p. 7, col. 3.
137 *Reports of the Superintendent and Chaplain for the Year 1885*, p. 17.
138 Golding, *Music and Moral Management*, p. 78.
139 *Reports of the Superintendent and Chaplain for the Year 1885*, p. 17.
140 Hide, *Gender and Class*, p. 91.
141 Anne Shepherd, 'The Female Patient Experience in Two Late-Nineteenth Century Surrey Asylums', in Jonathan Andrews & Anne Digby (eds.), *Sex and Seclusion, Class and Custody: Perspectives on Gender and Class in the History of British and Irish Psychiatry* (New York: Rodopi, 2004), pp. 223–48, p. 244.
142 Cara Dobbing, 'The Circulation of the Insane: The Pauper Lunatic Experience of the Garlands Asylum, 1862–1913' (unpublished PhD Thesis, University of Leicester, 2019); Shepherd, 'Victorian Madmen', p. 158.
143 'Female dormitory in 1867', *Illustrated London News*, 24 August 1867, image by kind permission Mark Stevens, Berkshire Record Office, Reading, Berkshire.

Chapter 6

1 Anna Shepherd, *Institutionalizing the Insane in Nineteenth-Century England* (London: Pickering & Chatto, 2014), p. 41.
2 BCLA-BRO, D/H14/D2/2/2/259, Case File: Elizabeth Carr, 'Letter 26 September 1877'; D/H14/D2/2/2/251, Case File: Martha Baines.
3 Louise Hide, *Gender and Class in English Asylums, 1890–1914* (Basingstoke: Palgrave Macmillan, 2014), p. 92.
4 Daniel H. Tuke, *Chapters in the History of the Insane in the British Isles* (London: Kegan Paul, Tench & Co., 1882).
5 Akihito Suzuki, *Madness at Home: The Psychiatrist, the Patient, and the Family in England, 1820–1860* (London: University of California Press Ltd., 2006), pp. 4–5.
6 Michel Foucault, *History of Madness*, trans. J. Murphy & J. Khalfa (London & New York: Routledge, 2006).; Andrew Scull, *The Most Solitary of Afflictions: Madness and Society in Britain, 1700–1900* (New Haven: Yale University Press, 1993).
7 Michel Foucault, *Madness and Civilisation: A History of Insanity in the Age of Reason*, trans. Richard Howard (London: Tavistock, 1985).
8 Foucault, *Madness and Civilisation*, p. 234.
9 Foucault, *History of Madness*.
10 Scull, *The Most Solitary of Afflictions*, p. 179.
11 Thomas Dixon, 'Patients and Passions: Languages of Medicine and Emotion 1789–1850', in Fay Bound Alberti (ed.), *Medicine, Emotion and Disease, 1700–1950* (Basingstoke: Palgrave Macmillan, 2006), pp. 22–52, p. 43.

12 Ibid., p. 42.
13 Anne Digby. *Madness, Morality and Medicine: A Study of the York Retreat, 1796–1914* (Cambridge: Cambridge University Press, 1985).
14 Ibid., p. 53.
15 Ibid., p. 179.
16 Ibid., p. 43.
17 Hide, *Gender and Class*, p. 92.
18 Dixon, 'Patients and Passions', p. 40.
19 Michael Brown, *Performing Medicine. Medical Culture and Identity in Provincial England c.1760–1850* (Manchester: Manchester University Press, 2011).
20 Dixon, 'Patients and Passions', p. 41.
21 Shepherd, *Institutionalizing the Insane*, p. 41.
22 Ibid., p. 173.
23 Ibid., p. 52.
24 Alison Moulds, 'Making Your Mark in Medicine: The Struggling Young Practitioner and the Search for Success in Britain, 1830s–1900s', *History*, vol. 104, no. 359 (2019), pp. 83–104.
25 Hilary Marland, 'Languages and Landscapes of Emotion: Motherhood and Puerperal Insanity in the Nineteenth Century', in Fay Bound Alberti (ed.), *Medicine, Emotion and Disease, 1700–1950* (Basingstoke: Palgrave Macmillan, 2006), pp. 53–78, p. 68.
26 John C. Bucknill, M.D., 'Correspondence on the Theory of Emotional Insanity', *Journal of Mental Science*, vol. 20 (1874), pp. 484–6.
27 Dixon, 'Patients and Passions', pp. 40–1.
28 Hide, *Gender and Class*, p. 46.
29 Charles Mercier M.D., FRCS worked at Buckinghamshire County Asylum in Stone, near Aylesbury, Assistant Medical Officer at Leavesden Hospital and at the City of London Asylum, Dartford, Kent. He was the resident physician at Flower House Asylum in Catford. In 1902 he became a lecturer in insanity at the Westminster Hospital Medical School. 'Charles Arthur Mercier', *Munks Roll*, vol. 4, Royal College of Psychiatrists, p. 463.
30 Charles Mercier, *Lunatic Asylums: Their Organisation and Management* (London: Griffin & Co., 1894), pp. 197–8.
31 Jukes de Styrap, *The Young Practitioner: Practical Hints and Suggestions on Entering Private Practice* (London: H.K. Lewis, 1890), p. 32.
32 Moulds, 'Making Your Mark', pp. 83–104.
33 Douglas Small, 'Masters of Healing: Cocaine and the Ideal of the Victorian Medical Man', *Journal of Victorian Culture*, vol. 21, no. 1 (2016), pp. 3–20, p. 18.
34 Dixon, 'Patients and Passions', p. 40.

35 Michael Brown, 'Redeeming Mr Sawbone: Compassion and Care in the Cultures of Nineteenth-Century Surgery', *Journal of Compassionate Health Care*, vol. 4, no. 13 (2017), Open Access pp. 1–7.
36 Brown, *Performing Medicine*.
37 Sir William Charles Hood, 1824–1870, *Munks Roll*, vol. 4, Royal College of Psychiatrists, p. 136 www.munksroll.rcp.ac.uk.
38 John Meyer 1814–1870, *Munks Roll*, vol. 4, Royal College of Psychiatrists, p. 136 www.munksroll.rcp.ac.uk.
39 Richard Lansdowne, 'William Orange CB, MD, FRCP, LSA: A Broadmoor Pioneer', *Journal of Medical Biography*, vol. 23, no. 2 (2015), pp. 114–22.
40 Ralph Partridge, *Broadmoor* (London: Chatto & Windus, 1953), p. 89.
41 Ibid.
42 Jade Shepherd, '"I Am Very Glad and Cheered When I Hear the Flute": The Treatment of Criminal Lunatics in Late Victorian Broadmoor', *Medical History*, vol. 60, no. 4 (2016), pp. 473–91, p. 488.
43 Phil Fennell, *Treatment without Consent, Law, Psychiatry and the Treatment of Mentally Disordered People since 1845* (London & New York: Routledge, 1996), p. 59.
44 Kim Forester, *Inside Broadmoor* (CreateSpace Independent Publishing Platform, 2016), p. 17.
45 Richard Brayn, 'A Brief Outline of the Arrangements for the Care and Supervision of the Criminal Insane in England during the Present Century', *Journal of Mental Science*, vol. 47, no. 197 (April 1901), pp. 250–60, pp. 256–7.
46 First developed in the nineteenth century by Sir Francis Galton, an English scientist, Eugenics (meaning 'good birth') is the study of the method of improving the quality of the human race. Eugenic study suggested that this could be achieved by, amongst other methods, selective breeding.
47 Shepherd, 'I Am Very Glad and Cheered', pp. 489–90.
48 8 & 9 Victoria c. 126 County Asylums Act 1845.
49 Hide, *Gender and Class*, p. 52.
50 *Household Words* (15 August 1857), p. 147.
51 Dr Thomas Kirkbride, Superintendent of Philadelphia Hospital for the Insane, Philadelphia, P.A., U.S.A. quoted in Hide, *Gender and Class*, p. 52.
52 Edward G. O'Donoghue, *The Story of Bethlem Hospital from Its Foundation in 1247* (London: T. Fisher Unwin, 1914).
53 Mark Stevens, *Broadmoor Revealed: Victorian Crime and the Lunatic Asylum* (Barnsley: Pen & Sword Books Ltd., 2013), p. 23.
54 'Memorandum of Inspection', *Annual Reports upon Broadmoor Criminal Lunatic 1889*, p. 10.

55 Henry Morley, 'The Star of Bethlem', *Household Words*, vol. 16, no. 386 (15 August 1857), pp. 145–68, p. 147.
56 'Opening of the New Chapel at Fisherton House Asylum', *Salisbury and Winchester Journal* (28 May 1859), p. 7, col. 3.
57 'Dr Orange, C.B.', *The British Medical Journal*, vol. 1, no. 1327 (5 June 1886), p. 1075.
58 David Nicolson, 'Obituary: William Orange', *British Medical Journal*, vol. 13 (January 1917), pp 67–9, p. 67.
59 'Obituary: David Nicolson, M.D. CB.LL.D., MD.', *The British Medical Journal* (9 July 1932), p. 80.
60 Shepherd, *Institutionalizing the Insane*, p. 173.
61 Hilary Marland, *Dangerous Motherhood. Insanity and Childbirth in Victorian Britain* (Basingstoke: Palgrave Macmillan, 2004).
62 Shepherd, *Institutionalizing the Insane*, p. 173.
63 Brown, *Performing Medicine*.
64 Shepherd, *Institutionalizing the Insane*, p. 173.
65 BCLA-BRO, D/H14/D2/2/2/326/8.
66 BCLA-BRO, D/H14 2/2/2/107, Pryce.
67 BCLA-BRO, D/H14 2/2/2/107/4, Pryce, 'Warrant for Conditional Discharge'.
68 BCLA-BRO, D/H14 2/2/2/107/5, Pryce, 'Letter to Dr William Orange 27 February 1874'.
69 BCLA-BRO, D/H14 2/2/2/107/6, Pryce, 'Letter 11 March 1874'.
70 BCLA-BRO, D/H14/D2/2/2/189, Case File: Elizabeth Harris.
71 BCLA-BRO, D/H14/D2/2/2/189/6, Harris, 'Letter 16 April 1872'.
72 BRO, D/EX 1675, Records for The House of Mercy, Clewer, Windsor. The Community of St John the Baptist was an Anglican religious community established in 1852 Clewer to run a home for unmarried mothers and fallen women.
73 BCLA-BRO, D/H14/D2/2/2/189, Harris.
74 Kim Thomas, *Broadmoor Women: Tales from Britain's First Criminal Lunatic Asylum* (Barnsley: Pen & Sword History, 2022), pp. 130–1; BCLA-BRO D/H/D2/2/2/21, Case file: Rebecca Turton.
75 BCLA-BRO, D/H14/D2/2/2/189/6, Case File: Elizabeth Harris, 'Letter Dated 16 April 1872'.
76 BCLA-BRO, D/H14 2/2/2/303, Case File: Sarah Bates, 'Letter to William Orange, 12 July 1884'.
77 BCLA-BRO, D/H14/D2/2/2/299, Case File: Sarah Freeman, 'Letter from Alfred Freeman. 24 July 1916'.
78 BCLA-BRO, D/H14 2/2/2/111, Case File: Mary Bennett. 'Letter to William Orange (undated)'.
79 BCLA-BRO, D/H14 2/2/2/316, Case File: Sarah Bull, 'Handwritten Note 1883'.

80 William Orange, 'Twenty-Second Annual Report of the Medical Superintendent', in *Reports upon Broadmoor Criminal Lunatic Asylum with Statistical Tables for the Year 1884* (London: Eyre and Spottiswoode, 1885), p. 4.
81 BCLA-BRO, D/H14 2/2/2/567, Case File: Annie Florence Attree.
82 BCLA-BRO, D/H14 2/2/2/567/29, Attree, 'Copy of Letter to Charles Attree Dated 25 April 1901'.
83 BCLA-BRO, D/H14/D2/2/2/189/1, Harris, 'Letter from Richard Harris Dated 16 July 1872'.
84 BCLA-BRO, D/H14/D2/2/2/428 & 606 Case files Mary Ann Reynolds, Letter from William Reynolds Dated 11 January 1890.
85 Ibid.
86 BCLA-BRO, D/H14 2/2/2/567/57, Attree, 'File Memo JB Dated 24 March 1914'.
87 Diana Peschier, *Lost Souls, Religion and Mental Illness in the Victorian Asylum* (London: Bloomsbury Academic, 2020), p. 169.
88 Ute Oswald 'God, the Great Physician': Religious Activities in Nineteenth-Century British Asylums, European Association for the History of Medicine and Health (EAHMH), Leuven (Belgium), 7–10 September 2021.
89 'Opening of the New Chapel at Fisherton House Asylum', *Salisbury and Winchester Journal* (28 May 1859), p. 7, col. 3.
90 Ibid.
91 HO 45/9572/79056, *Rules for the Guidance of Officers*.
92 BCLA-BRO, D/H14/A2/1/4/1 Letter Book 1863–1875, p. 206, copy letter from the Office of Works for S.W. 20 June 1864.
93 Peschier, *Lost Souls*, p. 169.
94 Ibid., p. 8.
95 Chaplain's Report, *Reports of the Superintendent and Chaplain of Broadmoor Criminal Lunatic Asylum for the Years 1864 with Statistical Tables*, p. 8. Wellcome Collection.
96 Ibid.
97 Ibid.
98 Information from *Crockfords Clerical Directory:1868–1932*, www.ancestry.co.uk.
99 Ibid., p. 9.
100 'The Physicians' Report for the Year 1847: Ordered to Be Printed for the Use of Governors of The Royal Hospital of Bethlem', Wellcome Collection, p. 9.
101 BCLA-BRO, D/H14/B1/2/2/1, *Rules for the Guidance of Officers, Attendants and Servants,* 1863–1866, p. 1.
102 William Orange, 'Twenty-Third Annual Report of the Medical Superintendent', *Reports upon Broadmoor Criminal Lunatic Asylum with Statistical Tables for the Year 1885* (London: Eyre and Spottiswoode, 1887), p. 6.

103 TNA, HO 45/9572/79056, *Rules for the Guidance of Officers, Attendants and Servants of Broadmoor Criminal Lunatic Asylum* (London: Her Majesty's Stationery Office, 1869).
104 D/H14/A2/1/4/1 Letter Book 1863–1875, p. 383.
105 BCLA-BRO, D/H14/D2/1/2/2, Patient Casebook: Females admitted 1879–1901, Rebecca Bell Reg. no. 575, f. 105. (transcribed by BRO).
106 BCLA-BRO, D/H14/D2/2/2/575, Case File: Rebecca Bell, 'Letter from Mrs Sophia Lock 10 August 1900'.
107 Ibid.
108 BCLA-BRO, D/H14/D2/2/2/188, Case File: Annie Nicholls, 'Letter from R C Nicholls rec'd 15 April 1878'.
109 Jade Shepherd, 'Victorian Madmen: Broadmoor, Masculinity and the Experiences of the Criminally Insane, 1863–1900' (unpublished PhD Thesis, Queen Mary University London, 2013).
110 John Meyer, 'Superintendent's Report', *Reports of the Suprintendent and Chaplain of Broadmoor Criminal Lunatic Asylum for the Year 1864* (London: Eyre and Spottiswoode, 1865), p. 5. Wellcome Collection.
111 John Meyer, 'Superintendent's Report', *Reports of the Superintendent and Chaplain of Broadmoor Criminal Lunatic Asylum, for the year 1867* (London: Eyre and Spottiswoode, 1868), p. 6. Wellcome Collection.
112 Ibid., p. 7.
113 William Orange, 'Superintendent's Report', *Reports of the Suprintendent and Chaplain of Broadmoor Criminal Lunatic Asylum for the Year 1876* (London: Eyre and Spottiswoode, 1877), p. 11. Wellcome Collection.
114 Forester, *Inside Broadmoor*, p. 221.
115 Hide, *Gender and Class*, p. 46.
116 Ibid., p. 52.
117 Ibid., p. 49.
118 Shepherd, *Institutionalizing the Insane*, p. 173.
119 Shepherd, *Institutionalizing the Insane*; Lorraine Walsh, 'A Class Apart? Admissions to the Dundee Royal Lunatic Asylum. 1890–1910', in Jonathan Andrews & Anne Digby (eds.), *Sex and Seclusion, Class and Custody: Perspectives on Gender and Class in the History of British and Irish Psychiatry* (Amsterdam & New York: Rodopi, 2004).

Chapter 7

1 TNA, HO13/106/231, Home Office, Correspondence & Warrants, Letter Book. 1859–1862, 'Letter to the Governors of Bethlem Hospital 8 March 1859'.

2   TNA, HO13/106/11A, Letter Book, 1859–1862, 'Letter to the Governors of Bethlem Hospital 19 April 1859'.
3   BMM, CBC-02 Incurable & Criminal Patient Casebooks. 1778–1864, Sarah Jackson f. 168.
4   *Northampton Mercury* (17 January 1880), p. 2. col. 5.
5   BCLA-BRO, D/H14/D2/2/2/303. Case File (1): Sarah Bates, 'Warrant for Admission, 3 February 1880'.
6   BCLA-BRO, D/H14/D2/2/2/398, Case File (2): Sarah Bates, 'Letter from J. Bates, 19 July 1881; Letter from Dr Orange to J. Bates, 27 August 1884'.
7   BCLA-BRO, D/H14/D2/2/2/398, Bates, 'Letter from J. Bates to Dr Orange, 9 July 1886'.
8   BCLA-BRO, D/H14/D2/2/2/661, Case File (3): Sarah Bates, 'Warrant of Conditional Discharge, 6 July 1904'.
9   BCLA-BRO, D/H14/D2/2/2/661, 'Letter from Sarah Bates to Dr Brayn, 19 December 1904'; 'Revocation of Warrant, 14 January 1905'.
10 Jonathan Andrews, 'The Boundaries of Her Majesty's Pleasure: Discharging Child-Murderers from Broadmoor and Perth Criminal Lunatic Department, c.1860–1920', in Mark Jackson (ed.), *Infanticide. Historical Perspectives on Child Murder and Concealment, 1550–2000* (Farnham: Ashgate, 2002), pp. 216–49, p. 224.
11 David Wright, 'The Discharge of Pauper Lunatics from County Asylums in Mid-Victorian England: The Case of Buckinghamshire, 1853–1872', in Joseph Melling & Bill Forsythe (eds.), *Insanity, Institutions and Society, 1800–1914: A Social History of Madness in Comparative Perspective* (Abingdon: Routledge, 1999), pp. 93–113, p. 93.
12 Andrews, 'The Boundaries of Her Majesty's Pleasure', p. 224.
13 Ibid., p. 94.
14 Alison Pedley, 'Family Union and the Discharge of Infanticidal Married Mothers from Broadmoor Criminal Lunatic Asylum, 1863–1895', in James Gregory & Daniel J. R. Grey (eds.), *Union and Disunion in the Nineteenth Century* (Abingdon: Routledge, 2020), pp. 223–41.
15 David Nicolson, 'The Measure of Individual and Social Responsibility in Criminal Cases', *Journal of Mental Science*, vol. 24, no. 106 (July 1878), pp. 249–73, p. 272.
16 Ibid., p. 264.
17 William Orange, 'Twenty-Third Annual Report of the Medical Superintendent', in *Reports upon Broadmoor Criminal Lunatic Asylum with Statistical Tables for the Year 1885* (London: Eyre and Spottiswoode, 1887), p. 6.
18 Ibid., p. 16.
19 Cara Dobbing, 'The Family and Insanity: The Experience of the Garlands Asylum, 1862–1910', in Carol Beardmore, Cara Dobbing & Steven King (eds.), *Family Life in Britain, 1650–1910* (Basingstoke: Palgrave Macmillan, 2019), pp. 135–54, p. 136.
20 Ibid., pp. 149–50.

21 Andrews, 'The Boundaries of Her Majesty's Pleasure', p. 224.
22 46 & 47 Vict., c. 38. Trial of Lunatics Act, s2. By this act the verdict for cases where the defendant was found to be insane was changed from 'not guilty by reason of insanity' to 'guilty but insane at the time of the criminal act'. This change was in response to the concern of Queen Victoria, after an assault on her person, that the verdict of 'not guilty on the ground of insanity' was not a deterrent.
23 47 & 48 Vict., c. 64. Criminal Lunatics Asylum Act 1884.
24 47 & 48 Vict., c. 64. S4 Periodical report of Criminal Lunatics (1).
25 47 & 48 Vict., c. 64. S4 Periodical report of Criminal Lunatics (2).
26 BRHA, DDR-02 & DDR-03, Register of Discharges & Deaths; FHA-WHC, J7/176/2, Register of Discharges & Deaths 1845–1880; BCLA-BRO, D/H14/D1/1/1/1&2, Admission Registers, male & female vol. 1 1863–1871, vol. 2 1868–1900; D/H14/D1/15/1, Discharge Register – male & female 1864–1900; D/H14/D1/17 (3 volumes) Registers of Deaths – male & female 1864–1965.
27 All figures derived from the above registers.
28 23 & 24 Vict., c. 75. Criminal Lunatics Asylum Act 1860 ('The Broadmoor Act') amended in 30 & 31, Vict., c.100. Criminal Lunatics Act 1867.
29 Criminal Lunatics Asylum Act 1860. 'VIII: Provision for Discharge of Persons Confined after Their Term of Imprisonment Has Expired'.
30 HC, Twenty-first Report of the Commissioners in Lunacy to the Lord Chancellor, p. 14. House of Commons, Parliamentary Papers Online.
31 16 & 17 Vict., c.97. Lunatic Asylums Act quoted in Twenty-First Report of the Commissioners in Lunacy, p. 14.
32 23 & 24 Vict., c. 75. Criminal Lunatics Asylum Act 1860. 'IX: Secretary of State May Permit Any Lunatic to Be Absent from Asylum on Trial'.
33 Twenty-First Report of the Commissioners in Lunacy, p. 14.
34 BCLA-BRO, D/H14/A2/1/3/1, Superintendent's Journal, 1863–1870, p. 212.
35 BCLA-BRO, D/H14/A2/1/3/1, Superintendent's Journal, p. 389.
36 FHA-WHC, J7/131/1 bundle 3, Sample – 'Warrant for Conditional Discharge of Martha Hocken, 3 August 1867'.
37 FHA-WHC, J7/131/1, 'Warrant for the Removal of Ann Lacey and Others. 26 November 1867'.
38 BCLA-BRO, D/H14/D2/2/2/126, Case File: Sarah Lancastell; D/H14/D2/2/2/136, Case File: Emma Kirby; D/H14/D2/2/2/138, Case File: Harriet Goodliffe; D/H14/D2/2/2/139, Case File: Harriet Salmon; D/H14 D/2/2/2/166, Case File: Ann Lacey.
39 BCLA-BRO, D/H14/D2/2/2/136, Case File: Emma Kirby; D/H14/D2/2/2/138, Goodliffe.
40 BCLA-BRO, D/H14/D/1/15/1, Some patients were transferred to other asylums as 'ordinary lunatics', others were transferred to Rampton Criminal Lunatic Asylum, Nottinghamshire. In 1899, the Lunacy Commissioners decided an additional facility was required as Broadmoor had become overcrowded. Rampton was

opened in 1912, taking a number of patients including some women of my dataset. Some were transferred back to Broadmoor before their deaths. Information from Introduction to BRO, BCLA, D/H14 Catalogue.
41 BCLA-BRO, D/H14/D/1/15/1, The deaths recorded here are for those women who were never released, those who returned after initial discharge are not included.
42 BCLA-BRO, D/H14/D/1/15/1, 242 cases admitted in the period 1863 to 1895 for murder or attempted murder of their child.
43 FHA-WHC, J7/131/1 bundle 2, 'Transfer Warrant to Fisherton House Asylum Signed by Sir George Grey, Home Secretary on Behalf of Her Majesty's Privy Council dated 22 May 1863'.
44 TNA, HO13/107/247, Home Office, Correspondence & Warrants, 1859–1862, 'Letter to Mr George Harris from H. Waddington', 8 January 1864.
45 TNA, HO13/108/2 H. O. Correspondence & Warrants, 'Memorandum 18 July 1864'.
46 BCLA-BRO, D/H14/D2/2/2/73, Case File: Mary Ann Harris, 'Warrant of Parole Dated 14 July 1864'. 'Warrant for Discharge (signed Victoria R) 20 September 1864'.
47 BCLA-BRO, D/H14/D2/2/2/73, Harris discharged 14 July 1864; D/H14/D2/2/2/4, Mary Ann Raby discharged 12 October 1864; D/H14/D2/2/2/20, Jane Torkington discharged 16 October 1864; D/H14/D2/2/2/106, Sarah Rylands discharged 31 August 1866.
48 BCLA-BRO, D/H14/D/2/2/2/166, Case File: Ann Lacey, 'Warrant for Conditional Discharge 21 September 1868'.
49 Jade Shepherd, '"I Am Very Glad and Cheered When I Hear the Flute": The Treatment of Criminal Lunatics in Late Victorian Broadmoor', *Medical History*, vol. 60, no. 4 (2016), pp. 473–91, p. 489.
50 BCLA-BRO, D/H14/A2/1/3/1, Superintendent's Journal, 1863–1870.
51 Andrews, 'Boundaries of Her Majesty's Pleasure', p. 224.
52 BCLA-BRO, D/H14/D2/2/2/2/29, Case File: Sarah Allen, 'Warrant of Conditional Discharge 19 August 1872'.
53 47 & 48 Vict., c.64. Criminal Lunatics Act 1884. S6. 'Duty of Superintendent on Discharge or Expiration of Sentence'.
54 Andrews, 'Boundaries of Her Majesty's Pleasure', p. 254.
55 Pedley, 'Family Union', p. 224.
56 Ibid., p. 225.
57 Jade Shepherd, 'Victorian Madmen: Broadmoor, Masculinity and the Experiences of the Criminally Insane, 1863–1900' (unpublished PhD Thesis, Queen Mary University London, 2013).
58 Dr William Orange, *Reports of the Superintendent and Chaplain of Broadmoor Criminal Lunatic Asylum for the Year 1885* (London: George E. Eyre and William Spottiswoode, 1887), p. 7.
59 Ibid., p. 6.
60 Andrews, 'Boundaries of Her Majesty's Pleasure', p. 230.

61 BCLA-BRO, D/H14/D2/2/2/187, Case file: Hannah Mary Ryan.
62 David Wright, 'Getting Out of the Asylum: Understanding the Confinement of the Insane in the Nineteenth Century', *Social History of Medicine*, vol. 10, no. 1 (1997), pp. 137–55, p. 139.
63 TNA, HO13/106/27, H.O., Correspondence & Warrants, re Sarah Jackson.
64 London Metropolitan Archives (LMA), dro/004/a/01/067, London Church of England Burials, 1813–2003.
65 TNA, 1861 England Census, Class: RG 9, Piece: 800, Folio: 8, Page: 6; 1871 England Census Class RG10, Piece: 1345, Folio: 96, Page: 7; 1881 England Census Class: RG11, Piece: 1395, Folio: 85, Page: 10.
66 Dobbing, 'The Family and Insanity', pp. 138–9.
67 Louise Hide, *Gender and Class in English Asylums, 1890–1914* (Basingstoke: Palgrave Macmillan, 2014), p. 142; Wright, 'The Discharge of Pauper Lunatics', p. 107.
68 BCLA-BRO, D/H14/D2/2/2/111, Case File: Mary Bennett, 'Letter from H. Spence to Dr Orange, 30 July 1867'; 'Letter from E. Cooper to Dr Orange, 9 December 1875'; 'Letter from A. Stokes (M.P.) to Dr Orange, September 1876'.
69 BCLA-BRO, D/H14/D2/2/2/111, 'Letter from Dr Orange to Mrs E. Cooper, 21 December 1875'.
70 Andrews, 'Boundaries of Her Majesty's Pleasure', p. 243.
71 Pedley, 'Family Union', p. 232.
72 BCLA-BRO, D/H14/D2/2/2/276, Case File: Ann Amess, 'Report to Home Office by Dr Orange, 21 March 1882'.
73 BCLA-BRO, D/H14/D2/2/2/276, 'Report to Home Office by Dr Orange, 17 March 1886'.
74 BFHS, 3 January 1900 St John the Baptist, Crowthorne, Ann Amess (64) Berkshire Burial Records. (see Appendix 4).
75 Andrews, 'Boundaries of Her Majesty's Pleasure', p. 244.
76 BCLA-BRO, D/H14/D2/2/2/261, Case File: Agnes Martha Morris, 'Letter from Laces, Bird, Newton & Richardson (Solicitors), 15 January 1877'.
77 BCLA-BRO, D/H14/D2/2/2/261/55, 'Memorandum to Home Office, 4 April 1885'.
78 BCLA-BRO, D/H14/D2/2/2/261/22, 'Letter from Rev. R. Gough, 23 May 1878'.
79 Joseph Melling & Bill Forsythe, *The Politics of Madness: The State, Insanity and Society in England, 1845–1914* (London: Routledge, 1996), p. 100.
80 Dobbing, 'The Family and Insanity', p. 140.
81 Jade Shepherd, 'Life for the Families of the Criminally Insane', *The Historical Journal*, vol. 3, no. 63 (Cambridge University Press, Cambridge, 2019), pp. 603–32, p. 622.
82 BCLA-BRO, D/H14/D2/2/2/136/29, Case File: Emma Kirby, 'Letter from Miss Emily Kirby 5 October 1878'.
83 Andrews, 'Boundaries of Her Majesty's Pleasure', p. 237.
84 Ibid., p. 236.

85 Ibid.
86 BCLA-BRO, D/H14/D2/2/2/252, Case File: Emma Luke; Andrews, 'Boundaries of Her Majesty's Pleasure', p. 232.
87 BCLA-BRO, D/H14/D2/2/2/252. Various letters 1875–1878.
88 Pedley, 'Family Union', p. 227.
89 'Another Shocking Tragedy in Birmingham', *Worcestershire Chronicle* (23 October 1875), p. 7, col. 4.
90 'Insanity & Murder', *Worcestershire Chronicle* (18 December 1875), p. 5, col. 6.
91 BCLA-BRO, D/H14/D2/2/2/252, 'Draft Report for Home Office, May 1877'.
92 TNA, 1861 England Census, Class: RG9, Piece: 3104, Folio: 65, Page: 38.
93 TNA, 1901 England Census, Class: RG13, Piece: 2855, Folio: 188, Page: 3.
94 For example: Emma Griffin, *Bread Winner. An Intimate History of the Victorian Economy* (New Haven & London: Yale University Press, 2020); Ellen Ross, *Love and Toil: Motherhood in Outcast London, 1870–1918* (Oxford & New York: Oxford University Press, 1993); Susie L. Steinbach, *Understanding the Victorians. Politics, Culture and Society in Nineteenth-Century Britain* (London & New York: Routledge, 2012).
95 BCLA-BRO, D/H14/D2/2/2/136, Kirby, 'Draft Medical Report to the Home Office 21 February 1878'.
96 BMM, CBC-04, Criminal Patient Casebook, 1857–1862, Elizabeth William, Newspaper cutting attached to f. 49.
97 BCLA-BRO, D/H14/D2/2/2/14, Case File: Elizabeth Williams, W.O. annotation to letter dated 24 August 1880.
98 Ibid., Report on Health dated 23 December 1881.
99 BMM, CBC-03, Incurable & Criminal Patient Casebooks, 1850–1857, Emma Sanderson f. 185.
100 TNA, HO18/276, Home Office: Criminal Petitions: Series II, 'Letter from Thomas Sanderson 1 April 1852'.
101 BCLA-BRO, D/H14/D2/2/2/18, Case File: Ann Wilson, 'Warrant for Conditional Discharge. 5 September 1867'.
102 TNA, HO13/109/174, H.O., Correspondence & Warrants, 'Letter to Dr John Meyer, Broadmoor. 5 September 1867'.
103 BCLA-BRO, D/H14/D2/2/2/288, Case File: Annie Howell, 'Report to Secretary of State at the Home Office (draft) 10 July1879'.
104 BCLA-BRO, D/H14/D2/2/2/244, Case File: Louisa Ashley, 'Letter 30 March 1879 John Ashley to Dr William Orange'.
105 Pedley, 'Family Union', p. 230.
106 Shani D'Cruze, *Crimes of Outrage: Sex, Violence and Victorian Working Women* (London: UCL Press, 1998).
107 BCLA-BRO, D/H14/D2/2/2/344, Case File: Sarah Beagley, 'Schedule A: Statement to Accompany Each Criminal Lunatic 30 September 1882'.

108 BCLA-BRO, D/H14/D2/2/2/344, Beagley, 'Copy of Medical Report to Home Office, 26 June 1885'.
109 Ibid.
110 BCLA-BRO, D/H14/D2/2/2/344, Beagley, 'Letter from Pvt J. Beagley to Dr Nicolson, 21 February 1890'.
111 BCLA-BRO, D/H14/D2/2/2/344, Beagley, 'Warrant of Discharge, 12 August 1895'.
112 Andrews, 'Boundaries of Her Majesty's Pleasure', p. 242.
113 BCLA-BRO, D/H14/D2/2/2/365, Loveridge, 'Memorandum to Home Office signed DN, 30 September 1885' & 'Warrant of Discharge 4 November 1885'.
114 GRO, England & Wales, Civil Registration Death Index, 1916–2007. March 1922 vol. 5b, p. 211.
115 Pedley, 'Family Union', p. 231.
116 Ginger S. Frost, *Living in Sin: Cohabiting as Husband and Wife in Nineteenth-Century England* (Manchester: Manchester University Press, 2008), p. 89.
117 BCLA-BRO, D/H14/D2/2/2/246, Case File: Elizabeth Hillier, 'Report to the Home Office. 1 July 1881'.
118 BCLA-BRO, D/H14/D2/2/2/246, Hillier, 'Report to the Home Office. 1 July 1881'.
119 BCLA-BRO, D/H14/D2/2/2/274, Case File: Ellen Oldman, 'Letter from Charles Oldman to Dr Orange, 16 March 1881'.
120 BCLA-BRO, D/H14/D2/2/2/274, Oldman, 'Letter from Samuel Rainbird to Dr Orange, April 1880'.
121 Alison C. Pedley, 'A Deed at Which Humanity Shudders' Mad Mothers, the Law and the Asylum, c.1835–1895' (unpublished PhD Thesis, University of Roehampton, 2020). Case also quoted in Catherine L. Evans, *Unsound Empire. Civilization & Madness in Late-Victorian Law* (New Haven & London: Yale University Press, 2021), p. 139.
122 BCLA-BRO, D/H14/D2/2/2/2, Case File: Sarah Allen, 'Letter from Dr John Meyer. May 1872'.
123 BCLA-BRO, D/H14/D2/2/2/31, Case File: Sarah Allen.
124 BCLA-BRO, D/H14/D2/2/2/31, Allen, 'Letter from W. B. Allen 31 August 1872'.
125 LRO, LCLAR, M614 RAI/8/3, Case Books 1856–1860, Agnes Bradley.
126 TNA, HO13/106/8, H.O: Correspondence & Warrants, Rt. Hon. Thomas H. Sotheron-Estcourt, Home Secretary.
127 TNA, HO18/276, Home Office: Criminal Petitions, 'Letter to Lord Palmerston dated 1 April 1852'.
128 'The Case of Mrs Onions', *Coventry Evening Telegraph* (15 September 1893), p. 4., col. 3.
129 BCLA-BRO, D/H14/D2/2/2/463, Case file (1) Emma Onions.
130 BCLA-BRO, D/H14/D2/2/2/463, Onions.
131 'The Case of Mrs Onions' (15 September 1893).
132 BCLA-BRO, D/H14/D2/2/2/463, D2/2/2/625, D2/2/2/931. Case files Emma Onions.

133 Warwickshire, Coventry Workhouse Deaths 1845–1943, Register 8/5, Emma Onions 1862–21 May 1927. www.findmypast.co.uk.
134 BCLA-BRO, D/H14/D2/2/2/398, Case File (2): Sarah Bates, 'Letter from Rev. G. Harrison, 29 July 1884'.
135 BCLA-BRO, D/H14/D2/2/2/303, Case file (1): Sarah Bates, 'Letter from Thomas Britten to Dr Orange, 7 July 1882'.
136 BCLA-BRO, D/H14/D2/2/2/398, Bates (2), 'Annual Report to Home Office, 25 May 1886'.
137 BCLA-BRO, D/H14/D2/2/2/123, Case File: Mary Coleman, 'Letter Dated 18 March 1886'.
138 BCLA-BRO, D/H14/D2/2/2/123, Coleman.
139 BCLA-BRO, D/H14/D2/2/2/152, Case File: Sarah Fletcher.
140 BCLA-BRO, D/H14/D2/2/2/152, Fletcher.
141 BCLA-BRO, D/H14/D2/2/2/187, Case File: Hannah Ryan.
142 BCLA-BRO, D/H14/D2/2/2/187, Ryan, 'Letter Dated 7 August 1875 from Mrs Mary Brocklehurst, Stanhope Terr., Hyde Park'.
143 BCLA-BRO, D/H14/D2/2/2/442/8, Case File: Elizabeth White.
144 Ibid.
145 BCLA-BRO, D/H14/D2/2/2/442/8, White, Notes on reverse of 'Report of the Superintendent 31 July 1893'.
146 Steinbach, *Understanding the Victorians*, p. 132.
147 Andrews, 'Boundaries of Her Majesty's Pleasure', p. 236.
148 John Thomas Burt, *A Sermon in Behalf of the Birmingham Discharged Prisoners' Aid Society* (London: Longman & Company, 1859), p. vi. Preface.
149 BCLA-BRO, D/H14/D2/2/2/105, Case File: Lucy Thompson, Series of letters August 19/22/25, 18 September 1874 and 7 May 1875.
150 Graham Mooney, *Intrusive Intervention: Public Health, Domestic Space and Infectious Disease Surveillance in England, 1840–1914* (Rochester, NY: University of Rochester Press, 2015), pp. 15–16.
151 BCLA-BRO, D/14/D2/2/553, Case File: Elizabeth Keating: TNA, HO144/496/X42157/3, Home Office Registered Papers: Home Office Memorandum. 'Lunacy: Emily Harriet Wilson. Murder, Guilty but Insane. Conditional Discharge 1894'.
152 'A Closer Look at The Salvation Army's London Rescue Homes', *International Heritage Centre Blog*, February 2020. www.salvationarmy.org.uk.
153 Helen Johnston & Jo Turner, 'Female Prisoners, Aftercare and Release: Residential Provision and Support in Late Nineteenth-Century England', *British Journal of Community Justice*, vol. 15, no. 12 (2015), pp. 35–50.
154 'A Closer Look at The Salvation Army's London Rescue Homes', *International Heritage Centre Blog*, February 2020. www.salvationarmy.org.uk.
155 Ibid.

156 'Kevin', Archive Research Assistant, International Heritage Centre blog, February 2020.
157 BRO, D/EX 1675, Records for The House of Mercy, Clewer, Windsor; BCLA-BRO, D/H14/D2/2/2/189 Elizabeth Harris.
158 BCLA-BRO, D/H14/D2/2/2/550, Case File: Elizabeth Stapleton.
159 William Booth was founder of the Salvation Army. There are letters in various files from the office of his son and wife Bramwell and Florence Booth regarding the potential placements of discharged patients.
160 BCLA-BRO, D/H14/D2/2/2/152, Fletcher, 'Letter Dated 27 October 1896 to Mrs Constance Booth, Mare Street, Hackney'.
161 BCLA-BRO, D/14/D2/2/456, Case File: Eva Mary Lonnon.
162 TNA, Census Returns of England and Wales 1901, Class: RG13; Piece: 650; Folio: 82; Page: 25.
163 TNA, Census Returns of England and Wales 1911, Class: RG14, Piece: 5655, Schedule: 12.
164 BCLA-BRO, D/H14/D2/2/2/166, Case File: Ann Lacey, 'Letter Dated 8 July 1868'.
165 FHA-WHC, J7/190/9, Patient Casebook 1862–1871, Mary Ann Payne, ff. 170-2.
166 FHA-WHC, J7/190/9, Mary Ann Payne, f. 177.
167 TNA, 1871 England Census. Class: RG10; Piece: 251; Folio: 46; Page: 20. Islington, London.
168 BFHS, Parish Records, SS. Peter & Paul, Wantage. Mary Ann Payne, Death Date 31 December 1903.
169 Andrews, 'Boundaries of Her Majesty's Pleasure', p. 225.
170 BCLA-BRO, D2/2/2/337, Case File: Hannah Shawcross. 'Letter dated 25 June 1885 to Mr E Hibbert, Hyde, Cheshire re Hannah Shawcross'.
171 Other 'manias' relating to childbearing included lactational insanity and insanity of pregnancy. Should this have been highlighted in text? Avoid short notes like this.
172 47 & 48 Vict., c.64. Criminal Lunatics Act 1884. Sample Warrant BCLA-BRO, D/H14/D2/2/237, Case File: Hannah Shawcross, 'Warrant of Conditional Discharge 9 August 1890'.
173 BCLA-BRO, D/H14/D2/2/2/126, Case File: Sarah Lancastell, 'Annual Reports 1886–1891'.
174 BCLA-BRO, D/H14/D2/2/2/330, Case File: Kate Barrow, 'Letter from C. Barrow to Dr Nicolson, 5 January 1892'.
175 BCLA-BRO, D/H14/D2/2/2/330, 'Letter from Chief Constable, Birmingham Police, 19 August 1895'.
176 BCLA-BRO, D/H14/D2/2/2/330, Barrow; TNA, 1901 England Wales & Scotland Census. Class: RG13; Piece: 1809; Folio: 124; Page: 11; GRO, 1909 Death Index. Barrow, Kate (64) Q4 vol.6c. p. 29 Kings Norton (Worcestershire) England & Wales, BMD Death Index, 1837–1915.

177 BCLA-BRO, D/H14/D2/2/2/568, Case File: Sarah Newman, 'Letter from Daniel Newman to Dr R. Brayn, 5 January 1900'.
178 BCLA-BRO, D/H14/D2/1/2/2, Patient Casebook: Females admitted 1879–1901, Rebecca Bell Reg. no. 575, f. 105. (transcribed by Berkshire Record Office).
179 BCLA, D/H14/D2/2/2/575, Case File: Rebecca Bell, 'Letter from Mrs Sophia Lock 10 August 1900'.
180 BCLA-BRO, D/H14/D2/2/2/670, Case File: Caroline E Gardiner, 'Warrant of Conditional Discharge 7 December 1898'.
181 BCLA-BRO, D/H14/D2/2/2/670, Gardiner, 'Letter from Dr Brayn to Chief Constable of Kent. 2 November 1905'.
182 BCLA-BRO, D/H14/D2/2/2/670, Gardiner, 'Letter from Dr C A Kent. 2 November 1905'.
183 Shepherd, 'The Families of the Criminally Insane', p. 26.
184 BCLA-BRO, D/H14/D2/2/2/568, Newman, 'Warrant of Discharge 30 January 1900'; D/H14/D2/2/2/611, Sarah Bates.
185 BCLA-BRO, D/H14/D2/2/2/575, R. Bell. 'Death Notice 2 November 1905'; D/H14/D2/2/2/611, Bates, 'Death Notice 12 February 1911'; D/H14/D2/2/2/670, Gardiner, 'Death Notice 22 May 1918'.
186 Invalids' Day Room, Broadmoor Prison. Illustration for *The Police Encyclopaedia* by Hargrave L. Adam (Blackfriars Publishing, *c.* 1912). Credit: Look and Learn.
187 BCLA-BRO, D/H14/D2/2/2/136, Case File: Eliza Kirby; D/H14/D2/2/2/138, Case File: Harriet Goodliffe.
188 FHA-WHC, J7/190/12, Patient Casebook 1871–1875, Mary Ann Payne f. 177.
189 BCLA-BRO, D/H14/D2/2/2/111, Bennett, 'Medical Report 1868'.
190 BCLA-BRO, D/H14/D2/2/2/111, Bennett, 'Medical Reports 1875, 1880 and 1883'.
191 BCLA-BRO, D/H14/D2/2/2/111, Bennett, 'Death Notice 21 August 1884'; BHFS, Berkshire Burial Records 25 August 1884 St John the Baptist, Crowthorne, Mary Bennett (44). Berkshire Burial Records.
192 A total of 303 cases admitted to any asylum as a criminal lunatic in the period 1835 to 1900 for murder or attempted murder of their child. The number of deaths for the admissions in the period 1863 to 1900 includes the twenty-one women who were readmitted.
193 Hilary Marland, 'Under the Shadow of Maternity: Birth, Death and Puerperal Insanity in Victorian Britain', *History of Psychiatry*, vol. 23, no. 1 (2012), pp. 78–90.
194 Sarah York, 'Suicide, Lunacy and the Asylum in Nineteenth-Century England' (unpublished PhD Thesis, University of Birmingham, 2009).
195 Olive Anderson, *Suicide in Victorian & Edwardian England* (Oxford: Clarendon Press, 1987), p. 406; Anne Shepherd & David Wright, 'Madness, Suicide and the Victorian Asylum: Attempted Self-Murder in the Age of Non-Restraint', *Medical History*, vol. 46 (2002), pp. 175–96.

196 BCLA-BRO, D/H14/D2/2/2/316/23, Bull, 'Dr Orange to Commissioners in Lunacy 10 June 1884'.
197 BCLA-BRO, D/H14/D2/2/2/316, Case File: Sarah Ann Bull, 'Medical Report 15 June 1883'.
198 BCLA-BRO, D/H14/D2/2/2/316, Bull, transcribed suicide note.
199 BCLA-BRO, D/H14/D2/2/2/316/23, Bull, 'Dr Orange to Commissioners in Lunacy 10 June 1884'.
200 'Distressing Suicide at Broadmoor Asylum', *Reading Observer* (14 June 1884), p. 2.
201 Andrews, 'Boundaries of Her Majesty's Pleasure', p. 230.
202 BCLA-BRO, D/H14/D2/2/2/136, Kirby, 'Draft Medical Report to the Home Office 12 April 1877'.
203 BCLA-BRO, D/H14/D2/2/2/136, Kirby, Death notice 6 February 1887. Berkshire Family History Society (BHFS), Berkshire Burial Records, 10 February 1887 St John the Baptist, Crowthorne, Eliza Kirby (56).
204 Julie-Marie Strange, *Death, Grief and Poverty in Britain* (Cambridge: Cambridge University Press, 2005), p. 138.
205 Shepherd, 'The Families of the Criminally Insane', p. 28.
206 See Appendix 4: 'Burials at Broadmoor Criminal Lunatic Asylum'.
207 BCLA-BRO, D/H14/D2/2/2/168, Case File: Adelaide Freedman, 'Telegram from United Synagogue. 16 May 1902'.
208 Strange, *Death, Grief and Poverty*, p. 159.
209 Ibid., p. 193.
210 BCLA-BRO, D/H14/D2/2/2/147, Case File Emma Greenwood, 'Letter from William Greenwood 31 August 1879'; BHFS, Berkshire Burial Records. 8 August 1879 St John the Baptist, Crowthorne, Emma Greenwood (53); Photograph; Appendix 4.
211 Image Old Burial Ground Broadmoor, November 2022. Author's photograph.
212 Dobbing, 'The Family and Insanity', p. 150.

Chapter 8

1 Hilary Marland, 'Under the Shadow of Maternity: Birth, Death and Puerperal Insanity in Victorian Britain', *History of Psychiatry*, vol. 23, no. 1 (2012), pp. 78–90.
2 Hilary Marland, 'Languages and Landscapes of Emotion: Motherhood and Puerperal Insanity in the Nineteenth Century', in Fay Bound Alberti (ed.), *Medicine, Emotion and Disease, 1700–1950* (Basingstoke: Palgrave Macmillan, 2006), pp. 53–78, p. 59.
3 Joanne Begiato, *Manliness in Britain, 1760–1900. Bodies, Emotion and Material Culture* (Manchester: Manchester University Press, 2020), p. 21.

4   Katherine D. Watson, *Medicine and Justice: Medico-Legal Practice in England and Wales, 1700–1914* (London & New York: Routledge, 2020), p. 84.
5   Ellen Ross, 'Fierce Questions and Taunts: Married Life in Working-Class London 1870–1914', *Feminist Studies*, vol. 8 (Autumn 1982), pp. 575–602.
6   Barbara Leonardi, 'Introduction: The Family Metaphor', in Barbara Leonardi (ed.), *Intersections of Gender, Class and Race in the Long Nineteenth Century and beyond* (Basingstoke: Palgrave Macmillan, 2018), pp. 1–14, p. 4.
7   Dr William Orange, *Reports of the Superintendent and Chaplain of Broadmoor Criminal Lunatic Asylum for the Year 1885* (London: George E. Eyre and William Spottiswoode, 1887), p. 7.
8   Dr John Baker, 'Female Criminal Lunatics – A Sketch', *Journal of Mental Science*, vol. 48 (1902), pp. 13–28.
9   Catherine L.Quinn, 'Include the Mother and Exclude the Lunatic. A Social History of Puerperal Insanity, c1860–1922' (unpublished PhD Thesis, University of Exeter, 2003), p. 341.
10 Dr Gwen Adshead, forensic psychiatrist in *Lady Killers with Lucy Worsley*, bbc.co.uk podcast, April 2022.
11 Julie Wheelwright, '"Nothing in between": Modern Cases of Infanticide', in Mark Jackson (ed.), *Infanticide: Historical Perspectives on Child Murder and Concealment, 1550–2000* (Aldershot: Ashgate, 2002), pp. 270–85, p. 285.
12 'What Is Postpartum Psychosis?' Information page from the charity 'Action on Postpartum Psychosis' (APP) www.app-network.org.
13 'Postpartum Psychosis: Severe Mental Illness after Childbirth'. Royal College of Psychiatrists information leaflet. www.rcpsych.ac.uk.
14 '"Loving Mother" Who Killed Her Children', *Times*, 31 October 2012, p. 3., col. 4.
15 'Felicia Boots Admits Killing Her Two Babies', *BBC News Website*, 30 October 2012. https://www.bbc.com/news/av/uk-20145563/felicia-boots-admits-killing-her-two-babies.
16 'Mother Who Killed Her Two Babies … Returns Home', *Daily Mail*, 8 May 2014. MailOnline.
17 Postcard Female Airing Court, Broadmoor c1910, Kind permission, Mark Stevens, Berkshire Record Office, Reading, Berkshire.

Bibliography

Primary sources

Archives

Bethlem Royal Hospital Archive: Bethlem, Museum of the Mind, Monks Orchard Road, Beckenham

ARA-09 A11/3 Admission Register 1841–1842.
CB-063 Incurable Patients Book 1805–1893.
BHRA CBC-01 Incurable & Criminal Patient Casebooks 1778–1840.
BHRA CBC-02 Incurable & Criminal Patient Casebooks 1841–1849.
BHRA CBC-03 Incurable & Criminal Patient Casebooks 1850–1857.
BHRA CBC-04 Incurable & Criminal Patient Casebooks 1857–1862.
DDR 04 Register of Discharges & Deaths 1868–1877.

Broadmoor Hospital (Broadmoor Criminal Lunatic Asylum) Archive, Berkshire Record Office, Colney Avenue, Reading

Management and administration (A)
- D/H14/A2/1/1/1 Reports of the Superintendent and Chaplain of Broadmoor Criminal Lunatic Asylum for the Years 1864–1875 with Statistical Tables.
- D/H14/A2/1/1/2 – 12 (10 vols) Reports of the Superintendent and Chaplain of Broadmoor Criminal Lunatic Asylum for the Years 1876–1885 with Statistical Tables.
- D/H14/A2/1/1/12 Reports of the Superintendent and Chaplain of Broadmoor Criminal Lunatic Asylum for the Years 1886–1895 with Statistical Tables.
- D/H14/A2/1/3/1 Superintendent's Journal, 1863–1870.

Personnel (B)
- D/H14/B1/2/2/1 Rules for the Guidance of Officers, Attendants and Servants of Broadmoor Criminal Lunatic Asylum.

Patients' records (D)
Administrative records (D1)
- D/H14/D1/1/1/1 Admissions Register: males and females 1863–1871.
- D/H14/D1/1/1/2 Admissions Register: males and females 1868–1900.
- D/H14/D1/15/1 Discharge Register: males and females 1863–1900.

Clinical records (D2)
- D/H14/D2/1/2/1 Patients: Casebooks: females admitted 1863–1879 (closed to 2034).
- D/H14/D2/2/2 Female Patients' Case Files: – (74 files referenced).
    Allen, Sarah, D/H14/D2/2/2/2.
    Amess, Ann, D/H14/D2/2/2/276.
    Ashley, Louisa, D/H14/D2/2/2/244.
    Attree, Annie Florence, D/H14/D2/2/2/567.
    Baines, Martha, D/H14/D2/2/2/251.
    Barrow, Kate, D/H14/D2/2/2/330.
    Bates, Sarah, (3) D/H14 D2/2/2/303/398/606.
    Beagley, Sarah, D/H14/D2/2/2/344.
    Bell, Rebecca, D/H14/D2/2/2/575.
    Bennett, Mary, D/H14/D2/2/2/111.
    Bull, Sarah, D/H14 2/2/2/316.
    Burfield, Susan, D/H14/D2/2/2/385.
    Burt, Amelia Elizabeth, D/H/D2/2/2/11.
    Carr, Elizabeth, D/H14/D2/2/2/259.
    Cherry, Annie, D/H14/D2/2/2/411.
    Coleman, Mary, D/H14/D2/2/2/123.
    Cornford, May or Mary, D/H14/D2/2/2/321.
    Cummings, Margaret, D/H14/D2/2/2/177.
    Davenport, Margaret, D/H14/D2/2/2/212.
    Dawson, Catherine, D/H14 D2/2/2/113.
    Davies, Ellen, D/H14/D2/2/2/16.
    Dobbins, Sarah, D/H14/D2/2/2/384.
    Dudley, Lucille (2), D/H/D/2/2/2/457&528.
    Dyson, Mary Ann, D/H14/D2/2/2/101.
    Fletcher, Sarah, D/H14/D2/2/2/152.
    Freeman, Sarah, D/H14/D2/2/2/299.
    Freedman, Adelaide, D/H14/D2/2/2/168.
    Gardiner, Caroline E., D/H14/D2/2/2/670.
    Goodliffe, Harriet, D/H14/D2/2/2/138.
    Goring, Ann, D/H14/D2/2/2/318.
    Greenwood, Emma, D/H14/D2/2/2/147.
    Harris Elizabeth, D/H14/D2/2/2/189.
    Harris, Mary Ann, D/H14D2/2/2/73.
    Hillier, Elizabeth, D/H14/D2/2/2/24.
    Howell, Annie, D/H14/D2/2/2/288.
    Ingham, Annie, D/H14/D2/2/2/183.
    Keary, Lucy, D/H14/D2/2/2/284.
    Keating, Elizabeth, D/14/D2/2/553.

Kirby, Emma, D/H14/D2/2/2/136.
Lacey, Ann, D/H14/D/2/2/2/166.
Lancastell, Sarah, D/H14/D2/2/2/126.
Lee, Emily, D/H14/D2/2/2/341.
Loveridge, Rebecca, D/H14/D2/2/2/36.
Lonnon, Eva Mary, D/H14/D2/2/2/456.
Luke, Emma, D/H14/D2/2/2/252.
Lyons, Mary, D/H14/D2/2/2/119.
McNeil, Mary, D/H14/D2/2/2/12.
Meller, Mary, D/H14/D2/2/2/146.
Morgan, Mary Ann, D/H14/D2/2/2/362.
Morris, Agnes Martha, D/H/D2/2/2/261.
Myles, Bridget, D/H14/D2/2/2/150.
Nattrass, Margery, D/H14/D2/2/2/157.
Newman, Sarah, D/H14/D2/2/2/568.
Nicholls, Annie, D/H14/D2/2/2/188.
Oldman, Ellen, D/H14/D2/2/2/274.
Onions, Emma, D/H14/D2/2/2/463.
Parr, Mary Ann, D/H14/D2/2/2/1.
Patey, Sarah, D/H14/D2/2/2/71.
Pegg, Eliza, D/H14/D2/2/2/84.
Platts, Elizabeth, D/H14/D2/2/2/326/8.
Pryce, Elizabeth, D/H14/D2/2/2/107.
Reynolds, Mary Ann (2), D/H14/D2/2/2/428 & 606.
Rowe, Harriet, D/H14/D2/2/2/118.
Rylands, Sarah, D/H14 D2/2/2/106.
Salmon, Harriet, D/H14/D2/2/2/139.
Shawcross, Hannah, D/H14/D2/2/2/337.
Smith, Hannah, D/H14/D2/2/2/9.
Stapleton, Elizabeth, D/H14/D2/2/2/550.
Taylor, Eliza, D/H14/D2/2/2/270.
Thompson, Lucy, D/H14/D2/2/2/105.
Turton, Rebecca, D/H/D2/2/2/21.
White, Elizabeth, D/H14/D2/2/2/442.
Williams, Elizabeth, D/H14/D2/2/2/14.
Wilson, Ann, D/H14/D2/2/2/18.

Berkshire Family History Society (BFHS)
Berkshire Burial Index – St Michael and All Angels Parish Church, Sandhurst, Berkshire
- St John the Baptist Parish Church, Crowthorne, Berkshire
- SS Peter & Paul Parish Church, Wantage, Berkshire

Old Manor Mental Hospital (Fisherton House Asylum) Archive, Wiltshire and Swindon History Centre, Cocklebury Road, Chippenham

J7/131/1/40 Correspondence 'Criminal lunatics and their maintenance at Fisherton by the Commissioners in Lunacy'. 1854–1875. (4 bundles)
J7/170/4 Register of Admissions 1845–1868.
J7/170/5 Register of Admissions 1868–1877.
J7/170/6 Register of Admissions 1877–1887.
J7/171/3 Journal of Admissions and Discharges 1877–1890.
J7/176/1 Register of Discharges and Deaths 1845–1854.
J7/176/2 Register of Discharges and Deaths 1845–1880.
J7/190/2 Male and Female Patients' Casebook Nos 830–966 1849–1866.
J7/190/3 Male and Female Patients' Casebook Nos 967–1041 1850–1873.
J7/190/4 Male and Female Patients' Casebook Nos 1042–1172 1851–1877.
J7/190/5 Male and Female Patients' Casebook Nos 1173–1381 1853–1877.
J7/190/6 Male and Female Patients' Casebook Nos 1382–1509 1856–1880.
J7/190/7 Male and Female Patients' Casebook 1856–1881 (continuation book).
J7/190/8 Male and Female Patients' Casebook 1853–1866 (continuation book).
J7/190/9 Male and Female Case Books Nos 1649–1921 1859–1880.
J7/194/1 (1 bundle of 4) Particulars of Patients transferred from other asylums 1863; 1911–1917 (4 bundles).
J7/198/1 Reception Orders A-BOX.
J7/198/7 Reception Orders L-MEW.

Rainhill Hospital (Lancashire County Lunatic Asylum at Rainhill) Archive Liverpool Record Office, William Brown Street, Liverpool

M614 RAI/2/1 Criminal Lunatic Admission Papers 1874–1906.
M614 RAI/8/1 to M614 RAI/8/17 Casebooks: Female Patients. 1851–1913 (17 volumes).
M614 RAI/28/1 Medical Officer's Journal 1851–1870.
M614 RAI/40/1/1 Annual Reports of the Superintendent and Chaplain of Lancashire County Lunatic Asylum at Rainhill for the Years with Statistical Records 1881–1891 (1 volume).
M614 RAI/40/1/2 Annual Reports of the Superintendent and Chaplain of Lancashire County Lunatic Asylum at Rainhill for the Years with Statistical Records 1891–1892 (1 volume).
M614 RAI/40/2/1 Annual Reports of the Superintendents and Chaplains of Lancashire County Lunatic Asylums at Lancaster, Prestwich, Rainhill and Whittingham 1866–1870 (1 volume).
M614 RAI/40/2/2 Annual Reports of the Superintendents and Chaplains of Lancashire County Lunatic Asylums at Lancaster, Prestwich, Rainhill and Whittingham 1871–1874 (1 volume).
M614 RAI/40/2/3 Annual Reports of the Superintendents and Chaplains of Lancashire County Lunatic Asylums at Lancaster, Prestwich, Rainhill and Whittingham 1875–1878 (1 volume).

M614 RAI/40/2/4 Annual Reports of the Superintendents and Chaplains of Lancashire County Lunatic Asylums at Lancaster, Prestwich, Rainhill and Whittingham 1879–1882 (1 volume).

M614 RAI/40/2/5 Annual Reports of the Superintendents and Chaplains of Lancashire County Lunatic Asylums at Lancaster, Prestwich, Rainhill and Whittingham 1883–1886 (1 volume).

M614 RAI/46 Notes and other documents collected by Dr Millicent Regan for *A Caring Society, a Study of Lunacy in Liverpool and South-west Lancashire*. 1986.

The National Archives, Kew (TNA)

Records of Justices of Assize, Gaol Delivery, Oyer and Terminer and Nisi Prius: (ASSI).

ASSI 36/6/24 Assizes: Home, Norfolk and South-Eastern Circuit: Depositions. 1849–50. Surrey. Accused: E Goddard. Offence: Infanticide.

ASSI 36/6/50 Assizes: Home, Norfolk and South-Eastern Circuit: Depositions. 1849–50. Suffolk. Accused: M Robinson. Offence: Infanticide.

ASSI 36/8/24 Assizes: Home, Norfolk and South-Eastern Circuit: Depositions. 1853–56. Hertford. Accused: S. Newton. Offence: Murder.

ASSI 52/9 Assizes: Home, Northern Circuit: Depositions and case papers. 1887.

- Murder: Elizabeth Crean. (infanticide).
- Murder: Mary France.
- Murder: Mary Anthony.
- Murder: Harriet Rushton.

*Records relating to proceedings in court (**CRIM**).*

CRIM 1/20/6 1149328 Central Criminal Court: Depositions. Defendant: Levesley, Rose. Charge: Murder. Session: March 1884.

*Records created or inherited by the Home Office, Ministry of Home Security and other related bodies (**HO**).*

HO8/160 Quarterly returns of prisoners in convict prisons and criminal lunatic asylums, 1864.

HO13/104/193 Home Office Correspondence and Warrants. Copy letter to the Town Clerk of Portsmouth from Horatio Waddington. 10 December 1855.

HO13/106 Criminal Entry Books: Correspondence & Warrants, 1859–1862.

HO17/106/TX40 Home Office Criminal Petitions Series 1 'Letter from Robt. Hughes, Surgeon'. 6 August 1837.

HO17/106/TX40 Home Office Criminal Petitions Series 1 'Petition of George Colley'. 12 August 1837.

HO17/126/YX31 Home Office Criminal Petitions Series 1 'List of Criminal Lunatics in the Gaol at Stafford' 1837.

HO17/1776/464/2 1851 England and Wales Census. Springfield, Chelmsford, Essex.

HO18/276 Criminal Petitions: Series II Petitions (surnames of convicts, S-Z) (75 items). 29 April–9 May 1850

HO18/305 Criminal Petitions: Series II Petitions (surnames of convicts, H-Z) 27 May–June 4 1851; Petitions, 5–12 June; 1851 Petitions (surnames of convicts, A-K) 12–14 June; 1851 (64 items).

HO18/305 Home Office Criminal Petitions: Series II. 1850 'Surgeons' Recommendation of Removal of Milicent Page, Sarah Grout, Martha Prior and Esther Playle from Springfield Gaol, Essex to an Asylum'. 19 May 1850.

HO18/305 Home Office Criminal Petitions: Series II. The petition for Martha Prior's release was headed 'To the Queen's most Excellent Majesty in Council'. 'Petition of Charles Prior' 30 July 1851 and other supporting correspondence.

HO18/350 Criminal Petitions: Series II 1850 Amelia Burt. Letter to Secretary of State at the Home Office 28 February 1870.

HO18/305/31 Home Office Criminal Petitions: Series II, Letter from Orsett Union. 22 January 1855.

HO144/128/A33589 Home Office Memorandum. Home Office Registered Papers, Lunacy: Proposed acceptance of bail pending murder trial at Assizes. Criminal: Morgan, Marianne; Court: Swansea P.C.; Offence: Murder; Sentence: Criminal Lunatic. 1883–1884.

HO144/496/A340007 Home Office Registered Papers, Criminal: Agar, Elizabeth Matilda Wilson. Offence: Murder, of her one-month child; Sentence: Criminal Lunatic. 1883–1884

HO144/496/X42157/3 Home Office Memorandum. Home Office Registered Papers, Lunacy: Wilson, Emily Harriet. Murder, guilty but insane. Conditional discharge. 1893–1899.

HO144/579/A63301, ASS113/32. Regina v Worley. 1902–1903.

*Records created or inherited by the Ministry of Health and successors, local government boards and related bodies (**MH**).*

MH94/3 to MH94/26 UK Lunacy Patients Admission Register Vols. 1 to 66, County asylums and hospitals. 1846–1912.

*Records of the Palatinate of Lancaster- Records of the Crown Court (**PL**)*

PL 27/14 Palatinate of Lancaster: Crown Court: Depositions 1856–1858.

Official Publications & Parliamentary Papers: House of Commons (HC) House of Lords (HL)

Books (printed for Her Majesty's Stationery Office)

Sixth Report of the Commissioners in Lunacy to the Lord Chancellor. (pursuant to Acts 8 & 9 Vict., c. 100, s. 88) (ordered, by The House of Commons, to be printed 8th August 1851).

Rules for the Guidance of Officers, Attendants and Servants of Broadmoor Criminal Lunatic Asylum. (pursuant to act 23 & 24 Vict., c. 75, s. 5) (London: HMSO, 1863).
Twenty-first Report of the Commissioners in Lunacy to the Lord Chancellor. (pursuant to Acts 8 & 9 Vict., c. 100, s. 88) (London: HMSO, 1867).
Reports upon Broadmoor Criminal Lunatic Asylum, with statistical tables, for the year 1889 (London: H.M.S.O., Eyre and Spottiswoode, 1890).

Debates & select committee minute.
HC Punishment of Death – Parliamentary Debates. 3rd Series vol. 174. March 1865.
HL J16 (19 June 1843) M'Naghten's Case. House of Lords Decisions (1843).

Hansard 1803–2005.
HL Deb 18 May 1852, vol. 126, cc 1230–1244. 'Criminal Lunatics' House of Lords Debate 18 May 1852.
HC Deb 10 June 1856, vol. 142, cc 1231–1261. 1231 – Mr W. Ewart. House of Commons Debate 10 June 1856.

Statutes
21 Jac.I. c. 27 Infanticide Act (1624).
39 & 40 Geo. III c.94. Criminal Lunatics Act (1800).
43 Geo 3, c 58. 'Lord Ellenborough's Act' (1803).
6 & 7 Wm IV c 89. Attendance and Remuneration of Medical Witnesses at Coroners Inquests Act (1836).
3 & 4 Vict. c.54 The Insane Prisoners Act (1840).
8 & 9 Vict. c.100. Lunacy Act (1845).
23 & 24 Vict. c.75. Criminal Lunatic Asylum Act (1862).
42 & 43 Vict. c.22. Prosecution of Offences Act (1879).
46 & 47 Vict. c.38. Custody of Insane Persons Act (1883).
47 & 48 Vict. c.64. Criminal Lunatics Act (1884).
48 & 49 Vict. c.69. Criminal Law Amendment Act (1885).

Old Bailey Trial Proceedings Online (OBP)

Contemporary books
Burt, Rev John T., *A Sermon in Behalf of the Birmingham Discharged Prisoners' Aid Society* (London: Longman & Company, 1859)
Conolly, John, *Treatment of the Insane without Mechanical Restraint* (London: Smith, Elder & Co., 1856).
Hawkins Bt., Henry, with Richard Harris, K.C., *The Reminiscences of Sir Henry Hawkins, Baron Brampton* (London: Thomas Nelson, 1904).
Hood, Wm. Charles, *Suggestions for the Future Provision of Criminal Lunatics* (London, Soho: John Churchill, 1854).
Hood, Wm. Charles, *Statistics of Insanity. A Decennial Report of Bethlem Hospital from 1846 to 1855* (London: Batten, 1856).

Mercier, Charles, *Lunatic Asylums: Their Organisation and Management* (London: Griffin & Co., 1894).
Mercier, Charles, *Criminal Responsibility* (Oxford: Clarendon Press, 1905).
Nicolson, David, 'Twenty-seventh Annual Report of the Medical Superintendent', *Annual Reports upon Broadmoor Criminal Lunatic Asylum with Statistical Tables, for the Year 1889* (London: Eyre & Spottiswood, 1890).
O'Donoghue, Edward G., *The Story of Bethlem Hospital from Its Foundation in 1247* (London: T. Fisher Unwin, 1914).
Orange, William, 'Twenty-third Annual Report of the Medical Superintendent', *Annual Reports upon Broadmoor Criminal Lunatic Asylum with Statistical Tables for the Year 1885* (London: Eyre and Spottiswoode, 1887), pp. 4–8.
de Styrap, Jukes, *The Young Practitioner: Practical Hints and Suggestions on Entering Private Practice* (London: H.K. Lewis, 1890).
Taylor, Alfred Swaine, *Medical Jurisprudence* (London: L. N. Fowler, 1891).
Tuke, Daniel Hack, *Chapters in the History of the Insane in the British Isles* (London: Kegan Paul, Trench & Co., 1882).
Tuke, Samuel, *Description of the Retreat, an Institution Near York, for Insane Persons of the Society of Friends* (York: W. Alexander, 1813).

Contemporary articles
Baker, John, 'Female Criminal Lunatics: A Sketch', *Journal of Mental Science*, vol. 48 (January 1902), pp. 13–28.
Brayn, Richard, 'A Brief Outline of the Arrangements for the Care and Supervision of the Criminal Insane in England during the Present Century', *Journal of Mental Science*, vol. 47 (April 1901), pp. 250–60.
Nicolson, David, 'The Morbid Psychology of Criminals', *Journal of Mental Science*, vol. 19 (July 1873), pp. 222–32; ibid., vol. 20 (July 1874), pp. 167–85; ibid., vol. 21 (April 1875), pp. 18–31 and pp. 225–53.
Nicolson, David, 'A Chapter in the History of Criminal Lunacy in England', *Journal of Mental Science*, vol. 23 (July 1877), pp. 165–85.
Nicolson, David, 'The Measure of Individual and Social Responsibility in Criminal Cases', *Journal of Mental Science*, vol. 24 (April 1878), pp. 1–25 and pp. 249–73.
Nicolson, David, 'Some Observations on the State of Society, Past and Present, in Relation to Criminal Psychology', *Journal of Mental Science*, vol. 27 (October 1881), pp. 359–70.
Nicolson, David, 'Presidential Address Delivered at the Fifty-Fourth Annual Meeting of the Medico-Psychological Association, Held in London: 25th and 26th July, 1895', *Journal of Mental Science*, vol. 41 (October 1895), pp. 567–91.
Nicolson, David, 'An Address on Mind and Motive: Some Notes on Criminal Lunacy', *The Lancet*, vol. 182 (Originally published as Volume 2), no. 4698 (16 September 1913), pp. 783–850.
Nicolson, David, 'William Orange: Official and Personal: An Appreciation', *British Medical Journal*, vol. 1, no. 2924 (13 January 1917), pp. 68–9.

Orange, William, CB, MD, FRCP, LSA, 'An Address on the Present Relation of Insanity to the Criminal Law of England', *British Medical Journal*, vol. 2, no. 877 (13 October 1877), pp. 509–11 and pp. 553–4.

Orange, William, 'Presidential Address, delivered at the Annual Meeting of the Medico-Psychological Association, held at the Royal College of Physicians, London: July 27th, 1883', *Journal of Mental Science*, vol. 29 (October 1883), pp. 329–54.

Rogers, Thomas Lawes, M.D., M.R.C.P., 'An Address to the Section of Psychology of the British Medical Association in Liverpool. August 1883', *The British Medical Journal*, vol. 2, no. 1179 (4 August 1883), pp. 231–2.

Newspapers, periodicals and journals (www.britishnewspaperarchive.co.uk)
Banbury Advertiser
Belfast Telegraph
Birmingham Daily Post
British Medical Journal
Carlisle Express and Examiner
Chelmsford Chronicle
Cheshire Observer
Cornhill Magazine
Daily Mail
Daily Telegraph
Derby Mercury
Derbyshire Courier
Devizes and Wiltshire Gazette
Dublin Medical Press
The Era
Glasgow Herald
The Globe
Hampshire Telegraph
Herts Advertiser
Household Words
Huddersfield Daily Chronicle
Illustrated London News
Illustrated Police News
Journal of Mental Science
Kendal Mercury
Lady's Own Paper
Lancaster and General Advertiser for Lancaster, Westmorland and Yorkshire
Lancet
Leeds Mercury
Leicester Chronicle and Leicestershire Mercury
Lloyds Weekly Newspaper

Liverpool Mercury
Manchester Times
Morning Advertiser
Morning Chronicle
Northampton Mercury
Pall Mall Gazette
The Penny Illustrated
Penrith Herald
Reading Mercury
Reading Observer
Royal Cornwall Gazette
Salisbury and Winchester Journal
Saturday Review
Sheffield and Rotherham Independent
Southwark and Lambeth Ensign
South London Chronicle
South Wales Daily News
Sussex Chronicle
Standard
Times
Worcestershire Chronicle

Secondary sources

Books

Allderidge, Patricia, *Bethlem Hospital 1247–1997* (Chichester: Phillimore & Co Ltd, 1997).

Anderson, Olive, *Suicide in Victorian and Edwardian England* (Oxford: Oxford University Press, 1987).

Andrews, Jonathan, 'The Boundaries of Her Majesty's Pleasure: Discharging Child-murderers from Broadmoor and Perth Criminal Lunatic Department, c. 1860–1920', in Mark Jackson (ed.), *Infanticide: Historical Perspectives on Child Murder and Concealment, 1550–2000* (Aldershot: Ashgate, 2002), pp. 216–48.

Andrews, Jonathan, 'The Rise of the Asylum in Britain', in Deborah Brunton (ed.), *Medicine Transformed: Health, Disease and Society in Europe 1800–1930* (Manchester: Manchester University Press. Milton Keynes: The Open University, 2004), pp. 298–326.

Andrews, Jonathan & Anne Digby (eds.), *Sex and Seclusion, Class and Custody: Perspectives on Gender and Class in the History of British and Irish Psychiatry* (New York: Rodopi, 2004).

Andrews, Jonathan & Anne Digby, 'Introduction: Gender and Class in the Historiography of British and Irish Psychiatry', in Jonathan Andrews & Anne Digby (eds.), *Sex and Seclusion, Class and Custody: Perspectives on Gender and Class in the History of British and Irish Psychiatry* (New York: Rodopi, 2004), pp. 7–44.

Andrews, Jonathan, Asa Briggs, Roy Porter, Penny Tucker & Kier Waddington, *The History of Bethlem* (London: Routledge, 1997).

Appignanesi, Lisa, *Mad, Bad and Sad: A History of Women and the Mind Doctors from 1800* (London: Virago, 2008).

Arnot, Margaret L., 'Understanding Women Committing New-born Child Murder in England', in Shani D'Cruze (ed.), *Everyday Violence in Britain, 1850–1950: Gender and Class* (Harlow, England and New York: Longman, 2000), pp. 55–69.

Arnot, Margaret L., 'The Murder of Thomas Sandles: Meanings of a Mid-nineteenth-century Infanticide', in Mark Jackson (ed.), *Infanticide: Historical Perspectives on Child Murder and Concealment, 1550–2000* (Aldershot: Ashgate, 2002), pp. 149–67.

Arnot, Margaret, L. & Cornelie Usborne (eds.), *Gender and Crime in Modern Europe* (London: UCL Press, 1999).

Bach, Matthew, *Combating London's Criminal Class. A State Divided, 1869–95* (London: Bloomsbury Academic, 2020).

Bailey, Joanne, *Unquiet Lives. Marriage and Marriage Breakdown in England, 1660–1800* (Cambridge: Cambridge University Press, 2003).

Bailey, Joanne, *Parenting in England 1760–1830: Emotion, Identity and Generation* (Oxford: Oxford University Press, 2012).

Bailey, Victor, *'This Rash Act': Suicide across the Life Cycle in the Victorian City* (Stanford: Stanford University Press, 1998).

Barclay, Katie, *Men on Trial. Performing Emotion, Embodiment and Identity in Ireland, 1800–45* (Manchester: Manchester University Press, 2019).

Barrell, Helen, *Fatal Evidence. Professor Alfred Swaine Taylor & the Dawn of Forensic Science* (Barnsley: Pen & Sword History, 2017).

Bartlett, Peter, 'The Asylum and the Poor Law: The Productive Alliance', in Joseph Melling & Bill Forsythe (eds.), *Insanity, Institutions and Society, 1880–1914: A Social History of Madness in Comparative Perspective* (London: Routledge, 1999), pp. 48–67.

Bartlett, Peter, 'Community Care and Its Antecedents', in Peter Bartlett & David Wright (eds.), *Outside the Walls of the Asylum: This History of Care in the Community 1750–2000* (London and New Brunswick, NJ: The Athlone Press, 1999), pp. 1–18.

Bartlett, Peter, *The Poor Law of Lunacy: The Administration of Pauper Lunatics in Mid-Nineteenth Century England* (London: Leicester University Press, 1999).

Bartlett, Peter & David Wright, (eds.), *Outside the Walls of the Asylum: This History of Care in the Community 1750–2000* (London and New Brunswick, NJ: The Athlone Press, 1999).

Beardmore, Carol, 'Balancing the Family: Edward Wrench, Baslow G.P., c1862–1890', in Carol Beardmore, Cara Dobbing & Steven King (eds.), *Family Life in Britain 1650–1910* (Basingstoke: Palgrave Macmillan, 2019), pp. 113–34.

Beardmore, Carol, Cara Dobbing & Steven King (eds.), *Family Life in Britain 1650–1910* (Basingstoke: Palgrave Macmillan, 2019).

Begiato, Joanne, *Manliness in Britain, 1760–1900. Bodies, Emotion and Material Culture* (Manchester: Manchester University Press, 2020).

Bewley, Thomas, *Madness to Mental Illness. A History of the Royal College of Psychiatrists* (London: RPysch Publications, 2008).

Bound Alberti, Fay, 'Introduction: Medical History and Emotion Theory', in Fay Bound Alberti (ed.), *Medicine, Emotion and Disease, 1700–1950* (Basingstoke: Palgrave Macmillan, 2006), pp. xiii–xxviii.

Bound Alberti, Fay (ed.), *Medicine, Emotion and Disease, 1700–1950* (Basingstoke: Palgrave Macmillan, 2006).

Brand, Paul & Joshua Getzler, (eds.), *Judges and Judging in the History of the Common Law and Civil Law; from Antiquity to Modern Times* (Cambridge: Cambridge University Press, 2012).

Brown, Michael, *Performing Medicine. Medical Culture and Identity in Provincial England, c1760–1850* (Manchester: Manchester University Press, 2011).

Burney, Ian, *Bodies of Evidence: Medicine and the Politics of the English Inquest, 1830–1926* (London: Routledge, 2000).

Cannadine, David, *Class in Britain* (London: Penguin Books, 1998).

Cannadine, David, *Victorious Century: The United Kingdom, 1800–1906* (London: Penguin Random House, 2017).

Cossins, Annie, *Female Criminality: Infanticide, Moral Panics and the Female Body* (Basingstoke: Palgrave Macmillan, 2015).

Coleborne, Catharine, *Why Talk about Madness? Bringing History into the Conversation* (Cham: Palgrave Macmillan, 2020).

Conley, Caroline A., *Certain Other Countries: Homicide, Gender and National Identity in Late Nineteenth-Century England, Ireland, Scotland and Wales* (Columbus, OH: Ohio State University Press, 2007).

Cox, Catherine & Hilary Marland, *Disorder Contained: Mental Breakdown and the Modern Prison in England and Ireland, 1840–1900* (Cambridge: Cambridge University Press, 2022).

Crone, Rosemary, *Violent Victorians: Popular Entertainment in Nineteenth-Century London* (Manchester: Manchester University Press, 2012).

Crone, Rosemary, *Illiterate Inmates: Educating Criminals in Nineteenth Century England* (Oxford: Oxford University Press, 2022).

Cuming, Emma, *Housing, Class and Gender in Modern British Writing, 1880–2012* (Cambridge: Cambridge University Press, 2016).

Davidoff, Leonore & Catherine Hall, *Family Fortunes: Men and Women of the English Middle Class, 1780–1850* (London: Routledge, 2002).

D'Cruze, Shani, *Crimes of Outrage. Sex, Violence and Victorian Working Women* (London: UCL Press, 1998).

D'Cruze, Shani (ed.), *Everyday Violence in Britain, 1850–1950: Gender and Class* (Harlow, England & New York: Longman, 2000).

D'Cruze, Shani & Louise Jackson, *Women, Crime and Justice in England since 1660* (Basingstoke: Palgrave Macmillan, 2009).

Dobbing, Cara, 'The Family and Insanity: The Experience of the Garlands Asylum, 1862–1910', in Carol Beardmore, Cara Dobbing & Steven King (eds.), *Family Life in Britain, 1650–1910* (Basingstoke: Palgrave Macmillan, 2019), pp. 135–54.

Dobbing, Cara, 'Pauper Lunatics at Home in the Asylum', in Joseph Harley & Vicky Holmes (eds.), *The Working Class at Home, 1790–1940* (Cham: Palgrave Macmillan, 2022), pp. 193–211.

Digby, Anne, *Madness, Morality and Medicine: A Study of the York Retreat, 1796–1914* (Cambridge: Cambridge University Press, 1985).

Digby, Anne, *The Evolution of British General Practice, 1850–1948* (Oxford: Oxford University Press, 1999)

Eastoe, Stef, *Idiocy, Imbecility and Insanity in Victorian Society: Caterham Asylum, 1867–1911* (Cham: Palgrave Macmillan, 2020).

Eigen, Joel Peter, *Witnessing Insanity: Madness and Mad-Doctors in the English Court* (New Haven, CT: Yale University Press, 1995).

Eigen, Joel Peter, *Unconscious Crime: Mental Absence and Criminal Responsibility in Victorian London* (Baltimore & London: The Johns Hopkins University Press, 2003).

Eigen, Joel Peter, *Mad-Doctors in the Dock. Defending the Diagnosis* (Baltimore: Johns Hopkins Press, 2016).

Emsley, Clive, *Crime and Society in England 1750–1900*, 3rd edn (London: Pearson Longman, 2005).

Evans, Catherine L., *Unsound Empire. Civilization & Madness in Late-Victorian Law* (New Haven & London: Yale University Press, 2021).

Farrell, Elaine, *'A Most Diabolical Deed'. Infanticide and Irish Society, 1850–1900* (Manchester & New York: Manchester University Press, 2013).

Fennell, Phil, *Treatment without Consent: Law, Psychiatry and the Treatment of Mentally Disordered People since 1845* (London & New York: Routledge, 1996).

Foucault, Michel, *Madness and Civilisation: A History of Madness in the Age of Reason*, trans. R. Howard (London & New York: Routledge, 2001).

Foucault, Michel, *History of Madness*, trans. Jonathan Murphy & Jean Khalfa (London & New York: Routledge, 2006).

Forester, Kim, *Inside Broadmoor: Secrets of the Criminally Insane, Revealed by the Chief Attendant* (CreateSpace Independent Publishing Platform, 2016).

Frost, Ginger, *Living in Sin: Cohabiting as Husband and Wife in Nineteenth-Century England* (Manchester: Manchester University Press, 2008).

Frost, Ginger, *Illegitimacy in English Law and Society, 1860–1930* (Manchester: Manchester University Press, 2016).

Gale, Colin & Robert Howard, *Presumed Curable: An Illustrated Casebook of Victorian Psychiatric Patients in Bethlem Hospital* (Petersfield, UK & Pittsburgh, PA: Wrightson Biomedical Publishing Ltd, 2003).

Godfrey, Barry, *Crime in England, 1880–1945. The Rough and the Criminal, the Policed and the Incarcerated* (Abingdon: Routledge, 2014).

Godfrey, Barry & Paul Lawrence, *Crime and Justice since 1850* (London & New York: Routledge, 2015).

Golding, Rosemary, *Music and Moral Management in the Nineteenth-Century Lunatic Asylum* (Cham: Palgrave Macmillan, 2021).

Gordon, Harvey, *Broadmoor* (London: Psychology News Press, 2012).

Gregory, James, *Victorians against the Gallows: Capital Punishment and the Abolitionist Movement in Nineteenth Century Britain* (London: New York: I.B. Taurus, 2011).

Gregory, James, Daniel. J. R. Grey & Annika Bautz (eds.), *Judgment in the Victorian Age* (Abingdon: Routledge, 2019).

Gregory, James & Daniel. J. R. Grey (eds.), *Union and Disunion in the Nineteenth Century* (Abingdon: Routledge, 2020).

Grey, Daniel. J. R., '"No Crime to Kill a Bastard–Child": Stereotypes of Infanticide in Nineteenth-Century England and Wales', in Barbara Leonardi (ed.), *Intersections of Gender, Class and Race in the Long Nineteenth Century and beyond* (Basingstoke: Palgrave Macmillan, 2018), pp. 41–66.

Grey, Daniel. J. R., '"Monstrous and Indefensible?" Newspaper Accounts of Sexual Assaults on Children in Nineteenth-Century England and Wales', in Manon van der Heijden, Marion Pluskota & Sanne Muurling (eds.), *Women's Criminality in Europe, 1600–1914* (Cambridge: Cambridge University Press, 2020), pp. 189–203.

Griffin, Emma, *Bread Winner. An Intimate History of the Victorian Economy* (New Haven & London: Yale University Press, 2020).

Gutting, Gary, *Foucault: A Very Short Introduction* (Oxford: Oxford University Press, 2005).

Hamlett, Jane, Lesley Hoskins & Rebecca Preston (eds.), *Residential Institutions in Britain, 1725–1970* (London: Chatto & Pickering, 2013).

Hands, Thora, *Drinking in Victorian and Edwardian Britain. Beyond the Spectre of the Drunkard* (Basingstoke: Palgrave Macmillan, 2018).

Hammerton, A. James, *Cruelty and Companionship. Conflict in Nineteenth-Century Married Life* (London: Routledge, 1995).

Harley, Joseph & Vicky Holmes (eds.), *The Working Class at Home, 1790–1940* (Cham: Palgrave Macmillan, 2022).

van der Heijden, Manon, Marion Pluskota & Sanne Muurling (eds.), *Women's Criminality in Europe, 1600–1914* (Cambridge: Cambridge University Press, 2020).

Heywood, Colin (ed.), *In the Age of Empire. A Cultural History of Childhood and Family* (London: Bloomsbury, 2014).

Hide, Louise, 'From Asylum to Mental Hospital: Gender, Space and the Patient Experience in London County Council Asylums, 1890–1910', in Jane Hamlett, Lesley

Hoskins & Rebecca Preston (eds.), *Residential Institutions in Britain, 1725–1970* (London: Chatto & Pickering, 2013), pp. 51–64.

Hide, Louise, *Gender and Class in English Asylums, 1890–1914* (Basingstoke: Palgrave Macmillan, 2014).

Hurran, Elizabeth & Steven King, 'Cohabiting Couples in Nineteenth-century Coronial Records of the Midlands Circuit', in Rebecca Probert (ed.), *Cohabitation and Non-Marital Births in England and Wales, 1600–2012* (Basingstoke: Palgrave Macmillan, 2014), pp. 100–24.

Jackson, Louise, *Child Sexual Abuse in Victorian England* (London & New York: Routledge, 2000).

Jackson, Mark (ed.), *Infanticide: Historical Perspectives on Child Murder and Concealment, 1550–2000* (Aldershot: Ashgate, 2002).

Jackson, Mark, 'The Trial of Harriet Vooght: Continuity and Change in the History of Infanticide', in Mark Jackson (ed.), *Infanticide: Historical Perspectives on Child Murder and Concealment, 1550–2000* (Aldershot: Ashgate, 2002), pp. 1–17.

Johnston, Helen, *Crime in England, 1815–1880* (London & New York: Routledge, 2015).

Kilday, Anne-Marie, *A History of Infanticide in Britain, c.1600 to the Present* (Basingstoke: Palgrave Macmillan, 2013).

Kilday, Anne-Marie, 'Constructing the Cult of the Criminal: Kate Webster – Victorian Murderess and Media Sensation', in Anne-Marie Kilday & David Nash (eds.), *Law, Crime & Deviance Since 1700* (London: Bloomsbury, 2017), pp. 125–48.

Kilday, Anne-Marie & David Nash (eds.), *Law, Crime & Deviance Since 1700* (London: Bloomsbury, 2017).

Knelman, Judith, *Twisting the Wind: Victorian Murderesses and the English Press* (Toronto, Buffalo & London: University of Toronto Press, 1998).

Leonardi, Barbara (ed.), *Intersections of Gender, Class and Race in the Long Nineteenth Century and beyond* (Basingstoke: Palgrave Macmillan, 2018).

Loughnan, Arlie, *Manifest Madness: Mental Incapacity in Criminal Law* (Oxford: Oxford University Press, 2012).

Marland, Hilary, '"Destined to a Perfect Recovery": The Confinement of Puerperal Insanity in the Nineteenth Century', in Joseph Melling & Bill Forsythe (eds.), *Insanity, Institutions and Society, 1800–1914* (London & New York: Routledge, 1999), pp. 137–56.

Marland, Hilary, 'Getting Away with Murder? Puerperal Insanity, Infanticide and the Defence Plea', in Mark Jackson (ed.), *Infanticide: Historical Perspectives on Child Murder and Concealment, 1550–2000* (Aldershot: Ashgate, 2002), pp. 168–92.

Marland, Hilary, *Dangerous Motherhood: Insanity and Childbirth in Victorian Britain* (Basingstoke: Palgrave Macmillan, 2004).

Marland, Hilary, 'Languages and Landscapes of Emotion: Motherhood and Puerperal Insanity in the Nineteenth Century', in Fay Bound Alberti (ed.), *Medicine, Emotion and Disease, 1700–1950* (Basingstoke: Palgrave Macmillan, 2006), pp. 53–78.

Marten, James, 'Family Relationships', in Colin Heywood (ed.), *In the Age of Empire. A Cultural History of Childhood and Family* (London: Bloomsbury, 2014), pp. 19–38.

Marsden, Gordon (ed.), *Victorian Values: Personalities and Perspectives in Nineteenth-Century Society* (Abingdon: Routledge, 2014).
McDonagh, Josephine, *Child Murder and British Culture, 1720-1900* (Cambridge: Cambridge University Press, 2003).
Melling, Joseph & Bill Forsythe, *The Politics of Madness: The State, Insanity and Society in England, 1845-1914* (London: Routledge, 1996).
Melling, Joseph & Bill Forsythe (eds.), *Insanity, Institutions and Society, 1800-1914* (London & New York: Routledge, 1999).
Melling, Joseph, Bill Forsythe, & Richard Adair, 'Families, Communities and the Legal Regulation of Lunacy in Victorian England: Assessments of Crime, Violence and Welfare in Admissions to the Devon Asylum, 1845-1914', in Peter Bartlett & David Wright (eds.), *Outside the Walls of the Asylum: The History of Care in the Community, 1750-2000* (London & New Brunswick: The Athlone Press, 1999), pp. 153-80.
Mooney, Graham, *Intrusive Interventions: Public Health, Domestic Space and Infectious Disease Surveillance in England, 1840-1914* (Rochester, NY: University of Rochester Press, 2015).
Newbery-Jones, Craig, 'Judging the Judges: The Image of the Judge in the Popular Illustrated Press', in James Gregory, Daniel J. R. Grey and Annika Bautz (eds.), *Judgment in the Victorian Age* (Abingdon: Routledge, 2019), pp. 161-81.
Parry-Jones, William Ll, *The Trade in Lunacy: A Study of Private Madhouses in England in the Eighteenth and Nineteenth Centuries* (London: Routledge and Keagan Paul, 1971).
Partridge, Ralph, *Broadmoor: A History of Criminal Lunacy and Its Problems* (London: Chatto and Windus, 1953).
Peschier, Diana, *Lost Souls, Religion and Mental Illness in the Victorian Asylum* (London: Bloomsbury Academic, 2020).
Pedley, Alison, 'The Emotional Reactions of Judges in Cases of Maternal Child Murder in England, 1840-1890', in James Gregory, Daniel J. R. Grey & Annika Bautz (eds.), *Judgment in the Victorian Age* (Abingdon: Routledge, 2019), pp. 83-99.
Pedley, Alison, 'Family Union and the Discharge of Infanticidal Married Mothers from Broadmoor Criminal Lunatic Asylum, 1863-1895', in James R. Gregory & Daniel J. R. Grey (eds.), *Union and Disunion in the Nineteenth Century* (London & New York: Routledge, 2020), pp. 223-41.
Porter, Roy, *A Social History of Madness: Stories of the Insane* (London: Phoenix, 1999).
Porter, Roy, *Madness. A Short History* (Oxford: Oxford University Press, 2010).
Porter, Roy & David Wright (eds.), *The Confinement of the Insane: International Perspectives, 1800-1965* (Cambridge: Cambridge University Press, 2003).
Prior, Pauline M., *Madness and Murder: Gender, Crime and Mental Disorder in Nineteenth Century Ireland* (Dublin & Portland: Irish Academic Press, 2008).
Probert, Rebecca (ed.), *Cohabitation and Non-marital Births in England and Wales, 1600-2012* (Basingstoke: Palgrave Macmillan, 2014).

Reynolds, Melanie, *Infant Mortality and Working-Class Childcare, 1850–1899* (Basingstoke: Palgrave Macmillan, 2016).

Rose, Lionel, *The Massacre of the Innocents: Infanticide in Britain, 1800–1939* (London: Routledge, 1986).

Ross, Ellen, *Love and Toil: Motherhood in Outcast London, 1870–1918* (Oxford: Oxford University Press, 1993).

Rowbotham, Judith, Kim Stevenson & Samantha Pegg, *Crime News in Modern Britain. Press Reporting and Responsibility, 1820–2010* (Basingstoke: Palgrave Macmillan, 2013).

Rutherford, Helen, 'Unity or Disunity? The Trials of a Jury: R v John William Anderson: Newcastle Winter Assizes 1875', in James R. Gregory & Daniel J. R. Grey (eds.), *Union and Disunion in the Nineteenth Century* (London & New York: Routledge, 2020), pp. 242–58.

Saunders, Janet, 'Magistrates and Madmen: Segregating the Criminally Insane in Late Nineteenth Century Warwickshire', in Victor Bailey (ed.), *Policing and Punishment in Nineteenth Century Britain* (London: Croom Helm, 1981), pp. 217–41.

Schwan, Anne, *Convict Voices: Women, Class and Writing about Prison in Nineteenth-Century England* (Durham, New Hampshire: University of New Hampshire Press, 2014).

Scull, Andrew, *Museums of Madness: The Social Organization of Insanity in Nineteenth-Century England* (London: Penguin, 1982).

Scull, Andrew, *Social Order/Mental Disorder: Anglo-American Psychiatry in Historical Perspective* (London: Routledge, 1989).

Scull, Andrew, *The Most Solitary of Afflictions: Madness and Society in Britain, 1700–1900* (New Haven: Yale University Press, 1993).

Scull, Andrew, 'Rethinking the History of Asylumdom', in Joseph Melling & Bill Forsythe (eds.), *Insanity, Institutions and Society* (London & New York: Routledge, 1999), pp. 295–315.

Scull, Andrew, *Madness. A Very Short Introduction* (Oxford: Oxford University Press, 2011).

Scull, Andrew, *Madness in Civilisation* (London: Thames & Hudson, 2015).

Shanley, Mary Lyndon, *Feminism, Marriage, and the Law in Victorian England* (Princeton, NJ: Princeton University Press, 1989).

Shapiro, Barbara J., *Beyond Reasonable Doubt and Probable Cause: Historical Perspectives on the Anglo-American Law of Evidence* (Berkeley: University of California Press, 1991).

Shepherd, Anna, *Institutionalizing the Insane in Nineteenth-Century England* (London: Pickering & Chatto, 2014).

Shepherd, Anne, 'The Female Patient Experience in Two Late-Nineteenth Century Surrey Asylums', in Jonathan Andrews and Anne Digby (eds.), *Sex and Seclusion, Class & Custody in the History of British and Irish Psychiatry* (New York: Rodopi Clio, 2004), pp. 223–48.

Shepherd, Jade, 'Treating Mental Illness in Victorian Britain', in Nathan Wuertenberg & William Horne (eds.), *Demand the Impossible: Essays in History as Activism* (Washington, DC: Westphalia Press, 2020).

Showalter, Elaine, *The Female Malady: Madness, Gender and English Culture, 1830–1980* (London: Virago, 1987).

Sim, Joe & Tony Ward, 'The Magistrates of the Poor? Coroners and Deaths in Custody in Nineteenth-Century England', in Michael Clark & Catherine Crawford (eds.), *Legal Medicine in History* (Cambridge: Cambridge University Press, 1994), pp. 245–67.

Smart, Carol (ed.), 'Disruptive Bodies and Unruly Sex: The Regulation of Reproduction and Sexuality in the Nineteenth Century', in *Regulating Womanhood* (London: Routledge, 1992), pp. 7–32.

Smart, Carol (ed.), *Regulating Womanhood* (London: Routledge, 1992).

Smith, Leonard D., *Cure, Comfort and Safe Custody: Public Lunatic Asylums in Early Nineteenth-Century England* (London & New York: Leicester University Press, 1999).

Smith, Roger, *Trial by Medicine: Insanity and Responsibility in Victorian Trials* (Edinburgh: Edinburgh University Press, 1981).

Stedman Jones, Gareth, *Outcast London. A Study in the Relationship between Classes in Victorian Society* (London & New York: Verso, 2013).

Strange, Julie-Marie, *Death, Grief and Poverty in Britain, 1870–1914* (Cambridge: Cambridge University Press, 2005).

Steinbach, Susie, *Understanding the Victorians. Politics, Culture and Society in Nineteenth-Century Britain* (Abingdon: Routledge, 2016).

Stevens, Mark, *Broadmoor Revealed: Victorian Crime and the Lunatic Asylum* (Barnsley: Pen & Sword Books Ltd., 2013).

Suzuki, Akito, *Madness at Home, the Psychiatrist, the Patient & the Family in England, 1820–1860* (Berkeley, LA & London: University of California Press, 2006).

Thomas, Kim, *Broadmoor's Women* (Barnsley: Pen & Sword Books Ltd., 2022).

Taylor, Steven J., 'Conceptualising the "Perfect Family" in Late Nineteenth Century Philanthropic Institutions', in Carol Beardmore, Cara Dobbing & Steven King (eds.), *Family Life in Britain, 1650–1910* (Basingstoke: Palgrave Macmillan, 2019), pp. 155–78.

Tosh, John, *A Man's Place. Masculinity and the Middle-Class Home in Victorian England* (New Haven: Yale University Press, 2007).

Tosh, John, *Manliness and Masculinities in Nineteenth-Century Britain: Essays on Gender, Family and Empire* (London: Pearson Longman, 2005).

Turner, Jo, Paul Taylor, Sharon Morley & Karen Corteen (eds.), *A Companion to the History of Crime & Criminal Justice* (Bristol: Policy Press, 2017).

Wallis, Jennifer, *Investigating the Body in the Victorian Asylum. Doctors, Patients and Practice* (Basingstoke: Palgrave Macmillan, 2017).

Walker, Nigel, *Crime and Insanity in England: Volume 1 the Historical Perspective* (Edinburgh: Edinburgh University Press, 1968).

Walker, Nigel & Sarah McCabe, *Crime and Insanity in England: Volume 2 New Solutions and New Problems* (Edinburgh: Edinburgh University Press, 1973).

Walsh, Lorraine, 'A Class Apart? Admissions to the Dundee Royal Lunatic Asylum. 1890–1910', in Jonathan Andrews & Anne Digby (eds.), *Sex and Seclusion, Class and Custody: Perspectives on Gender and Class in the History of British and Irish Psychiatry* (Amsterdam & New York: Rodopi, 2004), pp. 249–70.

Ward, Tony, 'Legislating for Human Nature: Legal Responses to Infanticide, 1860–1938', in Mark Jackson (ed.), *Infanticide: Historical Perspectives on Child Murder and Concealment, 1550–2000* (Aldershot: Ashgate, 2002), pp. 249–69.

Watson, Katherine D., *Poisoned Lives: English Poisoners and Their Victims* (London: Hambledon Continuum, 2004).

Watson, Katherine D., *Forensic Medicine in Western Society: A History* (London & New York: Routledge, 2011).

Watson, Katherine D., *Medicine and Justice: Medico-Legal Practice in England and Wales, 1700–1914* (London & New York: Routledge, 2020).

Wheelwright, Julie, '"Nothing in between": Modern Cases of Infanticide', in Mark Jackson (ed.), *Infanticide: Historical Perspectives on Child Murder and Concealment, 1550–2000* (Aldershot: Ashgate, 2002), pp. 270–85.

Wiener, Martin J., *Men of Blood: Violence, Manliness and Criminal Justice in Victorian England* (Cambridge & New York: Cambridge University Press, 2004).

Wiener, Martin J., *Reconstructing the Criminal: Culture, Law and Policy in England, 1830–1914* (Cambridge: Cambridge University Press, 1990).

Williams, Lucy & Barry Godfrey, '"Find the Lady": Tracing and Describing the Incarcerated Female Population of London in 1881', in Manon van der Heijden, Marion Pluskota & Sanne Muurling (eds.), *Women's Criminality in Europe, 1600–1914* (Cambridge: Cambridge University Press, 2020), pp. 114–33.

Wright, David, 'The Discharge of Pauper Lunatics from County Asylums in Mid-Victorian England: The Case of Buckinghamshire, 1853–1872', in Joseph Melling & Bill Forsythe (eds.), *Insanity, Institutions and Society, 1800–1914: A Social History of Madness in Comparative Perspective* (London: Routledge, 1999), pp. 93–113.

Wright, David, *Mental Disability in Victorian England: The Earlswood Asylum, 1847–1901* (Oxford: Clarendon, 2001).

Wright, David, 'Delusions of Gender?: Lay Identification and Clinical Diagnosis of Insanity in Victorian England', in Jonathan Andrews & Anne Digby (eds.), *Sex and Seclusion, Class and Custody: Perspectives on Gender and Class in the History of British and Irish Psychiatry* (New York: Rodopi, 2004), pp. 149–76.

Zedner, Lucia, *Women, Crime and Custody in Victorian England* (Oxford: Clarendon Press, 1991).

Journal articles

Allderidge, Patricia, 'Criminal Insanity: Bethlem to Broadmoor', *Proceedings of the Royal Society of Medicine Section of the History of Medicine*, vol. 67 (1974), pp. 897–904.

Andrews, Jonathan, 'Case Notes, Case Histories and the Patients Experience of Insanity at Gartnaval Royal Asylum, Glasgow, in the Nineteenth Century', *Social History of Medicine*, vol. 11, no. 2 (1998), pp. 255–81.

Arnot, Margaret L., 'Infant Death, Childcare and the State: The Baby-Farming Scandal and the First Infant Life Protection Legislation of 1872', *Continuity and Change*, vol. 9 (1994), pp. 271–311.

Arnot, Margaret L., 'Perceptions of Parental Child Homicide in English Popular Visual Culture 1800–1850', *Law, Crime and History*, vol. 1 (2017), pp. 16–74.

Bailey, Joanne, '"Think Wot a Mother Must Feel": Parenting in English Pauper Letters c.1760–1834', *Family & Community History*, vol. 13, no. 1 (2013), pp. 5–19.

Bailey, Joanne, 'The History of Mum and Dad: Recent Historical Research on Parenting in England from 16th to 20th Centuries', *History Compass*, vol. 12, no. 6 (2014), pp. 489–507.

Barclay, Katie, 'Narrative, Law and Emotion: Husband Killers in Early Nineteenth-Century Ireland', *The Journal of Legal History*, vol. 38, no. 2 (2017), pp. 203–27.

Barclay, Katie, 'Performing Emotion and Reading the Male Body in the Irish Court, c. 1800–1845', *Journal of Social History*, vol. 51, no. 2 (Winter 2017), pp. 293–317.

Behlmer, George K., 'Deadly Motherhood: Infanticide and Medical Opinion in Mid-Victorian England', *Journal of the History of Medicine and Allied Sciences*, vol. 34, no. 4 (1979), pp. 403–27.

Breathnach, Ciara & Eugene O'Halpin, 'Scripting Blame: Irish Coroner's Courts and Unnamed Infant Dead, 1916–32', *Social History*, vol. 39, no. 2 (2014), pp. 210–28.

Brewer, John, 'Microhistory and the Histories of Everyday Life', *Cultural and Social History*, vol. 7, no. 1 (2010), pp. 87–109.

Brown, Michael, 'Redeeming Mr Sawbones: Compassion and Care in the Cultures of Nineteenth-Century Surgery', *Journal of Compassionate Health Care*, vol. 4, no. 3 (2017).

Chaney, Sarah, '"No 'Sane' Person Would Have Any Idea": Patients' Involvement in Late Nineteenth-Century British Asylum Psychiatry', *Medical History*, vol. 60, no. 1 (2016), pp. 37–53.

Cox, Catherine & Hilary Marland, 'Broken Minds and Beaten Bodies: Cultures of Harm and the Management of Mental Illness in Late Nineteenth Century England and Irish Prisons', *Social History of Medicine*, vol. 31, no. 4 (2018), pp. 688–710.

Cox, Catherine & Hilary Marland, '"Unfit for Reform or Punishment": Mental Disorder and Discipline in Liverpool Borough Prison in the Late Nineteenth Century', *Social History*, vol. 44, no. 2 (2019), pp. 173–201.

Cox, Catherine, Hilary Marland & Sarah York, 'Emaciated, Exhausted and Excited: The Bodies and Minds of the Irish in Nineteenth-Century Lancashire Asylums', *Journal of Social History*, vol. 46, no. 2 (2012), pp. 500–24.

Digby, Anne, 'Victorian Values and Women in Private and Public', *Proceedings of the British Academy*, vol. 78 (1990), pp. 195–215.

Eastoe, Stef, '"Relieving Gloomy and Objectiveless Lives". The Landscape of the Caterham Imbecile Asylum', *Landscape Research*, vol. 41, no. 6 (2016), pp. 652–63.

Eigen, Joel Peter, 'Diagnosing Homicidal Mania: Forensic Psychiatry and the Purposeless Murder', *Medical History*, vol. 54, no. 4 (2010), pp. 433–56.

Griffin, Emma, 'The Emotions of Motherhood: Love, Culture and Poverty in Victorian Britain', *American Historical Review*, vol. 123 (2018), pp. 60–85.

Higginbotham, Anne, '"Sin of the Age": Infanticide and Illegitimacy in Victorian London', *Victorian Studies*, vol. 32, no. 3 (1989), pp. 319–37.

Houston, R. A., 'A Latent Historiography? The Case of Psychiatry in Britain 1500–1820', *The Historical Journal*, vol. 57, no. 1 (2014), pp. 289–310.

Hunt, Aeron, 'Calculations and Concealments: Infanticide in Mid-nineteenth Century Britain', *Victorian Literature and Culture*, vol. 34, no. 1 (2006), pp. 71–94.

Hurren, Elizabeth T., 'Remaking the Medico-Legal Scene: A Social History of the Late-Victorian Coroner in Oxford', *Journal of the History of Medicine and Allied Sciences*, vol. 65, no. 2 (2010), pp. 207–52.

Johnston, Helen & Jo Turner, 'Female Prisoners, Aftercare and Release: Residential Provision and Support in late Nineteenth-Century England', *British Journal of Community Justice*, vol. 15, no. 12 (2015), pp. 35–50.

Kelly, Brendan D., 'Searching for the Patient's Voice in Irish Asylums', *Medical Humanities*, vol. 42, no. 2 (2016), pp. 1–5, published online 5 January 2016.

Lansdowne, Richard, 'William Orange CB, MD, FRCP, LSA: A Broadmoor Pioneer', *Journal of Medical Biography*, vol. 23, no. 2 (2015), pp. 114–22.

Marland, Hilary, 'Disappointment and Desolation: Women, Doctors and Interpretations of Puerperal Insanity in the Nineteenth Century', *History of Psychiatry*, vol. 14, no. 3 (2003), pp. 303–20.

Marland, Hilary, 'Under the Shadow of Maternity: Birth, Death and Puerperal Insanity in Victorian Britain', *History of Psychiatry*, vol. 23, no. 1 (2012), pp. 79–80.

Melling, Joseph, Bill Forsythe & Richard Adair, 'The New Poor Law and the County Pauper Lunatic Asylum: The Devon Experience 1834–1884', *Social History of Medicine*, vol. 9, no. 3 (1996), pp. 335–55.

Michael, Pamela & David Hirst, 'Recording the Many Faces of Death at the Denbigh Asylum, 1848–1938', *History of Psychiatry*, vol. 23, no. 1 (2011), pp. 40–51.

Moulds, Alison, '"Making Your Mark": The Struggling Young Practitioner and the Search for Success in Britain, 1830–1900', *History*, vol. 104, no. 104 (2019), pp. 83–104.

Porter, Roy, '"The Patient's View". Doing History from Below', *Theory and Society*, vol. 14 (1985), pp. 175–98.

Rosenwein, Barbara H., 'Problems and Methods in the History of Emotions', *Passions in Context. International Journal for the History and Theory of Emotions*, vol. 1, no. 1 (Spring 2010), pp. 1–31.

Scull, Andrew, '"Museums of Madness" Revisited', *Social History of Medicine*, vol. 6, no. 1 (1993), pp. 3–23.

Shepherd, Anne & David Wright, 'Madness, Suicide and the Victorian Asylum: Attempted Self-Murder in the Age of Non-Restraint', *Medical History*, vol. 46, no. 2 (2002), pp. 175–96.

Shepherd, Jade, '"I Am Very Glad and Cheered When I Hear the Flute": The Treatment of Criminal Lunatics in Late Victorian Broadmoor', *Medical History*, vol. 60, no. 4 (2016), pp. 473–91.

Shepherd, Jade, 'Life for the Families of the Victorian Criminally Insane', *The Historical Journal*, vol. 63, no. 3 (2020), pp. 603–32.

Smith, Leonard D., '"Your Very Thankful Inmate": Discovering the Patients of an Early County Lunatic Asylum', *Social History of Medicine*, vol. 221, no. 2 (2008), pp. 237–52.

Stevenson, Kim, 'Fulfilling Their Mission: The Intervention of Voluntary Societies in Cases of Sexual Assault in the Victorian Criminal Process', *Crime, History & Societies*, vol. 8, no. 1 (2004), pp. 93–110, p. 96.

Tosh, John, 'Masculinities in an Industrializing Society: Britain, 1800–1914', *Journal of British Studies*, vol. 44, no. 2 (April 2005), pp. 330–42.

Ward, Tony, 'The Sad Subject of Infanticide: Law, Medicine and Child Murder, 1860–1938', *Social and Legal Studies*, vol. 8 (1999), pp. 163–80.

Wannell, Louise, 'Patients' Relatives and Psychiatric Doctors: Letter writing in the York Retreat', *Social History of Medicine*, vol. 20, no. 2 (2007), pp. 297–313.

Weare, Siobhan, 'Bad, Mad or Sad? Legal Language, Narratives and Identity Constructions of Women Who Kill Their Children in England and Wales', *International Journal for the Semiotics of Law*, vol. 30 (2017), pp. 201–22.

Wiener, Martin J., 'Judges v. Jurors: Courtroom Tensions in Murder Trials and the Law of Criminal Responsibility in Nineteenth-Century England', *Law & History Review*, vol. 17, no. 3 (1999), pp. 467–506.

Wilczyynski, Ania, 'Mad or Bad? Child Killers, Gender and the Courts', *British Journal of Criminology*, vol. 37, no. 3 (1997), pp. 416–36.

Wright, David, 'Getting out of the Asylum: Understanding the Confinement of the Insane in the Nineteenth Century', *Social History of Medicine*, vol. 10, no. 1 (1997), pp. 137–55.

Zedner, Lucia, 'Women, Crime and Penal Responses: A Historical Account', *Crime and Justice*, vol. 14 (1991), pp. 307–62.

Theses and dissertations

Arnot, Margaret L., 'Gender in Focus: Infanticide in England 1840–1880' (unpublished PhD Thesis, University of Essex, 1994).

Chadwick, G. Roger, 'Bureaucratic Mercy: The Home Office and the Treatment of Capital Cases in Victorian England' (unpublished PhD Thesis, Rice University, Houston, TX, 1989).

Dobbing, Cara. 'The Circulation of the Insane: The Pauper Lunatic Experience of the Garlands Asylum, 1862–1913' (unpublished PhD Thesis, University of Leicester, 2019).

Grey, Daniel. J. R., 'Discourses of Infanticide in England, 1880–1922' (unpublished PhD Thesis, University of Roehampton, 2009).

Pedley, Alison C., '"A Painful Case of a Woman in a Temporary Fit of Insanity". A Study of Women Admitted to Broadmoor Criminal Lunatic Asylum between 1863 & 1884 for the Murder of Their Children' (unpublished MA dissertation, University of Roehampton, 2012).

Pedley, Alison C., 'A Deed at which Humanity Shudders; Mad Mothers, the Law and the Asylum, 1835–1895' (unpublished PhD Thesis, University of Roehampton, 2020).

Rutherford, Helen, 'The Coroner in an Emerging Industrial Society: John Theodore Hoyle and Newcastle upon Tyne 1857–1885' (unpublished PhD Thesis, University of Newcastle, July 2021).

Quinn, Catherine L., 'Include the Mother and Exclude the Lunatic. A Social History of Puerperal Insanity, c1860–1922' (unpublished PhD Thesis, University of Exeter, 2003).

Shepherd, Jade, 'Victorian Madmen: Broadmoor, Masculinity and the Experiences of the Criminally Insane 1863–1900' (unpublished PhD Thesis, Queen Mary University of London, 2013).

Wilson, Catherine, 'Mad, Sad or Bad? Newspaper and Judicial Representations of Men Who Killed Children in Victorian England, 1860–1890' (unpublished PhD Thesis, University of Essex, 2012).

York, Sarah, 'Suicide, Lunacy and the Asylum in Nineteenth-Century England' (unpublished PhD Thesis, University of Birmingham, 2009).

Conference papers

Ute Oswald, 'God, the Great Physician': Religious Activities in Nineteenth-Century British Asylums, European Association for the History of Medicine and Health (EAHMH), Leuven (Belgium), 7–10 September 2021.

Websites

Ancestry – www.ancestry.co.uk.
British History Online. www.british-history.ac.uk.
The British Newspaper Archive – www.britishnewspaperarchive.co.uk.
Find My Past – www.findmypast.co.uk.
Hansard – www.hansard.millbanksystems.com.
Munks Roll, Royal College of Psychiatrists – www.munksroll.rcp.ac.uk.
National Library of Australia – www.catalogue.nla.gov.au.
Old Bailey Proceedings Online – www.oldbaileyonline.org.
Oxford Dictionary of National Biography – www.oxforddnb.com.

Parliamentary Papers Online – www.parlipapers.proquest.com.
Royal College of Psychiatrists – www.rcpsych.ac.uk.
Salvation Army International Heritage Centre – www.salvationarmy.org.uk.
Vision of Britain – www.visionofbritain.org.uk.
Wellcome Trust – www.wellcomelibrary.org.

Index

Adshead, Dr Gwen 210 n.129, 210 n.133
Agar, Eliza, case 72–4
alcohol misuse 37–8
Allen, Sarah, case 87–8, 113, 150, 158
Alverstone, Richard Everard Webster,
    1st Viscount 11
Amess, Ann, case 107, 153
Anderson, Olive 170
Andrews, Jonathan 5, 21–2
Anglican Sisters of Mercy 162–3
Anthony, Mary, trial 43
arraignment cases 67–70, 73, 75
Ashe, Reverend Thomas 133
Ashley, Louisa, case 156 n.227
asylums 3–4, 10, 12, 17, 21–2, 78–81,
    127, 142, 147, 182. *See also
    specific asylum*
  and asylum care 57–9, 72, 76, 97,
    140–2
  case notes 20–2, 62, 88, 90–1, 95, 97,
    102, 105, 109–10, 113–14, 116,
    123–4, 141, 165, 172, 179
  chaplains 132–4, 137, 161–2
  chronic and terminal illness 93–7
  for criminally insane 13–16
  death in 97, 144, 168–72, 231 n.192
  discharge from 142–5 (*See also*
    discharge, protocols)
  environment of 19, 59, 77, 83, 126, 129
  financial considerations 64, 76
  leaving before 1867 145–7
  madness and 23, 80, 104
  moral management (*see* moral therapy
    and treatment)
  patient life in (*see* patient life
    (asylums))
  patient occupations 33, 39, 70, 72,
    107–10, 160
attendants 41, 81–2, 91, 97, 110–11, 115,
    118, 121, 123, 132, 134–7, 170–1
Attree, Annie Florence, case 74–5, 99,
    131–2

Bacopoulos, Alexandra 23
Baines, Martha, case 70–1, 102
Baker, Dr John 11, 59, 85–6, 132, 180
  Female Criminal Lunatics survey 85
Ballantine, William 159
Barrow, Kate, case 166
Bastian, Dr Henry 45
Bates, Sarah, case 33, 131, 139, 159–60, 167
Beagley, Sarah, case 156–7
Beck, Mary Ann Elizabeth, trial 31, 50
  husband, William T 31, 46
Begiato, Joanne 5
Bell, Rebecca, case 135, 167
Bennett, Mary, case 131, 153, 168
Bethel Hospital 75
Bethlem Royal Hospital 1, 10, 13–15,
    18, 20–2, 42, 60, 62–5, 69, 78–9,
    82, 87–8, 91, 94, 97, 101–2, 105,
    109–14, 117, 123–4, 126, 128, 134,
    136, 139, 148, 152, 155, 159, 165,
    168–9, 171, 174–5
  case book notes 20, 22, 62
  criminal patients 1, 15, 18, 22, 62, 91
  Incurable Casebook 94
  Physician's Report 81, 134
Beveridge, Mary Ann, case 64, 94, 114
Bingham Union Workhouse 53
Birkenhead, Martha Ellen, case 54
blame 29–33, 62, 104–6, 157
  blame-shifting 47, 49
Booth, Florence Bramwell 164
Booth, William 230 n.159
Boots, Felicia, case 183
Borley, Maria, case 87, 111
Bradley, Agnes, case 50, 64–5, 158
Brand, Emily 25
Brayn, Richard 80, 115–16, 126–7, 131,
    164, 167, 219 n.45
Brett, William 70
Brewer, John 24
Broadmoor Criminal Lunatic Asylum
    1–2, 5, 10–14, 16, 19–23, 27, 33–4,

36, 38, 42–5, 53, 76, 78, 80–2, 86, 89, 91–5, 97, 99, 101–3, 106–8, 110, 116–18, 123–4, 126, 128, 130–3, 136–7, 139–41, 147, 152, 154–6, 159–61, 163–8, 171–2, 180, 190 n.98, 191 n.115, 211 n.4, 225 n.40
Annual Reports 107–9, 112, 214 n.67
arraignment cases 68–9
before 1835 to 1863 60–6
burial 153, 172–3
case files 23, 97, 104, 124, 171
causes of death 169–70
discharges 141, 147–51, 162–3, 167
1835 to 1863 57–8
1863 to 1901 66–7, 69, 75
Female Airing Ground 184
friendships 115
Jewish patients 118, 172
press reports 18
Queen's pleasure patients 12, 77, 93, 95, 101, 103–4, 127
retention in 151
Rules for the Guidance of Officers, Attendants and Servants 135
'Schedule A – Statement respecting Criminal Lunatics' 67
statistics 11
Women's Division at 100, 180
Brookwood Asylum 92
Bruce, Sir Gainsford 71
Buckinghamshire County Asylum 218 n.29
Bucknill, Dr John 124
Bull, Sarah, case 131, 170
Burfield, Susan, case 33, 49, 69–70
Burney, Ian 29, 32
Burt, Amelia, case 1–2, 109
Burt, Reverend John 133, 161
Byrom, Ann, case 113

Cannadine, David 3, 5
Capital Punishment Commission 54
Central Criminal Courts trials 24, 28–9, 53, 73
  Old Bailey trials 24, 44–5, 72, 94, 106, 183
Chadwick, Roger 59
chaplains 93, 118, 132–4, 137, 161–2
Cherry, Annie, trial 45, 72

child homicide 2–3, 7–10, 19, 20, 25, 28–9, 35, 37–8, 41–2, 50–1, 54, 57, 60, 64, 67–8, 71, 76, 86, 177, 180, 182–4.
  See also infanticide
Chitty, Maria, case 88, 105
Chorley Union Workhouse 92
Clark, Eliza, case 109, 111, 113
Clarke, Maria, case 114
Claybury Asylum 110
Cole, Adelaide, case 94–6
Coleborne, Catharine 23
Coleman, Charles 137
Coleman, Mary, case 87, 160
Coleridge, John, 1st Baron Coleridge 47
Colley, Ann, case 61–2, 170
confinement 1–2, 11, 35, 43, 49, 57, 66–7, 74–5, 80, 84, 90–2, 103, 147, 151, 158
  of child murderers 71
  of insane women 59, 63, 66
  restraint and 81
Conolly, Dr John 86
Convict Lunatic Asylum at New Norfolk 126
convict lunatics 11–12, 16, 18, 103–4, 146
Cornford, Mary, case 115
coroners 7, 28–33, 46
  courts 28, 31, 35, 49
  juries 24, 29, 32, 35, 46
County Asylums Act (1845) 127
Coventry Evening Telegraph 159
criminal class 18, 101, 103–4, 179
criminal insanity 10–11, 20–1, 25, 52, 55, 80, 103
  asylums for 13–16, 76, 78, 140
  delusion and 36–7
  female 2–3, 9–13, 19, 25, 28, 34, 57, 59–60, 63, 77, 80, 87, 94, 121, 123, 137, 141, 165, 177, 182
criminal justice system 8–9, 183
criminal lunatic(s) 11, 22, 27, 44, 58, 60, 62, 65, 70, 101, 113, 127, 140, 143, 175, 177, 231 n.192
  asylums 2, 15, 19, 70–1, 73, 77, 79–80, 99, 123, 129, 138–9, 145, 149, 165
  care 140, 143
  class 11
  facilities 2, 6, 17–20, 27–8, 60, 78, 81, 90–1, 102, 161–2, 175, 180–1
  ordinary 103, 144
  retention and detention 63–4

Criminal Lunatics Act (1800) 69, 203 n.55
Criminal Lunatics Act (1867) 145, 147, 149, 224 n.28
Criminal Lunatics Act (1884) 143, 150, 166, 225 n.53, 230 n.172
Criminal Lunatics Asylum Act (The Broadmoor Act, 1860) 16, 111, 145, 224 n.28
criminal responsibility
  and awareness 73
  and defence of insanity 34–9, 50
  and delusion 28, 35, 37, 39
  and incarceration 72, 74
  unconscious impulse and 57, 68
Crimmings, Margaret, case 93, 104
Cuming, Emma 5–6

David, Catherine, case 97
Dawson, Catherine, case 92
Day, Sir John Charles 29
delirium tremens 39, 43, 165
Denman, Thomas, 1st Baron Denman 52
Department for Public Prosecutions 59
Dickens, Charles 128
Dickenson, Sarah, case 110, 113
Digby, Anne 4, 17, 122
Discharged Prisoners' Aid Societies 161–2
discharge, protocols 21, 60, 66, 76, 138–9, 175
  admissions between 1863 & 1900 148
  between 1835 and 1900 143–4
  Broadmoor 141, 147–51, 162–3, 167
  conditional 142–3, 150, 156, 164–5, 175
  of criminal lunatics 143, 165
  expectations of spouses 155–8
  family involvement 141, 148, 151–5, 173
  leaving asylum before 1867 145–7
  by marital status 145
  patronage and references 158–61
  philanthropy and charitable intent 161–4
  of pre-1863 admissions 146
  procedure and 2, 13, 60, 138, 140–2, 150, 152, 174
  relapse and return 164–7
  Royal Pardons 65, 113, 139, 145–6, 165, 175
  Warrant of Conditional Discharge 166–7

Dixon, Thomas 122
Dobbing, Cara 154
Dobbin, Sarah, case 92
doctor-patient relationship 124, 138
Dodwell, Henry 128
domestic abuse/violence 9, 46–7, 87, 105, 156, 178
Doyle, Bridget, case 110
Dudley, Lucille, case 115–16

Eigen, Joel Peter 10, 24, 41
emotions 6, 41, 122, 129
  and emotional involvement with patients 41, 123–5, 137, 140
  emotional relationships 181–2
  lay witness evidence 46
  moral 31
  and sentimentality 24, 55
Essex County Gaol at Springfield 63–4
eugenics 127, 219 n.46

family relationships 5, 23, 51, 87, 104–7, 179
Fauvel, Aude 23
female criminal insanity. *See* criminal insanity
Fiddington House 126
Finch, Charles 15, 136
Finch, Sarah Martha 189 n.88
Finch, William Corbin 15, 22, 79, 82, 91, 102–3, 108–10, 128, 133, 136, 161, 189 n.88, 215 n.92
Fisherton House Lunatic Asylum 1, 13–15, 20–2, 60, 65, 69, 78–83, 87–9, 95–7, 104, 106, 108–14, 117, 123–4, 127, 132, 136, 147–8, 161, 165, 168–9, 171, 174, 189 n.88, 215 n.92
  case books 88, 91, 97, 102, 113
  management 92
Fletcher, Sarah, case 160, 164
Forsythe, Bill 154
Foucault, Michel 17–18, 122
Freeman, Sarah, case 48–9, 52, 131
friendships and companionship (asylums) 75, 114–16, 130
Fulford, Sir Adrian 183

Galton, Sir Francis 127, 219 n.46
Gardiner, Caroline, case 167
Garlands (Cumberland and Westmorland Joint Counties Lunatic Asylum) 154

Gerrard, Jane, case 110
The Globe 18
Goddard, Elizabeth, case 94, 105–6
Gooch, Dr Robert 85
    Observations on Puerperal Insanity 85–6
Goodliffe, Harriet, case 147
Goring, Ann, case 97
Gover, Dr Robert Mundy 44
Greenwood, William, case 172
Grey, Daniel 4, 8
Grey, Sir George 149
Griffin, Emma 6
Griffith-Jones, George C. 18–19
Griffiths, George 19, 107–8
Grout, Sarah, case 45, 48, 63–4
Gunn, Simon 3–4, 31

Hammerton, James 4
Handler, Phil 200 n.164
Hanson, Sarah Ann, trial 43
Hanwell Asylum 93
Harcourt, Sir W. Vernon 73
Hardy, Sir Gathorne 156
Harris, Elizabeth, case 130–1, 163
    husband Richard 149
Harris, Mary Ann, case 147–9
Hatton Asylum 159
Hawkins, Sir Henry 51, 58, 72–4
Hillier, Elizabeth, case 157
Hocken, Martha, case 91
Holloway Sanatorium, Egham 75
Home Office (HO) 2, 11–15, 22, 34, 36, 40, 57, 59–60, 65–8, 71–3, 75–6, 96, 103, 106, 116, 139–41, 146, 149, 152, 154–6, 158–61, 163–5, 174–5
homicidal mothers 6, 8, 19, 21–2, 28, 31, 46, 55, 58–60, 68, 71, 74, 76–8, 83, 110, 119, 121, 123–4, 137–8, 145, 151, 155, 182. *See also* infanticide
    discharges 141, 165
    incarceration for 61
Hood, Dr Charles 10, 22, 42, 58–9, 79, 91, 101, 105, 126, 128, 136, 139, 156, 212 n.12
Horsemongers Lane Gaol 1, 95
Howell, Annie, case 156
Hoxton House Asylum 63–4
Hoyle, John Theodore 193 n.6
Huddleston, Sir John 44, 69–70

Hughes, Dr Robert 61–2
Hurst, Ann, case 104

Illustrated London News 18
incarceration 2, 11, 28, 35, 51–2, 57–9, 67–8, 76–7, 88, 99, 101, 104, 115, 119, 122, 125, 131, 134, 141, 143–4, 149, 151, 165, 169
    cause of death 169
    choice of initial 64
    criminal lunatic asylums 99
    of criminally insane 15, 28, 57, 66
    criminal responsibility and 72, 74
    for homicidal mothers 61
    place of punishment 58, 73
indictments 28, 33, 36, 53
    attempted suicide 27, 32, 65, 106, 131, 155, 159, 162–3
    concealment 7–10, 81
    wilful murder 1, 7, 31–2, 49, 62, 94
infanticide 4, 10–11, 20, 25, 54, 58, 76, 85, 91, 117, 177
    maternal 3–4, 9, 20, 28–9, 37, 58, 63, 76, 91, 107, 123, 129, 138, 179–80, 182
    and moral outcry 7–9
Infanticide Act (1922) 7, 187 n.48
Insane Prisoners Act (1840) 15, 34, 59, 195 n.41, 201 n.12
insanity 1, 10, 27–8, 31, 39–41, 43, 46, 49, 55, 62, 122, 153, 178, 181. *See also* criminal insanity
    cause and effects of 57, 67–8, 117
    criminal accountability and 57
    defence and criminal responsibility 34–9
    definitions and explanations of 87
    diagnosis and causes of 67, 78, 83–8, 117, 179
    hereditary degeneracy 181
    homicidal mania 42–3
    intense anxiety 154
    manifestation and characteristics of 43–4
    medical knowledge of 178
    plea in trials 42, 51, 188 n.68
    religious mania 117
    symptoms of 94, 104
institutional care 58, 126, 144, 162
Ipswich County Asylum 75
Isaacs, Dr John 132, 155

Jackson, Louise 50
Jackson, Sarah, case 139, 152, 174
Jervis, Sir John 53
Johnstone, Helen 162
Jones, Sir W. Quaile 27, 163
Jordison, Dr Robert 45
Journal of Mental Science 90
judges 29, 32, 35–6, 43, 46, 51–5, 57–8, 60–1, 65, 68–9, 71–4, 158, 163, 182–3. *See also specific judges*
juries 6, 24, 27, 29–35, 37, 40, 43, 45–7, 49, 50–5, 60, 67, 69–70, 73, 75, 159
    coroners juries 6, 29–30, 32, 46
    grand juries 53, 69–70
    magistrates juries 6, 46
    petit juries 53

Keary, Lucy, case 110
Keating, Elizabeth, case 162–3
Kilday, Anne Marie 8
Kirby, Eliza, case 147, 154–5, 171
Kirby, Emma, case 49
Kirkbride, Dr Thomas 220 n.51

Lacey, Ann, case 87–8, 147, 149–50
Lack, Esther, case 95–6, 183, 210 n.129, 210 n.133
Lancashire County Lunatic Asylum at Rainhill 20, 43, 65, 80
Lancastell, Sarah, case 32, 147, 166
Lawrence, Hannah, case 48
Lee, Emily, case 87
Leicester Asylum 88
Lewis, Emma 47
Lewis, Martha Ann, case 32, 50, 112–13
Lewis, Sir George 152
Lindley, Lord Nathaniel 39, 54, 70
Lipscomb, J. T. N. 70
Liverpool Assizes 39, 43, 54
Liverpool Mercury 54
Lloyds Weekly Newspaper 27
Lonnon, Eva, case 164
Loughnan, Arlie 10, 41
Loveridge, Rebecca, case 106, 157
Luke, Emma, case 154–5
    husband Thomas 154–5
Lunacy Commissioners 16, 22, 82, 112, 118, 128, 147, 170, 215 n.92, 224 n.40
Lunatic Asylum Act (1853) 147

lunatic criminals 12–13, 16, 104, 143, 146
Lush, Dr John Alfred 15, 189 n.88
Lush, Sir Robert 39
Lyons, Mary, case 38–9, 43, 48, 107

madness 9, 23, 25, 32, 40, 44, 46, 64, 76, 80, 87–8, 95, 104, 117, 122
magistrates' courts 28, 33–5, 41, 70, 72, 159
Marchant, Elizabeth, case 42, 47
Marland, Hilary 21, 59, 77, 85, 170
McNaughton Rules 35–6, 73
McNeil, Mary, case 87
medical evidence 28–31, 33–5, 37–9, 52–3, 55, 59, 65, 68–9, 73, 130, 138, 150, 162, 171, 179, 188 n.68, 210 n.129, 210 n.133
    in criminal courtrooms 39–45
    witness evidence in all courts 46–51
medical opinion 4, 9, 11, 28, 42–3, 45–6, 49, 58–60, 64, 67–8, 73–4, 76, 78, 80, 92, 132, 138, 149, 156, 178
medical superintendents 1, 11–13, 15–16, 20–2, 36–7, 42–5, 58, 65–6, 69, 72–4, 80, 82, 84, 89–92, 96–7, 101, 103, 105–6, 110, 112, 115, 117–18, 121, 123, 126–7, 137–8, 149, 153, 156, 160, 180. *See also specific medical superintendents*
    and medical officers 124–32
    paternal responsibility 123
    as protector and benevolent mentor 130
    sui generis 125
medical testimony 34, 45, 52, 69, 134
medico-legal system 2, 4, 9–10, 20, 29, 33, 42, 51, 55, 59–60, 75, 179–81, 188 n.68
Medico-Psychological Association 127
Melling, Joseph 154
mental illness 13, 30, 41, 55, 59, 67, 85, 89–90, 114, 127, 157, 168, 178–9
    cause of 105
    curability 77
    postnatal 86
    psychotic behaviour and 179
Mercier, Dr Charles 84, 125, 137, 218 n.29
Merritt, Dr Augustus 42
Metcalf, William James QC 75
methodology and sources 19–25
    database 19–20
    microhistory 20, 24–5, 181

Meyer, Dr John 1, 108, 126, 128, 136, 149, 158
middle-class 3–6, 8, 17, 23, 37–8, 46–7, 88, 107, 154, 159, 178, 182
    Christian virtues 5
    criminal patients 75
    culture 153, 174
    ideals 6, 46, 118, 129, 137, 142, 153, 162, 179, 182
    impoverished 101
    life and relationships 123, 137
    male authorities 179
    respectability 47
    society 37, 74
Mooney, Graham 162
moral therapy and treatment 17–19, 79–83, 97, 107–8, 110, 118–19, 122, 126–7
    bourgeois system of 18
    in criminal lunatic facilities 17–19
    employment and occupation 107–10
    moral management 18, 79
    and spiritual health 117
Morgan, Mary Ann, case 33–4, 71, 74, 88
Morison, Alexander 79
Morley, Henry 128
Morris, Agnes Martha, case 39, 103, 153
motherhood 2, 10, 40, 85, 180, 182
    childbearing and 177
    female decency 4
    ideals of 182
    natural maternal behaviour 58
Myles, Bridget, case 96, 107

Nattress, Margery 89
Newbery-Jones, Craig 198 n.117
Newman, Sarah, case 166–7, 174
Nicholls, Richard 136
Nicolson, Dr David 11, 13, 66, 90–1, 97, 101, 103, 117, 126, 128–9, 131, 140, 157, 166, 183
'nolle prosequi' 72, 203 n.73
Norfolk County Asylum 81–2

Office of the Director of Public Prosecutions (DPP) 40
Oldman, Ellen, case 114, 158
Onions, Emma, case 50, 159
Orange, Dr William 1, 11, 36–7, 43–5, 66, 72–4, 82, 89, 92, 97, 103, 106, 110, 115–16, 126, 128–31, 133, 135–6, 141, 149, 151–5, 157–8, 160, 165, 170–1, 180
Ormerod, Dr Henry 160
Oxford Movement 163

Page, Milicent, case 63–4
Palmerston, Lord 64, 159
parenthood 23, 180
Parr, Mary Ann, case 53
Partridge, Ralph 126
paternalism and patriarchy 76, 83, 96, 123–4, 126
Patey, Sarah, case 96
patient life (asylums)
    appearance 113–14
    conduct and agency 110–13
    employment and occupation 107–10
    family relationships 104–7
    friendships and companionship 114–16
    ordinary lunatics 63, 144, 174, 224 n.40
    patient-staff relationships 81, 119
    physical well-being and health 22, 89–90, 107, 115, 123, 128, 135, 143
    repercussions of former lives 116–18
    social status, privileges and class 100–4
Payne, Mary Ann, case 89, 91, 165, 168
Pegg, Eliza, case 81–2, 111
Platts, Elizabeth, case 38, 99, 116–17, 129
Player, Annie, trial 44–5, 48
Playle, Esther, case 63–4
Poor Law Union 33, 64, 92
Porter, Roy 22–3
pregnancy and childbirth 83, 86, 90–3, 156, 183, 230 n.171
    criminal lunatic facilities 91
    and early motherhood 78
    and lactation 85–6, 90, 180
    and puerperal mania 87
prerogative of mercy 59
Price, Sarah, case 102, 117
Prior, Martha, case 52, 63–4
The Prison Act (1865) 62–3, 67–8
prison doctors/surgeons 41, 44, 61–4, 66–7, 69, 76. *See also specific doctors*
Privy Council 65, 145–6, 159
proper behaviour 85, 179
Prosecution of Offences Act (1879) 40, 59, 66
Pryce, Elizabeth, case 115, 130

psychiatric pessimism 80, 126
puerperal insanity 41, 59, 73, 85, 127, 151–2, 166, 180, 183
   causes 84, 86
   cure 59, 74, 117
   deaths of women 170
   definitions 84
   diagnosis 41, 43, 84–5, 180
   infanticide 10, 85
   mania 10, 41, 59, 72, 74, 77, 84–7, 93, 106, 110, 129, 180
   medical views of 59
   melancholia 43, 73, 85–7, 90, 107, 129, 159
   postpartum psychosis 183
   prevention of 127, 166
   symptoms 86, 88

Rainhill County Lunatic Asylum. *See* Lancashire County Lunatic Asylum at Rainhill
Rampton Criminal Lunatic Asylum 224 n.40
rehabilitation 19, 58, 83, 109, 118, 162
respectability 2, 22, 37, 46–8, 50, 87–8, 100, 102, 121, 124, 129, 142, 154, 160–1, 174
   of behaviour and backgrounds 178
   and class 3–7, 142
   definitions 3
   and female violence 180
   ideals 46, 97, 138
   intellectual capability and 142
   inter- and intra-class perceptions 181
   middle-class 47
   social status and 2, 22, 50, 153, 178, 181–2
   working-class 5
Reynolds, Mary Ann, case 132
Rogers, Dr Thomas Lawes 43, 65, 80, 99
Rose, Leonard 8
Ross, Ellen 5
Rowe, Harriet, case 45
Rutherford, Helen 193 n.6, 200 n.163
Ryan, Hannah, case 48, 151, 160

Salmon, Harriet, case 91–2, 147
Salvation Army 116, 118, 162–4
Sanderson, Emma, case 156
   husband Thomas 49, 156, 159

Savell, Catherine, case 91, 102, 113
Saville, Mary Ann, case 117
Scull, Andrew 18, 108, 122
separate spheres 4
Shaftesbury, Lord 16
Sheffield Daily Telegraph 38
Shepherd, Anna 92, 100, 123
Shepherd, Anne 170
Shepherd, Jade 12, 23, 77, 80, 126–7, 151, 154, 219 n.42
Smart, Jane 48–9
Smith, Hannah, case 61–2
Smith, Roger 9–10, 57
social responsibility 141, 161
sociocultural environment 4, 78, 155
Sotheron-Estcourt, Sir Thomas 139
Stafford County Asylum 62
Stafford Summer Assizes 61
Stapleton, Elizabeth, trail 27, 163–4
Steinbach, Susie 161
Stephen, Sir James Fitzjames 54
Straight, Sir Douglas 42, 47
Strange, Julie-Marie 6, 172
suicide 1, 3, 27, 32, 45, 48, 139, 184
   in asylum 65, 131, 170
   attempted suicide 27, 32, 65, 106, 131, 155, 159, 162–3
   in prison 61–2, 65
Surrey County Lunatic Asylum 126
Swansea Lent Assizes 71

Taylor, Alfred Swaine 36, 43, 195 n.52
   Medical Jurisprudence 36
Taylor, Mary Ann, case 106
Taylor, Steven 6
Thew, Elizabeth, case 112
Thompson, Lucy, case 115, 162
Times 7, 24, 50
Tosh, John 4
tranquilisers and hypnotic drugs 83
Treasury Solicitor 40–1, 43–4, 72
Trial for Felonies Act (Prisoners' Counsel Act, 1836) 39–40
Trial of Lunatics Act (1883) 143, 224 n.22
Tuke, Dr Daniel Hack 117, 122
Tuke, Samuel 17, 19, 83, 107, 110, 122
Turner, Jo 162
Turton, Rebecca, case 106, 130

Vyse, Ann Cornish, trial 42, 91, 102–3

Waddington, Sir Horatio 158
Wales
  asylum systems 2–3
  child-homicide 8, 19
  institutional systems of 20, 181
Walker, Nigel 9, 68
Wallis, Jennifer 89–90
Walsh, Lorraine 100
Warwickshire County Lunatic Asylum 113
Watson, Katherine 9
Weiner, Deborah E. 191 n.115
Westmorland Spring Assizes 70
Wheelwright, Julie 183
Wiener, Martin 10, 24, 46
Wigan Observer 54
Wightman, Sir William 1
Wilcox, Matilda, case 72
Willes, Sir James Wilcox 65, 158
Williams, Elizabeth, case 155
Wilson, Ann, case 147, 156
Wilson, Emily Harriet 71, 162–3
Winslow, Forbes Benignus 42, 197 n.85
witnesses. *See also specific courts*
  lay evidence 46–51
  medical 24, 29, 31, 36–7, 40–1, 43, 69 (*see also* medical testimony)
  statements 181
women 6, 71, 97, 139, 142, 178, 184
  and criminal insanity 2–3, 9–13, 19, 25, 28, 34, 57, 60, 80, 87, 93–4, 121, 177
  female dormitory 120
  ideals of womanhood 4, 55, 76, 182
  intemperance and insobriety in 106, 116
  middle-class 38, 182
  patients 18–19, 21, 81, 86, 95, 101, 108, 129, 151
  physical appearance 113–14
  sterilization of 127
  suicidal 3, 65, 159
  'unfit to plead' cases 67–75
  working-class 5, 48, 112, 179, 182
Wood, Reverend Hugh 133
working class society 5, 37, 48, 154, 159, 174, 179
  educated 101, 113
  emotional ties 6, 23
  family relationships 23, 179
  home-lives 179
  living conditions of 5
  lower 177, 182
  lower-middle and 102
  mothers 5, 179, 182
  parenthood 23
  respectability 5
Wright, David 151, 170

The York Retreat 17
York, Sarah 170

Zedner, Lucia 4, 9

www.ingramcontent.com/pod-product-compliance
Lightning Source LLC
Chambersburg PA
CBHW071813300426
44116CB00009B/1293